Research Methods in Mass Communication

Edited by

Guido H. Stempel III   &   Bruce H. Westley

Ohio University   *University of Kentucky*

PRENTICE-HALL, INC., Englewood Cliffs, N.J. 07632

Library of Congress Cataloging in Publication Data

Main entry under title:
Research methods in mass communication.

Includes bibliographical references and index.
1. Communication—Methodology—Addresses, essays,
lectures. 2. Mass media—Methodology—Addresses,
essays, lectures. I. Stempel, Guido Hermann
II. Westley, Bruce H.
P91.R43   302.2′3   80-39609
ISBN   0-13-774240-1

Printed in the United States of America

10   9   8   7   6   5   4

Editorial/production supervision and interior design by Marybeth Brande
Manufacturing buyer: Harry P. Baisley
Cover design by Edsal Enterprises, Ltd.

Prentice-Hall International, Inc., *London*
Prentice-Hall of Australia Pty. Limited, *Sydney*
Prentice-Hall of Canada, Ltd., *Toronto*
Prentice-Hall of India Private Limited, *New Delhi*
Prentice-Hall of Japan, Inc., *Tokyo*
Prentice-Hall of Southeast Asia Pte. Ltd., *Singapore*
Whitehall Books Limited, *Wellington, New Zealand*

Contents

About the Authors

LEE B. BECKER is an associate professor in the School of Journalism and a member of the graduate faculty of the Department of Communication at Ohio State University. He received an A.B. degree in journalism and an M.A. in communication at the University of Kentucky and a Ph.D. in mass communication at Wisconsin-Madison. He is a member of the Editorial Board of *Journalism Monographs* and the Editorial Advisory Board of *Journalism Quarterly.*

JAMES W. CAREY is dean of the College of Communications at the University of Illinois at Champaign-Urbana. He received a B.A. from the University of Rhode Island and M.S. and Ph.D. degrees from the University of Illinois. He is a member of the Editorial Board of *Journalism Monographs,* the Editorial Advisory Board of *Journalism Quarterly* and the Advisory Board of the Sage Annual Reviews of Communication Research. He is a contributing editor to the *Journal of Communication* and book review editor of *Communication Research.*

CLIFFORD G. CHRISTIANS is an associate professor of communications in the College of Communications, University of Illinois, Urbana-Champaign. He received an A.B. degree in classical studies from Calvin College, a Bachelor of Divinity from Calvin Theological Seminary, a Master of Theology from Fuller Theological Seminary, an M.A. in sociolinguistics from the University of Southern California and a Ph.D. in communications from the University of Illinois. He is a former Director of Communications for the Christian Reformed Church.

GEORGE COMSTOCK is S. I. Newhouse professor in the school of the same name at Syracuse University, returning to academe in 1977 after a nine-year absence serving as a social psychologist and later senior social psychologist for the Rand Corporation at Santa Monica, Calif., interspersed with a two-year stint as science advisor and senior research coordinator for The Surgeon General's Scientific Advisory

Committee on Television and Social Behavior. After obtaining a B.A. in journalism and M.A. and Ph.D. degrees in communications from Stanford University, he was research director in Colombia for the Peace Corps Educational Television Project under contract to Stanford's Institute for Communication Research. He was senior editor of all five volumes of *Television and Social Behavior* (The Surgeon General's Report) and numerous Rand Corporation reports. His latest is *Television and Human Behavior* (with Steven Chaffee, Natan Katzman, Maxwell McCombs, and Donald Roberts).

HUGH M. CULBERTSON is professor of journalism at Ohio University. He received a Bachelor of Science degree from Michigan State University, a Master of Science degree from the University of Wisconsin in Agricultural Journalism and went back to Michigan State for the Ph.D. in communications. He is a member of *Journalism Quarterly's* Editorial Advisory Board.

WAYNE A. DANIELSON is professor of journalism at the University of Texas-Austin. He received a B.A. degree from the University of Iowa and M.S. and Ph.D. degrees from Stanford. He has done extensive consulting with news organizations, especially with respect to research and computer applications. He is past president of the Association for Education in Journalism.

EVERETTE E. DENNIS is dean of the School of Journalism at the University of Oregon. He received a B.S. degree from Oregon, an M.A. from Syracuse University and a Ph.D. from Minnesota. He is the author of *The Magic Writing Machine: Student Probes of the New Journalism* and *Other Voices: The New Journalism in America* (with William L. Rivers). He is a member of the Editorial Board of *Journalism Monographs* and the AEJ Standing Committee on Teaching Standards.

LEWIS DONOHEW is professor of communication and former director of the School of Communication and director of graduate studies at the University of Kentucky. He received an A.B. in journalism and an M.A. in political science at the University of Kentucky and a Ph.D. at the University of Iowa. He is the author (with Richard W. Budd and Robert K. Thorp) of *Content Analysis of Communications* and (with Joanne M. Parker) of *Impacts of Educational Change Efforts in Appalachia*.

ROBERT S. FORTNER is an assistant professor of communication at SUNY-Plattsburgh. His A.B. degree is from Otterbein, his M.A. is from Indiana, and his Ph.D. is from the University of Illinois.

DONALD M. GILLMOR is a professor of journalism at the University of Minnesota. His B.A. degree is from the University of Manitoba, his M.A. and Ph.D. degrees from Minnesota. He is the author, with Jerome A. Barron, of *Mass Communication Law: Cases and Comment* and of *Free Press and Fair Trial*. He served on the AEJ elected Standing Committee on Professional Freedom and Responsibility.

BRADLEY S. GREENBERG is chairman of the Department of Communication at Michigan State University. After receiving a B.S. degree at Bowling Green State University he received M.A. and Ph.D. degrees from the University of Wisconsin-Madison. He has authored *The Kennedy Assassination and the American Public* (with Edwin B. Parker) and *Use of the Mass Media by the Urban Poor* (with Brenda Dervin). He is a member of the Editorial Advisory Board of *Journalism Quarterly* and of the Editorial Board of *Journalism Monographs* and is a Review Editor for *Human Communication Research.*

MAXWELL E. McCOMBS is John Ben Snow Professor of Newspaper Research and heads the Communications Research Center in the S. I. Newhouse School of Public Communications at Syracuse University. He also heads the News Research Center of the American Newspaper Publishers Association, also at Syracuse. He received a B.A. from Tulane University and M.A. and Ph.D. degrees from Stanford. He is the author of *Handbook of Reporting Methods* (with Donald L. Shaw and David Grey) and with Donald L. Shaw edited *The Emergence of American Political Issues: The Agenda-Setting Function of the Press.* A former associate editor of *Journalism Quarterly,* he serves on the Editorial Board of *Journalism Monographs.*

HAROLD L. NELSON is a professor emeritus and former director of the School of Journalism and Mass Communication at the University of Wisconsin-Madison. He received B.A. and M.A. degrees in journalism from the University of Minnesota and was the first recipient of the Ph.D. degree in Mass Communication from that institution. He is the author of *Law of Mass Communications* (with Dwight L. Teeter) and of *Freedom of the Press from Hamilton to the Warren Court.* He is a past president of the Association for Education in Journalism.

DAVID PAUL NORD is assistant professor of journalism at Indiana University. He was graduated from Valparaiso University and received an M.A. in American business and labor history from the University of Minnesota where he was a Woodrow Wilson Fellow. He received his Ph.D. in mass communication and American history from Wisconsin-Madison.

PHILIP PALMGREEN is an associate professor of communication and chairman of the Department of Communication at the University of Kentucky. He received an A.B. degree in English and an M.A. in communication from the University of Kentucky and was the first to receive the Ph.D. in mass communication at the University of Michigan.

KEITH R. STAMM is associate professor of journalism and director of the Communication Research Center at the University of Washington. He received B.S., M.A. and Ph.D. degrees from the University of Wisconsin.

GUIDO H. STEMPEL III is a professor of journalism and director of the Bush Research Endowment at Ohio University. He received A.B. and A.M. degrees in journalism from Indiana University and was the first candidate to receive the Ph.D. in mass communication from the University of Wisconsin. He has been editor of *Journalism Quarterly* since 1972.

PHILIP J. TICHENOR is professor of journalism and mass communication at the University of Minnesota. His M.S. degree is from the University of Wisconsin-Madison and his Ph.D. in communications is from Stanford University. With F. Gerald Kline, he edited and contributed to *Current Perspectives in Mass Communication Research.* He is a member of the Editorial Advisory Board of *Journalism Quarterly,* the Editorial Board of *Journalism Monographs* and Advisory Board of the Sage Annual Reviews of Communication Research.

SERENA E. WADE is professor of journalism and mass communication at San Jose State University. She has B.A. and M.A. degrees from the University of California at Los Angeles and a Ph.D. from Stanford University. She is an associate editor of *Journalism Quarterly.*

DAVID H. WEAVER is an associate professor in the School of Journalism at Indiana University and heads the School's Bureau of Media Research. He received A.B. and M.A. degrees in journalism at Indiana University and the Ph.D. in mass communications from the University of North Carolina. He is a member of the Editorial Board of *Journalism Monographs* and the Editorial Advisory Board of *Journalism Quarterly.*

BRUCE H. WESTLEY is emeritus professor of journalism at the University of Kentucky. He received a Ph.B. degree from the University of North Dakota and an M.S. in journalism from Columbia University and did advanced graduate work in social psychology at the University of Michigan. He is the founding editor of *Journalism Monographs* and was for several years the associate editor of *Journalism Quarterly.* He is a past president of the Association for Education in Journalism. He co-authored *The Dynamics of Planned Change.*

MARYANN YODELIS SMITH is a professor in the School of Journalism and Mass Communication at the University of Wisconsin-Madison. She holds a B.A. from Briarcliff College and M.A. and Ph.D. degrees from Wisconsin. She is a member of the Editorial Advisory Board of *Journalism Quarterly* and the Editorial Board of *Journalism Monographs* and AEJ's elected standing Committee on Professional Freedom and Responsibility.

Research Methods
in Mass Communication

The Systematic Study
of Mass Communications

Bruce H. Westley and
Guido H. Stempel III

This book is the third in thirty years devoted specifically to mass communication research methods. Each has reflected rather clearly the state of the field at the time of its publication.

When *An Introduction to Journalism Research*, edited by Ralph O. Nafziger of the University of Wisconsin and Marcus M. Wilkerson of Louisiana State University, appeared in 1949, it signaled a new era in journalism education. Prophetically, it had chapters by Frank Luther Mott of the University of Missouri, Chilton R. Bush of Stanford University, and Fred S. Siebert of the University of Illinois. They, along with Nafziger, were among a small group of men who were creating doctoral programs at their schools that would produce a new breed of researcher.

That book made it clear where journalism research was headed. Nafziger said in the introduction:

> But perhaps the most significant development in the study of journalism has been recent progress in the use of new methods and research tools. Journalism has profited with other disciplines by one of the great modern advances in the field of learning: the invention and adoption of more precise means of studying human behavior in all of its manifestations.[1]

[1]Ralph O. Nafziger and Marcus M. Wilkerson, eds., *An Introduction to Journalism Research* (Baton Rouge: Louisiana State University Press, 1949), p. 3.

1

Chapters by Bush on statistics and Earl English of the University of Missouri on interviewing supported that thrust. However, there also were chapters on historical research by Wilkerson and legal research by Siebert. Thus, while Nafziger clearly reflected the behavioral research perspective that had begun to emerge in journalism research in the 1940s, the book also was in a sense a guarantee of the coming diversity in journalism research. That diversity made a multiauthored book even then the logical approach.

But if the Nafziger-Wilkerson book seemed to say that journalism research was on its way, the convention program of the Association for Education in Journalism and the pages of the AEJ's official publication, *Journalism Quarterly*, seemed to say it had not arrived. At that time, *Jouralism Quarterly* typically ran twelve to fourteen articles an issue, or about half the number it does today. The difference in the type of article is reflected in Percy Tannenbaum's finding in a study of *Journalism Quarterly* footnotes that only 2 percent of the citations in the pre-1950 era were to behavioral journals. In the 1950s, that figure rose to 18 percent, and the references to trade journals and general publications decreased.

The breakthrough in the convention program took a while. In 1955, a group of researchers organized their own program for the day after the last day of the AEJ convention at Boulder. The group became known officially as the Quantitative Research Group and unofficially as the rump group. Gradually, the group worked its way into the AEJ program proper. However, it was not until the reorganization of the AEJ in 1965 that the Quantitative Research Group was fully assimilated. It became the Division on Communication Theory and Methodology, and under the new constitution it had full status and full rights within the AEJ. It was from the very beginning one of the three largest divisions, a fact that reflects the growth of mass communication research.

In 1958, the second book appeared. Edited by Nafziger and David Manning White of Boston University, it was entitled *Introduction to Mass Communications Research.*[2] Although only nine years after the Nafziger and Wilkerson book, a whole new group of authors was included—Wilbur Schramm of Stanford University, Malcolm S. MacLean, Jr., of Michigan State University, Percy H. Tannenbaum of the University of Illinois, Roy E. Carter, Jr., of the University of Minnesota, Paul J. Deutschmann of Michigan State University, and Bruce H. Westley of the University of Wisconsin. Chapters on such topics as experimental method, measurement, and scientific method reflected the change that had occurred in the relatively few years between the two books. In many ways, *Introduction to Mass Communications Research* reflected the gains of a decade of experience in the field. And while Nafziger and White said in the introduction that it was "not intended to be a comprehensive textbook on communication research or even the special

---

[2]Ralph O. Natziger and David Manning White, eds., *Introduction to Mass Communications Research* (Baton Rouge: Louisiana State University Press, 1958), p. vi.

area to which it is confined," still it was noticeably more comprehensive—though less eclectic—than the earlier book. Just as the research output of the field was expanding, so the know-how about research was expanding, especially in the behavioral sciences. There was a deliberate decision to omit chapters on historical and legal methods. This did not reflect any reduced interest in those areas, but probably did reflect the content of courses then burgeoning in graduate programs across the country.

Parenthetically, it should be noted that the second edition of Nafziger and White was not the result of any profound change in the field. (The only new chapter was one on content analysis by Wayne Danielson.) It was believed that a flood in the basement of the Louisiana State University press building had wiped out the remaining flats!

That this book should come two full decades after the Nafziger and White book says something else about what has been happening in our field. As mass communication research has grown, it has grown closer to related disciplines. Mass communication researchers have drawn on the methodological insights of scholars in such fields as sociology, political science, and psychology. Another linkage has grown up between journalism scholars interested in communication processes broadly and like-minded persons in departments of speech, communications, speech-communications, and the like. At the same time those interested in historical and legal research in mass communication have found appropriate models in the base disciplines. As part of this process, text materials from other fields have become increasingly in evidence in mass communication research courses.

Yet, when we surveyed about 100 mass communication research methods teachers while this book was being planned, we found the majority eager for a new mass communication research methods book. They made it clear, however, that what they sought was an eclectic book. They sought a book broader in scope and yet deeper in detail than the two previous texts. That is what we have tried to provide. (A few still used Nafziger and White.) Their dissatisfaction with the half dozen or so books really intended for sociology equaled their dissatisfaction with a book as dated as Nafziger and White. The problem seemed to be that, even though the methods we employ are quite similar, these books were not really about mass communications research.

SYSTEMATIC STUDY

When we speak of "the systematic study of mass communications," we mean any research discipline that can shed new light on mass communication processes, effects, institutions, and institutional change, its legal constraints, its constitutional imperatives, its technology, its changing response to new challenges. And we mean to get a start, at least, on an appreciation of how these methods differ and how they are similar, how they are changing and how they remain the same.

In opting for an eclectic approach, we knew that we were complicating things for the student. How could we organize such a tale so that the student could move from one area to the next with ever-widening knowledge and understanding? What comes first? What comes next?

We begin with a chapter by Phillip Tichenor on the logic of social and behavioral science. Tichenor is one of the seminal theorists of mass communication institutions and processes whose work is known far beyond the world of mass communications. His chapter is meant to be introductory to the entire book because it raises questions about the nature of knowledge and, especially, how social and behavioral scientists contribute to knowledge, taking up such questions as how we deal with causality, how we use induction and deduction, how we choose between micro- and macro-system models, and how we move toward verification. It is also introductory in particular to the part of the book devoted to behavioral and social science methodology, which follows.

We focus first on theories and theory construction. Lewis Donohew and Philip Palmgreen, whose previous collaborations include a well-known revision of Festinger's cognitive dissonance theory, discuss the nature and role of theory in behavioral science and the process of theory "building." We are not talking about "building models" in the manner of graphic representations of communication processes, but the patient work of devising theories to account for data. We often speak of theory *and* methodology, signifying their separateness. Donohew and Palmgreen stress their interconnectedness, which should answer the expected question: why talk about theory in a book about method?

We usually test hypotheses derived from theories by means of statistical inference. So the leap from theory building to statistics should not be too difficult. David Weaver was surely given this book's most difficult assignment: to cover in a single chapter the "basic statistical tools" of our craft. His own facility in using statistics creatively in treating many journalistic topics is well known. His chapter ranges from descriptive to inferential statistics, from normative to nonparametric, from small-sample to large-scale survey statistics, from the t test to the F test, from R factor analysis to Q. It is a huge task for the author and demands much of the student.

Measurement, like statistics, is often the subject of entire courses and series of courses, yet, like Weaver, Keith Stamm has undertaken to cover its essentials in a single chapter. Measurement belongs logically between theory building and statistical inference. The reason is that theory generates concepts, concepts require operations, and operations is what measurement is about. In turn, measures are validated by resort to statistical inference, which is what statistics is about. However, the measurement chapter follows the statistics chapter here because it is easier to understand measurement after the rudiments of statistics are under control. For example, validity and reliability are both tested by means of correlation, and may more easily be understood once correlation is understood. Stamm's qualifications for the task are based on a record of productive research over a wide range of communications problems.

Closely allied to measurement and statistics and a powerful tool for research people of all kinds is data processing with the help of computers. Like measurement and statistics, computer use poses hard learning tasks for students, but the payoff is usually worth the effort. For, as Danielson points out, computers not only save time but allow us to perform much more sophisticated and searching analyses than are remotely possible without them. Danielson himself was one of the first among us to become involved with computer capabilities and has carried out some strikingly innovative work with them.

The next six chapters concern themselves with the three most frequently used modes of inquiry in mass communication research—content analysis, the sample survey, and the controlled experiment. Each poses distinct problems. Each mode is given a general introduction by authors with years of experience in that specialty, in turn, Guido Stempel, George Comstock and Maxwell McCombs, and Bruce Westley. Each introductory chapter is followed by a chapter devoted to the choice of research and statistical designs appropriate to that research strategy. Stempel does the chapter on designs for content analysis, Serena Wade the chapter on designs for survey research, and Hugh Culbertson the chapter on designs for experiments. All are prolific researchers in these subfields. They build on the statistics and measurement chapters as well as the basic methodology chapters devoted to each, since each poses its own problems and characteristically employs different kinds of statistics. These chapters are essential, but may be a little advanced for some introductory courses. To these has been added a chapter on secondary analysis by Lee Becker. While the three "special methods" chapters have been found in all the mass communication books that preceded this one, secondary analysis is a new topic; it was included at least in part because of the excellent work Becker has done in this area. Secondary analysis is not new to the field, but, as Becker points out, the opportunities to use it were never better now that vast accumulations of social science data are available in highly accessible form to any qualified scholar. (Why spend $100,000 to do a nationwide survey when the answers sought may already be available?) Becker offers guides to where the data are to be found and how to make use of them.

The section on the behavioral sciences of mass communication could end here, but one more significant issue remains to be discussed: the ethical issues that arise, particularly between the investigators and their respondents or subjects, issues respecting the relationship between investigators and their colleagues. This, too, is a new departure in books of this kind. Bradley Greenberg, one of the most prolific publishers of research of all behavioral varieties, seemed best qualified to write on this topic.

There is an abrupt shift at this point to the other methods that characterize research and scholarship in this field: history, legal scholarship, and qualitative studies. They are grouped together because they have much in common and because they are different enough from the methods discussed above to require separate treatment. They are not "last" in any sense of priority. In fact, if we ordered these chapters on a historical basis, they would come first. Historical, legal, and qualitative studies have been around much longer than behavioral science, as we shall see.

This block of chapters begins with "The Logic of Historical Research," by David Paul Nord and Harold L. Nelson, which contains some surprises for social and behavioral scientists—and perhaps some journalism historians as well. In the Nafziger and White book, the historians were not themselves involved, as we have said, but Westley's chapter explained "scientific method" in terms of how it differed from traditional historiography.[3] The happy surprise here is that historiography is moving closer to the methods of the social and behavioral sciences, so a great deal more may now be said about how they are similar. While "humanistic" history still has an important place in contributing to historical insight, Nord and Nelson make it plain that history now uses concepts much as the social scientist does, that is, organizes them into theoretical postures of a tentative nature while evidence is adduced to find support for the theory—or its disconfirmation. They seek quantitative data where feasible and they sometimes use statistical tests. It is an exciting new frontier that these authors explore. Nelson is, of course, one of the more prolific students of Colonial journalism and its milieu and has been much cited on historiography since his thoughtful paper on "guided entry."[4]

Nelson's former graduate students have contributed a large part of the productive scholarship in journalism history and one of the most prolific of them, MaryAnn Yodelis Smith, takes up the story in Chapter 16. While Nord and Nelson give us the big picture, Yodelis Smith gets down to cases. It was her assignment to talk about how historians proceed: how they authenticate data from primary and secondary sources, how they select analytical strategies, and how both documentary and quantitative analysis contribute to the emergence of "an integrated discipline."

History and law is a frequently encountered combination of research interests, as it is with Nelson himself, Yodelis Smith, and others. But the similarity between the systematic study of communications history and communications law may be more apparent than real. In their chapter, "Legal Research in Mass Communication," Donald Gillmor and Everette Dennis do not dwell on these similarities and differences. But they do point out that legal scholars are perhaps even more eclectic than historians, employing the methods of history and sociology, among others. They also make the point that legal research is at once a scholarly pursuit and a professional set of tools. The legal scholar in mass communications works mainly in selected areas of the law, for ex-

[3]"Scientific Method and Communication Research," in Nafziger and White, *Introduction to Mass Communications Research.*
[4]"Guide to Morasses in Historical Research," *Journalism Educator,* 19(2):38–42 (1964).

ample, torts and administrative and constitutional law. But they, too, stress the increasing convergence between what legal scholars do and what behavioral scientists do, at the same time acknowledging that "theory" plays a somewhat different role in the law. The student (and perhaps the instructor as well) will find important detail on the principal legal sources and how to use them.

"Qualitative research" was not mentioned in the two books cited above. It is at once the newest and the oldest of the research disciplines discussed here. For example, the qualitative group is the youngest interest group among AEJ divisions. Yet Clifford Christians and James Carey show that the research tradition may readily be traced to the work of the eighteenth-century philosopher Giambattista Vico—perhaps even earlier. Qualitative is not to be taken as an opposite to quantitative, they emphasize, but rather gives expression to the humanistic tradition with its emphasis on devising "intellectual strategies that not only reveal the world of human activity but contribute as well to the enhancement of freedom and the dignity of human life." For those of us who may have said "qualitative research—whatever that is," the answer lies here. Carey was well known long before the qualitative research group gained identity in AEJ—for such work as his oft-quoted study of Marshall McLuhan and Harold Innes[5]—and Christians, his student at the University of Illinois, is gaining recognition for such studies as his of Jacques Ellul's "fifth theory" of mass communications.[6] Christians and Robert Fortner carry the discussion of qualitative research a step further in the next chapter, "Separating Wheat from Chaff in Qualitative Studies," which discusses methods for qualitative studies.

The last chapter is another new departure, and we think a significant omission in previous books. Scholars have an obligation to spread their work before their colleagues. In fact, all scientific or scholarly endeavor must be open and accessible around the world. For new knowledge to accumulate requires regularized and open channels for reporting new theories, methods, and results. This chapter, by the editors of this volume, who are also the editors of the two AEJ-sponsored scholarly publications, is meant to be helpful to the student preparing a thesis or research report for publication, especially for publication in scholarly journals.

It might be assumed from its eclectic nature that the goal of this book is a truly Renaissance Man of mass communication scholarship, one who moves easily from the law library to the museum to the computer center, exuding confidence all the way. We have a few scholars who are actually able to range widely across the spectrum of methods,

[5]"Harold Adams Innis and Marshall McLuhan," *Antioch Review*, 21:5–39 (Spring 1967).

[6]"Jacques Ellul and Democracy's 'Vital Information' Premise," *Journalism Monographs* No. 45, August 1976.

equally at home in all, or nearly so. Our purpose is not to emulate them, but instead to give the student a broad introduction to the entire field, to pose alternatives in choice of method—a choice that may be made much later. These choices include methodologies useful to the university-based productive scholar, to be sure, but they also include other career choices available to competent research people. They may become archivists of mass media collections or writers of official media histories. They may become survey research specialists in opinion or marketing research firms or copy testers applying their experimental skills in an advertising agency or their survey research skills to the market characteristics of magazine audiences. They may become interpretive reporters with special skills in what we now call "precision journalism"—journalism that obtains at least part of its facts by means of systematic sampling of the community. In all these examples, and there are many more, what qualifies the person particularly is competence in and commitment to a method—a systematic means of studying mass media processes and institutions and human communication behavior.

So, although we assume the student must specialize eventually, we believe there should be a wide and sympathetic introduction to *all* the ways that new knowledge may be uncovered in our field. If students cannot be expected to produce in all these areas, at least they can be expected to read the literature. The danger inherent in specialization is the risk of insularity—that in gaining commitment to a methodology we see our phenomenal world only in the terms given by that methodology. Because other methods may work in different ways toward goals somewhat different than ours, we easily fall into the trap that turns commitment into a sort of methodological chauvinism.

But even the student who does not go into a research career is likely to meet research somewhere in his or her professional future. More research is being done by and about media than ever before. More decisions are based on research. More news is being gathered through the use of research, and more news stories are about research. The questions is not "if," but "when." The aim of this book is to start preparing you for that moment when you find yourself needing knowledge about research methods to carry out your duties.

Scholarship is an "adversary proceeding," a reality that should be more apparent after this book has been studied than before. The historian begs to differ—finds an interpretation based on new source materials. Legal scholars beg to differ—from old interpretations and flawed interpretations of the law. Communication theorists attack the assumptions of their predecessors and erect new theories that account for everything the earlier theory did and some new findings as well. This is adversarity with a high purpose. It is as much a matter of showing that what we thought we knew is wrong and it is a matter of finding what is right. New knowledge comes hard and it thrives on contest. In fact, the careful student may find points in this book where our authors are in some measure disagreeing. For example, Westley and Culbertson have different views of how we generalize from experimental data. What the student should recognize is that each author is writing from his or her own perspective and that it is for the student to resolve these matters in his or her own way.

But to be productive the contest should be between like-minded workers toiling in the same vineyard. Effort devoted to vilifying "those other people" with their quaint and stodgy searches through dusty archives or those young smartalecks who have substituted Cobol or Fortran for English, or those airy qualitative types who love to display their erudition—such effort is largely wasted. The goal of this book is to offer the best information we can muster from people who are committed to the search for new knowledge; we hope that they will impart their commitment and enthusiasm along with some knowledge of the research discipline they espouse. We ask the student to give them all a hearing, to enter the task with an open mind and some sensitivity to the differing ways that we move from evidence to inference.

2

The Logic of Social and Behavioral Science

Phillip J. Tichenor

Science owes its uniqueness as a mode of knowledge production to its blending of abstraction and empirical observation. Science is neither theory alone nor pure gathering of evidence in the absence of higher-order reasoning. Science requires both, pursued in an atmosphere of rigor in logic and measurement that allows others to determine whether they, using that combination of reasoning and procedure, would come to similar conclusions.

Deciding upon the particular blend of abstraction and empiricism to be used constitutes the most basic set of intellectual decisions that a scientist makes. In the investigation of a problem, the scientist must make a series of decisions about the types of abstractions to be used and the amount of his or her effort to devote to abstractions of any type. The scientist must make some choices about empirical methods to be used and about the way those empirical methods will be tied to the abstractions.

When we talk about "theory," we are using abstraction, which means a drawing back from experience and observation so as to conceptualize a problem in general terms. "Social status," "social conflict," and "self-esteem" are abstract concepts that may have particular operational definitions for given research purposes. "Cosmopolitan leadership" as an ideal type is a particular type of abstraction, as is any definition of a typical social role. "Attitude" is an abstraction in the sense that it refers to a predisposition that is not observed directly, but is inferred from a series of observations about a person's behavior.

How are abstractions and empiricism jointly employed in the production of scientific knowledge? The answer is that there is no one way of blending the two, nor is there a single form of abstract reasoning or empirical methodology that scientists do or must employ. There is, however, agreement that both abstractions and empirical methods must be used under a high degree of control. In fact, the term "control" is basic to science, starting with the control arising from rigor in statements of problems, of concepts, and of conceptual schemes and hypotheses. Science means controlled observation and/or experimental methods that may be replicated by others. It is controlled use of language in presenting statements of theory and procedure that can be understood uniformly by others. Terms that are called the "jargon" of a discipline are necessary consequences of rigorous use of language for scientific purposes. Such a pattern of control in all phases of intellectual and procedural activity sets science apart from what is called "commonsense" knowledge gained from everyday experience.

DEFINING RESEARCH PROBLEMS

Identification of a problem for social and behavioral research is itself a process of abstraction. From the complexity of events of concern in a topical area of interest, an investigator selects and formulates a problem in terms that give it some generality and make it amenable to systematic study.

The process may seem at first glance to involve few if any abstractions. It might start, for example, with a question based on the need to develop an effective campaign strategy for a political candidate. The question might be: How much do Milwaukee citizens know about candidate X? Or how can citizens of Milwaukee be better informed about the qualifications of candidate X? Thus far, these questions do not yield to much abstraction and pursuing them will not add much to general knowledge either, if the investigator seeks only to discover a recipe for political success in a particular campaign. Trying out or testing a variety of ingredients until one combination works is one way to get results; such an approach is often called "cut and try" experimentation.[1] Knowledge based on this procedure, however, is not the ultimate knowledge that a scientist seeks, because it is not systematic and it does not by itself uncover systematic principles. To state a problem that will produce systematic, generalizable knowledge requires abstraction, a stepping back from the immediate case at hand, to see what principles are involved and how they might better be understood.

Suppose the question about the political campaign is restated as: What is the relationship between level of television coverage of candi-

---

[1]James Conant, *Science and Common Sense* (New Haven, Conn.: Yale University Press, 1951).

dates and audience familiarity with candidates? Now the question is both more abstract and more likely to contribute to general knowledge. "Candidates" and "audience" are now treated as concepts of social roles, in the abstract, and may appear in a variety of situations.

The importance of abstraction in defining research problems is apparent even in situations that may seem to require immediate, concrete answers, such as social policy areas. As Greer[2] points out, such problems are among the foremost in stimulating social research. Part of the value of abstraction in these areas comes from the fact that policy problems reflect value concerns in society. An example is the study of violence in media content and consequences for members of audiences exposed to that content. Studying violence for its own sake, and in isolation, is not likely to add much to knowledge. However, the topic takes on greater import when it is seen as relating to questions about the code of conduct for young people and, therefore, to the entire question about socialization of adolescents—the problem of growing up.

Much of the justification for research on dramatic television portrayals, as well as on portrayals in other media, may be based upon a desire for social control of adolescents and lower status groups. Similarly, research on information campaigns is frequently based on a value assumption, usually that citizens should have a maximum amount of information about matters that affect their individual or collective welfare. The conflict between such values and the observed failure of publicity campaigns to meet stated goals for, say, improving eating habits is commonly cited as justification for research on information flow and diffusion.

While research problems have their roots in such value and policy concerns, abstraction of the problem not only gives it some generality but also serves to put the investigator in a more detached position. This helps protect his objectivity. Some examples may be seen in other areas of research on communication. There are many value and policy reasons why a better understanding of communication relationships between persons may be desirable, and there are many ways of studying those relationships. Research on co-orientation[3] (the extent to which communicators and their audiences perceive a situation in similar ways) puts self-other perceptions into a framework that is both abstract and, presumably, generalizable to a wider range of situations. Sherif's[4] work on group processes in reduction of ambiguity and of judgmental processes is another example of abstraction in developing a research model that offers generalizability in the interpretation of results.

Still another example is the question of the relationship between at-

[2]Scott Greer, *The Logic of Social Inquiry* (Chicago: Aldine Publishing Co., 1969).

[3]Steven H. Chaffee and Jack M. McLeod, "Sensitization in Panel Design: A Coorientation Experiment," *Journalism Quarterly*, 45:661–669 (Winter 1968).

[4]Muzafer Sherif, "The Formation of a Norm in a Group Situation," in Muzafer Sherif, *The Psychology of Social Norms* (New York: Harper & Row, Inc., 1936).

titudes and knowledge. In this case, the question may be raised in largely theoretical terms although some of the policy implications may be readily apparent. That is, social psychologists may conceive of the question in terms of relationships between "cognitive" and "affective" components of perceptions. In that sense, it touches on a central problem of social psychology. On the other hand, the question may be seen as relevant to the common assumption in politics and public relations that, say, persons who are more informed about the proposed Panama Canal treaty will be more supportive of it.

Whether a research problem is one of policy (such as how to inform electors about a candidate) or is meant to solve a disciplinary issue (such as the effect of knowledge on attitudes) is really up to the investigator. There may well be ingredients of both in a project, and one may lead to the other. But the problem must be stated in general terms if it is to be subjected to scientific inquiry.

A research problem in social and behavioral science requires a specification of phenomena that either vary or are subject to variation. Even if the investigator starts with a "why" question, variation is at the heart of the concern. If the question is "Why do television stations broadcast entertainment containing violent content?" there is the implied assumption that the content might under some conditions be different. Or if the question is about the consequences of violent content for viewers, there is the implication of variation across content and viewers. When a characteristic has different values for different cases or individuals, it is referred to as a *variable*. Amount of viewing of violent content will not be the same for all members of a given audience; it varies from one person to another. "Amount of viewing," then, is variable, as are level of education, degree of alienation of individuals, and degree of urbanization of communities, to mention a few.

ISSUES IN SOCIAL AND BEHAVIORAL SCIENCE

In conducting social and behavioral research, the investigator must go beyond the general standards of scientific inquiry, that is, beyond the norms of rigor, objectivity, and controlled measurement. The investigator must first define a problem in a way that makes that problem amenable to study. In conceptualizing that problem, the investigator must face and resolve a number of issues, which include these:

1. Causation versus prediction.
2. Induction versus deduction.
3. Positivism, reductionism, and holism.
4. Micro versus macro models.
5. The problem of verification of knowledge.

These issues and questions force a choice about the perspective or frame of reference used in approaching a research problem. The choices that are made may have ramifications for the scope of the problem to be addressed, the specific hypotheses to be tested, and the selection of evidence to be gathered. The choices and decisions to be made may encompass some thorny questions, but they cannot be avoided.

While these issues are considered sequentially here, they are not necessarily decided upon in any particular order. Together, however, their resolution ordinarily requires an intellectual posture that must be taken early in research planning. The issues may be reconsidered at some stage, such as when one project is complete and the researcher moves on to a new stage of inquiry.

CAUSATION VERSUS PREDICTION

Causation is an idea that has led to so much debate among scientists and philosophers that many investigators avoid use of the term altogether. Some point out that science is both causal and predictive, but emphasize prediction as the demonstration of causality. In its most narrow sense, prediction means accounting for the future status of something, but, more particularly, stating under what conditions that situation may be expected to occur. A projected estimate of the number of television sets in U.S. households in 1999 is a prediction. Or one might base a prediction upon the convergence of two or more variables. The number of television sets in a nation might be predicted from the level of income, level of education, and availability of programming at a given time in a particular nation, based upon evidence already gathered from a sample of nations.

Important as prediction is, it would be difficult to argue that prediction alone is the goal of scientific research without concern for explanation of causes. In fact, some observers (e.g., Hage)[5] see prediction as constituting only a small part of the concern of social science, apart from economics. A fundamental goal is explanation, which implies analysis of causes. Some notion of causation is back of most research activity as well as conscious activity in general, as MacIver[6] pointed out. This is not to imply that "causation" means the same thing to a scientist as it does to a nonscientist. The intrusion of a commonsense notion about a single cause-and-effect link for any phenomenon may encourage many investigators to abandon the idea of causes. Bronowski[7] is one observer who went so far as to insist that causation is not an essential part of scientific activity and has not been so historically.

Nevertheless, in most research some idea of causation is fundamental. When we ask about the effects of violent media content, about why

[5]Jerald Hage, *Techniques and Problems of Theory Construction in Sociology* (New York: John Wiley & Sons, Inc., 1972).

[6]R. M. MacIver, *Social Causation* (New York: Harper & Row, 1942); R. M. MacIver, *Community: A Sociological Study* (London: Cass Press, 1970).

[7]Jacob Bronowski, *The Common Sense of Science* (New York: Random House, Inc., 1962).

soap operas are viewed, about how people decide to adopt an innovation, or whether newspapers set public agendas, we are asking causal questions. What we need not accept—and ordinarly *should* not accept— is the idea of single causes and single effects. The answer to the question "why?" in social and behavioral science is much more complex than the idea of single causation would suggest.

Some of the more commonly used versions of causal thinking tend to emphasize single causes even when a more thorough analysis indicates greater complexity. MacIver pointed out some of the dangers of such oversimplification in causal thinking by his illustrations of *precipitants* and *incentives* as causal mechanisms.

Consider first the notion of precipitant as it might apply in a particular setting to the question of television and aggressive behavior. Suppose an 11-year-old boy is apprehended in the act of breaking a jewelry store window and stealing merchandise after seeing a television drama in which a similar theft occurred. Even the object he used to break the window is the same as the one used on television. It might be concluded from clinical observation that the prior viewing of the television drama precipitated the theft, and that the adolescent was known previously to be highly aggressive and predisposed to such acts. The television drama then is one of many potential precipitants and is part of a causal pattern, even though a full answer to the question of *why* the adolescent broke the window requires a far more extensive analysis.

In a mining community, there may be a volatile atmosphere, with unionized workers meeting regularly to discuss going on strike in protest over what they feel are unsafe working conditions. A televised speech by a corporation executive stating that economic conditions preclude changes in safety equipment or procedures may be followed by a walkout the next day and, subsequently, intense labor-management conflict with overtones of violence. Did the television report "cause" the walkout? In the sense that it was a precipitating act that grew out of a long history and complex set of conditions, the media coverage was part of the causal pattern, but only a part. It is entirely defensible to study the role of television or other media in precipitating such events, but the burden is on the investigator to point out that unless the other factors are considered, causation is being studied in such circumstances only in a very limited sense.

A very familiar causal interpretation in the social and behavioral sciences leans on incentives or motives. Incentives might in turn be seen as related to perceptions of need, to modes of tension reduction, or to pleasure-seeking of one type or another. The recent emphasis on the "uses and gratifications" approach to studying media behavior (e.g., Blumler and Katz)[8] is in this tradition. Certain types of media behavior

[8]Jay G. Blumler and Elihu Katz, eds., *The Uses of Mass Communications: Current Perspectives on Gratifications Research,* Volume 3, Sage Annual Reviews of Communications Research (Beverly Hills, Calif.: Sage Publications, Inc., 1973).

are explained as serving certain functions, foremost among which may be fulfillment of certain desires and specific wishes. Studies of soap opera listening, such as Herzog,[9] and of reasons for newspaper reading such as Berelson,[10] lean on causal explanations of this type. Similarly, certain studies of gatekeeper behavior, such as White[11] and Pool and Shulman[12] are based at least partly on interpretations of motivational causes.

Like the precipitant explanation, the incentive or motivation approach to causation may leave some questions unanswered. Explaining soap opera viewing by means of incentives may deal with only one or a cluster of factors, leaving aside the questions, among others, of social reinforcement, family and community setting, available content, communicative skills, and the symbolic characteristics of the soap operas themselves. Again, this is not to imply that any one investigator is not justified in concentrating on incentives or motivation in the study of such phenomena. What the illustration indicates, instead, is that a motivational explanation is inherently a *partial* explanation of causal forces, just as a selection of any one of the other factors suggested here *also* would be a partial explanation. The obligation of the scientist is to recognize that fact when it occurs.

In view of the multiple aspects of causation, a more basic approach is to consider the necessary and sufficient conditions for an event. A necessary condition is one without which the event in question will *not* occur. A sufficient condition is one whose presence always implies that the event will occur. While the difference between these two types of conditions may seem very clear in a logical sense, specifying them for a particular research problem is at once one of the most important and difficult tasks the investigator faces. One reason is that conditions are often mutually dependent, meaning that a particular condition may be one of a number of conditions that are jointly sufficient for an event to occur. There may be another set of conditions that, as a set, is also sufficient, meaning then that neither set of factors is, as a whole, necessary. For example, there may be many different sets of conditions, each of which might be sufficient to lead the adolescent to break in a jewelry store window. In each set or combination of conditions, there are factors that may be necessary in the sense that without each one the others would not suffice. When we speak of the violent television program as a precipitant for the break-in, we mean that the television

[9]Herta Herzog, "What Do We Really Know About Day-time Serial Listeners?" in Bernard Berelson and Morris Janowitz, eds., *Reader in Public Opinion and Communication* (New York: The Free Press, 1953), pp. 352–365.

[10]Bernard Berelson, "What Missing the Newspaper Means," in Wilbur Schramm, ed., *The Process and Effects of Mass Communication* (Urbana: University of Illinois Press, 1955), pp. 36–47.

[11]David Manning White, "The 'Gatekeeper,' A Case Study in the Selection of News," *Journalism Quarterly*, 27:383–390 (Fall 1950).

[12]Ithiel de Sola Pool and Irwin Shulman, "Newsmen's Fantasies, Audiences, and Newswriting," *Public Opinion Quarterly*, 23:145–158 (Summer 1959).

program must be considered jointly with other conditions without which the television show itself would not have led to the same result.

CAUSATION AND THE FUNCTIONAL APPROACH

In many areas of the social and behavioral sciences, causes are dealt with through functional analysis. Functionalism was introduced in social science largely by anthropologists who, like Radcliffe-Brown[13] and Malinowski,[14] conceived of "functions" of activities or processes to the maintenance of the system. Stinchcombe[15] goes a step further. He regards a functional explanation as one in which the consequences of some behavior are essential ingredients of the *causes* of that behavior. If soap opera viewing is functional for tension reduction in a particular family situation, the viewing may be continued for that reason. Functions may or may not be acknowledged or recognized directly by participants in a process.

As Stinchcombe has also pointed out, a functional explanation may be especially appropriate when the outcomes of action are quite uniform and the behavior causing those consequences is highly varied. This situation, in which different processes or acts produce the same result, is often referred to as *equifinality* by some systems theorists. A variety of leisure-time behaviors, such as television viewing and comic-book reading, may fulfill an escapist function. Similarly, a wide variety of conventions for reporting news in a community (and not reporting certain kinds) may have identical consequences for maintaining a low level of tension there. It is helpful in such causal analysis to remember that there are many roads to Rome.

Functional explanations have been widely used in communication research, at both individual and system levels. Berelson's[16] "What Missing the Newspaper Means" was an early example of a functionalist explanation for audience use of a mass medium. The "uses and gratifications" research mentioned earlier is equally functionalist (Wright; Blumler and Katz).[17] Much of the literature on impact of mass media on social systems is functionalist (e.g., Lasswell).[18]

[13]A. R. Radcliffe-Brown, "The Functional Unity of Social Systems: Is MI Incompatible with This Hypothesis," *American Anthropologist*, 37:394–402 (1935).

[14]Bronislaw Malinowski, *Magic, Science and Religion* (Boston: Beacon Press, 1948).

[15]Arthur L. Stinchcombe, *Constructing Social Theories* (New York: Harcourt Brace Jovanovich, Inc., 1968).

[16]Berelson, "What Missing the Newspaper Means."

[17]Charles R. Wright, "Functional Analysis and Mass Communication," *Public Opinion Quarterly*, 24:605–620 (Winter 1960); also see Blumler and Katz, *The Uses of Mass Communication*.

[18]Harold D. Lasswell, "The Structure and Function of Communication in Society," in Wilbur Schramm, ed., *Mass Communications* (Urbana: University of Illinois Press, 1949), pp. 102–115.

INDUCTION VERSUS DEDUCTION

Even if an investigator is satisfied with a particular kind of causal interpretation, there is the question of the logic, or reasoning, to be used in arriving at hypotheses about causes or appearance of phenomena. The principal debate about this logic is between induction and deduction.

A great deal of emphasis in the research literature of the social and behavioral sciences, particularly a decade or so in the past, was placed on deductive reasoning, in which a hypothesis or conclusion is implied in the premises. One proceeds, then, from the general to the particular. From a set of assumptions, sometimes called axioms or higher-order postulates, one deduces the hypothesis that, for example, the more aggressive the media content to which persons are exposed, the more likely these individuals are to engage in subsequent aggressive behavior. Such reasoning might be compared to *inductive* reasoning in which one proceeds inferentially from particulars to more general statements. Induction is used continuously, both in problem definition and in interpretation of results. An investigator might observe a case in which tension in one individual leads to avoidance of certain communications and, as a result, infer a general relationship between tension and avoidance. That would be a rather extreme case of inductive reasoning, but conceivable if the tension-avoidance relationship is then considered as a hypothesis for further testing. Also, generalization from measured results is an inductive process, such as when behavior among a sample of individuals is generalized to a larger population.

Heavy emphasis on empirical methods in behavioral and social research in recent years apparently contributed to concentration on deductive reasoning as *the* highest mode of scientific logic. The most specific example is the philosophical and procedural perspective often termed *hypothetico-deductive empiricism,* in which specific empirical hypotheses were deduced from a (presumably) specific set of higher-order statements taken as assumptions.[19]

There are several reasons why a rigid adherence to the hypothetico-deductive approach alone, as *the* mode of scientific reasoning, is not entirely satisfactory. One is that the basic statements (axioms, postulates, or assumptions) are not necessarily arrived at themselves by a previous chain of deductive reasoning, but may have involved a considerable degree of inductive logic as well. There are the "creative leaps" of reasoning upon which science depends so heavily.[20] Also, the process of generalizing from a given set of evidence to a larger set of events or circumstances is largely an inductive process, and generalizing is a vital

[19]Bruce H. Westley, "Scientific Method and Communication Research," in Ralph O. Nafziger and David Manning White, eds., *Introduction to Mass Communications Research* (Baton Rouge: Louisiana State University Press, 1961), pp. 238–276.

[20]Grover Maxwell, "Induction and Empiricism: A Bayesian-Frequentist Alternative," in Grover Maxwell and Robert M. Anderson, Jr., eds., *Induction, Probability, and Confirmation,* Vol. 6 of Minnesota Studies in the Philosophy of Science (Minneapolis: University of Minnesota Press, 1975), pp. 106–165.

phase of scientific activity. It therefore seems more reasonable to conclude that both induction *and* deduction are used, either simultaneously or alternately, in scientific activity. One might deduce that, given a set of assumptions about the joint consequences of age, social experience, and imitative behavior at particular developmental stages, aggressive activity is more likely to occur following one kind of media content than another. However, consideration of this reasoning might lead to the realization, arrived at inductively, that such content may have other consequences as well. The investigator may have observations indicating that violent content of a certain type leads some viewers to turn off the program and telephone their objections to the station. Generalizing from these observations (an inductive process), the investigator may reconsider some of the original assumptions about age and social experience and then make another try at the deductive scheme.

Rejecting a *rigid* deductive approach to the process does not mean denying the importance of either deductive logic or of hypotheses. Both are basic to research. It is more reasonable, however, to recognize that a deductive chain of reasoning is often a *reconstructed* logic, imposed on a set of statements that themselves were arrived at by both induction *and* deduction. An ultimate test of a chain of reasoning may be whether it is consistent from a deductive perspective, not whether it was *reached* that way in all its particulars.

POSITIVISM, REDUCTIONISM, AND HOLISM

With its heavy emphasis on empirical tests, the question of hypothetico-deductive empiricism is closely linked to the issue of logical positivism, sometimes referred to as the *classical empiricist* point of view. The positivistic view is that all knowledge derives from experience or, more specifically, from observational experience. Historically, the move toward positivism may well have counteracted what its adherents objected to as purely speculative reasoning.[21] While there are many consequences of a positivist outlook, one of the most frequently stated (and most hotly debated) is that theoretical concepts are defined entirely in terms of things that can be observed or determined empirically.[22] In the most extreme version of positivism, a concept may be broken down into its observational terms, with no surplus meaning.

Positivism has been an issue in social and behavioral research in several ways. One version of the controversy is at the individual level and

---

[21]Herbert Feigl, "Some Major Issues and Developments in the Philosophy of Science of Logical Empiricism," in Herbert Feigl and Michael Scriven, eds., *The Foundations of Science and the Concepts of Psychology and Psychoanalysis*, Vol. 1 of Minnesota Studies in the Philosophy of Science (Minneapolis: University of Minnesota Press, 1956), pp. 3–37.

[22]Paul K. Feyerabend, "On the Interpretation of Scientific Theories," in Richard E. Grandy, ed., *Theories and Observations in Science* (Englewood Cliffs, N.J.: Prentice-Hall, Inc., 1973), pp. 147–153.

may be illustrated by the difference between a Freudian approach and a classical learning-theory approach to an understanding of, say, aggressive behavior. An interpretation based on Freudian psychoanalytic theory may state that gratification from viewing an aggressive television drama is based on acting out impulses derived from traumatic childhood experience and resultant suppressed guilt feelings. A large portion of such an explanation might rest on an inferred but nonobservable conception of *ego defenses*. If the individual later behaves in an aggressive manner, the Freudian interpretation would locate that behavior within a complex pattern of ego defense mechanisms.

A more positivist approach, such as might be taken from a learning-theory perspective, would produce a hypothesis that is more clearly limited to observables and research operations. The hypothesis might take a form such as, "The more intense the aggressive stimulus, the more likely the subsequent response will be aggressive." Both stimulus intensity and response aggressiveness would be defined in terms of observable characteristics. The hypothesized impact of violent television programming on viewer behavior is then treated largely as a stimulus-response process, without any explanation in terms of anxieties, defense mechanisms, or repressed guilt.

There are other approaches to the question of television and aggressive behavior that might strike a compromise between these extremes, but it is correct to say that much social psychological research swings toward the positivistic end of the continuum. Similarly, much mass communication research has been strongly influenced by the positivist tradition. The rationale for positivism rests on the generally accepted view that observation is an indispensable requirement of scientific investigation.

One objection to the extreme version of positivism is that complete reduction of concepts to measurable indicators implies an unrealistic notion of what scientific theories are or can become. A frequently stated perspective portrays an integrated theory as a network of concepts and propositions that are linked in only a few places to observational data.[23] In this portrayal, a body of knowledge or theory is depicted as a system of postulates that hovers or floats above a plane of empirical data.[24] The basic theoretical terms are "primitive" expressions that are implicitly defined by the postulates in which they occur. A lower layer of defined concepts may be identified, and they, in turn, are linked to operational concepts that refer to items that may be observed.

According to this "layer cake" perspective, the primitive terms in the postulates can be given only a partial interpretation, meaning that they and the defined concepts are not reducible to operations or observa-

[23]Feigl, "Some Major Issues."
[24]Herbert Feigl, "The Orthodox View of Theories: Remarks in Defense as Well as Critique," in Michael Radner and Stephen Winokur, eds., *Analysis of Theories and Methods of Physics and Psychology*, Vol. 4 of Minnesota Studies in the Philosophy of Science (Minneapolis: University of Minnesota Press, 1970), pp. 7–16.

bles alone. It has sometimes been argued that such a view of theory is simply testimony to the current state of development of the social and behavioral sciences. It must be remembered, however, that this idea of a floating and partially uninterpreted postulate system, only partially linked to observables, has been stated largely for the physical, rather than social and behavioral, sciences.[25] The implication is that the linkage between a postulate system and the plane of observation is fundamentally the same, regardless of the substantive field involved.

MICRO AND MACRO MODELS AND REDUCTIONISM

Another choice an investigator faces in designing research is between the more microscopic and macroscopic conceptual approaches. At the microscopic level, the emphasis is primarily on the individual as a unit of analysis. At the macroscopic level, a holistic approach is taken, and the unit of analysis tends to be a collective or larger social unit, such as an organization, a community, or a social system. A distinction must be made here between the unit of observation and the unit of analysis. Gathering data among individual persons does not necessarily mean that the individual is the unit of *analysis*. One might, for example, do a study of community differences in communication patterns across ten different communities according to a holistic approach, with a hypothesis about community characteristics as they affect, say, television habits. Data for this study may come from samples of individuals from the general population of the communities and of persons in leadership roles in the communities. From these data, community characteristics might be determined, such as the overall level of education (which involves averaging) and the type of conversational pattern in the village (which may *not* involve averaging). The main analytic unit may be the community, even though individuals were measured.

There is no correct answer to the question, which is better? The individualistic approach can account for phenomena that a macroconceptual approach may not encompass. Similarly, a macroconceptual approach may provide insights and interpretations that are not possible with a microconceptual scheme. The choice between these approaches should be made in full knowledge that neither necessarily accounts for all the behavior or phenomena of concern. Suppose an investigator is studying performance of reporters in the coverage of local political events. A certain amount of the variance in that performance might be explained by structural characteristics of the communities and by organizational characteristics of the various newspapers for which the reporters write.[26] Reporters on newspapers in large, diverse urban centers might cover political affairs in quite different, and pre-

[25]Ibid.
[26]George A. Donohue, Phillip J. Tichenor and Clarice N. Olien, "Mass Media Functions, Knowledge and Social Control," *Journalism Quarterly*, 60:652–59 (Winter 1973).

dictable, ways from reporters on newspapers in small rural communities. Or political coverage might be different in communities with single newspapers under single ownership than in communities where there is direct competition. At the same time, there may be additional variance in reporter performance than can best be explained by a study of individual characteristics, such as reporter background, adherence to professional values, and personality characteristics. In some cases, it may be possible to determine empirically which approach provides a better explanation. Ordinarily, however, the chosen perspective leads initially to research operations that emphasize one approach or the other throughout the design.

The difference between the two approaches may be illustrated by two contrasting approaches to the study of effects of violence in the media. In many ways, the popular questions raised about effects of media violence have been in a micro framework. The general question, of whether violent media content produces more violence in society, has been conceptualized frequently as: Does violence in media content produce more violent behavior in the *individuals* exposed to that content? Conceptually, individual effects from exposure to aggressive content have been viewed as psychological processes, such as imitation, disinhibition, and acquisition.[27] In a number of studies, the results have supported the hypothesis that the more aggressive the content, the more aggressive the consequent behavior of individuals exposed to that content. (This is developed further by Donohew and Palmgreen in the next chapter.)

A quite different, and more macroconceptual, approach to the question of violent content in media has been taken by Gerbner and Gross.[28] Instead of starting with the question of the impact on individuals, Gerbner and Gross ask what the long-term consequences of televised drama are in American society. Their approach is both macroconceptual and functionalist, based on a fundamental assumption about maintenance of cultural values and norms through symbolic content. Television, as a medium different from all its predecessors in scope and kind, is conceived of as a "cultural arm" of American society, presenting symbolic rituals of oughts and naughts in the social order, and a reminder of who wins and who loses in the game of life. Dramatization of these rules requires direct, unambiguous portrayals of transgression of rules and the costs of so doing, and violence is one of the cheapest and most effective dramatic forms available for that purpose. In this setting, say Gerbner and Gross, the occasional effects of televised violence on individual aggression are less important than are the long-run societal effects, which are to create and reinforce the belief that society is a dangerous place to live. Viewers tend to identify more with victims of televised violence than with the perpetrators. In

[27]George Comstock, *Television Portrayals and Aggressive Behavior* (Santa Monica, Calif.: Rand Corporation, 1976).

[28]George Gerbner and Larry Gross, "Living with Television: The Violence Profile," *Journal of Communication*, 26:173–199 (Spring 1976).

support of their model, Gerbner and Gross present data indicating that the higher the level of viewing of television, the greater the perceived danger of their being involved in violence and the greater the perceived number of police. One of their main conclusions is that a long-run consequence of televised violence is to reinforce social control measures for containing and repressing violence, thereby increasing the likelihood of societal support for authoritarian measures.

In the cases described briefly here, both the micro and macro approaches include data gathered on individual respondents. The difference is in conception of the problem and in the way research problems are stated. The micro approach depends largely on assumptions about individual behavior and motivations; the macro approach depends on assumptions about social and cultural processes, particularly about societal patterns of organized social control. Hypotheses from both approaches may (and do) find support in different bodies of data. There is no more logical inconsistency between these models than there is between micro and macro approaches in other scientific fields.

There is a long-standing and deeply seated division of thinking over the related questions of holism and reductionism. Investigators favoring a macroconceptual approach generally take the holistic view that elements of the larger social system, such as organizations, communities and institutions, have existences as whole which cannot be reduced to behaviors of the actual individuals with them. Quite literally, the whole is seen as greater than the sum of its parts.

A reductionist view, often termed "methodological individualism," would hold that collective social units are nothing more than aggregations of individuals and may be so treated for methodological purposes. There is often a strong link between methodological individualism and the logical positivist view, which regards statements about social systems as nonscientific to the extent that they are not empirical.

The merit of the reductionist pattern is debated widely in the philosophy of science literature.[29] Hyland and Bridgstock conclude that the debate continues to be a crucial one, pointing out that it *is* reductionist to state that institutions are reducible to *actual* individuals, but *not* reductionist to hold that statements about institutions can be restated in terms of typical individuals.[30] The key term here is *typical,* meaning "ideal" types rather than statistical averages and "average" individuals. The ideal type, Weber[31] said, is an abstract characterization, and a typical individual in this sense could be a characterization of a role. Such a type is constructed and described by the researcher on the basis of a theoretical model and may not be found in reality. The difference between actual and typical individuals is of fundamental im-

[29]May Brodbeck, "Methodological Individualism: Definition and Reduction," in May Brodbeck, ed., *Readings in the Philosophy of the Social Sciences* (New York: Macmillan, 1968), Chapter 16.

[30]Michael Hyland and Martin Bridgstock, "Reductionism: Comments on Some Recent Work," *Philosophy of the Social Sciences,* 4:197–200 (1964).

[31]Max Weber, *The Methodology of the Social Sciences* (New York: Free Press, 1949).

portance, since social systems are generally conceived of as interacting configurations of social roles. Merton[32] offered one of the best known ideal types in communications research in his characterization of "local" influentials and "cosmopolitan" influentials. "Gatekeeper" as an abstraction is also a role type when used in the general sense. Although the Weberian language of "ideal type" is not used in every case, the characterization of "advocacy" roles, "channel" roles and "behavioral" (audience) roles in the Westley-MacLean[33] model is another case of abstraction in the interest of conceptualizing a social system.

OBSERVATION AND HYPOTHESES

As indicated repeatedly, a primary requirement of any scientific discipline is ultimate dependence on observation and experience. This requirement holds for the reductionist and holistic perspectives as well. Two investigators who differ widely in their choice of abstractions will, according to the scientific norm, accept specific observations in the same light. That is, regardless of their models concerning the consequences of televised violence, they would ordinarily be expected to agree on the fact that in a given experiment, say, 53 percent of the subjects behaved in a specific way. There may be differing interpretations of the meaning of those behaviors, but the observed empirical facts themselves are, in the norms of science, the same for all. The only concern about the empirical data is whether they meet the conventional norms of reliability and validity.

The important principle here is that regardless of one's overall perspective, one's theory must be grounded in observation at some point. Findings must stand the test of interobserver agreement and reproducibility, meaning that observers using the same procedures should get the same result.

Observation alone, however, is not a sufficient criterion for a scientific procedure. The observations must be relevant to a theory, meaning that in the specific case they must bear on one or more hypotheses. A hypothesis is a statement of relations, based on the best that can be derived from more general assumptions and prior evidence. While hypotheses take different forms, they are generally of the "If A, then B" form. They may be qualified in various ways, depending on the conditional relations between A and B. Is A hypothetically sufficient for B to occur? Or is it necessary without being sufficient? Or, as still another alternative, is A a contributory condition, *increasing* the *likelihood* of B?

Establishing a hypothesis for research may be an arduous task, occasionally prompting one to ask whether it is really essential. Instead

[32]Robert Merton, "Patterns of Influence: Local and Cosmopolitan Influentials," in Robert Merton, *Social Theory and Social Structure* (New York: Free Press, 1957).

[33]Bruce H. Westley and Malcolm S. MacLean Jr., "A Conceptual Model for Communications Research," *Journalism Quarterly*, 34:31–38 (Winter 1957).

of hypothesizing a relationship between level of education and, say, amount of television viewing, one might find it expedient to simply ask: How does level of education affect television viewing? Then one might go directly to measures without further cogitation.

The difficulty with the foregoing approach is that the question itself may well be part of an investigator's preliminary thinking, but it is not by itself an adequate guide for research. Hypotheses are central to the scientific process. As Kerlinger[34] and others have pointed out, the act of stating a hypothesis forces one first to have the basic problematic statement in hand and clearly defined. Second, stating a hypothesis requires thinking out the contingent conditions under which the hypothesis should hold and the linkages between this and other hypotheses. Third, the process of establishing a hypothesis forces the investigator to demonstrate how the hypothesis may be deduced from a more general body of theory and higher-order statements. Where, for example, does television viewing fit in the total pattern of leisure-time behavior available to a media audience? Is it reasonable to hypothesize about television viewing in general, or does it depend on what *kind* of viewing one is studying? Does higher education lead to an increase in certain kinds of television viewing and to a decrease in another kind of viewing? By considering such questions in stating and clarifying hypotheses, the investigator increases the likelihood of generating more *specific* knowledge and the likelihood of developing generalizations as well.

Furthermore, stating a hypothesis provides the specific points of reference for evidence, or data. *Testability* is a basic criterion of a theory, and the hypothesis leads the investigator toward identifying the operations for making the tests. Suppose the above question of television viewing is expressed in a hypothesis, such as: "The higher the level of education of viewers in a metropolitan area, the higher the viewing of documentary programs." Then if, in a sample of viewers in Cleveland, the investigator finds a high positive correlation between number of years of formal schooling and frequency of viewing such programs as "CBS Reports," the conclusion would be that the evidence *supports* the hypothesis.

VERIFICATION OF HYPOTHESES

When can a hypothesis be said to be "fully verified?" The answer in a sense is "never," since all empirical knowledge is tentative. There is always the possibility that a hypothesis, however strongly it may be held among scientists at a given time, may be rejected or modified some time in the future. One reason is that hypotheses are themselves generalizations, and future research may turn up situations in which the

---

[34]Fred Kerlinger, *Foundations of Behavioral Research* (New York: Holt, Rinehart and Winston, Inc., 1973).

generalization does not hold. Nevertheless, there is a point at which it is necessary to take stock of the evidence and theories about an issue so important that it may have engaged dozens or hundreds of investigators and an enormous commitment of funds and other resources over a period of years or decades. What *can* be said today, for example, about the impact that political content of mass media has on voter behavior? What *does* one conclude about the forces affecting whether certain kinds of content gets into newspapers, television programs, and magazines in the first place? The evidence at any given stage must be evaluated, and how should that be done?

The commonly adopted (and conservative) procedure is to evaluate hypotheses according to degree of support, which ordinarily means a joint consideration of amount of testing and the outcome of that testing. Practically, it means testing variations of a hypothesis. In the case of violent media content and individual behavior, there is now a great deal of evidence supporting the general hypothesis that the more aggressive the content viewed, the more likely the subjected individual is to behave aggressively later on.[35] This general hypothesis has received support in settings involving movies, cartoons, adult programming, and news and entertainment formats. At the same time, the media-aggression hypothesis has been sharply qualified and delimited. It has become a series of interrelated hypotheses, couched in an increasingly complex series of conditional statements. This is an example of normal progression in development of knowledge and in building theory. An initial hypothesis may be neither rejected nor supported in all tests and instances. Additional and accumulative research often leads, as it has in this case, to a specification of the conditions under which the hypothesis holds and when it does not hold.

As a result, accumulated research and evidence rarely provide a definitive answer to whether one or the other of competing theories is more correct. There has been, for example, the "aggression arousing" hypothesis concerning violent media content, as discussed. A countervailing hypothesis is one based on the *catharsis* principle: viewing violence may, through the vicarious acting out of aggressive impulses, lead to a draining off of tensions in a way that leaves the individual *less* inclined toward aggressive behavior later. Which is more correct? To date, the evidence as a whole provides far more support for aggression arousal than for catharsis. There is still the possibility, however, that the catharsis hypothesis may be correct for some situations and at least one body of evidence has been interpreted as supporting it.[36] It is also possible that catharsis effects may occur among some individuals in an audience even while the predominant effect is one of aggression arousal. If and when such conditions are specified, the answer to the

[35]Comstock, *Television Portrayals.*

[36]Seymour Feshback, "The Stimulating Versus Cathartic Effects of a Vicarious Aggressive Activity," *Journal of Abnormal and Social Psychology*, 63:381–385 (1961); Seymour Feshback and R. D. Singer, *Television and Aggression* (San Francisco: Jossey-Bass, Inc., 1971).

question "Which theory is correct?" will become increasingly complex. Also, however, the state of knowledge will be much more complete. Specification of complexity is a common outcome of the pursuit of knowledge.

CUMULATIVE BUT TENTATIVE KNOWLEDGE

The final test, in the assessment of the state of knowledge, is conducted in the arena of debate among peers of the scientific community. Behavioral and social science research depends upon confrontation of theories with evidence, and confrontations of the interpretations of that evidence by skeptical outsiders. In any specialized field or subfield, there is an array of procedural and methodological rules for measurement and for increasing the precision of that measurement. Yet, interpretation of evidence must ultimately meet the critical appraisal of others. A theory and its supporting evidence must stand the test of debate. The outcome of this debate is rarely conclusive to all, but it increases the likelihood that the theory and the associated evidence will add to the body of knowledge.

Scientific debate and criticism go beyond maintaining intellectual honesty, although they may serve that purpose as well. Debate forces rigor on the presentation and defense of hypotheses, data, and their interpretation. Knowing in advance that a paper will be subjected to peer review and criticism forces the investigator to anticipate weaknesses. The process may well stimulate alternative conceptualizations, strategies, and interpretations that enrich the final product of the research in question.

Criticism and debate have deep roots in the traditions of science and academic inquiry generally. They serve as continual reminders that science is an enterprise of uncertainty whose current knowledge is, therefore, tentative. When investigators regard a question as "settled," that generally means they are willing to accept a given body of evidence, for the time being, as supporting a particular generalization or set of generalizations. They may even regard a particular generalization as a "law," although few social and behavioral scientists today seem inclined to use that expression.

There are some generalizations that approach the status of laws. There may be widespread acceptance in behavioral and social research of the hypothesis that "the higher the level of education, the higher the use of print forms of mass media." The evidence for this hypothesis may be extensive enough to justify it as an assumption in design of other studies. Yet nearly any student of the subject can specify conditions under which this hypothesis might not be supported. The two variables do not occur in isolation, but operate in a social setting and are jointly affected by other conditions. There is also the possibility that new conditions might appear in the future under which the hypothesis would generally not be supported. So when scholars do accept the relationship between education and print media as an assumption, they are implicitly making still other assumptions about the related conditions.

A similar result occurred several decades ago with Lund's "law of primacy," to the effect that the first side in a debate has the persuasive edge. After systematic studies on the question, the Yale research group[37] concluded that under certain conditions a primacy effect would occur. But under other conditions, a recency effect was more likely.

Knowledge accumulates but never loses its tentative nature. There is no final or ultimate knowledge from science, only the *best* knowledge and the best interpretation that can be provided at a given time. Knowledge, like other products of human endeavor, always faces the possibility of obsolescence.

[37]Carl I. Hovland, *The Order of Presentation in Persuasion* (New Haven, Conn.: Yale University Press, 1957).

The author wishes to acknowledge the helpful suggestions and criticisms of earlier drafts of this chapter by Michael Root and Roy E. Carter, Jr. of the University of Minnesota.

3

Conceptualization and Theory Building

Lewis Donohew and Philip Palmgreen

A theory is a tentative explanation invented to assist in understanding some small or large part of the "reality" around us, as Tichenor pointed out in the previous chapter. Ideally, its concepts are measurable and its propositions testable and therefore subject to refutation. A theory comes into prominence when it is noticed and pursued by the scientific community, and it passes into history when better explanations are found.

Kaplan observes that, in its simplest sense: "A theory is a way of making sense of a disturbing situation."[1] As such, theory building appears to be a natural behavior of our complex species and an extension of the way our brains work as they interact with our environments. We are constantly building and testing mini theories in our minds as we try to make sense out of what goes on around us. The theories help us understand why it is that "if we do this, then this possibly will happen." As J. Z. Young describes this process in the human system:

> The brain is continually searching for fresh information about the rhythm and regularity of what goes on around us. This is the process that I call doubting, seeking for significant new resemblances. Once they are found

[1]Abraham Kaplan, *The Conduct of Inquiry* (New York: Harper & Row, Publishers, Inc., 1964), p. 295.

they provide us with our system of law, of certainty. We decide that this is what the world is like and proceed to talk about it in these terms. Then sooner or later someone comes along who doubts, someone who tries to make new comparisons; when he is successful, mankind learns to communicate better and to see more.[2]

Young likens this cycle of doubt and certainty to cycles of doubt and certainty in science, in which we offer explanations and predictions about our worlds, then somewhat better explanations and predictions, then more new ones as the testing of our theories against the empirical world continues and our level of information grows.

Theory building is a goal of all scientific disciplines, yet there have been relatively few contributions in this direction from those whose central research focus is communication. Steven H. Chaffee, a communication researcher noted for his work in a variety of areas ranging from models of interpersonal communication to effects of the mass media, has observed:

At least once each year an active communication researcher can expect to get invited to a conference to discuss what ought to be done on some facet of mass communication. In recent years I have thus conferred on topics as various as political campaigns, TV violence, consumer socialization, the Nielsen ratings, and education for journalism. The upshot is inevitably the same: there is no intellectual perspective to guide the thinking of the group, no matter how it has been constituted.[3]

By "intellectual perspective" Chaffee meant "theory," and although his later remarks made clear that he did not think the field of mass communication suffered from a total lack of theory, still he felt our theories were inadequate. In this Chaffee seemed to be expressing the consensus of his colleagues: that despite the vast amount of research on communication processes over the last three decades we somehow have fallen short in our attempts to construct theories that would both organize the results of this research and point the way for future research efforts. There is agreement that the *range* of past research efforts is impressive; researchers have delved into such topics as agenda setting, political persuasion, diffusion, selective exposure, advertising effects, and information processing, to name a few. But although theories exist in each of these areas, most communication researchers seem to feel they are inadequate, and despite chronic shortages of research funds, measurement problems, sampling deficiences, and the like, researchers are nearly unanimous in their opinion that the *major* problem in the field is the shortage of good theories.

[2]*Doubt and Certainty in Science: A Biologist's Reflections on the Brain* (New York: Oxford University Press, 1968), p. 11.

[3]Steven H. Chaffee, "Theory, Research, and Researchers: The Pictures in Our Head," Newsletter of the Theory and Methodology Division, Association for Education in Journalism, August, 1977.

But why, we may ask, is there all this concern over "theory"? And why should the problem be addressed in a book devoted to research methodology? As Tichenor has pointed out in Chapter 2, and as this chapter also emphasizes, theory and methodology are often taught separately but are, in fact, inseparable. Theory poses the questions that methodology tries to answer. Theories are not highly abstract webs spun by intellectuals in ivory towers. Kerlinger has pointedly observed that "the basic aim of science is theory"; not "practical results," not "the betterment of mankind," but theory.[4] But if this is true, then the "ivory tower" stereotype of theory must be incorrect, or at least partly so. Why is theory the ultimate goal of scientists, including those identified as communication researchers? The remainder of this chapter attempts some answers to this question.

THE RELATION BETWEEN THEORY AND RESEARCH: CONSTRUCTING AND TESTING THEORIES OF COMMUNICATION

As Tichenor pointed out in the previous chapter, two approaches to theoretical explanation are the deductive and the inductive. In the deductive approach, we proceed from the general to the specific. We begin with a fundamental law or basic assumption and deduce from it propositions about behaviors under specified conditions, then convert these propositions to operational statements, which are tested through use of a statistical probability procedure. In the inductive approach, we proceed from the specific to the general. Here, a set of interrelationships has been observed to occur under certain conditions with a frequency which makes it very likely that some general law is operative. This most frequently used approach in the behavioral sciences is explanatory, but its falsity cannot be demonstrated directly.

According to Kerlinger:

> A theory is a set of interrelated constructs (concepts), definitions, and propositions that present a systematic view of phenomena by specifying relations among variables, with the purpose of explaining and predicting the phenomena.[5]

This definition highlights the two major purposes of any theory: explanation and prediction. It goes beyond this, however, to indicate just how such goals are achieved. We achieve explanation and prediction by developing *concepts,* the building blocks of theory, and linking them in certain systematic ways. The concepts by themselves possess no ex-

---

[4]Fred N. Kerlinger, *Foundations of Behavioral Research* (New York: Holt, Rinehart & Winston, 1973), p. 8.

[5]Ibid, p. 19. Consult Carl G. Hempel, *Aspects of Scientific Explanation* (New York: Free Press, 1965), which is drawn on here.

planatory or predictive powers. Their interrelationship in the form of theoretical propositions performs these functions.

Where do such concepts come from? How do we relate them to one another to form a theory? Where does research enter into all this? An example drawn from the effects of televised violence should help to answer these questions, thus putting further detail in place using the example cited by Tichenor.

A Hindsight Theory of Television Violence Effects

Building an adequate theory requires a dash of intuition and at least a modicum of foresight. Although a vast amount of theorizing and research have been devoted to televised violence, let us assume that we are starting from scratch. Where should we begin? What steps should we follow in constructing and testing a theory of the effects of televised violence?

A reasonable description of what takes place is represented by the following outline.

1. Observe.
2. Develop concepts.
3. Relate concepts to form theoretical propositions.
4. Develop operational definitions of concepts.
5. State research hypotheses in operational terms.
6. Design a research study to test these hypotheses.
7. Evaluate the theory in terms of the outcome.

Let us examine each step in detail.

Observe. Most theory building begins with rather crude observations of events or other phenomena that seem to be related. At first, the scientist does not know exactly what to look for. Observation at this point tends to be rather unstructured and informal. But let us assume that we notice that all the children we know who spend most of their free waking hours immersed in video violence pattern their nonviewing behavior after a "hit" man in "The Godfather." On the other hand, each child of our acquaintance who avoids such fare in favor of "Sesame Street" and "Mr. Rogers' Neighborhood" appears to be a candidate for canonization. On the basis of this admittedly limited and possibly biased sample, we might surmise that the differences in observed behavior are due to the differences in exposure to television violence, using the inductive processes described by Tichenor. At this point we have moved very quickly through the next two steps of the theory construction process.

Develop concepts; relate concepts to form theoretical propositions. The observational stage is very unstructured, although not totally without its governing principles. Our perception of events is influenced by concepts acquired previously. Thus we are likely to perceive the nonviewing behavior of the violence viewers in our previous example as "aggression," and the aspect of their viewing behavior that may contribute to this aggression as "exposure to television violence." It is with such concepts that we build theories. Concepts that have been defined as unambiguously as possible and put to use in theories are known as *constructs.* Taken individually, however, such concepts or constructs can aid only in *description;* they cannot *explain.* We must relate concepts to each other in a systematic fashion before the explanatory apparatus that we call "theory" emerges.

In our example, we have proposed that "exposure to television violence" leads to or is a proximate cause of "aggression." (This is what Tichenor describes as a "precipitator.") This relationship between two abstract concepts is called a *theoretical proposition,* or *hypothesis.* Actually, this proposition, together with the definitions of the concepts involved and certain underlying axioms whose truth is assumed (e.g., "Television content can influence the behavior of those exposed to such content"), constitute a theory in its simplest form. However, at this stage the "theory" has little explanatory value. It does not tell us *how* or *why* exposure to televised violence might lead to aggression. Obviously, our theory requires some elaboration.

One common way in which theories are elaborated to increase their explanatory power is through the addition of "intervening" concepts. To illustrate in an abstract sense, we might insert concept Y between concepts X and Z to help explain why X and Z should be related. Then, instead of the theoretical proposition (X $\longrightarrow$ Z), we have (X $\longrightarrow$ Y $\longrightarrow$ Z). With regard to exposure to television violence (X), we might ask what mechanism or mechanisms (Y) could account for subsequent aggressive acts (Z) apparently related to that exposure. A possible mechanism, of course, is learning, especially observational learning of aggressive acts depicted on television. This may range from a young child's learning how to administer a karate chop to an adult's learning an intricate scheme for robbing a bank. We might expect such learning to be particularly prevalent among young children, since they spend so much time watching television and have relatively little personal experience with violence. Although we need not expect that all aggressive behaviors acquired while viewing television actually will be performed, it is plausible to assume that the larger the repertoire of learned aggressive acts, the greater the probability that some such acts will be performed in appropriate situations. The many recent accounts of murders, robberies, hijackings, and assaults whose details have closely matched events depicted in television drama provide some support for such a rationale.

Hence, observational learning of aggressive acts seen on television is one plausible explanation for the connection between exposure to televised violence and aggression. But could such exposure instigate or trigger *nonimitative* aggression, that is, aggressive acts which do not closely parallel the behavior seen on television? Could, for example, viewing a brutal murder on television cause someone to rush out of the house and commit armed robbery? Perhaps viewing any kind of aggression lowers our inhibitions against aggression in general, thus making it more likely we will behave aggressively. Or perhaps viewing televised aggression is physiologically arousing. Some theories treat arousal as a drive state serving to activate behavior. (This is what Tichenor calls "incentives" in the previous chapter.) If the cues in the postviewing environment seem to call for aggression, any arousal state generated by viewing television violence might serve as the motivational impetus for such aggression. Thus both "disinhibition"[6] and "arousal" emerge as plausible concepts that might intervene between viewing of televised violence and subsequent aggression.

But do these expectations square with what is already known? Before testing our own version of this prediction we must review the literature. We will not find the answers here, but it would be foolish and wasteful to proceed to our own test of a three-element theory without knowing what the research of others has told us about each element and the relations among them. There is a large literature on incidental learning, for example, and indeed the propositions stated in our example are based on that literature.

Part of the reason for the literature review is to decide which of the many intervening constructs we might find most promising. We might have chosen another among many intervening constructs that might have found support in the literature. Indeed, other researchers might well have reached the same point and decided to insert some other intervening construct and put the resulting hypotheses to test. We cannot include them in our own theory because any theory must meet the test of consistency. That is, any theory must be capable of yielding one and only one prediction linking any single set of independent and dependent variables.

This underscores a critical fact about the way a science progresses. One experimenter casts his lot with an incidental learning explanation as to why the viewing of television violence may lead to aggressive behavior. Another investigator may cast his or her lot with a "disinhibition" explanation, for example, that persistent viewing of television violence impairs inhibitions to aggressive behavior which a society has included in its customary socialization processes. Hence Television viewing ⟶ Disinhibition ⟶ Aggression. Another investigator, believing that the evidence really tells us that viewing of aggressive acts on television actually leads to a reduction in tendencies toward aggressive behavior, erects between independent and dependent variables the intervening construct "catharsis." For that theory, Viewing ⟶ Catharsis ⟶ Reduced tendency to aggress. The whole point is that science is, in essence, an adversary proceeding, in which each theorist

---

[6]For a good review of this literature, see Winnifred S. Rayburn, "The Effects of Viewing Patterns on Desensitization to Televised Violence," unpublished M.A. thesis, University of Kentucky, 1977.

does her or his best to find support for a particular view and points to flaws in the work of others, yet clings to a position only until the evidence plainly shows that another explanation is superior.

The only test of a theory is to see whether reality is indeed consistent with what the theory says. We must somehow derive predictions from our theory concerning the way in which certain real-world phenomena are related, and then make systematic observations to see if these predictions are supported. (As Tichenor points out in Chapter 2, prediction is the means we employ to identify a causal relation.) This process is referred to as *hypothesis testing.* But to make such observations requires first that we take the next step.

Develop operational definitions of concepts. Operational definitions are the crucial links between theory and reality that make theory testing possible. An operational definition specifies the "operations" or procedures necessary to measure or manipulate a concept. Kerlinger[7] sees two kinds of operational definitions: (1) *measured,* and (2) *experimental.*

A *measured* operational definition describes how an abstract concept is quantified, for example, "intelligence" as measured by the Stanford-Binet IQ test or "mass media exposure" to information on a certain topic by counting the number of media messages on that topic that a respondent can recall having encountered.[8] In our television violence example, "aggression" may be measured by observing and counting the number of times children perform aggressive acts against toys in a playroom setting; we might index "arousal" by measuring heart rate, galvanic skin response, or blood pressure change. (A lie detector uses two or more of these same measures to infer arousal as a consequence of lying.) In doing so we have defined abstract and thus unobservable concepts in terms of concrete observations that we can quantify. Quantification is important because it lends precision to our predictions, and permits mathematical and statistical operations to be applied to the data. A good portion of this book is devoted to such mathematical and statistical operations, but the raw material for such procedures is the product of measured operational definitions.

An *experimental* operational definition specifies not how to measure a concept, but how to *manipulate* it in an experiment. For example, we might manipulate "exposure to television violence" by randomly assigning subjects to two groups, exposing one to a ten-minute television sequence portraying a predetermined number of violent acts and exposing the other (*control*) group to a benign nature film.

But how can we be sure that an operational definition truly represents the abstract concept it is designed to represent? How do we know that an IQ test is a reasonable indicator of "intelligence," or that the

---

[7]Kerlinger, *Foundations,* p. 31.

[8]For an example of the use of such a "message discrimination" technique, see Philip Palmgreen, "Mass Media Use and Political Knowledge," *Journalism Monographs* No. 61, May 1979.

number of times a child subject in an experiment strikes a bobo doll is a measure of "aggression"? When we ask the question "Are we measuring (manipulating) what we think we are measuring (manipulating)?" we are concerned with the *construct validity* of our operational definition. Stamm treats this topic in greater detail in Chapter 5. We should emphasize here, however, that without valid operational definitions of concepts it is impossible to test the relations among those concepts specified by a theory. And the task of constructing valid operational definitions is a difficult one. As Blalock has observed,

> We shall take the commonly accepted position that science contains two distinct languages or ways of defining concepts, which will be referred to simply as the theoretical and operational languages. There appears to be no purely logical way of bridging the gap between these languages. Concepts in one language are associated with those in the other merely by convention or agreement among scientists.[9]

Closely tied to the construct validity question is the topic of reliability. Not only do we want, for example, our measures of "aggression" to reasonably tap what we ordinarily mean by that concept in the abstract, we also want those measures to do so consistently and reliably. This topic, too, is treated in detail by Stamm.

Operational definitions, then, are the primary tools of all scientific research, because as Kerlinger says, "they enable researchers to measure variables and because they are bridges between the theory-hypothesis-construct level and the level of observation."[10] They are also critical to the process of *replication*. Any finding that is obtained in a particular laboratory must be subjected to further scrutiny. Others must repeat the experiment to test the validity of the results. The finding itself is, as always, tentative, its plausibility estimated by the likelihood that when the experiment is repeated the same result will be found. As Weaver points out in Chapter 4, a result reported at the probability level of 0.05 means that there is one chance in twenty that the same result might not be found. So, while statistics estimate the likelihood, replication tests whether such a finding can be obtained repeatedly. The importance of operational definitions, then, is that they provide a precise answer as to what we did to obtain our result—both how we measured our attributes and how we manipulated our subjects—so that others may test them. Without operational definitions, replication would be impossible.

State research hypotheses in operational terms, design a research study to test these hypotheses, reevaluate the theory in terms of the outcome. Now that we have discussed the nature of the links between theory and observable

[9]Hubert M. Blalock, Jr., *Causal Inferences in Nonexperimental Research* (New York: W. W. Norton & Co., 1964), p. 6.

[10]Kerlinger, *Foundations*, p. 32.

reality we are in a position to describe the predictions or *research hypotheses* that such links make possible. *We do not test a theory or its propositions directly.* We test it indirectly through the predictions we make about reality that follow from the theory. We might test, for example, the theoretical proposition "the greater the exposure to televised violence, the greater the physiological level of arousal" indirectly through the research hypothesis: "Subjects exposed to a 10-minute violent sequence of 'Hawaii Five-O' will manifest greater mean physiological arousal as indexed by conductance measures of galvanic skin response than subjects exposed to a nonviolent nature film."

The *theoretic* hypothesis is stated in terms of abstract concepts and is thus untestable in any direct sense, while the *research* hypothesis is stated in terms of operational definitions (one "experimental" and the other "measured") and is therefore testable.

We must now face the troublesome fact that there are three levels at which hypotheses are stated. Our first statement of expectations was the *theoretic hypothesis,* the hypothesis stated in terms of the theory. The second statement was the *research hypothesis,* the same hypothesis stated in terms of the operations to be performed and the relations to be tested by the research. The third-level statement may be termed the *statistical hypothesis* and refers to the technical form in which the hypothesis is stated for purposes of a statistical test. Contrasted with each of these forms is the *null hypothesis,* which in fact restates the positive research hypothesis (for example, that subjects in the experimental group will exhibit increased physiological arousal while those in the control group will not) in negative form. The research hypothesis predicts a difference. The null hypothesis makes a statement of no difference. When there is a statistically significant difference, we "reject the null hypothesis," that is, we find positive evidence for our prediction. If we must accept the null hypothesis, this means failing to find positive evidence for the predicted relationship. (The null hypothesis is explained more fully by Weaver in Chapter 4.) Being in a position to reject the null hypothesis means we have indirect support for the theory that generated the hypothesis, provided, of course, that our operational definitions are valid.

Note that we did not use the word "proof" in our discussion. One cannot "prove" a theory. We can only accumulate evidence "in support of" a particular theory. If most of the research hypotheses generated by the theory are supported in most cases, then we usually *accept* the theory as a reasonable representation and explanation of how certain phenomena are interrelated. This acceptance is always tentative, because a new theory with better empirical support may come along at any time, as we have said.

The reader may have noticed that we have not discussed step six in the theory-research process, *design a research study to test the hypotheses.* Given that a substantial portion of this book is devoted to research design (see Chapters 7 through 12), we do not deal with that topic in detail here. As the material in these chapters should make clear, it is a gross oversimplification to reduce such a complex undertaking to one "step." Research design is but one aspect of the overall theory-data-theory process, or "scientific method." It cannot be reduced to choices between experiment and survey or between chi square and correlation. These are important decisions, certainly, but they are only links in a long chain of decisions that constitutes the entire process. It is this decision chain that makes the research process inherently creative. To begin with, any number of concepts might be chosen and these concepts might be related to one another by theoretical propositions in any number of ways. There are many ways each concept may be operationalized and literally hundreds of research designs from which to choose and hundreds of analysis techniques to pick from depending on the research design selected.

But for all its complexity the process is characterized by a single underlying structure (see Figure 3–1). Basically, the process involves a continuous shuttling back and forth between two planes, the abstract plane of theory and the earthly plane of the empirical world. We begin with relatively informal observations of some phenomenon in the real world. To explain and predict phenomena, we engage in conceptualization, an inductive step by which we develop concepts and link them in a theoretical structure. To test the propositions of this structure, we must again descend to the real world, over the bridge created by our operational definitions. It is important to recognize the essentially arbitrary nature of these definitions. Our operational definitions enable us to make new observations, this time of a highly structured kind. We then examine these observations and, based on the relationships among them, we make inferences concerning the "truth" or "falsity" of our original propositions. If certain propositions did not receive empirical support, then we need to alter the theory, or correct our methodological procedures, or both, and put the theory to test once again. This process of reconceptualization prompted by research findings is what Selltiz, Wrightsman, and Cook term "retroduction":

> Retroduction is no bastard of science, but its progenitor. We fit data into patterns retroductively; we elaborate the patterns deductively and test them inductively, but the propositions that endure are usually retroduced, not deduced or induced. The scientist shuttles back and forth between data and theory. How else could it be?[11]

Ideally, this process should continue until an ideal theory emerges, one which is highly explanatory and that repeatedly withstands rigorous testing and replication. Unfortunately, this level of explanation is rarely attained.

[11]Claire Selltiz, Lawrence S. Wrightsman, and Stuart W. Cook, *Research Methods in Social Relations* (New York: Holt, Rinehart & Winston, 1976), p. 35.

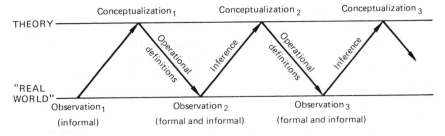

Figure 3–1

A Recent Example of Theory Building

Theory building need not be global, however, as an innovative conceptualization of agenda setting by McCombs and Weaver[12] will indicate. Agenda setting refers to the mass media tendency to select and emphasize particular issues and thereby focus attention on them, potentially resulting in these issues being placed high on the public's "agenda." The major concept in McCombs and Weaver's theory-building effort is *need for orientation,* in which an individual has a need to fill in enough details about the environment to become oriented and find his or her way around.

This concept is derived primarily from cognitive "utilitarian" theories, which "view the individual as a problem solver who approaches any situation as an opportunity to acquire useful information or new skills for coping with life's challenges.[13] The authors also drew upon Berlyne's[14] description of thinking as a reaction to a *gap* in a cognitive map, in which a person needs some additional information before being able to bring about closure, or completion, of some idea or thought. Awareness of this gap in one's information would trigger information search. The developers of the need for orientation concept reasoned that to be aware that a gap exists would necessitate some knowledge of a topic.

However, some gaps seemed likely to be more motivating than others. McCombs and Weaver then drew upon Jones and Gerard[15] for the proposition that motivation to seek information would increase with

[12]Maxwell McCombs and David Weaver, "Voters' Need for Orientation and Use of Mass Communication," paper presented to International Communication Association, Montreal, 1973. See also Maxwell McCombs, "Editorial Endorsements: A Study of Influence," *Journalism Quarterly* 44:545–48 (1967).

[13]William J. McGuire, "Psychological Motives and Communication Gratification," in Jay G. Blumler and Elihu Katz, eds., *The Uses of Mass Communications: Current Perspectives on Gratifications Research* (Beverly Hills, Calif.: Sage Publications, Inc., 1974), p. 181.

[14]D. E. Berlyne, *Conflict, Arousal, and Curiosity* (New York: McGraw-Hill Book Company, 1960).

[15]Edward E. Jones and Harold B. Gerard, *Foundation of Social Psychology* (New York: John Wiley & Sons, Inc., 1967).

(1) degree of uncertainty, (2) importance, or relevance, of the information for action decisions, and (3) the likelihood that a reliable source of information is available. The developers then reasoned that the wide availability of the mass media and their broad political coverage made the third proposition unnecessary in their study of political agendas. Their early reasoning, later revised,[16] was that if relevance and uncertainty are preconditions for arousal of a need for orientation, relevance should precede uncertainty in time.

All this resulted in the following summary of their propositions:

> Increased need for orientation leads to increased mass media use, which in turn leads to increased agenda-setting effects by media. As an individual strives to map political (or other) issues through the use of mass media, he is more susceptible (at least in many situations) to the agenda-setting effects of the media.[17]

The deductive model they constructed (Figure 3–2) describes levels of need for orientation in terms of differing levels of relevance and uncertainty.

Operational definitions were developed for each concept. For example, a subject's degree of uncertainty (assumed to be triggered by presence of a gap) was indexed by measuring (1) consistency (or lack of it) in a person's voting record over the previous four presidential elections, (2) strength of political party identification, and (3) degree of certainty about choice of a presidential candidate. Sources of data were field surveys of random samples of registered voters and content analysis of newspapers and television news shows in the area studied, the latter to compare rank orderings of issues identified by voters with rank orders of issues covered by the media. The resulting hypotheses were:

H₁: Group I [high need for orientation] subjects more frequently use newspapers and television for political information than Group II [moderate need] subjects. In turn, Group II subjects more frequently use newspapers and television for political information than Group III [low need] subjects.

$$(I > II > III: \text{use of newspapers and TV})$$

H₂: The agenda of national political issues among Group I subjects will more closely approximate the agenda of issues provided by newspa-

---

[16]See David H. Weaver, "Voters' Need for Orientation, Media Uses and Gratifications, and Learning of Issue Importance During the 1976 Presidential Campaign," paper presented to Speech Communication Association, Washington, D.C., 1977.

[17]David H. Weaver, "Political Issues and Voter Need for Orientation," in Donald L. Shaw and Maxwell E. McCombs, eds., *The Emergence of American Political Issues: The Agenda-Setting Function of the Press* (St. Paul, Minn.: West Publishing Company, 1977), p. 108.

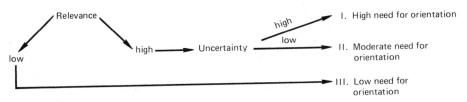

Antecedents of Need for Orientation

Relevance

low

high — Uncertainty — high / low

I. High need for orientation

II. Moderate need for orientation

III. Low need for orientation

Figure 3–2   Antecedents of Need for Orientation.

pers and television than will the agenda of Group II subjects. . . . In turn, the agenda of national issues among Group II subjects will more closely approximate the agenda of issues provided by newspapers and television than will the agenda of Group III subjects.

(I > II > III: agenda-setting)

This is as far as we need to go in this illustration. In general, the hypotheses about uncertainty were supported and have been supported in subsequent studies. But the findings permit less confidence about the time order of relevance and uncertainty. Through what we earlier described as retroduction, the conceptualization has been revised so that one does not need to precede the other.[18]

Much of the voluminous research done thus far in mass communication has been based on *implicit* theory; that is, their theoretical basis has not been stated in detail. McCombs and Weaver developed concepts and related them in *explicit* ways to form their theoretical propositions.

The "Crucial" Experiment

The ideal research design is one that considers not only the investigator's own theoretical explanation of some phenomenon, but at the same time takes into account alternative theories. Such a procedure is called a *crucial experiment* and, as noted by Stinchcombe,[19] "is a description of a set of observations which will decide between two alternative theories, both of which according to present knowledge are quite likely." He states that this method adds considerably more to the credibility of one's theory than studies that merely eliminate alternatives at random.

The present authors once became involved in such a study as part of a series of investigations into the factors that influence human in-

[18]Weaver, "Voter's Need," p. 5. See also Maxwell McCombs, "Agenda-Setting Research: A Bibliographic Essay," *Political Communication Review* 1:1–7 (1976), p. 5.

[19]Arthur L. Stinchcombe, *Constructing Social Theories* (New York: Harcourt Brace Jovanovich, Inc., 1968), p. 25.

41

formation processing.[20] We were concerned with a dissonance theory proposition which states that information discrepant with an individual's beliefs, attitudes, and values will induce greater dissonance (psychological stress) than will supportive information. From this is derived the well-known selective exposure hypothesis, which holds that people will avoid discrepant information and seek out supportive information. While the selective exposure hypothesis itself had received a great deal of research attention prior to our study, no previous investigation had directly tested the dissonance-induction proposition.

We might have tested this proposition simply by exposing one group of randomly assigned subjects to supportive information and another group to discrepant information, examining the levels of dissonance induced. We recognized, however, that certain individuals appear able to withstand the supposed discomfort produced by discrepant information better than others. In particular, dogmatism theory states that highly dogmatic individuals are characterized by a general rigidity of thought and an intolerance for ambiguity.[21] From this we might deduce that such individuals would display higher levels of dissonance when exposed to discrepant information than would low dogmatics. It would follow that high dogmatics should display a greater aversion for discrepant material than would low dogmatics (a prediction supported by research).

The expectation that high dogmatic individuals would display greater dissonance than low dogmatics when exposed to discrepant information was deduced from "conventional" dogmatism theory. However, it seemed to the authors that there existed another plausible model of dogmatism dynamics that generated an opposite prediction, that a low dogmatic or open-minded person may actually perceive herself or himself to be open-minded. In other words, low dogmatic persons might possess an open-minded perception of themselves. As such, we would expect them to be motivated to expose themselves to and evaluate fairly all types of information, both discrepant and supportive. This process, however, of attempting to evaluate opposing arguments fairly and even to consider restructuring one's cognitions should be highly stressful to the low dogmatic person. The high dogmatic or closed-minded person, lacking such an "open-minded" cognition, should feel no motivation to "try to see the good points" of opposing arguments and should thus experience less stress when actually confronted with discrepant material. In other words, the high dogmatic individual might actually close his or her mind and admit few incon-

[20]Lewis Donohew and Philip Palmgreen, "A Reappraisal of Dissonance and the Selective Exposure Process," *Journalism Quarterly* 48:412–20 (1971); Donohew and Palmgreen, "An Investigation of 'Mechanisms' of Information Selection," *Journalism Quarterly* 48:627–39, 666 (1971); Donohew and John R. Basehart, "Information Selection Processes and Galvanic Skin Response," *Journalism Quarterly* 51:33–39 (1974). The description here quotes liberally from these articles.

[21]Milton Rokeach, *The Open and Closed Mind* (New York: Basic Books, Inc., 1960).

sistent cognitions into the "arena of psychological debate." It was thus hypothesized as an alternative to the "conventional" dogmatism interaction hypothesis that it would be the low dogmatic subjects who would experience the greater stress upon exposure to discrepant material. By this interpretation, low dogmatics should expose themselves more than high dogmatics to discrepant material, as other investigators have found. But this would not be because low dogmatics experience less stress when confronted by inconsistency—as had been the general assumption—but instead because the low dogmatic person possesses an open-minded cognition to expose himself or herself to and evaluate opposing arguments, even though that is stress producing.

Employing the Rokeach dogmatism scale, we divided our subjects into high and low dogmatic groups and exposed half of each group (randomly chosen) to supportive information and the other half to discrepant information about the Vietnam War. Our results supported the "open-minded cognition" model of dogmatism, in that low dogmatic individuals displayed significantly higher dissonance (as measured by a "mood" scale) when exposed to discrepant information than did high dogmatics (no dogmatism-related differences were observed for supportive information). Our investigation thus constituted a *crucial experiment* in that it provided at least initial grounds for choosing between two competing and apparently equally plausible information-processing models.

Whenever theories in a particular substantive area contradict one another, crucial experiments are the ideal way to proceed. Of course, in every well-conceived experiment the built-in controls help eliminate competing explanations of the research findings that might be ascribed to individual differences, distractions in the laboratory setting, and so on. The reader is referred to Chapters 11 and 12 for further discussion of controls. In surveys, a certain amount of *statistical* control is also possible over potential "spurious correlation" explanations due to individual differences. As we have seen, all theoretical research is devoted to attempts to find support for certain theoretical explanations while discounting or eliminating others. Occasionally, though, this problem is made even more critical when two or more well-defined theories are in direct competition; then the crucial experiment is called for.

Theory before Data or Data before Theory?

There is some disagreement among students of scientific method over which should come first, data or theory. In the seven-stage description of the process given here we put observation first, followed by tentative formulations of constructs and propositions. Such observations may, of course, arise unaided by research. But it is more likely that they arise from observations of data, our own and those of others. We scan data for signs of regularity and of anomaly. (Some are better at this than others. The late Paul Deutschmann, for example, was noted for astuteness in finding suggestive relationships in relatively unreduced data.)

Both Westley[22] and Reynolds[23] offer perspectives of the process that identify three stages. For Westley, whose ideas are summarized in Figure 3–3, the first stage is one of relatively crude observation and highly intuitive interpretation. At this stage observation and interpretation are more or less inseparable, just as in perception observation is guided by expectation.

It is at stage II (inductive empiricism) that we begin to refine our observations (through measurement), treat them systematically (through statistical reduction), and begin to refine constructs and develop operational definitions. This is more or less the correlational stage where we seek as much order as the data provide us, working entirely inductively. Thus what we carry to stage III is a combination of observation and interpretation. (Stage III is more or less the process as it is described here.)

Reynolds' three stages (exploratory, descriptive, explanatory) are in many ways similar:

(1) *Exploratory.* Research is designed to allow an investigator to just look around with respect to some phenomenon. The researcher should endeavor to develop suggestive ideas, and the research should be as flexible as possible. If possible, the research should be conducted in such a way as to provide guidance for procedures to be employed in research activity during stage two.

(2) *Descriptive.* The goal at this stage is to develop careful descriptions of patterns that were suspected in the exploratory research. The purpose may be seen as one of developing intersubjective descriptions, i.e., empirical generalizations. Once an empirical generalization is developed, it is then considered worth explaining, i.e., the development of a theory.

(3) *Explanatory.* The goal at this stage is to develop explicit theory that can be used to explain the empirical generalizations that evolve from the second stage. This is a continuous cycle of:

  (a) Theory construction;
  (b) Theory testing, attempts to falsify with empirical research;
  (c) Theory reformation, back to step 3a.

This formulation is also quite consistent with the position taken here.

Searching for Ideas

Now that we have described the steps in theory construction and discussed assumptions, how does one come up with ideas for communi-

[22]Bruce H. Westley, "Scientific Method and Communication Research," in Ralph O. Nafziger and David M. White, eds., *Introduction to Mass Communications Research* (Baton Rouge: Louisiana State University Press, 1963), p. 260.

[23]Paul Davidson Reynolds, *A Primer in Theory Construction* (Indianapolis: Bobbs-Merrill Co., Inc., 1971), pp. 154–55.

Figure 3–3 Schematic representation of three levels of empirical investigation.[a]

Level (Stage)	Purpose	Formal System	"Mapping" Devices	Theoretical System	"Mapping" Devices	Reality System	Approached "End Product"
I Orientation, Problem setting	Orientation: problem setting, "hypothesis hunching." Intuitive (no certainty) knowledge of loosely defined segment of reality.	"Common sense." Inductive logic.	"Common sense."	Fragmentary, intuitive constructs. Plausible hypotheses and explanations. "Interpretations."	Verbal definitions. Subjective relations between observations and constructs.	Sweeping, inclusive, holistic, interpretative observations (wholly uncontrolled).	Description; insight; "wisdom." Orientation.
II Inductive empiricism	Orientation: problem setting, hypothesis formulating. Conceptual clarity. Low-certainty knowledge of a more or less defined segment of reality.	Inductive logic.	Concepts loosely related to formal properties.	Hypothetical constructs of increasing refinement. Emerging hypotheses.	Measurement of attributes. (Operational definitions?) Normative (probability) statistics.	Observations defined by operations (statistical control).	"Observed dependencies" leading to testable hypotheses.
III Hypothetico-deductive empiricism	Dependable (high-certainty) knowledge of a strictly defined segment of reality.	Deductive logic.	Formal derivation.	Assumptions, postulates, and derived hypotheses.	Measurement of attributes. Operational definitions. Normative and nonnormative statistics.	Observations strictly defined by operations. Controlled observation (statistical and/or laboratory controls).	Verified generalizations, statable as laws, and inferring causal connections.

[a]This may also be treated as stages in the development of a science or as stages in the advancement of a particular investigation.

cation theories? We noted earlier that there is a shortage of theory in the field, yet this does not indicate a lack of research over a wide range of topics. In the preface to the third edition of *Theories of Mass Communication,* sociologists Melvin DeFleur and Sandra Ball-Rokeach have observed that

> various sources have yielded an amazingly diverse set of trends, specialized interests, subareas, and directions. In fact, the heterogeneity of the field has sometimes proved to be an embarrassment of riches. No one can be sure at any given time, or can be sure at the present time, precisely what constitutes the study of mass communication.[24]

Cole and Bowers asked the twenty-four most productive scholars in the field and the deans of the twenty-five most research-productive schools: "What are the important areas in which we should involve ourselves and in which theory should be developed?" The researchers gave thirty different answers and the deans gave twenty-five, with no area receiving more than three mentions.[25]

DeFleur and Ball-Rokeach are not disturbed by this diversity. They write that although heterogeneity exists, it would be superficial to conclude that investigators in mass communication are less capable or more indecisive in choosing modes of inquiry than persons in other disciplines. They argued that:

> The diversity characteristic of this area of study arises because of the fundamental nature of the communication process itself, and the tremendous importance that mass communication plays in modern society. Students of human nature, whatever their disciplinary identification or theoretical orientation, cannot study human behavior without recognizing at the outset that communication processes are as vital to human beings as are biological processes. The latter permit them to function as living creatures; the former permit them to function as *rational* creatures. The principles of human communication, not the principles of biological functioning, most sharply distinguish human beings from other living organisms.[26]

Within the body of literature represented by the several journals dealing with communication, two annual reviews describing perspectives and new thinking in communication research,[27] a number of special publications, and work in related fields, there is considerable raw material for developing new concepts and reconceptualizing old ones.[28]

---

[24]Melvin L. DeFleur and Sandra Ball-Rokeach, *Theories of Mass Communication,* 3rd ed., (New York: David McKay Co., Inc., 1975), p. ix.

[25]Richard R. Cole and Thomas A. Bowers, "An Exploration of Factors Related to Journalism Faculty Productivity," *Journalism Quarterly* 52:638–44 (1975). See also Cole and Bowers, "Research Article Productivity of U.S. Journalism Faculties," *Journalism Quarterly* 50:246–54 (1973).

[26]DeFleur and Rokeach, *Theories,* p. x.

[27]F. Gerald Kline and Peter Clarke, eds., *Sage Annual Reviews in Communication Research* and Brent Ruben, ed., *Communication Yearbook.*

[28]In recent years, the study of communication has tended to be divided into three sys-

It also is possible to get some notion about what is likely to be supported in this new perspective, and why, through review of data reported in the tables accompanying these articles and chapters.

Reynolds has suggested that a "new idea" or paradigm may incorporate either or both of the following:

> (1) The invention of a new theoretical concept that can be used as part of a theory, either hypothetical (imaginary) or one that has empirical referents (can be measured with operational definitions). In the example of the jigsaw puzzle, this is tantamount to cutting the picture into a new set of pieces.

> (2) A suggestion of new ways of organizing the causal relationships among "old" or "old" and "new" theoretical concepts. Following the analogy, this is like putting the pieces of the puzzle together in a new way.[29]

In communication we often have borrowed the theories of others as we have sought to understand, explain, and predict behaviors associated with communication. But there are no patents on disciplinary boundaries to theories, and there is nothing to prevent us from going further and inventing new concepts or reorganizing old ones in new ways that allow us to explain in greater detail or in greater depth the phenomena that interest students of mass communication.

---

tem levels. See C. David Mortensen, *Communication: The Study of Human Interaction* (New York: McGraw-Hill Book Co., 1972). These may be described as (1) *intrapersonal,* in which the unit of analysis is the individual, (2) *interpersonal,* in which the unit of analysis is the dyad or small group, and (3) *social system,* in which the unit of analysis is some larger unit, such as a neighborhood, a community, a metropolitan area, or a developing nation.

[29]Reynolds, *Primer in Theory,* p. 151.

4

Basic Statistical Tools

David H. Weaver

Many students interested in journalism and mass communications express a dislike or fear, or both, of anything quantitative. One typical comment from such a student is: "I never was any good at math; that's why I decided to go into journalism."

This comment reflects a misunderstanding about the nature and uses of statistics in mass communication research. Statistics and mathematics are not the same, and one need not necessarily be adept at mathematics to use statistics effectively in mass communication research.

In most cases in mass communication research, we use statistics to reduce complicated sets of findings or data to simpler terms. We usually are trying to answer one of two questions: (1) how strong is the relationship between variables, or (2) is this difference real, or is it due to chance? We might, for example, find that modernization of format by newspapers is related to increase in circulation. A correlation coefficient, which we know can range from -1.0 to $+1.0$, enables us with one number to summarize the relationship we have found between modernization of format and circulation. Or we might find that readership of editorials in our survey is on the average 5 points higher for men than for women. A *t*-test will enable us to find out whether that is merely a difference that happened by chance in this sample or a real difference we might expect to find with all readers of that paper.

Although it used to be argued that one needs to be somewhat familiar with mathematics to calculate various statistics, this is less true as electronic calculators and computers become more available, and as preprogrammed statistical packages (such as SPSS, the statistical package for the social sciences)[1] become easier to use. Unless one wants to invent a new statistic, there are preprogrammed calculators and computer packages to produce just about any commonly used statistic from raw data.

This is not to say that an extended knowledge of mathematics is irrelevant or useless, but only to suggest that it is ordinarily not needed in conducting most quantitative mass communication research.

A knowledge of the mathematical principles and procedures underlying statistics is very valuable in interpreting statistical results and in checking the packaged programs used to calculate various statistics. But it is not essential for one to be highly proficient in mathematics to understand and use statistics.

DESCRIPTIVE STATISTICS

A primary use of statistics in quantitative mass communication research is to summarize large and complicated sets of data. Why are such summaries needed?

Consider a survey of 500 persons or an analysis of 500 court documents. If only ten questions are asked of each person or each document, such a study produces at least 5,000 pieces of information. The hundreds of answers to each question, in their raw form, are very difficult, if not impossible, to interpret without the help of some summary measures, or statistics. This becomes more and more the case as the size and the complexity of a set of data increase.

There are basically two ways to summarize or describe a set of data: (1) according to how the individual pieces of information *cluster* together (measures of central tendency), and (2) according to how individual cases *spread apart* (measures of dispersion).

Measures of Central Tendency

The three most common measures of clustering, or central tendency, are the *mean* (average), the *median* (midpoint), and the *mode* (most frequent value, or values).

Mean. This is the most common measure of central tendency. It is simply the sum of the individual values for each variable divided by the number of cases. It should be used with interval data. By interval, we mean that the scale of measurement contains equal intervals.

---

[1]See Norman H. Nie and others, *SPSS: Statistical Package for the Social Sciences,* 2nd ed. (New York: McGraw-Hill Book Company, 1975).

Height measured in inches, for example, is an interval measurement because all inches are the same size.

Thus, if we interview twenty persons and assign them scores based on how often they use newspapers, radio, and television for news, we find the mean, usually represented as $\bar{X}$, by adding the scores and dividing by the number of cases (twenty in this example). In other words,

$$\bar{X} = \frac{\text{sum of scores}}{\text{number of scores}} \quad \text{or} \quad \bar{X} = \frac{\Sigma x}{N}$$

Once the mean is calculated it tells you the *balance point,* or the average, of the set of values you are interested in summarizing. There are not necessarily an equal number of scores above and below the mean, as is true of the median, but the mean is sensitive to the value of each score and the distance of each score from every other score. With a normal distribution, there will tend to be the same number of scores both above and below the mean (see Figure 4–1). When there are a few very high or very low scores, however, the mean will be pulled toward those extreme scores and will not be as accurate an indicator of the central clustering, or midpoint, of these scores as it would be if there were no extreme scores (see Figure 4–2).

Distributions of scores with a few very high members are said to be *positively* skewed, whereas distributions with a few very low scores are said to be *negatively* skewed. In positively skewed distributions, the mean is likely to be misleadingly high (see Figure 4–2). In negatively skewed distributions, the mean is likely to be misleadingly low (see Figure 4–3).

In short, the mean is an extremely sensitive measure of clustering and is also a very accurate measure of central tendency when the set of measures is fairly equally distributed above and below the midpoint, as in Figure 4–1. In addition, the mean is the most important statistically of all the measures of central tendency, as will become more apparent in the discussions of the *t*-test and the analysis of variance.

Median. The median is the midpoint of a set of ordered numbers. To find the median, arrange the numbers from smallest to largest. Thus, if we had the numbers 1, 5, 8, 7, and 3, we would arrange them 1, 3, 5, 7, and 8. The median would be the middle number, 5. If we

Figure 4–1 A Normal Distribution.

6						×					
5					×	×	×				
4				×	×	×	×	×			
3			×	×	×	×	×	×	×		
2		×	×	×	×	×	×	×	·×	×	
1	×	×	×	×	×	×	×	×	×	×	×
	1	2	3	4	5	6	7	8	9	10	11

Mean = 6.0

Figure 4–2   Positively Skewed Distribution.

				Modes							
5		×	×		×						
4		×	×		×						
3		×	×	×	×	×	×	×			
2	×	×	×	×	×	×	×	×	×	×	×
1	1	2	3	4	5	6	7	8	9	10	11

Mean = .5.04

add a number, say 10, to the series, then we would have 1, 3, 5, 7, 8, and 10. We would use a slightly different procedure. We would now take the two middle numbers, 5 and 7, and take the midpoint between those two numbers, or 6, as our median. Like the mean, the median can be used with interval data. It also can be used with ordinal data. If instead of measuring height in inches, we line people up according to height and rank them from tallest to shortest, those ranks will be ordinal measures.

Because the median depends only on the number of measures in a distribution and not their value, it is quite useful as a measure of central tendency for distributions that are positively or negatively skewed, but it is not as useful as the mean in more complicated statistical tests where one is interested in the odds of certain differences occurring by chance.

Mode. The mode is simply the most frequent score, or scores, in a distribution and may be calculated for variables measured at any level. In the case of a "normal" distribution, as illustrated in Figure 4–1, there will be only one mode and it will equal the mean and the median. In some distributions that are not normally arranged, however, there may be several measures that tie for the most frequent score, and thus several modes (see Figures 4–2 and 4–3). In distributions where all scores are equal, there will be no mode.

Why use the mode? What does it tell you that the mean and median do not?

In a normal distribution, the mode offers no additional information to that conveyed by the mean and the median. In a skewed distribution, however, where the mean, median, and mode may all take on different values, the mode tells you not only the most frequent value(s)

Figure 4–3   Negatively Skewed Distribution.

						Modes					
5											
4						×			×	×	
3						×			×	×	
2		×	×	×	×	×	×	×	×	×	
1	×	×	×	×	×	×	×	×	×	×	×
	1	2	3	4	5	6	7	8	9	10	11

Mean = 6.54

but also how far from the midpoint (median) and balance point (mean) the most frequent value, or values, occur.

It is useful to compare the values of the mean, median, and mode for any distribution of scores or values of any kind. If these three statistics are fairly equal, the chances are that the distribution is fairly normal. If they are substantially different, the chances are that the distribution is skewed in some manner. If the mean is larger than the median and the mode, this usually indicates a positively skewed distribution (see Figure 4–2). If the mean is smaller than either the median or the mode, this usually indicates a negatively skewed distribution (see Figure 4–3).

Measures of Dispersion

The three most common measures of scatter, or dispersion, are the *range,* the *variance,* and the *standard deviation. Percentiles* are also considered measures of scatter by some researchers.

Range. This is the simplest measure of dispersion. It is calculated by subtracting the lowest score (minimum) from the highest score (maximum) in a distribution of values. It is not at all sensitive to the distribution of scores falling between the minimum and maximum, and so provides very limited information about how a set of scores is dispersed.

Variance. Sometimes referred to as s^2, variance is a measure of the dispersion of values around the mean. Unlike the range, the variance is sensitive to every score in a distribution of scores, and thus provides more information about the dispersion of a set of scores than does the range.

The variance is the average of the squared deviations from the mean. To calculate the variance, the mean must first be determined. Once this is done, each score is subtracted from the mean, and the difference is squared to eliminate any negative values and to give additional weight to extreme cases. These squared differences are then added together and divided by the number of scores in the distribution to get the average squared deviation:

$$s^2 = \frac{\Sigma (x - \bar{X})^2}{N}$$

where Σ means "the sum of," x equals each individual score, $\bar{X}$ equals the mean of the set of scores, and N equals the number of scores in the distribution (see Figure 4–4).

Thus the variance provides a measure of scatter which is sensitive to all the values in a distribution. The larger the variance, the more spread out the scores in a distribution. In addition, variance is important in many other statistical tests and procedures. In mass communi-

Figure 4–4 Calculation of the variance and the standard deviation.

Scores (x)	Frequency	$(x - \bar{X})$	$(x - \bar{X})^2$	$(x - \bar{X})^2 \times$ Frequency
6	1	-4	16	16
7	2	-3	9	18
8	4	-2	4	16
10	6	0	0	0
12	4	2	4	16
13	2	3	9	18
14	1	4	16	16
	20			$\Sigma(x - \bar{X})^2 = 100$

$$\bar{X} \text{ (mean)} = \frac{\Sigma x}{N} = \frac{200}{20} = 10$$

$$s^2 \text{ (variance)} = \frac{\Sigma (x - \bar{X})^2}{N} = \frac{100}{20} = 5$$

$$s \text{ (standard deviation)} = \sqrt{\frac{\Sigma (x - \bar{X})^2}{N}} = \sqrt{\frac{100}{20}} = \sqrt{5} = 2.24$$

In a distribution of scores where more than one score has the same value, one must remember to multiply each score by its frequency when adding the scores and to divide by the total frequency of scores rather than the number of different scores. So, in calculating the mean, one multiplies each score by its frequency and gets a total of 200, which is divided by the total frequency of scores (20) to yield a mean of 10.

Each score is then subtracted from the mean of 10, and the difference is squared: $(x - \bar{X})^2$. Then the squared differences are multiplied by the frequency of each score and added to produce the sum of the squared differences about the mean: $\Sigma (x - \bar{X})^2$. This sum (100 in this case) is divided by the total frequency of scores (20) to yield a variance of 5.

The standard deviation is calculated simply by taking the square root of the variance of 5, yielding a value of 2.24 (rounded to two decimal places).

cation research, one of the main goals is to "explain variance" in dependent variables by locating other independent variables which can account for why some cases deviate more or less from the mean. (A "dependent" variable is one for which the value depends on an "independent" variable. For example, if we hypothesize that the amount of time a person spends reading magazines depends on the person's level of reading ability, then reading ability is the independent variable and time spent reading magazines the dependent variable.)

Standard deviation. This is the most commonly used measure of dispersion because it is expressed in the *same* measurement units as the scores it summarizes. The standard deviation is simply the square root of the variance, and is often expressed as *s*. The values of the standard deviation are smaller and easier to work with than those of the variance, and the standard deviation values have more intuitive meaning because they are expressed in the same units as the original scores. That is, if the variance of the annual income of a sample of workers is 250,000, then we are really talking about 250,000 squared dollars. A standard deviation of 500, though, refers to 500 dollars.

The standard deviation is calculated in exactly the same manner as the variance, except that one additional step is required—taking the square root of the final figure:

$$s = \sqrt{\frac{\Sigma(x - \bar{X})^2}{N}}$$

where Σ means "the sum of," x equals each individual score, $\bar{X}$ equals the mean of the set of scores, N equals the number of scores in the distribution, and $\sqrt{}$ means "the square root of" (see Figure 4–4).

In addition to being sensitive to every score, or value, in a distribution and being expressed in the same measurement units as the original scores, the standard deviation is very important in estimating the *probability* of how frequently certain scores can be expected to occur in random sampling. In other words, the standard deviation is very important in calculating sampling error and confidence intervals. This will be discussed in more detail in the next section on inferential statistics, where measures of association and differences are included.

Percentiles. Perhaps the most common measure of dispersion, percentiles are useful for describing how an individual score is related to other scores in a distribution. For example, if you know that an individual score is at the eightieth percentile, you know that nearly four-fifths of the scores fall below this score and one-fifth of the scores fall above it.

To compute percentiles, rank the scores from lowest to highest. Take the rank of the score you want the percentile for, divide it by the total number of items, and multiply by 100. For example, we have these scores: 6, 6, 8, 9, 10, 12, 14, 15, 18, and 19. We want to know the percentile value of 15. Ranking the scores, we find that 15 ranks eighth. There are ten scores, so our computation is $\frac{8}{10} \times 100$ or 80.

Summary of Descriptive Statistics

Descriptive statistics are summaries of distributions of measures or scores. These summaries are often needed in mass communication research because of the large and complex nature of different quantitative studies, be they surveys, content analyses, or experiments.

Measures of central tendency (the mean, median, mode, and others) are used to summarize how the individual scores or values cluster together, whereas measures of dispersion (the range, variance, standard deviation, and percentiles) are used to summarize how the individual measures scatter, or spread apart.

When using measures of central tendency, one should not automatically rely on only the mean, or average, but should check the value of the median to see how close it is to that of the mean. If the median differs substantially from the mean, this is probably a sign that the distribution is skewed. A further check of the skewness statistic, if available, should confirm whether the distribution is skewed. If so, the median should probably be used as a measure of central tendency rather than the mean, unless the median differs appreciably from the mode.

If the median does differ substantially from the mode, and there is only one clear mode, it may be that the mode is the truest measure of clustering in a highly skewed distribution.

If the mean, median, and mode are all fairly equal, however, it is best to use the mean because of its usefulness in statistical tests of differences, such as the t-test and the analysis of variance.

When using measures of dispersion, one should not rely only on the range, because it is not sensitive to the scores between the lowest and highest points of the distribution. Percentages are useful for comparing one score or a category of scores with the other scores in a distribution, but percentages cannot provide a single measure of how spread out a set of scores is from the mean, as can the variance or the standard deviation.

In general, the standard deviation is more useful as a single measure of dispersion than is the variance, because the standard deviation is expressed in the same units of measurement as the original scores and can be directly related to the probability of certain scores occurring in random samples, as will be discussed in the next section. The variance, on the other hand, is more useful in statistical tests of relationships and differences among two or more variables.

INFERENTIAL STATISTICS

Inferential statistics differ from descriptive statistics because they are used not only to summarize characteristics of sets of data and relationships between various sets of data, but also to make estimates of how likely it is that such characteristics or relationships exist in the universe (or population) of all possible cases that make up the sets of data, whether these cases be people, cities, newspaper articles, or whatever.

Mass communication researchers usually study only a *sample* of the universe of all possible cases, whether they are persons in a survey, documents or articles in a content analysis study, or cities in a field experimental study. Descriptive statistics, such as the median, mean, and standard deviation, are usually used to describe characteristics of these samples. If these samples are drawn on a *random* basis, such that each case in the universe has an approximately equal chance of falling into the sample, then sampling error may be calculated to make estimates of how these descriptive statistical summaries apply to a universe of all possible cases.

Because most mass communication researchers are interested in generalizing beyond their particular samples, and because they are usually more interested in *relationships* between measures (or variables), rather than simply describing each set of measures individually, measures of associations and differences are needed to summarize the strength of such relationships and to provide an estimate of how likely it is that such relationships exist in the universes from which the samples were drawn.

Thus, inferential statistics differ from descriptive statistics in two fundamental ways: (1) They are usually concerned with the strength of *relationships* (associations or differences) among two or more sets of measured variables, and (2) they have accompanying tests of statistical significance which indicate how likely it is that a particular relationship would occur by chance, given a certain sized sample.

Before discussing various measures of association and difference, it is necessary to distinguish between statistics and parameters and to briefly review some of the underlying principles of random sampling. A more detailed account of various forms of sampling appears in Chapter 9.

Statistics and Parameters

Simply put, statistics refer to various characteristics of a *sample,* such as the mean, median, and mode, and parameters refer to various characteristics of a *universe.* Statistical inference is the process of estimating parameters from statistics. For example, if we interview a random sample of 400 college students and find that they read an average of four issues of the college newspaper a week, we are dealing with a statistic, a mean of four issues read a week. If we know that a random sample of 400 cases has a certain error due to sampling, and we take this into account in estimating the average number of issues read each week by all 33,000 students, we are estimating a *parameter*—the average number of issues read each week by the universe (all students enrolled on a certain campus).

It is important to remember that parameters are *fixed* values and are generally *unknown* because we can rarely interview all persons in a certain universe (all citizens of a certain city, all students attending a given college) or examine all issues of a certain newspaper. Statistics, on the other hand, tend to vary somewhat from one sample to another and, of course, are known quantities.

Random Sampling

If statistics (characteristics of samples) vary from one sample to another, how is it possible to estimate parameters (characteristics of universes) from one sample? The answer, in its simplest form, is that random samples of the same universe, if drawn over and over again, are distributed in a *normal* fashion, and this normal pattern of distribution allows us to calculate the probability of a universe parameter falling within a certain range of values. By random sample we are referring to a sample where each member of a certain universe has an *equal chance* of being included. An example of this is the familiar technique of putting names in a hat and drawing a certain number of names without looking at them.

In other words, if repeated random samples are drawn from a certain universe of persons, newspaper issues, court documents, or whatever, the means of each sample will be distributed in the shape of a normal curve, with the overall mean for all samples coming very close to the actual universe mean (see Figure 4–5).

We also know from two mathematical theorems, the law of large numbers and the central limits theorem, that the larger the size of the samples, the more likely it is that the overall mean for repeated random samples (the mean of the sampling distribution) will be identical to the actual universe mean and the spread of sample means about the overall mean will be less. This is true *even though the universe itself may not be normally distributed.*[2]

Figure 4–5 illustrates a nonnormal universe distribution and an accompanying normal sampling distribution, with equal means. Remember that the universe distribution is made up of many individual cases (persons, newspaper issues, court documents), and the sampling distribution is made up of the means from many repeated random samples. Why is it so important that the sampling distribution take the shape of a normal curve?

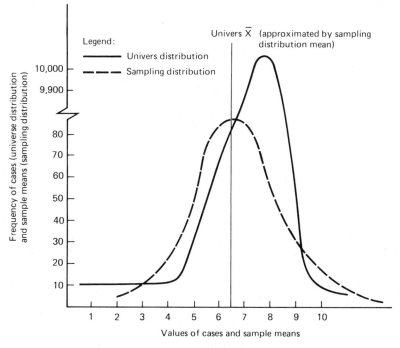

Figure 4–5 Nonnormal Universe Distribution with an Accompanying Normal Sampling Distribution.

[2]See William L. Hays and Robert L. Winkler, *Statistics: Probability, Inference, and Decision* (New York: Holt, Rinehart & Winston, 1971), pp. 285–292, for a discussion of the law of large numbers and the central limits theorem.

Because statistics from repeated random samples are arrayed in a normal distribution about universe statistics, it is possible to estimate the amount and the probability of the error contained in a single sample. This is so because the normal curve has certain known properties. For example, we know that about 68 percent of the cases in a normal curve fall within plus or minus one standard deviation from the mean. We also know that slightly more than 95 percent of the cases fall within plus or minus two standard deviations from the mean (see Figure 4–6).

This means that if random samples were drawn from the same universe over and over again for an infinite number of times, about 95 percent of these samples would have means falling within plus or minus 1.96 standard deviations of the overall mean. Therefore, we can be 95 percent certain that when we draw a random sample it will be one of those samples falling within plus or minus 1.96 standard deviations from the overall mean. Likewise, we can be 99 percent certain that when we draw a random sample it will fall within plus or minus 2.58 standard deviations from the overall mean of the sampling distribution.

It should be remembered that the samples must be of a fairly large size for their means to be distributed in a normal manner. That is, the samples should include at least 50 and preferably 100 cases.[3] Samples

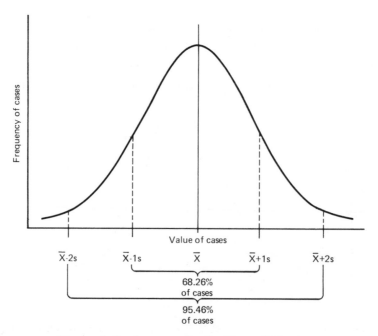

Figure 4–6 Areas under the Normal Curve.

[3]See Hubert M. Blalock, *Social Statistics* (New York: McGraw-Hill Book Company, 1960), p. 142, for a discussion of sample size and the assumption of normality.

with fewer than 50 cases cannot be assumed to be normally distributed; therefore, calculating sampling error for such samples is not recommended.

Calculating Sampling Error

Knowing that 95 percent of fairly large random samples fall within plus or minus 1.96 standard deviations from the sampling distribution mean is very useful, but it is not enough information to be able to calculate the amount of sampling error. An additional piece of information is required: the value of the standard deviation of the sampling distribution for any given sample. This value varies with the size of the random sample. As mentioned earlier, the spread of repeated sample means about the overall mean for the sampling distribution decreases as the sample size increases. Thus, the standard deviation of a sample distribution decreases as the sample size increases (and increases as the sample size becomes smaller). This means that the amount of sampling error decreases as the sample becomes larger, as one would intuitively suspect.

The value of the standard deviation ·of a sampling distribution is also known as the *standard error*. Although the standard error cannot be computed exactly because one cannot draw an infinite number of random samples of the same size from a given universe, it can be estimated by dividing the standard deviation of a single sample by the square root of the number of cases in the sample.[4] In other words,

$$\text{Standard error} = \frac{\text{standard deviation}}{\sqrt{N}}$$

or

$$s_m = \frac{s}{\sqrt{N}}$$

However, the computation of the standard error as discussed thus far assumes an *interval* level of measurement, a continuous scale. Often in mass communication research, the variables we are interested in are measured at the *ordinal* or *nominal* levels. In other words, we are often dealing with proportions (percentages) when calculating sampling error rather than means and standard deviations.

How is it possible, then, to estimate the value of the standard error for a certain sized random sample?

By treating proportions as special cases of means, much of the previous discussion of the standard error still applies. It can be shown from the general formula for the standard deviation that the formula for the standard error of a given random sample is $s_m = \sqrt{\dfrac{pq}{N}}$ where s_m equals the standard error for a given sized sample, p equals the proportion of the sample falling into a certain category (say, 30

---

[4]Hays and Winkler, *Statistics*, p. 284; Nie and others, *SPSS*, p. 184.

percent), q equals 100-p (70 percent in this example), and N equals the size of the sample.[5]

Once the value of the standard error is calculated, either by using the standard deviation or the proportions formula, one is ready to calculate the sampling error. This is usually done either at the 95 percent level of confidence or the 99 percent level of confidence. Because we know that 95 percent of large random samples will fall within plus or minus 1.96 standard deviations of the overall sampling distribution mean, we multiply the standard error by 1.96 to calculate the sampling error at the 95 percent level of confidence:

Sampling error $= 1.96 \; s_m$

or

$$\text{Sampling error} = 1.96 \sqrt{\frac{pq}{N}} \text{ (using the proportions formula)}$$

At the 99 percent level of confidence, the same formula holds, but 2.58 is substituted for 1.96, because we know that 99 percent of large random samples will fall within plus or minus 2.58 standard deviations of the sampling distribution mean (our estimate of the universe mean).

It should be emphasized that repeated large random samples fall *both above and below* the sampling distribution mean, so a plus or minus sign ($\pm$) should be inserted before any estimate of sampling error. That is, if the sampling error for a sample of 300 cases is calculated at 5.6 percent using the 95 percent level of confidence, this means that we are 95 percent confident that the true universe value lies somewhere between the sample value (say, 30 percent) *plus or minus* 5.6 percent. In other words, in this example we are 95 percent certain that the true universe value falls between 24.4 and 35.6 percent (30 $\pm$ 5.6 percentage points). This interval (24.4 to 35.6 percent) is known as a *confidence interval,* in this case, a 95 percent confidence interval.

One way of simplifying the calculation of sampling error for an entire study, using the proportions formula, is to assume that p equals 0.5 (or 50 percent) for each variable, and therefore q equals 0.5, making pq equal to 0.25 (0.5 $\times$ 0.5). This is the largest value the standard deviation can assume, using the proportions formula, and therefore is a conservative estimate. If 0.25 is substituted for pq, the formula for sampling error (using the proportions formula for the standard error) becomes

$$\text{Sampling error} = \pm 1.96 \sqrt{\frac{0.25}{N}} \text{ (for the 95\% level of confidence)}$$

In this formula, all that is needed is the sample size (N) to complete the calculation of sampling error.

Through random sampling and the calculation of sampling error

[5]Blalock, *Social Statistics,* pp. 149–153.

and confidence intervals, it is thus possible to estimate parameters from statistics—to generalize from one sample to the universe from which the sample was drawn.

RELATIONSHIPS

As noted earlier, mass communication researchers typically are interested in going beyond the generalizing of certain descriptive statistics of sample variables (e.g., the mean, median, or percentages) to various universes. Researchers are also very much interested in looking at the strength of *relationships* between various sample variables (e.g., level of education and mass media use) and in being able to estimate how likely it is that such relationships exist in the universes from which the samples were drawn.

An examination of relationships in a sample is important for at least three major reasons: (1) for testing research hypotheses, such as "The more education a person has, the more time he or she will spend reading newspapers"; (2) for answering research questions, such as "Do persons who spend much time reading newspapers tend to be more interested in politics than those who spend little time reading newspapers?" and (3) for suggesting new research hypotheses and/or questions (see Chapter 2 for a more detailed discussion of hypothesis testing).

There are two basic ways of looking at relationships among mass communication variables. One can look for *associations* or for *differences.* That is, one can ask if one variable increases (or decreases) as another increases, or one can ask if there are significant differences in one variable that may be due to differences in other variables.

Once one has decided to look for associations and/or differences in sample data, two additional questions must be answered: (1) How strong are the associations and/or differences? and (2) How likely is it that these associations and/or differences exist in the universe from which the sample was drawn? The second question applies *only* to sample data. If one collects data from every member of the universe (e.g., U.S. senators in 1965), only the first question is of interest.

There are many different statistical measures designed to indicate the strength of association between two variables. The choice of which one(s) to use depends largely on the *level of measurement* of the variables being related (see Chapter 5 for a detailed discussion of different levels of measurement).

Before discussing specific measures of association, it is necessary to briefly review the nature of correlation and cross-tabulation.

Correlation

When we speak of a *correlation* (positive or negative) between two variables, we are talking about things that are measured on the *ordinal level* or higher; that is, they range from low to high or from few to many. Such variables might include frequency of newspaper readership (measured in number of issues read each week or the amount of each issue read), level of political interest (ranging from low to high), or amount of time spent watching television each week.

A *positive correlation* between political interest and frequency of newspaper readership means that high levels of political interest tend to be associated with high levels of newspaper readership, and low levels of political interest are linked with low levels of newspaper readership. A *negative correlation* between political interest and frequency of newspaper readership would indicate that high levels of political interest are associated with low levels of newspaper readership, and vice versa.

Most correlational measures range from −1 to +1, with −1 indicating a perfect *negative* correlation (all low values of one variable are associated with all high values of another variable), 0 indicating *no* correlation (there is no pattern of association between low and high values of the two variables), and +1 indicating a perfect *positive* correlation (all high values of one variable are associated with all high values of another variable, and all low values of one variable are linked with all low values of the other).

In mass communication research it is very unlikely, given the crudeness of our measures and the lack of any hard and fast linear "laws," that you will find perfect correlations (either positive or negative). Most correlations will range from −0.65 (a moderately strong negative correlation) to +0.65 (a moderately strong positive correlation).

Significance Levels

In addition to indicating the *strength* of a relationship (from −1, a very strong negative correlation, to +1, a very strong positive correlation), most correlational statistics also include a *significance level,* which indicates how likely it is that the relationship could have happened by chance. This significance level may range from almost 0 (which indicates that there is almost no likelihood that the relationship could have occurred by chance) to 1 (which indicates that it is certain that the relationship could have occurred by chance).

Significance level varies not only with the strength of the relationship (high correlations have higher significance levels, indicating that they are less likely to occur by chance), but also with the size of the sample. In large samples, even weak relationships may by statistically significant, while in small samples only high correlations will be significant. Therefore, the choice of a significance level depends upon the size of the sample, among other factors.[6]

There are no hard rules regarding the choice of a significance level

[6]For a discussion of other factors influencing the choice of a significance level, see Sanford Labovitz, "Criteria for Selecting a Significance Level: A Note on the Sacredness of .05," *American Sociologist,* 3:220–222 (August 1968).

in mass communication research, but 0.05 is generally accepted for samples of 500 or less, and 0.01 is generally more appropriate for larger samples.

A significance level of 0.05 simply indicates that the relationship has a probability of occurring by chance 5 percent of the time, or 5 times in 100 samples. Likewise, a significance level of 0.01 indicates that the relationship would occur by chance only 1 time in 100 samples.

It should be stressed that statistical significance levels only indicate the likelihood that an observed relationship actually exists in the universe from which the sample was drawn. They do not tell how strong the relationship is. Thus, a statistically significant relationship may not be substantively important. One should consider *both* the strength of the relationship and the statistical significance level before concluding that the relationship is meaningful.

Cross-tabulation

There are two major methods of obtaining measures of association and their accompanying significance levels: (1) from cross-tabulation or contingency tables, and (2) from scatterplots or scatter diagrams. In mass communication research, where most variables take on only a limited number (three to seven) values, cross-tabulation tables are more common than are scatter diagrams, because scatter diagrams are more appropriate for continuous variables that have many values measured on an interval or ratio scale (e.g., income or temperature).

A cross-tabulation table is simply a joint frequency distribution of cases according to two or more variables (see Table 4–1). The two variables being related are taken from an opinion survey of students en-

Table 4–1 College class standing and frequency of watching television news.

Class Standing	1–2 Times a Week	3–4 Times a Week	5 or more Times a Week	Total
Freshmen and sophomores	30 37.5%	34 42.5%	16 20.0%	80 100%
Juniors and seniors	25 26.0%	43 44.8%	28 29.2%	96 100%
Graduate students	9 20.5%	7 15.9%	28 63.6%	44 100%
Total	64	84	72	220

Chi square = 27.76, 4 df, p = 0.0000
Cramer's V = 0.25
Contingency coefficient = 0.33
Kendall's tau$_b$ = 0.24, p = 0.0000
Gamma = 0.37

rolled on the Bloomington campus of Indiana University. Each person in the survey who indicated his or her class standing *and* who indicated how often he or she usually watches the evening network and/or local news on television is sorted into one of nine categories on the basis of the answers to both questions.

In Table 4–1, only the row percentages are included because of the nature of the two variables being compared. Class standing is considered to be an *independent variable* (a predictor of watching television news), and frequency of watching evening television news is considered to be a *dependent variable* (the behavior being predicted or being studied).

Correlation and Causation

It is important to remember that correlations and cross-tabulations, especially with data gathered at one point in time, do *not* indicate a causal relationship. Just because a person's educational level is strongly correlated with his or her time spent reading newspapers does not mean that increased levels of education cause increased use of newspapers. It may be that a third factor, such as income or kind of job, can account for the high correlation between level of education and reading a newspaper. It may also be true that increased newspaper reading may lead to a higher level of education, although this seems intuitively unlikely.

The point is that the designation of independent and dependent variables is often somewhat arbitrary, depending upon the researcher's interests, and should not be interpreted to mean that the independent variable really *causes* the dependent variable in a real-world setting.

To prove causality, not only must we be able to establish that the correlation between our variables is nonspurious (that it holds even when we control for as many other factors as possible), but also that the cause preceded the effect in time, and that there is a plausible rationale for why one variable should be a cause of another. Even if all these conditions are met, a causal relationship cannot be proved by one study. If the evidence from numerous studies all supports a causal relationship, we can have more faith that such a relationship exists.[7]

Returning to Table 4–1, then, it is obvious that class standing is considered the independent variable and frequency of watching television news the dependent variable, because the percentages are calculated on the totals for the class-standing categories. Whenever trying to decide which percentages to use, remember to base them on the totals for the *independent* variable categories—the variable that your research question or hypothesis implies is predicting the other variable.

[7]For a more complete discussion of the necessary and sufficient conditions for inferring causal relationships, see Claire Selltiz and others, *Research Methods in Social Relations*, rev. ed. (New York: Holt, Rinehart & Winston, 1959), pp. 80–88; and Sanford Labovitz and Robert Hagedorn, *Introduction to Social Research* (New York: McGraw-Hill Book Company, 1971), pp. 1–12.

Looking at the percentages in Table 4–1, it is clear that there is a positive correlation between class standing and the watching of television news. As class standing increases (from freshman to graduate student), greater proportions of students fall into the highest category of television news viewing (five or more times a week). Conversely, lower levels of class standing are associated with lower levels of television news viewing; that is, greater proportions of underclassmen fall into the lowest category of television news viewing.

Even if we know that the sampling error at the 95 percent level of confidence for a random sample this size (220) is about ±6.7 percentage points and therefore differences in individual percentages should be 13.5 percent or greater to ensure that they really exist in the overall universe of Bloomington students, we still do not know how strong the *overall relationship* between class standing and watching television news is, nor do we know how likely it is that this relationship exists in the universe from which the sample was drawn.

Measures of Association

At this point, we need to turn to specific statistical measures of association to determine both the strength of the relationship and the likelihood that it exists in the universe of all Bloomington students.

Chi square. This measure makes no assumption about the level of measurement. The variables need not be ranked from high to low, or from few to many. They may simply contain discrete categories (e.g., sex, religion, political party) which are not ranked in any way. Chi square may be applied to tables with variables measured at a higher level (ordinal, interval, or ratio), but chi square is calculated as if the variables are measured at the nominal level.[8]

Chi square is primarily a test of statistical significance, rather than a measure of the strength of an association, because its value can range from very small to very large depending upon the size of the table (the number of rows and columns) and the size of the sample.

In Table 4–1, for example, the value of chi square is 27.76, which by itself says nothing about the strength of the relationship between class standing and watching television news. However, when we also know that there are 4 degrees of freedom (4 df) for this particular table (number of rows minus 1 times number of columns minus 1), then we can check a table of chi-square probabilities to see what the chances are of getting a chi square of 27.76 in a table with 4 degrees of freedom.[9] It turns out that the chances are equal to 0.0000 (carried out to

[8]Nie and others, *SPSS*, p. 223.

[9]As with other tables of probabilities, chi-square tables can be found in the back of most statistics books. See, for example, Frederick Williams, *Reasoning with Statistics: Simplified Examples in Communications Research* (New York: Holt, Rinehart & Winston, 1968), pp. 174–175; Sidney Siegel, *Nonparametric Statistics for the Behavioral Sciences* (New York: McGraw-Hill Book Company, 1956), p. 249; and Blalock, *Social Statistics*, p. 452.

only four decimal places), or less than 1 in 10,000 (a significance level of 0.01 indicates 1 chance in 100; a level of 0.001 indicates 1 chance in 1,000; a level of 0.0001 indicates 1 chance in 10,000).

Obviously, the odds are very good that the relationship in Table 4–1 is not due to chance and therefore *does* exist in the universe from which the sample was drawn.

The logic behind the chi-square measure is rather simple: the *actual* values in each cell of a table are compared to the *expected* values. The expected value for each cell is calculated by multiplying the column total for that cell by the row total for that cell, and dividing the product by the total number of cases in the table. Once each cell's expected value has been calculated, it is subtracted from the actual (or observed) value, and the difference is squared and divided by the expected value for the cell. The final figures for all cells in the tables are summed to get the value of chi square.

In other words,

$$X^2 = \sum \frac{(f_o - f_e)^2}{f_e}$$

where X^2 equals chi square, f_o equals the observed (or actual) frequency in each cell of the table, f_e equals the expected value for each cell, and Σ indicates that the values for all cells are summed to equal the overall value of chi square.

The expected frequency for each cell, f_e, is calculated with this formula:

$$f_e = \frac{(c_r)}{N}$$

where c equals the column total (or marginal) for a particular cell, r equals the row total for that cell, and N equals the total number of cases in the table.

As can be seen from the formula for chi square, the larger the discrepancies between the actual and expected values for each cell, the greater the value of chi square and the less the probability that the relationship indicated in the table is due to chance.

It should be noted that chi square assumes randomly sampled data, so is not appropriate for data gathered from an entire universe.[10] Also, the chi-square test requires that the expected frequencies in each cell not be too small. In general, for a two-by-two contingency table (two rows and two columns), the total number of cases should be greater than forty, and all *expected* cell frequencies should be five or more. In a larger table (more than two rows and two columns), chi square may be used if fewer than 20 percent of the cells have an *expected* frequency

[10]Although this seems to be the most widely held view, there are some scholars who argue otherwise. See, for example, Robert J. Winch and Donald T. Campbell, "Proof? No. Evidence? Yes. The Significance of Tests of Significance," *American Sociologist*, 4:140–143 (1969).

of less than five and if no cell has an *expected* frequency of less than one.[11]

If the expected cell frequencies are less than five, the researcher may combine categories of the table to increase the expected frequency of the cells (if possible), or employ the Fisher exact probability test for a two-by-two table.[12] In all two-by-two tables, the formula for chi square should be corrected for continuity.[13]

As mentioned earlier, chi square is not a measure of the strength of a relationship because its value fluctuates greatly according to the size of the table, and to the differences between the actual and expected values in each cell. However, when chi square is adjusted for these factors, it can serve as an indicator of the strength of association between two variables.

Phi. This statistic, which is based on chi square, is appropriate for two-by-two contingency tables. It corrects for the fact that the value of chi square is directly proportional to the total number of cases by adjusting for the number of cases in the table. The formula for phi is

$$\phi = \sqrt{\frac{X^2}{N}}$$

where ϕ equals phi, X^2 equals chi square, and N equals the total number of cases in the table. Phi takes on the value of 0 when no relationship exists and $+1$ when the variables are perfectly related, that is, when one value of the first variable is associated with just one value of the second variable, and the other value of the first variable is associated with the other value of the second variable (see Table 4–2). It should be remembered that phi, like chi square, is most appropriate for *nominal-level* variables, so a value of $+1$ does not indicate positive

Table 4–2 Chain ownership of newspapers and modern design (hypothetical data).

	Ownership	
Design	Chain, %	Not Chain, %
Traditional	0	100
Modern	100	0

Phi $= +1$
Chi-square significance $= 0.0000$ (assuming random sample data)

Note that if the relationship were the opposite—that is, if all chain papers were traditional and all non-chain papers modern—phi would still be $+1$. This underscores the necessity of looking at the actual contingency table when using nominal-level measures such as phi, Cramer's V, and the contingency coefficient.

[11]See Siegel, *Nonparametric Statistics*, p. 110, for a more detailed discussion.
[12]Ibid., pp. 94–110.
[13]Nie and others, *SPSS*, p. 243; and Siegel, *Nonparametric Statistics*, p. 110.

or negative correlation; it simply indicates a perfect association of some kind. It is necessary with all nominal-level measures of association to examine the contingency table to see what kind of relationship is (or is not) present. With ordinal-level (ranked) variables and those measured at interval or ratio levels, it is possible to look only at the measure of association to tell if the association is positive, negative, or nonexistent.

It is recommended that chi square be obtained whenever using any nominal measure of association with random sample data.

Cramer's V. Like phi, Cramer's *V* is based on chi square and assumes a nominal (categorical) level of measurement. Unlike phi, Cramer's *V* is appropriate for tables with *more* than two rows and two columns. It ranges from 0 to +1, as does phi, with 0 indicating no relationship and +1 indicating a perfect relationship.

Like phi and other nominal measures of association, Cramer's *V* may be applied to tables with variables measured at a higher level, but a positive value of *V* does not necessarily indicate a positive correlation. It simply indicates that the variables are related in some manner. In Table 4–1, where two ordinal variables are being related, *V* equals 0.25, indicating some sort of association, and the chi-square significance level (0.0000) suggests that this relationship holds in the universe of all Bloomington students, or that it is not due to chance. A look at the table suggests that the association is positive: as class standing increases, so does the frequency of watching television news (see Table 4–1).

The formula for computing Cramer's *V* is

$$V = \sqrt{\frac{\phi^2}{\min{(r-1)}, (c-1)}}$$

where *V* equals Cramer's *V*, ϕ^2 equals phi squared, and min $(r-1)$, $(c-1)$ indicates that ϕ^2 is divided by either the number of rows minus 1 *or* the number of columns minus 1, depending on which is smaller. One advantage of Cramer's *V* is that it varies between 0 and 1, even when the number of rows and columns in a table is not equal.

Contingency coefficient. This is another nominal measure of association based on chi square, but it is not as useful as phi or Cramer's *V*, even though it can be used with a table of any size. Like phi and *V*, the contingency coefficient has a minimum value of 0 (when no association between two variables is present), but its maximum value varies with the size of the table. In a two-by-two table, for example, the maximum value is 0.71. The contingency coefficient cannot attain an upper limit of 1 unless the number of categories for the two variables is infinite.[14]

Because its maximum value varies with the size of the table, it cannot be directly compared to other measures of association, which vary in range from 0 to +1 or from −1 to +1. Also, the contingency coefficient cannot be used to compare tables of differing sizes.

[14]Hays and Winkler, *Statistics*, p. 804.

In Table 4–1, for example, the contingency coefficient of 0.33 is not directly comparable to Cramer's V, Kendall's tau_b, or gamma, because all these measures have an upper limit of $+ 1$.

The formula for calculating the contingency coefficient is

$$C = \sqrt{\frac{X^2}{X^2 + N^2}}$$

where C equals the contingency coefficient, X^2 equals the value of chi square for the table, and N equals the total number of cases in the table.

Although chi square itself is not a measure of strength of association and should be used only with random sample data, the other measures based on the chi square (phi, Cramer's V, and the contingency coefficient) may be used as estimates of the strength of an association between two variables, even if the data are based on the entire universe. If the data are based on all cases in the universe, however, the chi-square significance level is meaningless and should not be computed.

Other nominal-level measures of association are discussed by Blalock, Hays and Winkler, and Siegel.[15]

We turn now to a discussion of measures of association appropriate for variables measured at the ordinal (ranked) level.

Kendall's Tau$_b$ and Tau$_c$. Kendall's tau and two other measures of association between ordinal-level variables (gamma and Somers' D) employ a similar calculating procedure. They all consider every possible *pair* of cases in a table to see if the relative ordering on the first variable is the same (concordant) as the relative ordering on the second variable or if the ordering is reversed (discordant).

In Table 4–1, for example, a junior who watches television news three times a week is "higher" on both variables (class standing and television news) than a freshman who watches television news two times a week. This is a *concordant* pair because the first person is higher on both variables than the second person. But a freshman who watches television news five times a week compared with a graduate student who watches three times a week is a *discordant* pair because the first person is lower on one variable (class standing) than the second person, but higher on the other variable (television news watching). If two persons in Table 4–1 are in the same position on one or two of the variables, the pair is *tied*.

Kendall's tau$_b$, which is appropriate for square tables (the same number of rows and columns), ranges from $- 1$ (a perfect negative correlation) to $+ 1$ (a perfect positive correlation), with a value of 0 indicating no association between the two variables. Tau$_c$ is appropriate for *rectangular* tables (those with a different number of rows and columns) and also ranges from $- 1$ to $+ 1$.

[15]See Blalock, *Social Statistics*, pp. 212–241; Hays and Winkler, *Statistics*, pp. 801–813; and Siegel, *Nonparametric Statistics*, pp. 95–111 and 196–202.

The first step in calculating either tau_b or tau_c is to compute the number of concordant pairs (P), the number of discordant pairs (Q), the number of ties on the row variable (T_1), and the number of ties on the column variable (T_2).[16]

Once these quantities are determined, the formula for Kendall's tau_b is

$$\text{Tau}_b = \frac{P - Q}{\sqrt{[\frac{1}{2} (N^2 - T_1^2) \frac{1}{2} (N^2 - T_2^2)]}}$$

where N equals the total number of cases in the table.

It can be seen that if P (number of pairs ordered in the same direction on both variables) is larger than Q (number of discordant pairs), the final statistic will be positive, indicating a positive correlation between the variables. Conversely, tau_b will be negative if Q is larger than P, and will equal 0 if Q equals P.

The formula for tau_c, which is used in a rectangular table, is

$$\text{Tau}_c = \frac{2m(P - Q)}{N^2(m - 1)}$$

where m equals the number of rows or columns, whichever is smaller, and N equals the total number of cases in the table.

One advantage of Kendall's tau over other ordinal measures of association such as gamma is that both tau_b and tau_c take ties into account and are generally more conservative measures of association than the other ordinal measures. In Table 4–1, for example, Kendall's tau_b equals 0.24, but gamma equals 0.37.

Another advantage of Kendall's tau is that a significance test may be calculated, assuming random sample data. Finally, Kendall's tau can also be used in partial correlation, where one is measuring the strength of association between two variables while statistically controlling for a third variable.[17]

Gamma. This ordinal-level measure of association makes no adjustments for either ties or table size. Therefore, it tends to be higher in value than Kendall's tau, and it can assume a value of +1 (perfect correlation) even if all cases do not fall along the major diagonal of a table. Like Kendall's tau, gamma ranges from −1 to +1.

Gamma is simply the number of concordant pairs (P) minus the number of discordant pairs (Q) divided by the total number of concordant and discordant pairs ($P + Q$). This means it is easier to calculate than either Kendall's tau_b or tau_c, but gamma tends to inflate the strength of an association between two variables because it does not take ties into account.

[16]For more detailed discussions of these computing procedures, see Siegel, *Nonparametric Statistics*, pp. 213–223; Blalock, *Social Statistics*, pp. 319–324; and Hays and Winkler, *Statistics*, pp. 845–849.

[17]For the formula for computing a partial Kendall's tau, see Siegel, *Nonparametric Statistics*, pp. 223–229.

The formula for calculating gamma, once the number of concordant and discordant pairs has been calculated, is

$$\text{Gamma} = \frac{P - Q}{P + Q}$$

Because it does not take into account the number of tied pairs, gamma should not be used with tables where most of the cases fall into one column category or one row category. The cases should be fairly evenly spread among the column and row categories.

Spearman's Rho. This is a very commonly used measure of association between two sets of rankings. It, too, varies from -1 (a perfect negative correlation) to $+1$ (a perfect positive correlation), but it is generally *not* used with cross-tabulation tables where each variable has several categories.

Instead, Spearman's rho is usually used to measure the strength of association between two sets of rankings (see Table 4–3). When used in this manner, rho is an estimate of the value of Pearson's correlation coefficient (discussed in the next section).

In Table 4–3, Spearman's rho, also designated ρ_s, equals 0.83, indicating that the two sets of rankings are strongly, but not perfectly, correlated. A quick look at the rankings themselves bears out this strong correlation. Five of the eight rankings are identical, and the largest difference between ranks is three (on the issue of government scandal). Clearly, these two rankings are highly similar, and the high value of Spearman's rho reflects this similarity.

Spearman's rho, like Kendall's tau, requires the use of rankings rather than the absolute values of the variables. Hence the first step in

Table 4–3 Issues emphasized by the *Charlotte* (N.C.) *Observer* and "CBS Television News" during the 1972 U.S. Presidential Campaign.[a]

Issue	Charlotte Observer	CBS News
Vietnam war	1[b]	2
Economy and inflation	3	3
Human rights and welfare	2	4
Government scandal	4	1
Environment and ecology	6	6
International relations	7	7
Crime and violence	5	5
Busing	8	8

Spearman's rho = 0.83

[a]Data are taken from Donald L. Shaw and Maxwell E. McCombs, *The Emergence of American Political Issues: The Agenda-Setting Function of the Press* (St. Paul, Minnesota: West Publishing Co., 1977), p. 139.

[b]The *Charlotte Observer* ranking of issues was established by tabulating the column inches, excluding headlines. The CBS ranking of issues was determined by adding up seconds devoted to each "issue" story. In both cases, a 1 indicates the issue given most coverage.

computing rho is to rank order the values of the variables from lowest to highest.

In the case of tied ranks, the ranks are averaged and the same value assigned to each of the tied values of the variable. For example, if three values of the variable are tied for second place, each value is assigned the rank of 3 (the average of ranks 2, 3, and 4), and the next value is assigned the rank of 5 because ranks 2, 3, and 4 have already been used.

Once the ranks have been assigned to each value of the two variables for each case (person, issue, or whatever), one rank is subtracted from the other, the difference is squared, and the squared differences for each rank are added together. Then the following formula is used to adjust this sum of squared differences so that its value will be $+1$ whenever the rankings are in perfect agreement, -1 when they are perfectly opposite, and 0 when they are not related in any way:

$$\rho_s = 1 - \frac{6 \Sigma d^2}{N(N^2 - 1)}$$

where ρ_s equals Spearman's rho, Σ means the "sum of," d^2 equals the squared difference between the ranks for each case, and N equals the number of cases or ranks (eight in the case of Table 4–3).

So this formula simply says that one multiplies the sum of the squared differences between the ranks by 6, divides this number by the number of ranks times the number of ranks squared minus 1, and subtracts this number from 1.

How does one decide whether to use Spearman's rho or Kendall's tau to measure the strength of association between two rankings? If one knows that the distances between ranks are unequal (in terms of the absolute values of the variables) and if there are a few cases with extremely low or high ranks, Kendall's tau is a more appropriate measure of association than Spearman's rho. On the other hand, if the data are distributed fairly equally among a fairly large number of ranks (eight or more), Spearman's rho is a better estimate of the degree of correlation between the rankings.

Before moving on to a discussion of the Pearsonian correlation coefficient, we want to make a few brief comments about *nonparametric statistics*. In general, the measures of association considered thus far (chi square, phi, Cramer's *V*, contingency coefficient, Kendall's tau, gamma, and Spearman's rho) are nonparametric statistics because they are appropriate for categorical data (nominal and ordinal), they do not assume that the scores being related were drawn from a population distributed in a certain way (such as a normally distributed population), and they are generally easier to calculate than more complicated parametric statistics such as the Pearsonian correlation coefficient.[18]

---

[18]Ibid., p. vii, for a more extended discussion of the difference between parametric and nonparametric statistics.

Another advantage of nonparametric statistics is that they are useful with small samples. For generalizations from a sample to a universe, however, nonparametric statistics require random sampling just as parametric statistics do. So the use of nonparametric statistics does not mean that one can draw convenience or quota samples and still generalize to a given universe. Random sampling is necessary for generalizing to a universe, regardless of whether nonparametric or parametric statistics are being used. The disadvantages relate to the relatively low power of nonparametric statistics, a concept that is explained by Stamm in Chapter 5.

Pearsonian correlation coefficient. This well-known measure of association between two variables, also known as Pearsonian *r*, assumes that the variables being related are measured at the interval or ratio levels (that we know the distance between different values, as well as the fact that one value is larger or smaller than another), and that the relationship between two or more variables is *linear;* that is, as one variable increases, the other either increases or decreases in a constant manner.

Pearsonian *r* also assumes that the variables being related have many values (that they are more nearly continuous than discrete) and that the joint distribution of two variables is a bivariate normal distribution.[19] When this is the case, it can be shown that Pearsonian *r* calculated from random sample data is the best estimator of the actual correlation in the universe from which the samples were drawn.[20]

Although Pearsonian *r* assumes at least interval-level data, it is often used by mass communication and other researchers with ordinal-level variables. In fact, some social science methodologists have argued that Pearsonian *r* and other interval-level statistics (such as factor analysis) should be used with ordinal-level data so as not to miss relationships that less powerful nonparametric statistics would not detect.[21] There is no widespread agreement about this, however, so Pearsonian *r* should be used cautiously, if at all, with ordinal data.

We have mentioned that there are two major methods of obtaining measures of association, from contingency (cross-tabulation) tables and from scatter diagrams or scatter plots. Although cross-tabulation tables are more common in mass communication research because the variables under study usually have a limited number of values, there are some interval-level, continuous variables in mass communication research that require scatter diagrams and Pearsonian *r* as a measure of association (e.g., percentages of literate adults in a country and daily newspaper circulation per 1,000 adult population).

Instead of creating a separate table cell for the intersection of each value of one variable with each value of the other variable, one plots

[19]Ibid., pp. 195–196.
[20]See Hays and Winkler, *Statistics,* p. 601, for a discussion of why this is true.
[21]See, for example, Sanford Labovitz, "Statistical Usage in Sociology: Sacred Cows and Ritual," *Sociological Methods and Research,* 1:13–37 (August 1972).

the joint values on a two-dimensional plane, with the horizontal axis defined by one variable and the vertical axis defined by the other.

One way to summarize a scatterplot is to draw a straight or curved line through the middle of the points so as to summarize the pattern of points (see Figure 4–7). In the case of a rather clear and consistent linear pattern, a straight line may be used to summarize the relationship between the two variables. This line is placed so as to minimize the vertical distances of all the points from the line, a procedure known as least-squares regression. (See Chapter 10 for a more detailed discussion of regression.)

Pearsonian r is a measure of the degree to which a linear regression line (a straight line) fits the data displayed in a scatter diagram. If all the points fall on the line, r equals either $+1$ or -1, depending on the direction of the line. As the squared vertical distance from each point to the line becomes greater, the value of r comes closer to zero. An r of zero indicates that there is no *linear* relationship between the variables, but it does not mean that there is no relationship. There may be a well-defined curvilinear relationship between the two variables.

The calculation of the Pearsonian correlation coefficient is more complex than that required for most of the other measures of association discussed thus far, but the principle behind r is rather simple. Pearsonian r is the ratio between the maximum amount of variability

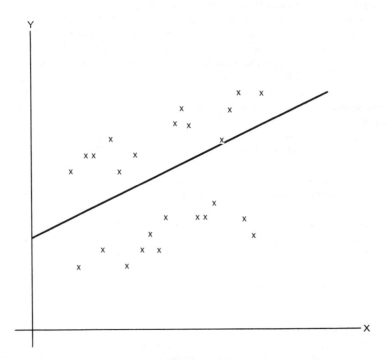

Figure 4-7

that two measures could have in common and the amount that they actually have in common. In other words, r is the ratio of the covariation (the amount of variation two measures have in common) to the square root of the product of the variation in both variables.[22]

Thus r^2 (which is also known as the coefficient of determination) can be interpreted as the percentage of variability in one variable explained by the other variable.[23] Both Pearsonian r and r^2 vary from -1 to $+1$, but the interpretation of r and r^2 is considerably different.

Pearsonian r is simply a measure of the strength of the linear relationship between two variables. An r of 0 denotes no linear relationship, whereas an r of -1 denotes a perfect negative linear relationship (as one variable increases, the other steadily declines), and an r of $+1$ denotes a perfect positive linear relationship (as one variable increases, the other increases at a constant rate). It should be noted that an r of 0.80 does not signify a relationship that is twice as strong as an r of 0.40, because r is not an actual measurement scale.[24]

The interpretation of r depends on several factors, including the purpose of the research. With very large samples (say, 1,000 or larger), even small r's of 0.20 or less may be highly significant statistically. This does not mean that such correlations are journalistically significant. The researcher must consider whether the purpose of the study is to locate variables that are related to each other or whether the purpose is to predict from one variable to another. In the case of prediction, very strong correlations are required.

Guilford and Williams have suggested the following as a rough guide to interpreting the strength of a Pearsonian correlation coefficient:

less than .20	slight correlation; almost negligible relationship
.20–.40	low correlation; definite but small relationship
.40–.70	moderate correlation; substantial relationship
.70–.90	high correlation; marked relationship
more than .90	very high correlation; very dependable relationship[25]

Whereas r is interpreted as an indicator of the strength of a linear relationship between two variables, r^2 is interpreted as the proportion of variation in one variable explained by the variation in another. Thus an r^2 of 0.80 indicates that two variables have twice the variation in common as two variables with an r^2 of 0.40.

Pearsonian r may be calculated by the following formula:

$$r = \frac{\Sigma (X - \bar{X}) (Y - \bar{Y})}{\sqrt{[\Sigma(X - \bar{X})^2] [\Sigma(Y - \bar{Y})^2]}}$$

[22]For a more detailed discussion of Pearsonian r, see Blalock, *Social Statistics*, p. 287.

[23]For a more detailed discussion of r^2, see Blalock, *Social Statistics*, p. 298; and Dick A. Leabo, *Basic Statistics* (Homewood, Ill.: Richard D. Irwin, Inc., 1972), pp. 436–437.

[24]Williams, *Reasoning with Statistics*, p. 134.

[25]Ibid.; and J. P. Guilford, *Fundamental Statistics in Psychology and Education* (New York: McGraw-Hill Book Company, 1956), p. 145.

where r stands for the Pearsonian correlation coefficient, X equals each value of the first variable, $\bar{X}$ equals the mean of the first variable, Y equals each value of the second variable, $\bar{Y}$ equals the mean of the second variable, and Σ means "the sum of."

Measures of Difference

The various statistics we have considered thus far (chi square, phi, Cramer's V, contingency coefficient, Kendall's tau, gamma, Spearman's rho, and Pearsonian r) are useful for indicating either the strength of association between variables or the probability that the association occurred by chance or both.

But not all research questions and hypotheses are couched in terms of associations. Many are stated in terms of *differences* between individuals and/or groups. This is especially true in experimental research, where comparisons are made between groups that have and have not been exposed to certain experimental treatments (such as certain media messages or television programs).

In such a setting, instead of asking, "Do persons who spend much time reading newspapers tend to be more interested in politics than those who spend little time reading newspapers?" we might ask, "Is there a significant difference in political interest between those persons who spend much time reading newspapers and those persons who spend little time reading newspapers?"

Or instead of hypothesizing that "The more education a person has, the more time he or she will spend reading newspapers," we might hypothesize, "There is a significant difference in time spent reading newspapers between those persons with low levels of education and those persons with high levels of education."

To address these restated research problems, measures of difference are more appropriate than measures of association. We turn now to some specific examples of these measures of difference.

Difference of proportions test. This is one of the simplest measures of difference, both in terms of calculation and underlying assumptions. This test assumes only nominal-level data and random sampling. As was true in calculating sampling error, a difference between two proportions can be treated as a special case of a difference between two means. (See the section, "Calculating Sampling Error.")

When comparing two proportions from the *same* random sample, we can simply subtract one from the other and ask if the difference exceeds plus or minus the sampling error. In other words, if we have calculated the sampling error to be plus or minus 5 percentage points at the 95 percent level of confidence, we can simply ask if the two proportions differ by 10 points or more. If they do, we can be 95 percent sure that the difference between the proportions really exists in the universe from which the sample was drawn.

Remember that the formula for the sampling error at the 95 percent level of confidence (or the 0.05 level of significance, depending upon how you want to view it) is

$$\text{Sampling error} = \pm 1.96 \sqrt{\frac{pq}{N}}$$

where ± 1.96 equals the number of standard deviations within which 95 percent of large random samples will fall, p equals the proportion (or percentage) of cases in one category, q equals $1 - p$ (or $100\% - p$), and N equals the number of cases in the sample.

Another way of estimating the probability that the difference between two proportions in the same sample is real is to employ the formula

$$Z = \frac{p_1 - p_2}{\sqrt{\frac{pq}{N}}}$$

where Z equals the number of standard deviations from the mean in a normal curve, p_1 equals the first proportion, p_2 equals the second proportion, p equals either p_1 or p_2, depending upon which is closer to 50 percent, q equals $1 - p$ (or $100\% - p$), and N equals the number of cases in the sample.[26]

For example, if we draw a random sample of 125 newspaper issues from the files of the local newspaper for the past five years and we find that 60 percent of these issues contain editorials critical of local government and 65 percent contain editorials critical of national government, can we conclude that this is likely to be a real difference in all issues of this newspaper for the past five years?

Applying the formula,

$$Z = \frac{0.60 - 0.65}{\sqrt{\frac{(0.60)\,(0.40)}{125}}} = \frac{-0.05}{0.0438} = -1.14$$

Checking this Z-score in a table of areas under the normal curve, which can be found in most statistics books, we find that the odds of this difference occurring by chance are about 0.13, or 13 times in 100. If we have set our significance level at 0.05, we must conclude that this difference could have occurred by chance and therefore probably does not occur in the universe of the past five years' issues of the local newspaper.[27]

It is also possible to test the significance of the difference between two proportions taken from two independent random samples, but this procedure is more complicated and less often used in mass communication research. (For the computing procedure, the reader is referred to Blalock, pages 176–178; see note 3.)

---

[26]Blalock, *Social Statistics*, pp. 149–152.
[27]Ibid., p. 152. (See p. 441 for a table of areas under the normal curve.)

The chi-square test can also be thought of as a difference of proportions test because it compares expected values of nominal variables with their actual values. (See the section on chi square for a discussion of the computing procedure.)

T-test. This commonly used difference of means test is appropriate for two-group problems, that is, for situations where one is comparing the mean(s) of one group with the mean(s) of another group. For three or more groups of cases (persons, newspaper issues, etc.), analysis of variance should be used.

The *t*-test assumes interval-level data, random sampling, and a normally distributed population. It produces a *t* statistic with accompanying significance test, which enables the researcher to estimate the probability that a difference observed between sample means is a real difference in the universe from which the sample was drawn. If one is using data from an entire universe or from a non-random sample, the *t*-test should not be used.

Although the most common use of the *t*-test is to test the significance of the difference between two sample group means to estimate if such a difference exists in the universe, another use often made of the *t*-test is to measure the *change* in average scores of the *same* persons after being exposed to an experimental treatment of some kind.

For example, if a group of persons is exposed to a film on techniques of advertising, and their scores on an attitude measure about advertising are averaged before and after the film, the *t*-test may be used to determine the statistical significance (if any) of the difference between the before and after mean scores. This is sometimes called a *correlated t-test.* Again, the *t*-test does not indicate how *meaningful* the difference is; it simply indicates how likely the difference is to occur by chance, and therefore how likely it is that the difference would exist in the universe from which the sample of persons was drawn.

The *t*-test, sometimes called Student's *t*, is based upon a distribution similar, but not identical to, the normal distribution. This distribution is more appropriate for smaller samples (less than thirty or so) than is the normal distribution.[28] For larger samples, the difference between the *t* distribution and the normal distribution is trivial.

The calculation of the *t*-test is shown in Chapter 8.

As mentioned earlier, the *t* distribution is more appropriate for smaller samples than is the normal distribution, but this does *not* mean that the *t*-test may be used only with small samples. Blalock argues that it is always preferable to use the *t* distribution whenever the universe standard deviation is unknown and whenever a normal universe (population) can be assumed.[29]

In addition, there is no advantage to using analysis of variance over

---

[28]Nie and others, *SPSS*, p. 268; Blalock, *Social Statistics*, p. 145; and Williams, *Reasoning with Statistics*, p. 81.

[29]Blalock, *Social Statistics*, p. 149.

the t-test when only two groups are being compared because it can be shown that exactly the same conclusions will be reached in the two-sample case regardless of whether analysis of variance or the t-test is used.[30]

Analysis of variance. This test of the difference between sample means should be used when *three or more* means are being compared simultaneously. For example, subjects in an experiment may be randomly assigned to three different groups, one exposed to a very violent television program, one exposed to a moderately violent television program, and one exposed to a neutral (nonviolent) program. After viewing the television program, each group may be asked to complete a test measuring willingness to use violence to solve various problems in society.

In such an experiment, the researcher would be interested in the relationship between degree of violence in television programs and willingness to use violence in solving problems. To test this relationship, the researcher would ask if the mean problem-solving scores vary significantly among the three experimental groups. Analysis of variance would provide a single F test, with accompanying significance level, to tell the researcher how these sample means are likely to differ in the universe from which the samples were drawn.

Once having obtained an overall test for all three mean scores, the researcher could then use a t-test of difference to check on the statistical significance of the difference between *each pair* of means.

The preceding example is known as a *one-way* (or single-factor) analysis of variance because only one independent variable is involved—violence in television programs. It is possible, however, to examine the effects of two or more independent variables simultaneously on the mean scores of a dependent variable by using n-way (two-way, three-way, etc.) analysis of variance.

The assumptions required for analysis of variance are basically the same as those required for the t-test, but the computation of the F test is very different. Analysis of variance assumes interval-level measurement of the dependent variable, independent random samples (or independent random groups within a single sample), a normally distributed population or universe, and equal universe variances.[31] The independent variables (or factors) are usually categorical variables measured on the ordinal level (such as three levels of violence in a television program).

The F test underlying the analysis of variance is based on a comparison of the variation of scores *within* each category of each independent variable (factor) with the variation between the means of each category. Thus, the more variation *between* the means of each category of each independent variable (as compared to the overall mean for the sample)

---

[30]For a discussion of why this is so, see Blalock, *Social Statistics,* p. 253.
[31]Ibid., p. 242.

and the less variation of the scores *within* each category (about each category mean), the larger the value of F and the more certain we are that the differences between categories really exist in the universe from which the sample was drawn. And the more certain we are that the independent variable has a real effect on the dependent variable.

In other words, the value of the F test may be expressed by the formula

$$F = \frac{SS \text{ between } / (k - 1)}{SS \text{ within } / (N - k)}$$

where "SS between" stands for the sum of squared differences between the means of each category of each independent variable (factor) and the overall (grand) mean for the entire sample, k stands for the number of categories of each factor, "SS within" equals the sum of the squared differences between each score and its category mean, and N equals the total number of cases in the sample.

Another way of expressing the formula for the F test is

$$F = \frac{MS \text{ between}}{MS \text{ within}}$$

where "MS between" equals mean score between, which is the same as "SS between" divided by the number of groups minus 1, and "MS within" stands for mean score within, which is the same as "SS within" divided by the total number of cases in the sample minus the number of groups (or categories) of each independent variable. Analysis of variance is discussed further in Chapter 12.

Analysis of covariance. This is a modified version of analysis of variance, which enables one to statistically extract variance from the dependent variable that is accounted for by one or more measured control variables *before* assessing the effects of the various experimental factors on the dependent variable.

For example, in assessing the effects of televised violence on the tendency for children to act aggressively, a researcher would be interested in having groups of children as nearly alike as possible exposed to different levels of violence. As pointed out in Chapters 11 and 12, *control* is a primary goal of experimental research because without adequate controls one cannot be sure if the observed effects are due to the independent variable(s) or to other influences.

One way of ensuring that the children in each group are as alike as possible is to assign them randomly to each group, hoping that this procedure will tend to cancel out individual differences that might affect the level of aggressiveness in their behavior. Another way to control for individual differences is to match the children on as many characteristics as possible (sex, age, school grade level, etc.). Still another way to control for individual differences is to measure things you think might not be equal in the two groups and might affect the dependent variable; then use analysis of covariance to statistically control for these variables (covariates).

In assessing the effect of televised violence on children, the researcher might not be able to assign the children randomly to different groups receiving different amounts of violence or might suspect that differences remain even after random assignment. One way to remedy this lack of control would be to identify those differences thought to be crucial and devise measures for them.

For example, in the case of children exposed to televised violence, the researcher might want to obtain a measure of each child's tendency to act aggressively before the experiment (perhaps by unobtrusive observation) and then use analysis of covariance to control statistically for the pre-experiment tendency to act aggressively. This procedure would first eliminate the variance in the dependent variable accounted for by the children's pre-experiment tendency to act aggressively, and then perform a normal one-way analysis of variance to determine the effects of the televised violence on the children's tendency to act aggressively.

In applying analysis of covariance, it is necessary to assume that the covariates (the variables being controlled for) do not interact with the factors (the independent variables).

It should be noted that covariates must range from "low" values to "high" values, and they should be measured at the interval level. Therefore, measures of variables one wishes to control for in analysis of variance should ideally be as precise and continuous as possible.

Other measures of difference. The reader should not conclude that the statistics discussed thus far (difference of proportions test, *t*-test, analysis of variance and covariance) are the only tests of difference available to the mass communication researcher. Although these tests are commonly used, several others are useful, especially for variables measured at the ordinal level. These include the median test, the Mann-Whitney U test, the Kolmogorov-Smirnov test, the sign test, the Wilcoxon matched-pairs signed-ranks test, the Friedman two-way analysis of variance, and the Kruskal-Wallis one-way analysis of variance. The assumptions and computational procedures of these tests are discussed in Siegel.[32]

SUMMARY AND CONCLUSIONS

This chapter has attempted to provide an overview of descriptive and inferential statistics useful to mass communication researchers. The treatment of most of these statistics has been brief and, in some cases,

---

[32]Siegel, *Nonparametric Statistics.*

oversimplified. The reader is urged to consult some of the standard statistics books, such as Siegel, Blalock, McNemar, Williams, and Hays and Winkler for more details about the assumptions, calculation, and interpretation of these statistics.

Because the chapter was designed to focus on basic statistical tools, no description has been provided for more powerful multivariate techniques such as multiple regression (for assessing the effects of several independent variables on a dependent variable, controlling for the relationships between the independent variables), factor analysis (for locating patterns of relationships in the intercorrelations of a large number of variables), multidimensional scaling or cluster analysis (for locating dimensions, or patterns, of relationships in the associations of a large number of variables), canonical correlation (for simultaneously correlating one group of variables with another group), and discriminant analysis (for simultaneously relating a dependent variable with only two or three values to many independent variables—in other words, for finding independent variables that statistically distinguish between two or more groups of cases).

For additional information on these more sophisticated techniques, the reader is urged to consult the appropriate sections of the *SPSS* manual (see note 1) and more advanced statistics books such as Cooley and Lohnes, Van de Geer, Harman, Stephenson, Anderson, Kerlinger and Pedhazur, Duncan, Heise, Morrison, and Bock.[33]

Using Statistics to Describe Data

In trying to decide which descriptive statistics to use to summarize a distribution of data, there are two major considerations: (1) the level of measurement of the data (nominal, ordinal, interval, or ratio), and (2) the kind of summary desired (one emphasizing the clustering of the cases or one emphasizing the amount of scatter of the cases).

Figure 4–8 shows the relationship of these two major considerations to the individual descriptive statistics discussed in the first part of this chapter. Although the measures of central tendency seem to be used more often than the measures of dispersion in mass communication

[33]William W. Cooley and Paul R. Lohnes, *Multivariate Data Analysis* (New York: John Wiley & Sons, Inc., 1971); John P. Van de Geer, *Introduction to Multivariate Analysis for the Social Sciences* (San Francisco: W. H. Freeman, 1971); Harry H. Harman, *Modern Factor Analysis* (Chicago: University of Chicago Press, 1967); W. Stephenson, *The Study of Behavior* (Chicago: University of Chicago Press, 1953); T. W. Anderson, *Introduction to Multivariate Statistical Analysis* (New York: John Wiley & Sons, Inc., 1958); Fred N. Kerlinger and Elazar J. Pedhazur, *Multiple Regression in Behavioral Research* (New York: Holt, Rinehart & Winston, 1973); Otis Dudley Duncan, *Introduction to Structural Equation Models* (New York: Academic Press, Inc., 1975); David R. Heise, *Causal Analysis* (New York: John Wiley & Sons, Inc., 1975); Donald G. Morrison, "On the Interpretation of Discriminant Analysis," *Journal of Marketing Research*, 6:156–163 (1969); R. D. Bock, *Multivariate Statistical Methods in Behavioral Research* (New York: McGraw-Hill Book Company, 1975); Paul E. Green and Frank J. Carmone, *Multidimensional Scaling* (Boston: Allyn & Bacon, Inc., 1970); and Hubert M. Blalock, Jr., *Causal Inferences in Nonexperimental Research* (New York: W. W. Norton & Co., Inc., 1964).

Figure 4–8   Commonly used descriptive statistics in mass communication research.[a]

Level of Measurement of Data	Kind of Statistic	
	Central Tendency (Clustering)	Dispersion (Scatter)
Nominal (unranked categories)	Mode (most frequent value), p. 51	Range[b] (maximum to minimum), p. 52 Percentile[b] (100 equal portions), p. 54
Ordinal (Ranked categories)	Median (midpoint), p. 50	
Interval (known distance between ranks)	Mean (average), p. 49	Variance (Σ of squared deviations about mean/N), p. 52 Standard deviation (square root of variance), p. 53
Ratio (interval with a true zero point)	All of above	All of above

[a]Each statistic is listed under the lowest acceptable level of measurement, but it should be remembered that all statistics are appropriate for all higher levels of measurement. It should also be noted that many interval-level measures are commonly used with ordinal-level data.

[b]It can be argued that the range and the percentile are more appropriate for ordinal-level data because they both imply a ranking of values from "low" to "high." In practice, however, they may be used with nominal-level data.

research, it is recommended that both kinds of measures be used wherever possible.

Simply reporting modes, medians, and means without ranges and standard deviations does not give the reader enough information to compare these measures of central tendency from one distribution of data to another. And reporting only ranges, percentages, and standard deviations does not tell the reader much about the clustering of cases within distributions.

As pointed out earlier, when using measures of central tendency with interval data (or perhaps ordinal, if one suspects that the differences between ranks are not too great), one should not automatically rely only on the mean. In a skewed distribution of values, the median or mode may be more representative of the central clustering of cases then the mean. If the mean, median, and mode are fairly equal, there are statistical advantages in using the mean. When in doubt, report more than one measure.

When using measures of dispersion, one may be limited by nominal measurement to the range and percentiles (or percentages), but if the data are at least ordinal scale and there is no reason to suspect great differences in the distances between rankings, it is recommended that the standard deviation be reported as well.

In general, then, when reporting the mode or the median, it is recommended that the range and/or percentages also be reported. When reporting the mean, it is recommended that the standard deviation also be reported.

Using Statistics to Analyze Relationships

The choice of an appropriate statistic to analyze a relationship between variables is more complex than choosing a descriptive statistic for several reasons, including the greater number of inferential statistics, the more complex assumptions underlying the use of many of these statistics, and the nature of one's research questions and hypotheses.

Two major considerations in the choice of inferential statistics, however, should be dealt with before the others: (1) the level of measurement of the variables, and (2) the kind of relationship specified by one's research question or hypothesis: either an *association* between two variables or a *difference* between two or more groups. Figure 4–9 groups the individual measures of association and difference discussed in this chapter in terms of these two major considerations.

When considering Figure 4–9, one should remember that other considerations besides level of measurement and the kind of relationship enter into the selection of specific statistical tests. These considerations include whether random sampling was employed, whether the samples being related are independent or related, whether the universes from which the samples were drawn can be assumed to be normally distributed (as in the case of parametric statistics such as Pearsonian r and analysis of variance), the size of the contingency tables, and whether distinctions are made between independent and dependent variables. Many of these points are touched on in the descriptions of individual statistics, and these descriptions should be read before selecting a particular statistical test.

Figure 4–9 also assumes that both variables being related are measured at the same level (nominal, ordinal, interval, or ratio). In practice, this is often not the case. One may be relating a nominal independent variable (such as religion or selection of a specific newspaper) to an ordinal dependent variable (such as amount of political participation). There are specific statistical tests to handle such situations, such as Somers' d, but they are not discussed here because of the limited scope of this chapter.[34]

[34]For a more thorough and detailed guide for choosing specific statistical tests, see Frank M. Andrews and others, *A Guide for Selecting Statistical Techniques for Analyzing Social Science Data* (Ann Arbor, Mich.: Institute for Social Research, University of Michigan, 1974).

Figure 4–9 Commonly used inferential statistics in mass communication research.

Level of measurement of variables	Kind of relationship	
	Association	*Difference*
Nominal (unranked categories)	Chi square, p. 65 Phi, p. 67 Cramer's *V*, p. 68 Contingency coefficient, p. 68	Difference of proportions test, p. 76
Ordinal (ranked categories)	Kendall's tau, p. 69 Kendall's tau$_b$, p. 69 Kendall's tau$_c$, p. 69 Gamma, p. 70 Spearman's rho, p. 71	Median test, p. 81 Mann-Whitney U test, p. 81 Kolmogorov-Smirnov test, p. 81 Sign test, p. 81 Wilcoxon matched-pairs signed-ranks test, p. 81 Kruskal-Wallis one-way analysis of variance, p. 81 Friedman two-way analysis of variance p. 81
Interval (known distance between ranks)	Pearsonian correlation coefficient, p. 73	*T*-test, p. 78 Analysis of variance, p. 79 Analysis of covariance, p. 80
Ratio (interval with a true zero point)	All of above	All of above

If both variables are not measured at the same level, it is recommended that a statistical test be chosen according to the *lower* level of measurement. Thus, if one is looking for a measure of association between a nominal and an ordinal variable, it is recommended that one of the nominal measures of association be used, such as phi or Cramer's *V*. This rule applies whenever a nominal and an ordinal variable are being related, but the reader may choose to ignore it when an ordinal variable and an interval variable are being related because of the advantages of using more powerful parametric tests such as Pearsonian *r* and the *t*-test. When using analysis of variance or covariance, only the dependent variable need be measured at the interval level. The independent variables (factors) are typically measured at the ordinal, or perhaps nominal, level.

If in doubt, the researcher should apply more than one test of association or difference to the data. If the conclusions of the two tests are different, one should use the results from the more appropriate test (the one suited best to the lower level of measurement of the variables).

In looking for statistically significant relationships, the researcher should remember that at the 0.05 level of significance, 5 instances of every 100 relationships significant at this level may be due to chance. That is, 5 of 100 (or 1 of 20) statistically significant relationships at the 0.05 level may not actually exist in the universe from which the sample was drawn. At the 0.01 level, 1 of every 100 relationships may not exist in the universe from which the sample was drawn.

Finally, just because a relationship is statistically significant does not mean it is substantively important. A positive correlation of 0.20 indicates a weak relationship, regardless of the significance level. (See the section on the Pearsonian correlation coefficient for some guidelines for interpreting the strength of correlations.)

Conclusions

This chapter provides a foundation of commonly used statistics for describing mass communication variables and for relating them to one another. In using these statistics, the researcher should keep in mind the need to let the research questions and hypotheses dictate the kind of measurement employed and the specific statistics used. The use of statistics in mass communication research should not become mindless or an end in itself. Statistics should be used only to clarify the understanding of complex sets of findings and relationships, not to embellish and legitimize research reports.

5

Measurement Decisions

Keith R. Stamm

The numbers that researchers produce and manipulate seem to be what most sharply separates science from our professional and everyday lives. Anyone who has succumbed to this view of measurement and statistics is probably intimidated by the whole subject or at least has developed some defense mechanisms. Neither is very conducive to an understanding of the subject, so this chapter begins by describing some familiar uses of measurement outside of science, to show what they have in common with "scientific" uses.

Introductory textbooks in journalism often provide examples of the application of measurement to professional concerns. Measurement is basically a set of rules for assigning numbers to observations. Under this definition the rules that editors employ in counting headlines would qualify as measurement. One such instrument, described by Westley,[1] is as follows:

* Count all small letters 1 except *l, i, f, t,* which count ½, and *m* and *w*, which count 1½.

* Count all capital letters 1½ except *I*, which counts ½, and *M* and *W*, which count 2.

[1]Bruce H. Westley, *News Editing*, 2nd ed. (Houghton Mifflin Company, 1972), p. 145.

* Count all punctuation marks ½ except the dash, question mark, dollar sign, and percent sign, which count 1.

* Count all numbers 1.

* Count all spaces 1.

The basic question to be asked about this measuring instrument, or any other, is how well it serves its purpose. Editors use it to estimate the space a given headline will require—a tool to fit headlines to a designated space—and it usually provides sufficiently precise estimates. Some lack of precision can be tolerated because the headline does not have to fit the space exactly. But of course if it exceeds the allotted space, the headline will come back from the composing room for revision.

Within the scientific community, the precision (or "power") of a measuring instrument must also be appropriate to its purpose. Many "scientific" instruments are less precise than the headline count, either because the additional precision is not needed or because present techniques do not allow it. The scientist, like the editor, must be aware of this. Greater precision is not an end in itself. (Actually, in today's automated newsrooms, headlines are no longer counted in this way. Instead they are counted by a computer, which signals the editor working at a visual display terminal whether a line is too long or too short. This change has meant the difference between crude estimating and exact measurement.)

If the old headline count were to be used for scientific purposes, we would use different terms to describe the power of the instrument, but would actually be concerned with the same properties of the instrument. The scientist would note, for example, that characters assigned a value of 1 always occupy more space than those which count ½, but they do not necessarily occupy twice as much space, although the numbers might imply that they did. Scientists refer to this type of instrument as an *ordinal scale*. The power of an ordinal scale is limited in that the intervals between values are not equal. Thus, for example, a headline that counts 30 will always be longer than one which counts 15, but we cannot be sure that it is twice as long. Later we will consider how the inequality of intervals limits the mathematical operations that may be performed upon numbers derived from ordinal scales.

Ordinal scales reflect the magnitude or amount of a quality that is being observed. It is thus an instance of what we call *quantitative* measurement as compared to *qualitative*. A circulation manager who just wants to keep track of people who take the Sunday edition distinguishes them from those who do not by a simple measurement scheme employing two numerals. Each household that has the quality (of taking the Sunday edition) can be assigned the numeral 1, and each subscriber who does not can be assigned the numeral 2 (or 0 or any other numeral; it does not really matter).

In this example the numerals do not reflect the magnitude of the quality being measured. They are used only to distinguish the presence of a quality from its absence; a qualitative measurement is all that is needed in this case. We call this kind of measurement a *nominal scale,* because it names a quality and merely notes its presence or absence.

We can find other cases where the professional requires very powerful measurement tools. For example, a film script writer needs precise measures of the length of each scene to prepare a script that will fit the time each scene occupies. The film writer begins by constructing a shot list, which includes measures of the length of each scene. Measurements of length can be used because of the exact correspondence between the length of a scene (in feet) and the time it will occupy on the screen. Since film is projected at the rate of 24 frames per second, each foot of film will take 1.6 seconds on the screen. It is safe to say a scene 20 feet in length will take twice as much time as a 10-foot scene. Here the intervals between numbers (e.g., between 1 foot and 2 feet and between 2 feet and 3 feet) are equal, which is why this type of scale is called *equal interval.*

Actually, the number system underlying this last instance is more powerful than an equal-interval scale, and the reason is that both length in inches and time in minutes have meaningful zero points. That makes both of them what we call *ratio* scales, the most powerful of our scales of measurement. A ratio scale requires equal intervals *and a zero point.* There are common scales of measurement that have equal intervals but no meaningful zero. Temperature, whether given in Fahrenheit or Celsius, is an equal-interval scale but not a ratio scale. We may say that one scene is twice as long as another—in either feet or minutes. We cannot say that 40 degrees is twice as hot as 20 degrees.

To recapitulate, nominal scales are qualitative rather than quantitative: the numbers are arbitrarily chosen to indicate the presence or absence of a quality. Ordinal scales are quantitative but the numbers indicate order only, not magnitude. Interval scales order data, too, but in addition the intervals between values are equal. Ratio scales have these same properties and a meaningful zero.

In any situation where measurement is employed, professionally or scientifically, questions about the adequacy of the measurement scheme are bound to arise. Common questions include the following:

* Will the instrument give us the same result time after time?
* Will it give the same result no matter who uses it?
* How can we be sure it is measuring what it is supposed to be measuring?
* How can we be sure it is measuring *only* what it is supposed to measure?
* How can we know what it is that it is measuring?

THE RESEARCH CONTEXT

The basic concepts of measurement illustrated here in a professional context apply to decisions made in the course of any research project.

There are several different points at which important decisions about measurement must be taken.

Although we do not actually begin working with numbers until we reach the analysis stage, measurement must be part of the researcher's thinking from the moment a project is initiated. But for purposes of discussion, let us consider the role of measurement at four stages: (1) conceptualization, (2) operationalization, (3) analysis, and (4) discussion of results. At each of these stages, four basic measurement questions are raised: (1) power, (2) validity, (3) reliability, and (4) efficiency.

Conceptualization

Let us say the researcher is interested in the variable "attention to television." Is the concept meant to distinguish those who are attending from those who are not (at the moment a survey interviewer calls)? Or is it meant to distinguish those who attend much of the time from those who attend only a little? From the moment of conceptualization, measurement principles are involved, in this case the power of the number system appropriate to the concept. Whatever the hypothesis to be tested, whatever the relationship to be discovered, we must ask how much measurement power will be required to do the job, whether adequate measures can be obtained, and what time and resources will be needed to develop and pretest appropriate instruments.

There is insufficient space here to discuss all the relationships between concepts and measures. For example, Cronbach and Meehl did seminal work nearly twenty years ago that identified "construct validity" and distinguished it from other validity problems.[2] They argue that ultimately the validity of any measure rests upon the adequacy with which the concept is defined, including the hypothesized relations among observables. Such hypotheses must be sufficiently explicit to permit unequivocal interpretation of validating evidence.

A good example of the connection between conceptualization and measurement is provided by recent analyses of the concept of accuracy in interpersonal communication.[3] Since accuracy had not been adequately conceptualized, a number of measurement procedures were being employed that did not pertain to the same concept. In fact, it was often unclear exactly what was being measured, and therefore difficult to interpret the meaning of the accuracy scores obtained.[4] The

[2]Lee J. Cronbach and Paul E. Meehl, "Construct Validity in Psychological Tests," *Psychological Bulletin*, 52:281–302 (1955).

[3]Norman L. Gage and Lee J. Cronbach, "Conceptual and Methodological Problems in Interpersonal Perception," *Psychological Bulletin*, 62:411–22 (1965); Steven H. Chaffee, "Pseudo-Data in Communication Research," unpublished paper, 1971; Keith R. Stamm and W. Barnett Pearce, "Communication Behavior and Coorientational Relations," *Journal of Communication*, 21:208–20 (1972); Beth Hefner, "Communicatory Accuracy: Four Experiments," *Journalism Monographs* No. 30, August 1973.

[4]Daniel B. Wackman, "A Proposal for a New Measure of Coorientational Accuracy or Empathy," unpublished paper, 1969.

confounding of accuracy scores had to be untangled through sharper definition of the underlying attributes.

Another relationship between concepts and measures concerns the *stability* of the attribute. Most psychologists regard intelligence as a very nearly fixed characteristic of a person. In that case a very high degree of reliability can be expected. At the other extreme is a "mood scale," which measures a highly unstable condition, one that will have validity only if it is sensitive to moment-to-moment changes in feelings. The appropriate degree of stability lies in the concept itself, and that must be reflected in the research and statistical designs that use it.

The greatest contributions to the *efficiency* of a measure are also made at the conceptualization stage. A clean, focused definition of the attribute to be measured pays dividends in at least two ways. First, it prevents confounding the instrument with observations that have little or nothing to do with the concept. Second, clarity of definition leads more readily to standardization of the measurement procedures. When there is little doubt about what we want to measure, we can specify all the relevant observations ahead of time and determine what values should be assigned to each type of observation.

Operationalization

The operationalization stage is pivotal for the development of an adequate and appropriate measurement scheme. On the one hand, we look back to the conceptualization to ensure that the empirical operations are faithful to the concept(s). On the other hand, we look ahead to the analysis to be sure that the obtained measure will satisfy the demands of the analytical model. A danger at the operationalization stage is asserting more power than is justified by the concept. The power must be appropriate to the reality of the attribute being studied.

The technique of *indexing* offers a way of enhancing measurement power when measuring a qualitative attribute. One way to construct an index is to ask yes-no questions with respect to a quality and then combine them into an index on the basis of the number of "yes" answers. This converts nominal data into ordinal data and yields a more powerful measure. This process can also be reversed. We can ask the question on the basis of an ordinal scale of values, using, for example, the response categories "no influence," "slight influence," "moderate influence," and "strong influence." These could be combined into a single ordered metric, then collapsed into "high" and "low" influence categories at whatever point on the scale yields the nearest thing to equal frequencies in the two categories. It would still be an ordinal scale, of course.

The key to attaining control over measurement power is careful *pretesting* at the operationalization stage. Just as a skilled hunter sights in his rifle before the hunt, the power of instruments should be established before any data are gathered. What pretesting can do is illustrated by a recent study of newspaper use by new residents. The concept to be operationalized was "severity of dislocation." Since this was a new concept, it was given only a preliminary definition at the conceptualization stage. The initial purpose of pretesting was to identify dimensions of the attribute that would provide a basis for developing an instrument to measure the magnitude of dislocation. In-depth interviews with a number of recent relocators revealed that the severity of dislocation was expressed in terms of the amount of difference between the new location and a previous one, and in terms of how much thought was given to relocation concerns. Pretesting also showed that relocation concerns were very diverse. The magnitude of concern might be very strong along some dimensions (e.g., home and work) and moderate or weak in others (neighborhood, community, and leisure). Pretesting, then, provided a place to start in developing a measure of "severity of dislocation."[5]

In the second pretest, the investigators developed a set of items to tap each of five dimensions of relocation concerns that had been identified. Generally, there were six items for each dimension. For example, home concerns items asked about "things" in the home, "activities" in the home, and "people" in the home. In each case, two items were used, one item asking about differences between the new home and the previous one and one asking how often respondents thought about (things, people, activities) in the new home. An ordered scale was used with each item: either "very similar," "similar," "different," "very different," or "not at all," "not much," "some," "pretty much," "very much."

In total, thirty-four items were designed and administered to a small sample of students who had recently moved. This second pretest provided information pertinent to the validity of the prospective measure. In this case, the validity of the items was tested in two ways: (1) the extent to which each item correlated with other items on the test, and (2) the extent to which each item correlated with the average score for all items on the test. Two types of items were removed from the instrument at this point: (1) items that produced a number of very small or negative correlations with other items and/or the average test score, and (2) items that correlated too strongly with the average test score. The first type of item was removed because it could only reduce the instrument's reliability. The second type was removed because it contributed little to the discriminatory power of the instrument. A final consideration was that an adequate number of items be included to represent each of the five dimensions of severity of dislocation.

A somewhat different approach to measurement has been developed largely in the field of attitude measurement, but the general approach, called *scaling*, is applicable to a variety of other measurement problems. The logic of scaling is most easily explained in terms of the

[5]Keith R. Stamm, Kenneth M. Jackson, and Lawrence Bowen, "Newspaper Use Among New Residents," in *ANPA News Research Report No. 6* (Reston, Va.: ANPA Foundation, 1977).

Guttman scalogram technique, a technique widely applied in communication research.[6]

The basic objective of scaling is to develop a set of items ordered on the basis of a single dimension. With the Guttman technique this is achieved through extensive pretesting of items and an analysis that produces an ordering of the items and evidence of unidimensionality. Consider the following item set: *Answer yes or no:*

1. Do you watch television as much as 3 hours a day?
2. Do you watch television as much as 2 hours a day?
3. Do you watch television as much as 1 hour a day?

It is easy to see that there is an inherent order in these items. A person who says "yes" to the first item should give the same answer to the other two. To produce a unidimensional measure of television viewing time, we can ask several friends to answer the questions and construct a *scalogram* in which *both items and respondents are ordered:*

1. Columns are ordered from least to most often endorsed items.
2. Rows are ordered beginning with the respondent who endorsed the least number of items to the respondent who endorsed the greatest number.

The resulting scalogram would look like the matrix shown in Figure 5–1. The unidimensionality of this case is perfect. No one gave an answer that was inconsistent with the resulting ordering of the items. Of course, it will not always turn out that way. In fact, we would not normally go to the trouble of scaling such an attribute in this way.

But let us say we want to measure the strength of individuals' surveillance need because we want to study the relationship between surveillance need and time spent with various mass media. We pretest the following items:

1. Are you concerned that people will tell you things that are not true?
2. Are you concerned that important changes might take place without your knowing it?
3. Are you concerned that you will not anticipate problems that could come up?
4. Are you concerned that stores will charge you too much?

Figure 5–1   Scalogram of Television Viewing.

Resp.	Item		
	3	*2*	*1*
1	×		
2	×	×	
3	×	×	×

[6]Louis L. Guttman, "The Basis for Scalogram Analysis," in G. M. Maranell, ed., *Scaling: A Sourcebook for Behavioral Scientists* (Chicago: Aldine Publishing Co., 1974).

Here who to prioritize

Compared to the television viewing items, there are two important differences in this set. We cannot be sure that each item pertains only to surveillance. We have no idea what the ordering of the items might be, that is, which items are strong surveillance items and which are weak. Because of these uncertainties, it is generally advisable to begin pretesting with a very large sample of items, perhaps thirty or forty.

Scalogram analysis of the four items (see Figure 5–2) should tell whether they are unidimensional. If unidimensionality is not demonstrated strongly, we have no evidence for either the validity or reliability of these items as a measure. The extent to which a scalogram demonstrates unidimensionality may be estimated by calculating its *coefficient of reproducibility*. The coefficient has been calculated for the scalogram in Figure 5–2.

The reproducibility of the scale was computed by first counting the "errors" for each person on each item. An error is defined as any answer that would have been wrongly predicted on the basis of the person's scale score. The number of errors (four) is divided by the total number of responses (four items times ten respondents equals forty). The resulting fraction is then subtracted from unity to yield, in this case, a coefficient of reproducibility of 90 percent. In other words, 90 percent of the responses on the pretest are correctly predicted by the scores assigned to each person.

A reproducibility of 90 percent or better is generally taken as strong evidence of unidimensionality, particularly if the pattern of errors appears to be random.[7] However, if most or all of the errors had been confined to one of the four items, the coefficient is misleading and the thing to do is to remove that item from the scale and recompute re-

Figure 5–2 Scalogram of Surveillance Need.

		Item			
Resp.	*3*	*1*	*2*	*4*	*Score*
1	×				1
2	×				1
3	×		⊗		1
4	×			⊗	1
5	○	×			2
6	×	×			2
7	×	×	×		3
8	×	×	○	×	3
9	×	×	×	×	4
10	×	×	×	×	4
Errors	1	0	2	1	$R = 1 - \frac{4}{40} = 90\%$

[7]If the population reproducibility is at least 0.90, then the standard error of a sample proportion of reproducibility is at most 0.013. This allows a deviation in the proportion of at most 0.040 at the three standard error level of confidence. Guttman, "Basis for Scalogram Analysis."

producibility or pretest again with a revised set of items.[8] The advantage of beginning with a large sample of items is that the pretest can be used to eliminate those items that do not conform to the unidimensional pattern. Reproducibility is evidence of reliability but not validity, although the items often provide evidence for what we call *face* validity—plausible grounds for believing that the scale should measure what it is intended to measure.

In recent years, factor analysis has been commonly used as an alternative to scalogram analysis for assessing the unidimensionality of a set of items. Factor analysis correlates every item with every other item and then sorts the items into *factors,* each with *loadings* indicating what items share variance with other items. However, this practice is not advised for those who are not well trained in the use of factor analysis. Since factor analysis yields several dimensions, it is best used to identify them, not to try to order items on a single dimension (or factor). Besides, the nature of the dimensions obtained, and even the number, is largely dependent upon the type of factor analysis model employed, and there are several. This difficulty has been discussed by Carter in criticizing Osgood, Suci and Tannenbaum's argument for a three-dimensional interpretation of meaning. Carter showed that the number of dimensions obtained was largely a function of the factor analysis model employed.[9]

Of course, the validity and reliability of instruments may already exist at the time the researcher turns from concept to operations. It only requires a careful search to discover that a measure appropriate to a concept in which the investigator is interested has been used fruitfully many times and its properties as measurement well established. In the computer age, however, there is no reason not to check one's own experience with a measure, since a computer routine often will provide everything that is needed. (For example, *SPSS, the Statistical Package for the Social Sciences,* yields the kind of data that permit tests of reliability and encourage purification of measures by means of item analysis.)

The notion of validity raises two sorts of questions about measures. The first is whether the instrument actually taps the attribute it purports to measure. We will refer to this as *empirical validity.* The second question is much more difficult: it asks whether the instrument taps *only* the attribute in which you are interested. This question has been called *construct validity.*

To take the easier of the two questions first, we may begin by identifying the types of evidence that bear upon whether a measure ac-

[8]For additional advice on the interpretation of scalograms, consult B. W. White and Edi Saltz, "Measurement of Reproducibility," in Maranell, *Scaling,* pp. 172–97, and Carmi Schooler, "A Note of Extreme Caution on the Use of Guttman Scales," in Maranell, *Scaling,* pp. 223–30.

[9]Consult Richard F. Carter, "Communication and Affective Relations," *Journalism Quarterly,* 42:203–212 (Spring 1965); Charles E. Osgood, G. J. Suci and Percy H. Tannenbaum, *The Measurement of Meaning* (Urbana: University of Illinois Press, 1957).

tually measures what it is intended to measure. Three types of evidence must be considered: *face validity, concurrent validity,* and *predictive validity.*

We will begin with face validity. Generally, any measure of a communication variable is begun on evidence of face validity. All this means is that the content of the measure (e.g., its items) *appear* to represent the attribute being measured. Of course, the validity of a measure cannot rest on face validity alone.

To go beyond face validity requires us to relate to other measures of the same attribute. An instrument that correlates with scores on another measure of the attribute provides some evidence of concurrent validity. Indexing is one way of producing concurrent validation. Here several items, all designed to measure the same attribute, are correlated with one another over a sample of respondents. Such evidence for validity is normally obtained in a pretest. Until some evidence of concurrent validity is found, it is risky to use an instrument for extensive data gathering.

There are many other ways of obtaining concurrent validation. Where other instruments have been developed for measuring the attribute, such an instrument may be used together with an untested instrument in a pretest. If they correlate, this is further evidence of concurrent validity. Osgood and others[10] used this method in validating the semantic differential. For example, they showed high correlations between the location of concepts on the evaluative factor of the semantic differential and scores on standard attitude scales. Another approach, called "multiple operationism," has been gaining favor in the research literature recently. The basic argument behind this approach is that concurrent validation can be strengthened by comparing scores obtained through different types of observational procedures. For example, the validity of a paper-and-pencil test as a measure of the popularity of an exhibit might be checked against a measure of floor erosion in front of the exhibit.

Despite frequent exhortations to multiple operations by Webb and others and Campbell and Fiske,[11] among others, the actual use of multiple operations has not gained much popularity in communication research. This is probably not due to lack of a convincing argument or to ignorance on the part of researchers. Paisley and others[12] have shown that some concepts are adequately measured with a single op-

[10]Ibid.

[11]Eugene J. Webb and others, *Unobtrusive Measures: Non-Reactive Research in the Social Sciences* (Chicago: Rand McNally & Co.); Donald T. Campbell and D. W. Fiske, "Convergent and Discriminant Validation by the Multitrait-Multimethod Matrix," *Psychological Bulletin,* 56:81–105 (1959).

[12]Mathilda B. Paisley, W. A. Collins, and William J. Paisley, "The Convergent-Discriminant Matrix: Multitrait-Multimethod Logic Extended to Other Social Research Decisions," unpublished paper, Institute for Communication Research, Stanford University, Stanford, Calif., 1970.

eration, while others, such as "intelligence" and "ethnocentrism," require triangulation using multiple measures. There is no reason such communication concepts as "empathy," "agenda," "readership," "readability," or "use" and "gratification" could not also be validated by this method.

Campbell and Fiske[13] long ago described a method of concurrent validation which they called the "multitrait-multimethod matrix." Actually, this method is designed to demonstrate construct validity as well as concurrent validity. Concurrent validation is demonstrated with this method by the "convergence" of measures of the same attribute obtained through different methods. Construct validity is demonstrated through discrimination; that is, measures of different attributes obtained with similar methods should not be highly correlated. (If they are highly correlated, one suspects that something other than the trait in question is being measured by the instrument.)

Paisley and others have elaborated the Campbell and Fiske idea with their "convergent-discriminant matrix" and shown that other "double variation" strategies are also available, including cross-lagged correlation, "Q analysis" and profile analysis. These techniques are too specialized to receive full treatment here.

Turning now to *predictive validity*, the question is whether a measure relates to other measures as expected. Once again, it is at the conceptualization stage that one identifies variables which should be predicted by the measure in question. For example, it would be expected that a measure of the individual "news agenda" should be related to variables describing patterns of media use. Osgood and others demonstrated the predictive validity of the semantic differential by showing that ratings of Stevenson and Eisenhower could be used to predict how people would actually vote in the 1952 election.[14]

There are some things to keep in mind when testing predictive validity. First, when a measure is tested against an extensive list of criterion variables, it is likely that some significant relationships will appear by chance. After all, when we accept the usual p less than 0.05 criterion (see Chapter 4), we may expect one prediction in twenty to be significant by chance. Second, if the expected relationships are not found, we are left with the question: Is the measure invalid or is the theory that led to those predictions invalid? Lack of predictive validity calls for reassessment of the concept and perhaps the theory from which it is drawn.

Demonstrating construct validity is a complex process, and one is not expected to get more than a start on it in a single investigation. It can only occur in a theoretical framework in which the construct can be defined in terms of propositions about relationships to observable variables. As Cronbach and Meehl have stated, "The investigation of a

---

[13]Campbell and Fiske, "Convergent and Discriminant Validation."
[14]Osgood and others, *Measurement of Meaning*.

(measure's) construct validity is not essentially different from the general scientific procedures for developing and confirming theories."[15] Many types of evidence may be relevant to the construct validity of measures. But how such evidence is to be interpreted depends largely upon what the theoretical framework leads us to look for and what that evidence means in that framework. Here are some kinds of evidence that might be obtained in demonstrating construct validity:

1. *Group differences.* Does the theory lead one to expect that two groups should differ on the measure? If so, both populations should be sampled and compared on the measure.

2. *Internal structure* of the instrument. Evidence of the unidimensionality of the measure, as discussed in connection with scaling techniques (e.g., Guttman scalogram) supports construct validity.

3. *Change over instances.* If the theory suggests experimental manipulations that should produce changes in the measure, we may demonstrate that these changes actually occur.

4. *Logical consequences.* If the theory specifies a certain outcome, measures of that outcome may be related to some logical consequence. For example, when Flesch was first measuring "readability," he reasoned that a consequence of readability should be reading comprehension, which allowed him to correlate his scores with an existing comprehension measure.[16]

Construct validity is established through a continuing program of research involving the development of theory, the creation of hypotheses, and testing of these hypotheses by experiments and other means. The aim of construct validation is the development of a measure that reflects only the attribute in which we are theoretically interested. There are very few measures currently employed in communication research whose construct validity is firmly established.

The *reliability* of measures should also be established at the operationalization stage. Reliability points to a different source of measurement error, error due to lack of stability or consistency in the measuring instrument. To return to the headline example, a headline count that is a reliable measure would assure that two editors counting the same headline would come up with identical (or very similar) values. Or if the same editor counted the same headline another time, the values should be the same or similar. To the extent that these measurements differ, reliability is lacking. As with validity, it is generally best to pretest so that a preliminary assessment of reliability can be guided by results. These results may lead to changes in either the instrument or the measurement context of the study. The purpose is to increase prospects of obtaining acceptable reliability when the study goes into the field.

To be a little more specific about the difference between validity and

---

[15]Cronbach and Meehl, "Construct Validity."
[16]Rudolph Flesch, "The Marks of a Readable Style," Ph.D. dissertation, Columbia University, New York, 1944.

reliability, let us take the example of a caliper. A caliper should measure distance and nothing else. Its validity, thus, is obvious. A caliper should get the same answer every time (within stated tolerances) no matter in whose hands, no matter in what circumstances. That is reliability. In human measurement, validity must be established and so must reliability. The fact that we usually use correlation in both instances requires us to be quite self-conscious about what such correlations mean.

The previous discussion has shown that basically validity is established by demonstrating that the measure in question is positively correlated with some external criterion—some independent measure of the same thing. In establishing a measure's reliability we are really asking two questions. The first relates to *equivalence*. For example, will two versions of the same measure consistently yield the same answer when applied to the same subjects? The second is *stability*. Will the measure yield the same answer at different times?

To test for equivalence we usually are called upon to show that the items in the test in various combinations consistently give the same result. We may use a *split half method* in which items are alternately or randomly assigned to two versions. Then the scores on the two halves are correlated (for the same subjects). In checking the reliability of standardized tests, multiple versions are developed and their intercorrelations are taken as measures of reliability. To test for stability, we rely on the *test-retest method,* which requires using the measure (or different versions of the measure) on the same subjects at widely separated times.

The split-half method has the obvious flaw that it uses half the items and thus increases random error in relation to variance accounted for. (These terms are explained in the preceding chapter.) The test-retest method has the obvious flaw that "test learning" may inflate the correlation. But *item analysis* may come to the rescue. Item analysis simply means correlating item scores with the total score. This should be part of the development of any multi-item test, since any test is only as good as its items. "Purifying" a test by means of item analysis allows us to assure the test's internal consistency by removing items that correlate negatively with the total measure and replacing items that correlate poorly with the total measure. By creating a "pool" of, say, 120 items of known item reliability, we may then select ideal combinations of items in creating alternate versions of the measure with the highest attainable intercorrelations. Alternate forms take care of the test-learning problem in test-retest procedures (although they do not solve the "test wisdom" problem; test takers simply get wiser and wiser the more experience they have with a measure). It also solves the split-half problem by providing versions of optimal length.

A final advantage of item analysis is that it allows us to create versions of a test of varying length. Well-developed measures like the *F* (for Fascism) test of years ago were available in versions as short as 9 items and as long as more than 100. The shorter versions have lower reliabilities and lower validities than longer versions, as might be expected, but the tradeoff between interview time and cost and known values of these characteristics may determine what version is ideal in the circumstances.

Stability is especially important in longitudinal surveys and in experiments where the outcome is before-after change on a measure. It is very difficult to show that changes are due to experimental manipulations when employing a dependent variable that fluctuates due to low reliability. In fact, it is worth noting here that a measure's validity can never exceed its reliability. If that is not self-evident, the student is urged to stop at this point and think the matter through.

The preceding discussion has assumed that we are talking about multi-item measures. But in both survey and experimental research we often depend upon single-item measures. For identifying information for later analysis, we may use single questions to obtain age, occupation of head of household, political affiliation, and the like. Surveys may use single items to measure attitudes or expected behaviors (Do you favor Proposition 13?) (If the election were held today, . . . ?). In validating such items, we are really talking about validating an entire instrument, and Comstock and McCombs have a good bit to say on that question in Chapter 9. We can say that the method used is essentially test-retest. In surveys it is customary to check on the work of interviewers by calling a respondent and checking out answers to selected questions—a test-retest procedure. In coding survey responses, it is customary to do a certain amount of "check-coding." Coders unknowingly recode the work of others, another test-retest procedure in effect. One caution: test-retest reliability coefficients such as these are affected by instability of the variable over time, as well as by instability of the measure, making it difficult to separate "true" variability from measurement error.

One way to separate "true" variance from measurement error uses the test-retest method. Data are gathered at three times rather than just two.[17] Heise has developed a path analysis model by which the two sources of variability may be separated where three data points are available. Once the reliability coefficients between each pair of the three tests have been calculated, a measure of reliability that is free of temporal change effects may be obtained by the following formula:

$$r_{xy} = r_{12}r_{23}/r_{13}$$

Where there has been change between tests due to "true" change in the variable, this correction will result in a higher coefficient that is a more accurate reflection of the actual stability of the method.[18]

[17]James S. Coleman, "The Mathematical Study of Change," in Hubert M. Blalock, Jr., and A. B. Blalock, eds., *Methodology in Social Research* (New York: McGraw-Hill Book Company, 1968).

[18]Donald R. Heise, "Separating Reliability and Stability in Test-Retest Correlation," *American Sociological Review*, 34:93–101 (1969). Students are advised to study this reference closely before attempting to use Heise's method.

The *coefficient of agreement* is especially useful in content analysis in measuring intercoder reliability. Stempel discusses this method in Chapter 8. This coefficient is also useful in survey research. Consult Chapter 9.

Analysis

By the time we get to the analysis stage, all the critical decisions have been made. The plan has been drawn and it only remains to carry it out. But sometimes the analysis stage turns up problems—failures at earlier stages. A case in point may be found in the literature of schizophrenia. Controversy arose over findings that parental communication behaviors were linked with the onset of schizophrenic symptoms in the children.[19] It centered around a measurement problem. The index used to measure parental communication deviance was confounded: scores on the index were heavily dependent upon the sheer number of words spoken. Thus, the question had to be posed whether lack of validity (of the index) had produced an artifactual correlation.

An effort was made at this point to reinterpret the finding by statistically removing the source of confounding by means of analysis of covariance, which is discussed in Chapter 4. It turned out, however, that the sources of measurement error were so complex that a statistical correction was inappropriate. The only way to clear up the controversy was to go back and design a more valid index and collect new data.

Attention to conceptual clarity and use of pretesting in the operationalization stage should help avoid serious difficulties of this kind. It is likely, however, that the instrument will not perform exactly as it did under pretest conditions. The preliminary checks that were employed in pretesting must now be repeated to verify that the instrument has performed according to expectations. Also, evidence bearing on predictive validity may be available for the first time at this stage. We begin by rechecking the internal consistency of the instrument, whether a scale or an index. This procedure includes checking the frequency distributions of individual items. Items that are too strongly skewed or distributed bimodally should be candidates for exclusion (these terms are explained in Chapter 4). Next a scalogram analysis or interitem correlation analysis should be conducted. Finally, validity and reliability coefficients should be recalculated.

Some modifications in the measure may be suggested by this additional evidence. Items that detract from the internal consistency of the measure may be dropped. Refinements in scoring the instrument may also be possible, including the item analysis mentioned previously, or with an external criterion.

[19]J. A. Woodward and M. J. Goldstein, "Communication Deviance in the Families of Schizophrenics: A Comment on the Misuse of Analysis of Covariance," *Science*, 197:2096–97 (1977).

At the analysis stage, the power of measurement operations may be asserted in terms of the statistical transformations appropriate to the level of measurement achieved. This power should not be asserted merely to make certain statistical operations available. It is worth remembering that the power asserted should be consistent with the conceptualization of the attribute and with the nature of the empirical information conveyed by the scores.

For example, let us take the purely hypothetical attribute "orientation to local news" and assume that procedures have been developed which order people in terms of the strength of orientation. This information tells nothing about the size of the intervals between individuals. To assert an interval level of measurement in this case would not be consistent with either the conceptualization or the measurement operations.

In mathematical terms, the appropriateness of a statistical transformation is based upon a principle of invariance. This principle simply states that any transformation may be made that does not distort the empirical relations contained in the measure.[20] Suppose that you were to calculate the average score for ten people whose local news orientation had been measured by an ordering procedure. The value obtained would certainly represent the mean of those ten scores, but a person who obtained that score would not represent an average local news orientation for the ten persons measured. The use of statistics involves making different kinds of mathematical transformations upon the scores assigned. The question is whether these transformations can be made while preserving the empirical information contained in the measure. Some of the statistics that are most appropriate for the measurement models we have discussed are elaborated in Chapter 4 and are summarized in Figures 4–7 and 4–8.

A question that invariably comes up at the analysis stage is whether the measures obtained can be treated as satisfying interval-level measurement. Unfortunately, readily applied procedures for meeting the requirements of intervality are lacking. The established method of creating interval scales, Thurstone's method of paired comparisons, is laborious and requires an enormous investment in development. Its primary use in communication research has been as an outside criterion for checking the intervality claims of other measures, such as the semantic differential and Likert scales. This use of Thurstone scales is rather limited because so few of them are available.

In a recent review of the intervality question, Hewes observed that few of the measurement scales currently in use have been adequately tested for intervality, even though they are treated as interval scales. This in itself presents a serious problem for two reasons. First, not very much is known about the effects of violations of intervality: specifically, the use of interval-level statistical models in the analysis of ordinal

[20]S. S. Stevens, "Measurement," in Maranell, *Scaling.*

data. According to Hewes, this widespread practice runs the serious risk that both type I and type II errors may be increased.[21] Until further information is available on this question, the cautious researcher is justified in selecting less demanding statistical tools. (A type I error is accepting an hypothesis when in fact it is false. A type II error is rejecting an hypothesis when in fact it is true.) Second, there is usually no practical way to test the intervality of a measure after the fact. There are few established measures that can be used as standards for checking one's own instrument. Hewes has worked out a path analysis procedure by which a necessary condition for intervality may be tested, but there is not much payoff from conducting such a test unless there is strong reason to believe the measure will pass the test. (Path analysis is explained in Chapter 10.)

Reporting Findings

When it comes to reporting findings, the researcher should give attention to explaining the reasoning behind the measurement model and to describing evidence that pertains (positively or negatively) to the validity and reliability of measurement. The report should describe the conceptual basis for the measurement model and give a detailed description of the development of the measure, the kinds of observational procedures selected, the results of pretests, and what modifications were made in light of pretest results, what kinds of validating evidence were incorporated into the study design, what rules were adopted for scoring, and the like. A complete report requires a listing of the contents of any new instrument.

The discussion of results should include an evaluation of the adequacy of the measure. Evidence bearing upon validity and reliability should be fully reviewed, since interpretation of findings hinges on this evidence. The choice of a statistical model for analyzing results should also be linked to the measurement procedures. It is not a matter of defending the "correctness" of the approach used, but of the instrument used within the research context.

Despite careful pretesting, it may happen that the obtained validity and reliability turn out to be inadequate. When the evidence for reliability is flawed, there is no point in reporting the study. The same is true where the evidence for validity is flawed. No reportable results can flow from flawed instruments. But if the study requires accepting the null hypothesis, there may be grounds for reporting the study.[22] The failure to predict may have sprung from weak measures or it may

[21]Dean Hewes, " 'Levels of Measurement' Problem in Communication Research: A Review, Critique and Partial Solution," *Communication Research*, 5:87–127 (January 1978).

[22]Successful prediction contributes positive evidence for validity. But the only safe course is to have independent evidence for validity before risking the null hypothesis, for this provides the best basis for judging whether the failure should be attributed to the measure or the hypothesis.

have sprung from a weak or inadequate theory. Presenting the study may permit the researcher to explore what needs to be done to revise the theory, and invites others interested in the work to do so themselves.

For further suggestions on reporting research results, see Chapter 20.

To summarize, the most important decisions respecting measurement of communication variables are made during the first two stages of a study. The conceptualization of the variable clarifies the choice of measurement model and indicates the types of evidence that will be most relevant to validation of the instrument. Pretesting is important to efficiency. It provides needed information for guiding development of a useful instrument and prevents overinvesting resources in an unproductive measurement approach. Evidence supporting the validity and reliability of a measure is an integral part of any research project and vital to the interpretation of findings.

6

Data Processing

Wayne A. Danielson

Data processing, the *Britannica* tells us, consists of "operations involving the handling of data, usually in accordance with an implicit or explicit logical, mathematical or arbitrary set of rules, in a series of discrete steps."[1] Nachmias and Nachmias define data processing as "the link between data collection and data analysis."[2] In their view it "involves the transformation of the observations gathered in the field into a system of categories and the translation of these categories into codes amenable to quantitative analysis."[3] Data processing, thus, is the central part of any research project. If it is done well, it can add greatly to the quality of the overall results. If it is done poorly, it can result in aborted or partially completed projects or projects that are brought to completion long after the deadline has passed.

It has been our experience that on the college scene most failures to complete master's theses or doctoral dissertations stem from inadequacies in data processing by the student. It is difficult, therefore, to over-

---

[1]*Encyclopaedia Britannica*, Micropaedia, Vol. III. 15th ed. (Chicago: Encyclopaedia Britannica, Inc., 1974), p. 389.

[2]David Nachmias and Chava Nachmias, *Research Methods in the Social Sciences* (New York: St. Martin's Press, Inc.), p. 143.

[3]Ibid.

state the importance of good data processing, for it is from the proper collection, coding, and analysis of the data that we will find or fail to find the answers to the research questions we have posed.

PLANNING FOR DATA PROCESSING

An important rule of research in general—and a cardinal principle of data processing—is that the researcher should think through the total project at the beginning, planning for all the operations that will be necessary along the way. Only data that will contribute to the final product should be collected and stored. The "carrying along" of unneeded or extra data is a trap that has snared many an unwary researcher. In planning the study, the project director should concentrate on the main chance and not get sidetracked into "interesting" or "possibly significant" bypaths. A sound bit of advice to the prospective data processor is to envisage each table in the final report before the first bit of data is collected. Only by so doing can the researcher be sure that he or she will indeed collect and have available in usable form the data needed to answer the research questions.

Not all researchers agree with this stern approach. The late Malcolm MacLean, for example, used to recommend that his students collect a lot of data and "wade around in it."[4] He wanted his students to *discover* relationships in the data rather than to assemble data to prove or disprove already hypothesized relationships. Undoubtedly, many scientists work and work productively in MacLean's mode. It is often a time-consuming method, however, and it tends to be about as productive as the researcher is ingenious. To this observer, the safer, hypothesis-testing model is better for the young researcher. Serendipity can still occur, but its appearance is not essential to the successful completion of the study.

To alter slightly the *Britannica*'s definition, methods of data processing that envisage explicit logical, mathematical, or arbitrary rules are to be favored over methods that leave the rules implicit or unstated. Especially to be avoided are methods that advocate the collection and retention of loosely defined collections of data that leave the researcher wondering what to do next. Early and specific planning is essential to efficient data processing.

THE IMPORTANCE OF PRETESTING

Along with early planning goes pretesting of the methods to be used. From the data-processing point of view, it is a happy idea to take some pretest data and run it all the way through the proposed study. If sur-

---

[4]Malcolm S. MacLean, Jr., "Frontiers of Communication Research," a paper presented at the 1966 Journalism Institutes (Madison, Wis.: School of Journalism, University of Wisconsin, 1966), p. 3.

vey data are involved, this exercise may deliver important feedback on how questions can be reworded to be more productive. If a content analysis is planned, the pretest of data-processing techniques will assure the researcher that the definitions are working, that usable data are being produced, and that if the study is carried to completion interesting results will be forthcoming. Time spent in planning and pretesting is never wasted; it often is the most efficient and productive use of the researcher's time.

At the close of the pretesting period, the researcher should be able to give a specific answer to such questions as: Why am I gathering these data? How will I encode the data? What variables will I form from the data? In what tables will these variables appear? How will I accept or reject my hypotheses with data from these tables? What statistical tests will I use to analyze the data? Do I know how to interpret these statistics?

Unless you can answer all these questions, stop. Your planning and pretesting work is not finished. You are not ready to start collecting the main body of data.

THE MACHINERY OF DATA PROCESSING

Mention data processing today and most people think of computers, flashing lights, yards and yards of printouts, and complex multivariate statistics. Most people are wrong.

The real work of research goes on in the researcher's mind. A good hypothesis can often be tested in a variety of ways. Some of these ways may indeed involve hundreds of subjects, thousands of data cards, and complex computer operations. Others, however, may involve simple observations and paper-and-pencil calculations. The discovery of penicillin, after all, required only a petri dish, some staphylococcus bacilli growing in it, an airborne contaminant, and a scientist with a mind flexible enough to realize that a deadly bacterial growth was being halted by some substance in a common household mold.

The principle of Ockham's razor says that the simplest explanation of a set of phenomena is best. By analogy, the simplest test of a hypothesis is generally to be preferred. Beginning researchers almost instinctively want to use the most complex research methods they can command. They want to crush the null hypothesis with tons of data, massaged in the most sophisticated manner possible. Actually, however, a strong research hypothesis does not need all that "extra help." It will stand easily, supported only by a fourfold table and a chi-square test.

The first rule of data processing is not to try for overkill. Use the simplest hypothesis test that you can devise. Employ the simplest data-processing technique adequate to the task.

Hand processing of data may be as simple as recording data subject by subject (or case by case) on 3 by 5 inch cards and then sorting those cards into categories, adding up the results, and performing statistical tests on a hand-held calculator. The point is, there is nothing wrong with such methods; on the contrary, they are to be preferred if they produce the desired results and satisfactory levels of statistical significance. "Student," writing of the famous Lanarkshire milk experiment, demonstrated that results of the same precision that were obtained by a sample survey of 20,000 British schoolchildren could have been derived from a test using only 50 pairs of identical twins.[5]

For slightly more complicated projects, there is still a lot to be said for punched IBM cards and a counter-sorter machine. The data remain physically in or close to the hands of the experimenter and do not disappear into the bowels of a computer. The experimenter, by watching the cards fall along the sorter tray, gets an almost physical "feel" for the relationships among the variables being analyzed. Missing or incorrectly reported data often "fall out" in the counting process and thus are recognized and corrected, whereas they tend to be ignored in the more complicated and distant computer.

Nothing impresses on a young researcher's mind more vividly the necessity of having backup systems in data processing than a faulty counter-sorter. Having one's research project eaten alive by a cranky sorter—and knowing that you do not have a duplicate or backup deck of cards—is highly educational. All methods are fallible and all machines are fallible. Counter-sorters are excellent, if primitive, teaching machines for drilling this principle into the heads of novice researchers.

Computers are a various lot. From the first ENIAC developed at the University of Pennsylvania in 1946 to the latest wonder from IBM or Control Data or Honeywell, they are all capable of impressive feats of data processing. But each tends to have peculiar faults and virtues. Furthermore, the machines do not talk to each other across brand lines very well. As a result, a program that works on one campus will not necessarily work on another campus and another machine. To date, hardware (the machines themselves) has influenced software (the programs) more than the software has influenced the hardware. As a result, programs that attempt to transcend hardware and work on a variety of machines almost always have limitations imposed by local hardware configurations.

Meeting this problem for the first time, many young researchers stop looking for already developed software and begin writing their own programs. This approach is almost always a mistake. The young investigator winds up reinventing the wheel (or in this case the standard deviation). What the researcher should do is plan consciously to spend a considerable amount of time breaking the information barrier at the computer center. Almost always a specific program read about in a text or in a journal article proves to be unavailable at the computer site. However, almost always a variant model will be found there which, in the local situation, will do about the same thing.

[5]"Student," "The Lanarkshire Milk Experiment," *Biometrika,* 23:398–406 (1931).

Just as teachers learn to reject student papers that begin with the assertion, "No significant research has yet been attempted on my subject," so should the researcher also reject the initial response, "No one here has ever tried to do that on our computer." The fact is that there are many common elements in all research fields. Projects in such diverse areas as economics, engineering, microbiology, psychology, and communication face similar problems of testing differences, measuring the strength of relationships, and the like. The intelligent researcher, like the good newspaper reporter, perseveres, refuses to take "no" for an answer, and eventually finds existing programs that can be used to great advantage.

To program or not to program? There will come a time in your research when you cannot find a "canned" program that will do the work you want to do. Then you come face to face with the question of learning or not learning how to do computer programming. The best advice is to take the time to learn at least one of the modern programming languages appropriate to your work. If you do not, you will spend the rest of your days trying to explain to someone else just what it is you want. And the idea will never quite get through, either because you do not understand the problems the programmer is facing or because the programmer does not (and one is tempted to say cannot) understand the problems you are trying to solve. The author once hired a programmer who worked for an entire year on one program and still did not have it right. After learning to program, the author solved the problem—slowly and inefficiently, to be sure, but the way he wanted it solved—in a few afternoons at the computation center. Computer languages are getting easier and easier to learn. To the researcher who expects to do a lot of data processing in the next twenty years, it may be as important to speak FORTRAN as to speak French or German. As Guersey observes, "the attempt to take a short cut to the use of computers may end up denying the social scientist all the contributions they could make to his work."[6]

METHODS OF DATA PROCESSING

Data processing has much in common with communication. The data begin as ideas or elements in the possession of a source and not available for analysis. These elements must be encoded or transformed into physical signals or messages capable of existing in time and space. Once ideas are in message form in a communication channel, they are "data" that can be sorted, rearranged, stored, and retrieved at the will of the analyst. Before the raw signals or data are of much use to anyone else, however, they have to be summarized and presented in a

[6]Elwood W. Guersey, *Social Research and Basic Computer Programming* (Springfield, Ill.: Charles C Thomas, Publisher, 1973), p. xxiv.

form a receiver can once again transform into elements or ideas that can be understood at the destination.

As in any chain model, the data-processing model is no stronger than its weakest link. If the encoding methods are inefficient, the research will break down at that point. If the messages are lost or distorted in the channel, the resulting output will be incomplete or distorted. If the materials prepared for decoding are poorly presented, chances are the point of the project will be blunted or dulled or lost altogether at the intended destination. Generally, in data processing an attempt should be made to keep each task along the chain as simple as possible so as to reduce the chances for error to occur.

Let us follow a common newspaper research question about the relative popularity of comic strips along the data-processing chain. In data-processing terms, the worst way to develop data from a reader might be to use the open-ended approach and ask a survey question such as: "What is your favorite comic strip?"

Such a question would produce answers expressed in words and, typically, would be plagued by errors and difficult-to-understand replies. ("Animals," a respondent might say, leaving an editor later on with an impossible task of deciding what he meant. "I like the one about, you know, the kid who likes baseball." Did he mean Charlie Brown in "Peanuts" or someone else?) A coder would have to examine each answer and assign a numerical response, which would then be entered into the data-processing system for analysis. The potential for error is great.[7]

A slightly better procedure from the data-processing point of view might be to ask more specific questions about each comic strip you want to test. The following question form might be tried:

Please indicate how much you like each of the following comic strips by checking one of the answers provided.

Peanuts

_____ Like it a lot

_____ Like it

_____ Don't care either way

_____ Dislike it

_____ Dislike it a lot

Doonesbury

_____ Like it a lot

_____ Like it

_____ Don't care either way

_____ Dislike it

_____ Dislike it a lot

[7]For an excellent discussion of data editing and coding procedures, see John A. Sonquist and William C. Dunkelberg, *Survey and Opinion Research: Procedures for Processing and Analysis* (Englewood Cliffs, N.J.: Prentice-Hall, Inc., 1977).

For questions asked in this way, an editor would have to supply a number for each possible answer: 5 for "like it a lot," for example, 4 for "like it," and so on. Then the numbers would be encoded onto a punched card for data storage and analysis. Or, in some systems, it would be read into a computer tape through optical scanning. Systems of the future undoubtedly will enable the researcher to speak data into computers.

A further refinement, even more preferable from the data-processing point of view, would be to precode the questions, so that appropriate numbers are printed on the form for the use of the card punchers. The numbers would tell the card punchers in which column of the card each number is to go and what that number is. Our example questions might now look like this:

Please indicate how much you like each of the following comic strips by checking one of the answers provided.

Peanuts (Col. 7)

_____(5)   Like it a lot

_____(4)   Like it

_____(3)   Don't care either way

_____(2)   Dislike it

_____(1)   Dislike it a lot

Doonesbury (Col. 8)

_____(5)   Like it a lot

_____(4)   Like it

_____(3)   Don't care either way

_____(2)   Dislike it

_____(1)   Dislike it a lot

A respondent who said he "liked" "Peanuts" would probably check the (4) space on the questionnaire. A card puncher, looking at the form, would know that a 4 was to be punched in Column 7 of that respondent's data card (see Figure 6–1). Similarly, if the respondent "disliked" "Doonesbury," the puncher would know to punch the 2 hole in column 8 of the respondent's card.

An even further refinement would be to have the respondent encode his response into machine readable form himself either by using a standard mark-sense form (like the forms students often use in taking multiple-choice tests) or some other especially printed form capable of being read by an optical scanner. The Bureau of the Census uses the latter method for encoding data for the Decennial Census. Either approach usually takes elaborate advance planning, but the savings in editing and encoding time can be substantial in a large-scale project. There is a danger, however, that the form, when designed more for the machine than for human beings, will actually introduce error.

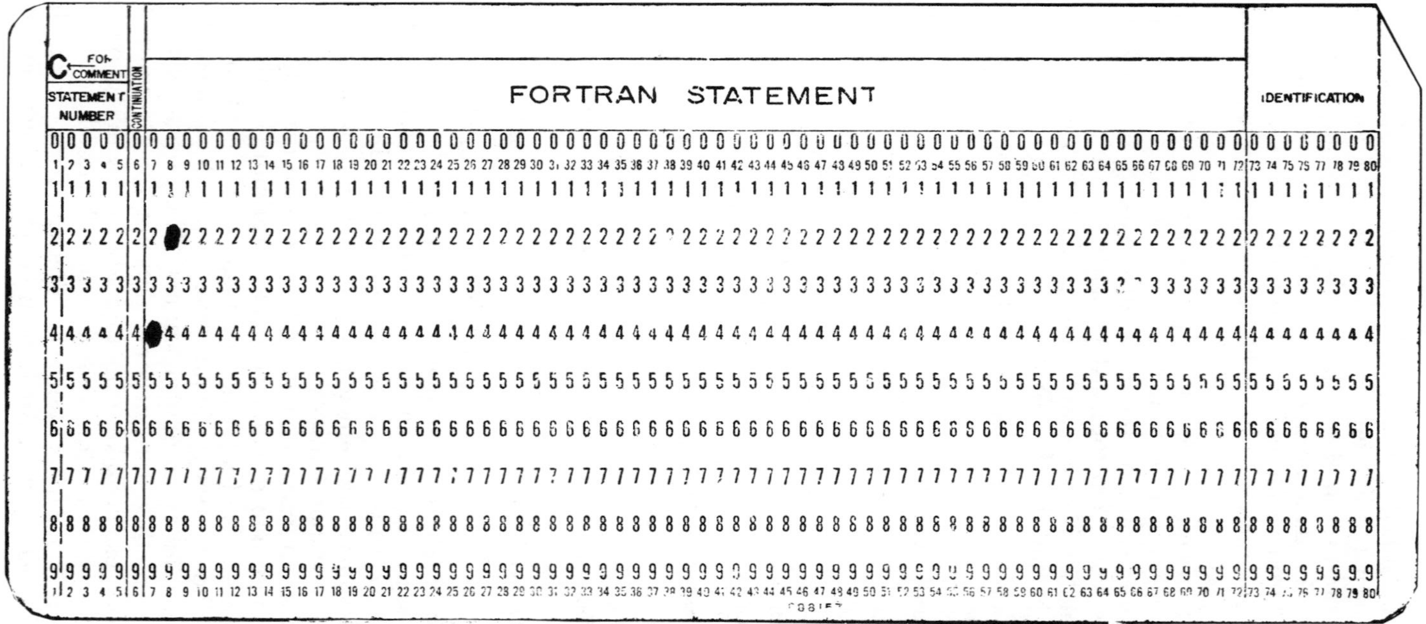

A *like* answer to the question on PEANUTS appears as a 4 punched in column 7 of the card. A *dislike* answer to the question on DOONESBURY appears as a 2 punched in column 8.

Figure 6–1 Punched Card Carrying Data from a Respondent on the Relative Popularity of Two Comic Strips.

Assuming for the moment that the data are in machine-readable form and on their way to machine or computer processing, what is the next thing to be done? The inexperienced data processor would probably say, "Make your first test runs." The more experienced data processor—older, wiser, sadder—would probably say, "Prepare a backup data file."

Any data-processing installation has its folklore about lost data. These stories are uniformly grim tales of graduate students or professors who have lost years' worth of data because an electrical storm blew the computer or because someone spilled coffee (with cream and sugar) on a card deck. In one case known to the author, a thief made off with a rental trailer which happened to have a graduate student's dissertation data in it along with the household clothing and the kids' bicycles. The thief was never caught. In another case, a box of cards, the student's only data deck, was left sitting temporarily on a waste basket. The data went to the campus dump and the student spent an entire weekend searching through tons of waste paper to recover his precious file. Wisdom demands that data be duplicated and the duplicate set be stored in a safe place, physically separated from the first set.

Second, take time to check the data for accuracy as soon as possible after getting it in machine-readable form. Cards can be duplicated erroneously, cards can be omitted, mysterious blanks can appear, enormous and disastrous errors can occur in the best-run facilities. You may never know that errors are present unless you take a careful look at the data. So look early and repeat the inspection often. Otherwise, you are almost certain to wind up reporting some results that prove embarrassing later on.[8]

Additional Thoughts on Error Reduction

Being neat, orderly, and organized is a problem for many researchers, young and old. But neatness does help. A few minutes spent cleaning up at the end of the day (or night) helps immensely when next you return to work, and may cut down on error.

A word needs to be said about keeping records of the decisions you make as you go through any data-processing procedure. It is a good idea to keep a record in a notebook of the steps you or your editors and coders take, the decisions you make, and the way you solve particular problems that come up. You should do this so that, if you should leave the project for a time, you can come back to it and quickly reconstruct everything that you did earlier. Such records also make secondary analysis of your data (see Chapter 13) possible for others. It is not uncommon for other researchers, after an article or book has been published, to criticize your work. It is helpful in replying to such criti-

---

[8]For a good discussion on "cleaning data," see Judith Rattenburg and Paula Pelletier, *Data Processing in the Social Sciences with OSIRIS* (Ann Arbor, Mich.: Survey Research Center, Institute for Social Research, University of Michigan, 1974), pp. 47–56.

cisms—which may appear months or even years after you have completed the task—to have a detailed record, or diary, to which you can repair to refresh your memory of "how we actually did it."

Planning for error.   Machines do make mistakes, and computers do err, but so do human beings. In the long run, most of us would probably agree that humans make mistakes more often. If the computer fails to work, our first inclination is to submit the run again instead of looking for *our* error. Almost always, the second run fails in exactly the same way the first one did. Then we have to start looking for the error, and all we have done is waste some valuable time. A wiser course would seem to be to plan for error, to expect it, and to be ready to cope with it. Coping probably will mean, among other things, (1) allowing additional time in the project for error correction, (2) being able to admit that we can make mistakes, (3) checking all work, (4) repeating key analyses, and (5) being cautious and humble in announcing findings.

Machine error and human error.   It is an accepted truism that machines cannot "think," and thus when they do make mistakes their mistakes are generally worse than the mistakes made by human beings. Usually, a human being would not send you an electric bill for $900,000 for one month's service for your apartment. A machine might. Human beings need to check the machines for the unreasonable mistakes they may make in their unthinking way. On the other hand, machines may be able to check human beings in the project for their "reasonable" errors, which are, as a matter of fact, just as wrong. And when the machines start making reasonable errors, watch out.

The first tables to be made from the data probably should be the "straight runs"—virtually simple tabulations of responses to each question. These straight runs enable the researcher to check the labeling procedures, the table organization, and so on. They also provide additional opportunities for checking for impossible ("wild") codes or other errors. If you are using the SPSS system mentioned by Weaver in Chapter 4 or a similar system, you will also want at this stage to obtain a graphic display of the data.[9] Such a pictorial account will provide an additional opportunity to detect errors that may have been missed in studying the numbers themselves.

LATTER STAGES OF DATA PROCESSING

Finally, you are ready to prepare your final tables. It is important at this time to be sure that all variables are neatly labeled and that the

[9]Two of the most widely available statistical packages are Norman Nie, Dale H. Bent, and C. Hadlai Hull, *Statistical Package for the Social Sciences* (New York: McGraw-Hill Book Co., 1970) and Wilfred J. Dixon, ed., *Biomedical Computer Programs* (Berkeley: University of California Press, 1973).

tables are as clean and intelligible as possible. In the well-written scientific article, the tables should stand alone. This means that the main ideas of the article should, as a rule, find expression in a set of key tables that can be read by themselves without reference to the text. A goal in data processing is to make tables so clear, so well labeled, so detailed that they are like a good news story; they answer the who, what, where, when, why, and how of the study by themselves. Take the time to rid your tables of mystifying abbreviations and code words that are intelligible only to the person who plows through the entire text and has a photographic memory. When in doubt, spell it out. Your readers will be grateful and you will enhance the usefulness of your study. (It goes without saying that your text should also be written so well that it can be read and understood without reference to the tables.)

The end result of data processing is usually a set of numbers that expresses relationships. Too often we rush to publish the numbers, which are exciting and meaningful to us, but not necessarily to others. Taking the time to show the results graphically will almost always be a real service to your reader. The underlying numbers must be there, of course, or the maps, charts, lines, and graphs will be insufficiently explicit, but a good picture of the results can be of immense benefit.

In the old days, data processing was so costly of human effort that only the key hypotheses were tested, only the main tables created. Modern data processing, in contrast, is so easy that hundreds of tables are produced in a few minutes and the analyst is given hundreds of relationships to ponder. Since the human brain has not kept pace with computer speeds, it still takes time to understand them. A danger is that we sometimes rush into print to report relationships that have not been properly thought through. When the tables are before us, the time for thinking has just begun. We study the results, go over them carefully and repeatedly, and *think* about them. We try to express the results in words. Only when the data have really been internalized— made our own in the deepest human sense—is it time to write the final paper or report.

A related issue involves the use of complex statistics by a researcher who may not know exactly what they mean. The ancient Romans, when they wanted to read the future, used to slay a chicken or an owl and look at its liver. As a method of forecasting the future, however, livers were not terribly reliable, and the term of office, even the life, of the average liver reader was short. People who use complex statistics without understanding them are our modern-day liver readers. Those mysterious numbers, which come pouring forth from the innards of a computer these days in such abundance, can be easily misinterpreted. It is better to stick to mean differences (if you understand mean differences) than to use the discriminant function just because it is there. Brier and Robinson wisely observe that "plausible-looking but quite erroneous results may be produced by a computer program which has been used as an act of faith rather than reason." They report that one error in a canonical correlation program distributed by IBM went unnoticed for ten years. The error was based on a mistake in a statistics book.[10]

"NATURALLY OCCURRING" DATA STREAMS

The observation was made earlier that data in general are like signals in a communication system. Usually data are special kinds of symbols in the special kinds of communication systems we use to conduct research. But how about getting permission to tap into a real communication system and extract some "naturally occurring" data of interest?

Almost all American newspapers and magazines and many books are now published in computerized typesetting plants. This means that all the words and numbers in those newspapers, magazines, and books are, at one point in the system, available in digital data form. Alert communication researchers who capture relevant data streams from such systems may have a large part of their data collection done for them. They do not need to repeat a single key stroke. Instead, they can devote their time and thought to other kinds of data processing—sorting, counting, and analyzing.

Suppose you are interested in readability formulas and that you have a new formula you would like to try out on a large data base. Where can you find a large body of words already in the form of digital data? The local daily paper may be able to give you a magnetic tape of all of yesterday's news stories. Or all of last week's. Or last month's. If you are imaginative and lucky, chances are you can quickly obtain at practically no cost all the data that you need.

G. C. Wilhoit of Indiana University was interested in testing some hypotheses about which U.S. senators got their names mentioned most often in the national news. He obtained permission from the Associated Press to collect a sample of its wire news. Then he wrote a computer program to search the data for AP's abbreviations for senator or senators, "Sen." or "Sens.," which the wire service always used with the names. He also got the computer to print out the words in a "window" before and after the key abbreviations. In this way, he was able to sort through a vast amount of news, isolate the data of special interest, and make some precise observations about the factors linked with the "visibility" of the senators.

A similar technique might be used to make a study of national coverage of various candidates in a presidential election. What words would you search for? How large should the window be? Over what time period would you collect data? How would you analyze the data? At what points should the data stream be tapped? Answering these

---

[10]Alan Brier and Ian Robinson, *Computers and the Social Sciences* (New York: Columbia University Press, 1974), pp. 133–34.

questions should give you an idea of the opportunities and the problems associated with the use of naturally occurring data.

Data in real communication systems are not limited to words. Think of the numbers being transmitted across the country and the world. Stock market transactions. Commodity and livestock markets. Money markets. These and other number flows provide a daily picture of the economic and social life of the nation. And they are all out there waiting to be used. It may even be possible in the years ahead to capture naturally occurring digital data streams containing photographs. (Even now, of course, the data from the weather satellites are available in digital form.) The Associated Press is presently sending its pictures from abroad via digitized images. Sometime in the next decade, the domestic picture service may switch to digital format as well, abandoning the analog format used for many years. Think of the millions of pixels (picture elements) passing by and the many ways in which you could analyze them.

Some of the small samples we see in published research could have been vastly enlarged if the researchers had thought to tap into naturally occurring data streams. In planning your future research, you might do well to ask, will the data I am after, *at any time,* be available naturally in digital form? If the answer is yes, ask yourself how you might gain legitimate access to them.

A word of caution. Words and numbers stored or transmitted as data are protected in the usual ways just as much as words or numbers printed on paper. Do not try to steal them. Ask first. You probably will find that the publisher, wire service, network, or other "owner" of the data will be happy to take part in your research project. And you won't be sued.

ETHICAL ISSUES

Cooking the Data

Almost any complex data-processing procedure has lots of moving parts. It is not difficult to fudge the data in the direction of your hypothesis. A few extra cards dropped in the deck here and there, a few ambiguous and embarrassing "outlyers" removed from a scattergram, and presto—instant results, just like a cake mix. Don't do it. If your deception is discovered, your career in research will be severely damaged at best and probably will be summarily terminated. If you succeed, you will have damaged something even more important than your own reputation; you will have damaged the honest search for truth that lies at the heart of all scholarship.

Honoring Pledges of Confidentiality

Much of the data we gather and process is obtained from people who cooperate with us under a pledge that personal information will not be given to others. Breaking the pledge of confidentiality through sloppy procedures is a serious breach of your responsibility. The future of social research in this country is tied up with data processing— the way we gather it, store it, and especially the way we share it with others. A pledge of confidentiality is a pledge, and it should be honored even though years may have elapsed since the data were collected. Greenberg discusses these matters in fuller detail in Chapter 14.

DATA PROCESSING CAREERS

For most of us, data processing is a means to an end—finding the answer to research questions in an efficient and accurate manner. To some, however, it is more than that, it is the doorway to a career. If you get a thrill when you look at a table of random numbers, if you automatically add any column of figures you see, if you look forward to balancing your check book at the end of the month, if you love number puzzles, then perhaps you may find a vocation in data processing. The world is filling up with data that need to be organized, synthesized, and reported on in an intelligent way for the rest of us. The jobs that are available pay well, as a rule. Those in them also tend to learn first what others learn later, and that can be satisfying. So if you think about data the way poets think about the moon, your future may lie in data processing.

7

Content Analysis

Guido H. Stempel III

Content analysis is a formal system for doing something that we all do informally rather frequently, drawing conclusions from observations of content. We express opinions about the adequacy of various kinds of coverage by newspapers, magazines, radio stations, and television stations. Those opinions are based on what we observe as readers or listeners.

Such opinions make interesting conversation, but we have seen in recent years that casual observations have been the basis for serious suggestions for major changes in the mass media. It has been, for example, the feeling by various observers that there is too much violence on television. It is such casual observation, rather than careful documentation of the amount of violence, that has sustained the attack on the television industry by public interest groups and politicians. There are by now some carefully documented statistics on television violence, but they are referred to much less frequently in the media and in Congress than the impressions of advocates. Likewise, discussions of network news and the effect of concentration of ownership have been dominated by casual observations about content.

The controversy over television violence may be interesting, but such controversies are seldom resolved. The impressions of those on both sides are colored by their perspectives. The critic watches a television program and sees nothing but violence. The television producer watches the same program and sees violence that is only incidental to the plot.

Such situations make the need for formal content analysis rather evident. Issues like television violence are too important to be resolved on the basis of people's impressions. Yet content cannot be ignored in that situation or in many others in mass communication. This suggests that we need a better way than merely recording the impressions of all those who have impressions about a given kind of content.

The place of content analysis in communication research is indicated by the following paradigm for communication research:

WHO says WHAT to WHOM with WHAT EFFECT

It is evident that communication research has not dealt equally with all four parts of this paradigm, but we did not introduce it here to make that point. Rather, we bring it up to suggest that communication research can realize its full potential only if it can relate content to communicator, audience, and effects.

DEFINITION OF CONTENT ANALYSIS

Berelson provided a classic definition of content analysis twenty-five years ago:

> Content analysis is a research technique for the objective, systematic, and quantitative description of the manifest content of communication.[1]

The key to understanding content analysis and performing it competently lies in understanding the meaning of *objective, systematic, quantitative,* and *manifest content.*

Objective to begin with means the opposite of subjective or impressionistic. Objectivity is achieved by having the categories of analysis defined so precisely that different persons can apply them to the same content and get the same results. If content analysis were subjective instead of objective, each person would have his own content analysis. That it is objective means that the results depend upon the procedure and not the analyst.

Systematic means, first, that a set procedure is applied in the same way to all the content being analyzed. Second, it means that categories are set up so that all relevant content is analyzed. Finally, it means that the analyses are designed to secure data relevant to a research question or hypothesis.

Quantitative means simply the recording of numerical values or the frequencies with which the various defined types of content occur.

---

[1]Bernard Berelson, *Content Analysis in Communication Research* (New York: The Free Press, 1952), p. 18.

Manifest content means the apparent content, which means that content must be coded as it appears rather than as the content analyst feels it is intended.

There has been little quarrel with the first two points in Berelson's definition. Certainly, some content analyses have not been objective and systematic, but no one has advocated that they should not be. With regard to content analysis being quantitative and dealing with manifest content, however, the story has been somewhat different.

There has been the recurring suggestion that content analysis should be qualitative rather than quantitative. This suggestion has incorrectly assumed that these were mutually exclusive. Those who have advocated qualitative content analysis have criticized published content studies for shallowness and lack of meaning. Such criticism, however, may well be an indictment of a study for failure to be systematic in the full sense of the word, as just defined.

Those who advocate qualitative rather than quantitative content analysis also seem to overlook what would be lost in meaning if a study were not quantitative. It is not, for example, particularly meaningful to say that *Newsweek* had references to both Jimmy Carter and Gerald Ford during the 1976 presidential campaign. The relative frequency of those references is a rather significant fact. It would also, of course, be useful to know such things as whether the references were favorable or unfavorable, attributed or unattributed, and issue-related or not. These points are matters of the system that is used, though, not of whether or not the analysis is quantitative.

The concept of *manifest content* has been criticized by those who balk at dealing with the apparent content when they are certain that the intent of the communicator is otherwise and are equally certain that they know what it is. This viewpoint has a certain appeal, but the question is whether objectivity can be maintained if manifest content is abandoned. The content analyst after all is at this point injecting a subjective interpretation. While he or she may feel that it is an obviously correct interpretation, whether or not others will see the situation in the same terms is another matter. If other coders do not agree, then obviously the criterion of two persons getting the same results when applying the categories to the same content will not be met.

Some researchers have expressed concern that taking content at its face value may distort reality. The concern, however, probably can be dealt with more effectively by interpreting the results accordingly than by giving up on manifest content. If two political candidates, for example, talk equally often about balancing the budget, it does not mean that their economic views are the same. It also does not mean, as has been amply demonstrated at all levels of government, that either of them really would balance the budget. What it does mean is that each candidate recognizes that speaking in favor of a balanced budget is what is expected, and that is how a sensible content analyst would interpret it.

CONTENT ANALYSIS PROCEDURE

The person who undertakes a content analysis study must deal with four methodological problems: selection of the unit of analysis, category construction, sampling of content, and reliability of coding.

Selection of the Unit of Analysis

What we are asking here is simply whether we are going to consider words, statements, sentences, paragraphs, or entire articles. The answer must be related to the purpose of the study. If our objective is to find out how much coverage newspapers give to South America, it would be silly to use the word as the unit of analysis and count each mention of South America or a South American country. We would learn as much by counting articles as by counting words, and it obviously would take considerably less work. Conversely, if our concern is with whether Jimmy Carter or Gerald Ford received more favorable coverage by network television news programs, we probably would want to use words or symbols. Most stories about either candidate would contain both favorable and unfavorable references, and while we probably could make an overall judgment, we would lose a great deal of information in doing that. Thus the decision about the unit of analysis depends primarily on what information is required for the purposes of the study.

Category Construction

Category systems already developed by other researchers may prove to be appropriate for your study. If you want to deal with television coverage of a presidential campaign, the symbol-coding system developed by Lasswell may be your answer.[2] That would involve simply identifying the pertinent symbols, which would be the names of the candidates and the parties, plus a set of directional categories such as favorable, unfavorable, and neutral. If you want to deal with the subject matter covered about South America in American newspapers, Deutschmann's categories would be appropriate.[3] His eleven categories that cover the full range of content in media are war and defense, popular amusements, general human interest, economic activity, education and classic arts, politics and government, crime, accident and disaster, public health and welfare, science and invention, and public moral problems. In other cases, you may be able to find a category system that has been used for a study similar to the one you have in mind. This is true even for some fairly narrow topics.

There are real advantages to using a category system that has been

[2]Harold Lasswell, Nathan Leites, and associates, *The Language of Politics* (Cambridge, Mass.: M.I.T. Press, 1965).
[3]Paul J. Deutschmann, *News-page Content of Twelve Metropolitan Dailies* (Cincinnati: Scripps-Howard Research, 1959), pp. 92–95.

used in other studies. First, you will know that it is a workable system. By looking at the results of other studies that have used the system, you will get some notion of the kinds of results that are likely. Validity and reliability will be lesser concerns. Yet, granting all this, you still may find that you need to create your own set of categories. The decision to create your own categories instead of using an existing set should be based primarily on the conclusion that no existing system will enable you to meet the objectives of your study.

As you set out to create a set of categories, you should keep three things in mind:

1. Categories must be pertinent to the objectives of your study.
2. Categories should be functional.
3. The system of categories must be manageable.

These three concepts are interrelated, and when a set of categories falls short on one of these, it is likely to fall short on all of them.

The simple test of whether or not categories are pertinent is whether or not the information they yield will answer the research questions of the study or permit the testing of the hypotheses of the study. For example, if your objective was to determine the adequacy of coverage of South America by American newspapers, you might want to consider where the stories are in the paper. It might be useful to have as categories "Page 1" and "other pages," because the distinction has some significance in assessing coverage. On the other hand, while you could create as categories "odd-numbered pages" and "even-numbered pages," such categories would not seem pertinent. Knowing the proportion of stories on odd-numbered pages would not really tell you anything meaningful about coverage. In many cases, whether or not a particular category is pertinent or not can be determined only by careful consideration of the hypotheses of the study. For example, to consider the subject matter of the stories about South American countries may or may not make sense. If the hypothesis is simply that the American public gets less information about South America than it does about Europe, then it does not seem important to note whether stories are about politics, economics, or accidents and disasters. If, on the other hand, the hypothesis is that coverage of South America, because of the way in which reporters are assigned, emphasizes disasters over political news, the distinction is vital.

In suggesting that categories are functional, we are assuming that a content study intends to say something about a media process and the decision making within that process. Our interest in how network television newscasts cover a presidential campaign assumes that through our content analysis we can gain insight into decisions that were made by reporters, cameramen, editors, or anchorpersons. If our categories include material over which these people have no control, we may not be able to achieve the objectives of our study. If, for example, we consider the coverage of crowd reaction to the candidate, we probably are dealing with something that is more related to the campaign itself than to what media personnel do in covering the campaign. If the newscast shows the crowd booing the candidate's statement on defense spending, that probably does not tell us anything about the cameraman.

Another problem in this area is the assigning of arbitrary numerical values to certain content characteristics. We might decide to assign a 4 to every story that has videotape or film, a 2 to every story that has still pictures, and a 1 to stories with no visuals. We presumably would do this on the grounds that the use of visuals increases impact. We might all agree with the underlying assumption in the numbers or weights assigned. However, it would be impossible to find substantiation for our assumptions of the relative impact. We would, in fact, be distorting reality, and we would have moved a substantial distance from the real choices available to newspersons. If the presence or absence of visuals is a real problem, it would seem that a set of direct descriptive categories would be more appropriate. It might be important to know that 75 percent of the videotape or film shown by a particular network is about the Republican candidate. And that statistic might be more informative than to say that the average visual value was 2.56 for the Republican candidate and 1.53 for the Democratic candidate.

Keeping the system of categories manageable is mostly a matter of limiting the number of categories. Once coders are familiar with the set of categories, they should be able to operate without frequent reference back to the list and the definitions. With a handful of categories, there should be no problem in achieving this. However, somewhere between ten and twenty categories you exceed the capacity of the coder. And if you go to 100 categories, you will find that more time is spent referring to the list of categories than in doing anything else. Keeping the system manageable depends a great deal on keeping objectives in mind. It is easy to become fascinated with all the possible categories and in the process forget about what it is that you set out to do.

Sampling of Content

In many respects, sampling in content analysis is no different from sampling in surveys. The major concern, often overlooked, is to make sure that the sample represents the population that it is intended to represent. The prime consideration is that each unit in the population must have the same chance of being represented in the sample. Unfortunately, in content analysis there has been a tendency to accept a less rigorous criterion—this unit is pretty much like any other unit in the population. It is on this basis that we accept the collection of daily newspapers at a university library as a representative sample. Even casual second thought should convince you, however, that the library's goal in selecting papers for its collection is not to create a representative sample and that, whatever the library's collection is, it is not a representative sample.

In sampling for content analysis, there is the additional consideration of sampling time as well as media. Thus, if you decide to study network news coverage of a presidential campaign, you must either take the total campaign or sample days from within the defined campaign period. Here, again, the guiding principle should be to give every day an equal chance of being drawn for the sample.

Beyond these fairly basic points of sampling, there are some special considerations in sampling for content analysis. These considerations tend to mean that stratified samples are necessary in some cases and that purposive sampling is useful in some cases.

The first of these considerations has to do with days of the week. Most newspapers have a fairly consistent pattern so far as number of pages is concerned. The number of pages is much larger in the middle of the week than at the beginning or end of the week. The exact details vary, depending on retail trade patterns in the newspaper's trade area, but in any case the variation in numbers of pages stems from variation in the volume of advertising. This makes it imperative to represent the days of the week equally. For example, if you decided to have twenty-four days in your sample, you should select four Mondays randomly, four Tuesdays randomly, and so on. Sundays, of course, are a whole separate problem, partly because Sunday papers are much larger and partly because many papers do not have Sunday editions. Some content analysts have dealt with this by excluding Sundays. That is not always a good idea, but if you include Sunday papers, you should be careful in making comparisons between papers with Sunday editions and papers that do not have Sunday editions.

Days of the week are a problem if you are studying radio or television, too, but for somewhat different reasons. Television maintains a constant amount of time for the news day after day. The problem variable here is the news itself, because news does not happen equally all days of the week. The worlds of commerce and government operate primarily on five-day, forty-hour weeks. All news does not come from these sources, but a substantial amount does. For broadcasters, the amount of available news between noon Friday and noon Monday is perceptibly less than it is for the rest of the week. Thus, if you are studying broadcast news, you need to have each day of the week appear equally often in your sample.

A second consideration is how news media and news gathering are organized. If, for example, you want to study coverage of South America by American newspapers, one approach is to simply take a random sample of American daily newspapers. You probably would want to take 100 of the approximately 1,760 daily papers. In doing that, however, you would be overlooking two things. First, the news of South America that comes to Americans comes from a very limited number of sources. There are the two major U.S. wire services, the Associated Press and the United Press International. Reuters, the British service, is also a factor. Beyond this, there are perhaps a dozen U.S. newspapers that maintain correspondents anywhere in South America. It would seem then that you might learn more by studying 15 carefully selected papers than by studying the random sample of 100. Second, papers that depend on wire service coverage have some choices that determine how much news of South America they will get. Those choices involve costs, and what a newspaper can afford is related to its revenue, which in turn is related to its circulation size. It is therefore predictable that the amount of news about South America available in newspapers with less than 50,000 circulation will be much less than the amount available in newspapers of more than 50,000 circulation. It is about at this circulation figure that newspapers find they can afford the national-international wire, rather than the condensed state compiled wire. It is also at this circulation figure that newspapers discover they can afford a second wire. Again it can be argued that a smaller sample chosen with reference to these considerations might yield more information.

A third consideration is availability. For the study of coverage of South America by newspapers, availability is not a major problem. Whatever American newspapers you want to study can be obtained through the circulation departments of those newspapers. For studies of broadcasting, however, the situation is somewhat different. Suppose that we want to know how television covered the last presidential campaign. It is a simple matter to draw a sample of television stations. Then what? How do I, living in Athens, Ohio, find out what was broadcast by WISH-TV in Indianapolis, to say nothing of KCST-TV in San Diego? The answer obviously is to obtain scripts or tapes, but that is easier said than done. We know of one national study, endorsed by the National Association of Broadcasters, that was able to obtain most of the scripts. That, however, undoubtedly was an exception, and the NAB endorsement probably was largely responsible for the high degree of cooperation.

A fourth and somewhat different concern relates to the question whether you intend to draw inferences about the behavior of news decision makers or whether you intend to draw inferences about what readers are exposed to in the media. In the first instance you are sampling newspapers, and a fair sample would represent all newspapers equally. In the second instance you would want to consider weighting newspapers by circulation size. The latter would require drawing newspapers randomly after stratification by circulation category. Otherwise, the very largest papers would be unlikely to turn up at all in a random selection of 100 newspapers among 1,600 plus. Or, conversely, a straight random sample of daily newspapers would tell us a great deal about the content of newspapers that reach few readers and very little about the content of newspapers that reach half a million readers or more a day. Once again it is a question of choosing the method that best suits the study's purposes.

How researchers generally have responded to this problem is unfortunately rather obvious. The studies we have of broadcast news content are largely of network news. It is, after all, relatively easy to monitor the three network newscasts, and it has been done by a number of re-searchers. Likewise, studies of the content of television entertainment have been of network offerings. The unfortunate result is that much of television news and entertainment has never been studied. The same can be said for radio, except that the problem is more serious there because network offerings comprise such a small portion of the total offerings.

These examples indicate that in many instances the researcher must accept less than the ideal sample because of limitations of availability.

Reliability of Coding

The fact that content analysis is defined as systematic and objective means that the researcher must be concerned with reliability. By relia-bility, we mean simply consistency of classification. If, for example, we have two coders viewing a network newscast in a study of presidential campaign coverage, we would expect them to agree on the number of times the Democratic candidate was mentioned and on whether a given mention was favorable or unfavorable. As a practical matter, we know that two coders will not agree completely, but unless we achieve some level of agreement, we obviously cannot claim that our study is system-atic or objective.

Disagreement between coders is usually the result of one of three things: (1) inadequate definition of categories, (2) failure of coders to achieve a common frame of reference, and (3) oversights. It is not un-common in the early stages of a study for there to be more disagree-ment than agreement among coders.

The researcher's primary concern needs to be with what he can do to increase reliability. The first step is to work out precise definitions of categories. The second is to go over these definitions and the coding procedure generally with the coders before they begin. Trial runs should be conducted, and the responses of coders should be compared item by item. This will contribute a great deal to the development of a common frame of reference among coders. As much practice coding as resources and the situation will permit should be done. It probably takes a group of coders a full week to reach a really common frame of reference.

Once coding has begun, spot checks should be made to make sure that the reliability level is not deteriorating. Briefings should be con-ducted to deal with problems that have come up that coders feel the definitions and instructions do not cover completely.

If you are doing all the coding for the study yourself, the reliability problem remains every bit as real, although perhaps not so complex. If possible, you should have a second person work with you initially and also have that person do some spot checking with you. By working with another person, you will have to clarify some definitions and proce-dures, and you will have to develop an objective approach.

For any content study, a reliability estimate ought to be calculated and reported. A minimum standard would be the selection of three passages to be coded by all coders. The person doing a content study by himself should, near the end of the work, recode some of the earlier material and compare. Also, if you have a second person working with you in the fashion suggested previously, you could use that person in making your reliability check. After the coding is completed, you should compare item by item. We believe that the appropriate thing to report here is simply the percentage of agreement between coders.

However, some content analysts argue that the complexity of the category system and the level of agreement that would be obtained by chance alone should be taken into account.[4] Still others use correlation approaches.[5] These more complex approaches have their merits. In most measurement situations, reliabilities are given in terms of correlation, and correlating coding distributions permits us to report values that are comparable to other measures. This also allows us to compute variance accounted for. Percentage of agreement has the further disadvantage of being arbitrary. What percent is acceptable is entirely a matter of judgment. Nevertheless, percentage of agreement is an accepted way of reporting reliability.

Training Coders

For studies using several coders, some things should be said about the selection and training of coders. The first suggestion is to try to find experienced coders, but while that may be obvious, it is not practical. The people you recruit to code will, in all probability, never have done any coding before. It probably is desirable to have people with somewhat similar academic backgrounds. We have found that a person's academic training does provide a perspective that is very evident in the early stages of coding. We once used as coders a group of college teachers in three fields, journalism, political science, and sociology. These are similar fields, and one might even suggest that college professors tend to be similar, but it was some time before we could get a unified approach. In the early work, the journalists performed pretty much alike, but distinctly differently from the political scientists, who in turn performed differently from the sociologists.

The major challenge in training coders is to develop the common frame of reference that is vital to the success of your study. It does not come quickly. No matter how carefully you define categories and instruct coders, there will be situations that coders do not perceive as being covered. Some of them will be fairly common. These situations need to be identified, discussed, and agreed upon. Bear in mind that the coder does not need to accept the rationale for handling a situation; he or she merely needs to know what the rule is. It is possible that

---

[4]W. A. Scott, "Reliability of Content Analysis: The Case of Nominal Scale Coding," *Public Opinion Quarterly*, 19:321–25 (1955).
[5]Lasswell, *Language of Politics*, Chapter 5.

you will have a coder who simply cannot develop the same frame of reference as the rest of the group. When that happens, of course, the coder should be dropped from the coding group. This happens usually because of major differences in background between one coder and the rest of the group. It is not a reflection on that person, but merely an indication of a different perspective.

Training will continue throughout a study. The work of coders needs to be checked as the study progresses. Opportunities should be provided for coders to discuss problems. A major value of such discussions is simply to promote the common frame of reference.

COMPUTERIZED CONTENT ANALYSIS

Computerized procedures for content analysis have been developed and used in some studies. Under optimal conditions, such procedures can save time and provide highly reliable coding. At the same time, you should recognize that there are many situations in which the computerized procedures will not be helpful. Our main purpose in discussing computerized content analysis is to help the reader recognize the potential of computerized procedures.

The strength of the computer is its ability to do fairly simple tasks extremely fast. Practically, what this means to the content analyst is that the computer is valuable for a study that involves recognition of words or even syllables. A good example of efficient use of the computer for content analysis is the study by Wilhoit and Sherrill[6] on visibility of U.S. senators in wire service copy mentioned by Danielson in Chapter 6. The computer's task in this study was basically to recognize 100 words (the names of the senators). Another good example is Anderson's use of key words as a way of identifying what news stories were about.[7] His assumption was that a properly constructed set of key words based on current news would enable him to make accurate comparisons of news coverage by different stations.

Still another example is Holsti's system for computerizing Osgood's evaluative assertion analysis.[8] What is necessary in such a study is to catalog certain evaluative adjectives. Holsti not only enumerated them, but assigned a numerical value to each evaluative adjective, as is required in evaluative assertion analysis. The procedure normally calls for a separate judgment on each assertion, but Holsti's procedure provided a standardized judgment for any one adjective.

[6]G. Cleveland Wilhoit and Kenneth S. Sherrill, "Wire Service Visibility of U.S. Senators," *Journalism Quarterly,* 45:42–48 (1968).

[7]James A. Anderson, *Broadcast Stations and Newspapers: The Problem of Information Control: A Content Analysis of Local News Presentation* (Washington, D.C.: National Association of Broadcasters, 1971).

[8]Ole R. Holsti, *Content Analysis for the Social Sciences and Humanities* (Reading, Mass.: Addison-Wesley Publishing Co., 1969), pp. 167–94; Charles E. Osgood, "The Representational Model and Relevant Research Methods," in Ithiel de Sola Pool, ed., *Trends in Content Analysis* (Urbana: University of Illinois Press, 1959), pp. 33–88.

What is not easy to do with the computer is to deal with context or with groups of words. It would, for example, be fairly simple to develop the set of words or symbols for a study of a presidential campaign. However, if we wanted a directional judgment based on the context, that would be extremely complicated. We could provide certain words or sets of words, but it would be difficult to build a complete list that would cover all the contexts that would occur on campaign coverage. We might, of course, simply have the computer print out all the statements and make the judgments ourselves, but that probably would not turn out to be a very efficient use of the computer.

If we wanted to tackle the problem of news coverage of South America, we could come up with a list of datelines and country names. Assuming that we had an easy way of getting content into the computer using the means suggested by Danielson in Chapter 6, this might be a highly efficient way to identify what would be a relatively small proportion of the total content.

This brings us to a major consideration in computerized content analysis: how we enter the computer. One way, of course, would be to key punch all the content that is to be analyzed, but that probably would take more time than simply hand coding. There might, however, be situations in which a number of people could be keypunching at the same time with some savings of time. Savings in compiling and computation time might actually make it possible for the group to finish the task more rapidly than if they all coded by hand. Still, this is almost a brute force kind of approach. Two easier ones exist.

First, as Danielson pointed out, the printing processes of many publications call for the punching of tape from which type is set. Once the type is set, that tape is no longer needed. Adapters are available that make it possible to read these tapes directly into the storage of a computer. That is a much faster and more efficient way for the content analyst to enter content. Of course, getting the tapes could be a problem. Cooperation from the media or wire services being studied would be required, and such cooperation is likely to be uneven.

Second, wire services are now transmitting directly into the storage of computers of member newspapers. If you have a way to tap into a wire, you could put the wire in your own storage. Or you could possibly get what you need on tape that could then be transferred into your storage. Combinations of any or all of these approaches may be practical in a given situation, depending on the available computer hardware. Interfacing (going from one system to another) is frequently a serious problem for the content analyst who wants to use a computer.

Optical scanning devices could be the long-range solution to the problem of entry into the computer. Present optical scanning devices are accurate only under specified conditions, notably only when certain typefaces are used. It is not, however, totally unrealistic to speculate about the possibility that an optical scanning device might be able to read a whole page of a newspaper or a book or a magazine into a computer's storage. We are not yet at that stage, however.

What we are suggesting here is that if you have a content analysis problem that can be answered by coding of words or symbols, and if you have a simple means of entry into a computer, then computerized content analysis makes a great deal of sense. For many content studies, however, computerized approaches really have little to offer. While computer content analysis certainly will become more common, it still will be used in a minority of studies for the foreseeable future.

A successful content analysis study is the result of a series of good decisions. The process must start with a clear statement of objectives and hypotheses. The necessary decisions cannot be made intelligently unless you know what it is you are trying to find out. Once you have determined that, you are ready then to move to the basic decisions about the unit of analysis, category construction, and sampling. Next comes the selection and training of coders. While all these matters can be and should be decided with careful deliberation well in advance of the start of the study, the need for little decisions will arise continuously throughout a study. These must be dealt with in a way consistent with the basic decisions, but not with total rigidity. Adjustments usually are needed simply because not every problem can be anticipated.

We have tried to indicate in this chapter some of the considerations that enter into these various decisions. It is important for you to remember that there will be more than one good choice in some instances. Researchers may differ as to which of several good choices is clearly the best. Your goal ought to be to make those decisions to the best of your ability, keeping the objectives of the study clearly in mind at all times. If you can achieve that, you undoubtedly will produce a good study.

8

Statistical Designs for Content Analysis

Guido H. Stempel III

The same statistical principles that apply to other areas of mass communication research apply to content analysis. Much of what you will read in Chapter 10 on statistical analysis of survey data and in Chapter 12 on statistical analysis of experiments applies equally to content studies. Yet it takes only a cursory look at the published research to discover that the statistical approaches used in content analysis studies are different. There are at least three apparent differences between how content data and how survey and experimental data are handled:

1. Statistical tests are used much less often in content analysis.
2. Nonparametric statistics are used a greater proportion of the time in content studies.
3. Multivariate analyses are used far less often in content studies.

In this chapter, we want to look at the reasons for these trends and to talk about appropriate ways to handle some common types of content data. We will suggest that the handling of content data should become more similar to the handling of survey and experimental study data. However, we also will point out some differences about content data that mean that they cannot be handled across the board in identical fashion with survey and experimental study data.

STATISTICAL TESTS

There are two reasons that statistical tests are used less often in content studies than in survey or experimental studies. One is legitimate, the other perhaps not.

The legitimate reason for not using significance tests in a content study is that in many instances a sample is not being used. For example, the author made a study of presidential campaign coverage by what were considered the fifteen best newspapers in the country, the prestige press of America.[1] This was not a sample of newspapers in the usual statistical sense of the word sample. The other 1,745 U.S. daily newspapers were not like these newspapers. These fifteen were the elite papers. What they did in covering the campaign was almost certainly not like what the rest of the press did. We did make the argument that what these papers did was in and of itself important. We could not and did not, however, extrapolate from our sample to the rest of the U.S. press by using statistical tests.

Likewise, in that study we analyzed all the issues published by each paper during the traditional campaign period of Labor Day to Election Eve. We did not sample time. The campaign coverage was not what we reported it to be for those papers plus or minus a sampling error. For the stated time period, it was exactly what we said it was. Any differences between papers were real.

In a later study, we did sample days out of this Labor Day to Election Eve time period, and we did use significance tests.[2] We did so because in that situation there were some differences that were the result of sampling error, not real differences between media. At the same time, in doing that, we made it clear that we were still dealing with the stated period of time from which we sampled.

Another kind of problem is raised by the study that covers only a block of time out of the total campaign period. A number of studies have covered the last four or five weeks of the campaign. The tendency then has been to infer that this represented the total campaign period. Significance tests have been used to support such inferences. Yet the appropriateness of significance tests for this purpose is doubtful. First, significance tests require that sampling be on a purely probability basis. Second, the assumption in using a significance test in this situation has to be that the coverage of the last four weeks can be expected to be like that of the entire campaign. There is ample evidence from studies that have reported figures for various time periods within

---

[1]Guido H. Stempel III, "The Prestige Press Meets the Third-Party Challenge," *Journalism Quarterly*, 46: 699–706 (Winter 1969).

[2]Dru Evarts and Guido H. Stempel III, "Coverage of the 1972 Campaign by TV, News Magazines and Major Newspapers," *Journalism Quarterly*, 51: 645–48 (Winter 1974).

a campaign that this is not the case.[3] The known characteristics of most campaigns would suggest this anyhow.

For example, in the 1976 presidential campaign, Gerald Ford made limited appearances in September because of the time he spent carrying out the duties of the office of the president. As the campaign wore on, he increased his political activity, partly by linking political and presidential activities. Jimmy Carter, on the other hand, maintained a high level of campaign activity throughout the campaign. If coverage did not reflect this difference in activity levels of the two candidates, it would be surprising.

Similar examples can be cited from other political campaigns. What we can expect is a systematic variation between time periods. Statistical tests cannot enable the researcher to deal meaningfully with such systematic variation, because they are not designed for that. The researcher must instead deal with the question by comparing the known characteristics of the campaign during the time covered by the data and the time for which there are no data. The test must be one of logic, not of statistics. On the basis of logic, the researcher must conclude either that there were substantial differences between time periods or that the two time periods were similar. The case must stand or fall on the merit of the evidence provided, not on statistical tests.

We also find in content analysis research a number of case studies. If one studies the reporting of crime in Houston, the conclusions that can be drawn are necessarily limited. Performing statistical tests will not change that fact. The content analysis case study can be valuable, and important insights may be drawn from such studies. However, those insights must be supported with logic.

We thus see that in content analysis we frequently are not dealing with samples and therefore have no need or justification for the usual statistical tests. This brings us to the other reason that some researchers do not report statistical tests. It is simply that they *assumed* they were not necessary. They do not see a content sample as in any way similar to a survey sample. They have seen many content studies reported without statistical tests and have not stopped to analyze, in the way we have done here, why tests were not used. They are likely to be surprised if anyone suggests that significance tests should be used. In fairness, one must recognize that there are borderline situations in which it may not be clear that standard sampling statistics are called for.

However, researchers who are doing content studies need to recognize that this is a matter that requires careful consideration. The research in print cannot be depended upon as a guide for appropriate practice. Researchers should think through the situation carefully to determine whether or not statistical tests are needed.

[3]Stempel, "Prestige Press"; Robert G. Meadow, "Cross-Media Comparison of Coverage of the 1972 Presidential Campaign," *Journalism Quarterly,* 50: 482–88 (Autumn 1973); John W. Windhauser, "Reporting of Ohio Municipal Elections by the Ohio Metropolitan Daily Press," *Journalism Quarterly,* 54: 552–65 (Autumn 1977).

PARAMETRIC VERSUS NONPARAMETRIC STATISTICS

The second difference we mentioned between statistical analysis of content data compared to survey or experimental data is the more frequent use of nonparametric statistics. If we look at a couple of fairly typical situations, we can see why.

Suppose that we are analyzing the coverage of the mayor by the *Daily Planet* for the month just completed. We have a constructed week of six days, and each day we found one story. We have classified the statements in those stories as follows:

	Favorable	Unfavorable
Monday	14	10
Tuesday	7	4
Wednesday	15	11
Thursday	11	5
Friday	9	6
Saturday	16	12

We thus find that 60 percent of the statements about the mayor were favorable and 40 percent were unfavorable. The question we must answer by use of an appropriate statistical test is whether the coverage really was more favorable than unfavorable or whether our result is possibly due to sampling error. Did we observe a real difference or a chance difference? One approach would be the *t*-test, which is a test of the significance of a difference between two means. The formula for this test is

$$t = \frac{\bar{X}_1 - \bar{X}_2}{s_p \ \sqrt{1/n_1 + 1/n_2}}$$

where

$$s^2_p = \frac{\Sigma X_1^2 - \frac{(\Sigma x_1)^2}{n_1} + \Sigma X_2^2 - \frac{(\Sigma X_2)^2}{n_2}}{n_1 + n_2 - 2}$$

The computation then becomes

$$s^2_p = (14)^2 + (7)^2 + (15)^2 + (11)^2 + (9)^2 + (16)^2 - \frac{(72)^2}{6} + (10)^2$$

$$+ (4)^2 + (11)^2 + (5)^2 + (6)^2 + (12)^2 - \frac{(48)^2}{6} \bigg/ 6 + 6 - 2$$

$$= \frac{928 - 864 + 442 - 384}{10}$$

135

$$= \frac{122}{10} = 12.2$$

$$s_p = 3.49$$

The computation of t then is

$$t = \frac{12 - 8}{3.49 \quad \sqrt{1/6 + 1/6}} = \frac{4}{2.01}$$

$$= 1.99$$

The value of t (1.99) needs to be compared with the value in a table of t. The table is entered for 10 degrees of freedom because that is the value in the numerator of the formula for s_p. We should use a two-tailed test because we have not predicted whether coverage would be favorable or unfavorable. (The two "tails" refer to the farthest right and left areas of the normal curve. When the hypothesis predicts the *direction* of a difference, *i.e.*, $\overline{X}_1$ is greater than $\overline{X}_2$, only one tail of the distribution is involved in accepting or rejecting the null hypothesis. When direction is not specified, *i.e.*, $\overline{X}_1$ is not equal to $\overline{X}_2$, both tails are involved.) The table value is 2.23. Since our t value is less than that, the interpretation is that the difference we have found is a chance difference. We cannot say that coverage of the mayor is more favorable than unfavorable.

With a difference this large (20 percentage points), this is a rather frustrating conclusion. Our chance of getting a significant t value here is limited by the rather small N of 6. That, of course, is due to the fact that we have six days and six stories. The t formula does not take into account the frequency of statements, which is really the root of our data. It matters not whether we have the 120 statements that we do have, or only 12 or 1,200. The N remains 6.

With chi square, however, the number of statements does enter in and does affect the computation. Chi square is a test of distribution of frequencies. The formula for chi square is

$$X^2 = \frac{(\text{observed frequency} - \text{expected frequency})^2}{\text{expected frequency}}$$

The observed frequencies are 72 favorable and 48 unfavorable, the number of statements. To test whether that difference could have been a result of chance, we calculate an expected frequency based on what chance would predict: that the statements are evenly divided. With 120 statements (72 + 48), an even split would be 60 and 60. Putting those values in the chi square formula, we have

$$\text{Chi square}_1 = \frac{(72 - 60)^2}{60} = 2.40$$

$$\text{Chi square}_2 = \frac{(48 - 60)^2}{60} = 2.40$$

Chi square total $= 4.80$

This value of chi square needs to be compared with the appropriate value from a chi square table. We have 1 degree of freedom because with a single classification the degrees of freedom is $N - 1$.[4] The chi square value at the 0.05 level for 1 degree of freedom is 3.84. Our value of 4.80 is larger than that, so our conclusion is that the difference in the number of favorable and unfavorable statements is a real difference, not a chance difference.

We thus have the anomaly of one statistical test telling us that we have a chance difference and the other telling us that we have a real difference. We should recognize that we were not testing the same thing with both tests, so in one sense the results are not in conflict. We found that the difference in the average number of favorable and unfavorable statements per story or per day was a chance difference, but that the difference between the total number of favorable and unfavorable statements was not a chance difference. The latter clearly comes closer to answering the question asked than the former.

But more than this is involved in the difference between the results of the t test and the chi square test. In a mechanical sense, the reason for the different findings is the different N. With the chi square computation, we were dealing with an N ten times as large as the one we had in the t test. One perhaps can argue that the N we are forced to use with the t test is unrealistically small, but that argument is tangential to the point that the researcher should observe: in any content study in which symbols or statements or themes are the coding unit, chi square is more likely to yield a finding of a significant difference. And in most cases the logic does not particularly favor one test over the other. In this case the logic favors the chi square test because it more clearly speaks to the question tested.

One other nonparametric test should be mentioned here because it can be applied so readily to this type of data. This is the sign test. The sign test simply deals with the distribution of direction. To use it with the data we have here, you would assign a plus sign for each story that has more favorable than unfavorable references and a minus sign for each story that has more unfavorable than favorable references. Since all six stories in our example had more favorable than unfavorable statements, we would have six plus signs and no minus signs. You then go to a sign test table and seek the entry for $N = 6$.[5] You would find that the chance of having all six stories in the same direction is less than 0.05. This then would indicate that the coverage really is more favorable than unfavorable and is thus consistent with the chi square result. This also, of course, is by far the quickest of the three tests we have discussed.

[4]The general rule for degrees of freedom of a χ^2 table is number of rows minus one times the number of columns minus one.

[5]See Sidney Siegel, *Nonparametric Statistics for the Behavioral Sciences* (New York: McGraw-Hill Book Co., 1956), p. 250.

In the situation we have been discussing, it is possible to use any of the three tests mentioned, but there are fairly common situations in content analysis in which chi square is a good deal more appropriate because it can be applied to more complicated sets of figures. For example, suppose that in addition to the data we already have presented about the *Daily Planet,* we have a similar set of data for the competing newspaper, the *Intelligencer.* Here are the figures:

	Favorable	*Unfavorable*
Monday	13	17
Tuesday	11	12
Wednesday	14	19
Thursday	8	16
Friday	7	8
Saturday	5	10
Total	58	82
Average	9.67	13.33

A *t* computation from these data would of course be the same mechanically as the earlier one, but there is a new complication. If we take the two *Daily Planet* figures and the two *Intelligencer* figures, there are in fact six possible *t* tests, since each *t* test involves only two means. If we are interested in comparing the coverage of those two papers, four of the six have some meaning.

1. *Daily Planet* favorable versus *Daily Planet* unfavorable.
2. *Daily Planet* favorable versus *Intelligencer* favorable.
3. *Daily Planet* unfavorable versus *Intelligencer* unfavorable.
4. *Intelligencer* favorable versus *Intelligencer* unfavorable.

There are 108 possible combinations of outcomes of these four *t* tests, only a few of which could be interpreted in any definitive fashion. You most likely would be left with a on-the-one-hand, on-the-other-hand kind of interpretation.

By contrast, chi square fits this situation very nicely. You simply construct a 2 by 2 table as follows:

	Favorable	*Unfavorable*
Daily Planet	72	48
Intelligencer	58	82

You then construct a table of expected frequencies, as indicated in Chapter 4.

	Favorable	*Unfavorable*
Daily Planet	60	60
Intelligencer	70	70

The chi square computation then would be

$$\text{Cell 1:} \quad \frac{(72 - 60)^2}{60} = 2.40$$

$$\text{Cell 2:} \quad \frac{(48 - 60)^2}{60} = 2.40$$

$$\text{Cell 3:} \quad \frac{(58 - 70)^2}{70} = 2.06$$

$$\text{Cell 4:} \quad \frac{(82 - 70)^2}{70} = 2.06$$

$$\text{Total chi square} = 8.92$$

Again we enter a chi square table at 1 degree of freedom and get the value of 3.84. Our value is larger than that, and so we conclude that there is a real difference in coverage between the two papers, not merely a chance difference. Chi square has enabled us to draw a simple, clear-cut conclusion.

An additional advantage with chi square is that you can apply it to a table of any size. Thus, if you wanted to compare four papers instead of two, you could use chi square as your significance test. Assuming that we were still dealing with coverage of the mayor, we then would have a 2 by 4 table instead of a 2 by 2, but the procedure would remain essentially the same. One caution, however: chi square requires that you have an expected frequency of at least 5 in each cell. This is a frequent problem with larger chi square tables. It is possible to use a correction for a single low frequency cell, however.

MULTIVARIATE ANALYSES

The main reason that multivariate analyses occur infrequently in reported content analysis studies is the nature of the measurement. The content study usually has a single measure and a single measured variable. There is, however, one multivariate approach that has proved useful with a variety of types of content data: factor analysis, which begins with correlation. It has as its purpose grouping like responses together to provide a simpler description. Deutschmann first demonstrated this application in his study of the content of papers in New York, Cincinnati, and Cleveland.[6] Here is the process that Deutschmann used:

1. News-editorial space was measured and classified, using a system of eleven categories that covers all news-editorial content.

2. For each newspaper, the categories were ranked according to how much space was in each category. Deutschmann called these "emphasis ranks."

[6]Paul J. Deutschmann, *News-page Content of Twelve Metropolitan Dailies* (Cincinnati: Scripps-Howard Research, 1959).

For each newspaper he then had a ranking by news categories from 1 to 11.

3. Rank correlations between newspapers were computed. For example, Deutschmann analyzed the seven daily newspapers in New York as a set. He computed the rank correlation between each pair of newspapers. That gave him the following correlation matrix:[7]

	NYT	HT	WTS	NYP	JA	NYN	NYM
New York Times							
Herald-Tribune	0.96						
World-Telegram-Sun	0.65	0.71					
New York Post	0.65	0.67	0.97				
Journal American	0.50	0.59	0.89	0.84			
New York News	0.22	0.41	0.56	0.57	0.53		
New York Mirror	0.04	0.20	0.53	0.52	0.73	0.71	

It is evident from this matrix that the *New York Times* and *New York Herald-Tribune* were highly similar to each other and not to any of the other papers. It is also evident that the *World-Telegram and Sun,* the *Post,* and the *Journal American* were highly similar to each other. Finally, the *Daily News* and the *Daily Mirror* were much alike, although the *Mirror* had a slightly higher correlation with the *Journal American* than it did with the *Daily News.* Deutschmann used linkage analysis to show these similarities, but presumably any factor analysis technique would separate out these three clusters of papers.

Deutschmann then went back to the emphasis ranks to determine what differences in news emphasis in these papers accounted for the clustering. Basically, it was the greater emphasis on politics, war, defense and diplomacy, and economic news that separated the *Times* and the *Herald-Tribune* from the other five papers. The *Daily News* and *Daily Mirror* were different in their much greater emphasis on crime news and human interest. The other three papers were somewhat in between these two extremes.[8]

The basic strategy here could be applied to a wide variety of content analysis situations. Of course, the specific correlation coefficient and factor analysis technique used might vary, depending on the nature of the data. Deutschmann used rank correlations (see Chapter 4 for a discussion of various rank-order correlations) because Pearsonian *r*, the most commonly used correlation coefficient, assumes a normal distribution, a condition not met in these data. Pearsonian *r*, however, could be used with some content data. For purposes of creating a correlation matrix for factor analysis, a variety of estimates of correlations would be permissible.

[7]Ibid., p. 92.

[8]To people who knew these papers at the time, these clusterings are simply stunning. NYT and HT were the morning prestige full-sized papers. WTS, NYP, and JA were all afternoon papers. NYN and NYM were both morning tabloids. But why was NYM more like JA? Both were Hearst papers.

A couple of other studies that have used factor analysis are worth looking at at this point because they suggest the variety of possibilities. The author used factor analysis to determine elements of news empirically.[9] This involved taking a group of news stories and checking to see which of twenty newspapers used those stories. Then 2 by 2 tables were formed between each pair of news stories and a fourfold r computed. From there, a factor analysis produced a six-factor solution, indicating six news elements being employed by those newspapers in making news decisions.

Lee used semantic differential scales as content categories and then factored Pearsonian correlations on a study of political coverage.[10] This technique enabled him to separate the newspapers into clusters according to characteristics of their political coverage. The extent to which papers of similar political leaning fell into the same clusters provided an indication of the effects of political leaning on coverage.

This approach might also be used for data concerning the symbols, issues, or themes in political coverage by different media. In such cases, factor analysis would provide an easy way to determine the extent of similarity between media. The connection between similarity of content and similarity of political leaning is, of course, frequently the main point of interest of such studies. Few techniques can illustrate such similarity in more striking fashion than factor analysis.

Other multivariate techniques have not been widely used in content analysis. Most seem to have limited possibilities, given the nature of content data. An example is regression analysis, which is now being widely used in communication research, although applications to content analysis are not too obvious. Price did attempt a regression approach to deal with display of political content.[11] However, he found that an index that combined several variables produced nearly the same result as simple space measurement. Others have proposed regression approaches to the matter of display of news and have even suggested equations. These, however, have been hypothetical constructs that have not been tied to other pertinent variables such as readership, political leaning, or news selection.

We began this chapter by indicating that there are three major differences in how content analysis data are analyzed compared to how other communication research data are analyzed. We have attempted to indicate some of the reasons for the differences and some of the problems posed by the particular character of content analysis data.

This has been, therefore, a somewhat limited view of the statistical possibilities for content studies. We would suggest, however, that the

---

[9]Guido H. Stempel III, "An Empirical Exploration of the Nature of News," in Wayne A. Danielson, ed., *Paul J. Deutschmann Memorial Papers in Mass Communications Research* (Cincinnati: Scripps-Howard Research, 1963).

[10]Jae Won Lee, "Editorial Support and Campaign News: Content Analysis by Q Method," *Journalism Quarterly*, 49: 710–16 (Winter 1972).

[11]Granville C. Price, "A Method for Analyzing Newspaper Campaign Coverage," *Journalism Quarterly*, 31: 447–58 (Fall 1954).

limitation comes not from us, but from the nature of the field of content analysis. Presumably, almost anything that is in the companion chapters on statistical analysis could in theory be applied to content analysis. Such speculation, however, is not too meaningful in the absence of measurement approaches that make such techniques appropriate.

We have tried instead to emphasize what some of the possibilities are for types of content data that are being gathered commonly now. Content analysis as a field suffers considerably from the failure of researchers to recognize the data analysis possibilities. Statistical analysis is not only appropriate, but also necessary, in content analysis. At the proposal stage, the content analyst should be dealing with the matter of statistical analysis just as the experimental researcher is; and should attempt to visualize what various statistical approaches might do to enhance the meaning of findings.

In this connection, particular emphasis should be placed on the use of factor analysis and other appropriate multivariate techniques. Multivariate approaches have not been used in most areas of communication research to the extent that they might well be.[12] We have passed from the era in which the computational complexity of some of these procedures severely limited the practical capability of the researcher to use them. Today the computer brings them within reach of a high percentage of communication researchers. Yet in content analysis, as in other areas, this greater access has not led to an appreciable increase in their use. Each content analyst needs to address this issue because of its significance for the future of the field.

STATISTICAL APPROACHES TO RELIABLITY

One statistical problem applies uniquely to the content analysis study. This is the question of how to measure reliability and how to treat the reliability data. There are two basically different approaches, and for one of those approaches, two different statistical strategies.

One approach is to deal with category frequencies, with the obvious statistical technique being to correlate frequency distributions of two or more coders on the same material. This is a fairly quick way to get a reliability estimate, but there is an inherent problem. If one simply compares the frequency distributions of two coders, one is overlooking some random fluctuation. Suppose, for example, that two coders code the direction of paragraphs of a political story in this way:

Paragraph	1	2	3	4	5	6	7	8
Coder 1	D	D	D	D	R	R	R	R
Coder 2	D	R	D	R	D	R	D	R

---

[12]Malcolm S. MacLean, "Some Multivariate Designs for Communications Research," *Journalism Quarterly*, 42: 614–22 (Autumn 1966).

The frequency distributions are the same, four Democratic and four Republican for each coder. However, it is evident that the two coders disagreed on half the paragraphs. This example exaggerates the problem, but it is nonetheless very real.

The solution to this problem suggests the other approach, which is item analysis. Item analysis takes longer, but we believe that the extra precision makes it worth the time. Using the preceding example, item analysis would pick up the fact that there was agreement on only four of the eight paragraphs.

How to interpret that result is the point of difference among content analysts. One can simply indicate that the percentage of agreement is 50 percent. That does tell the reader something about the consistency of coding. Some content analysts, however, suggest that the interpretation ought to deal with whether or not the extent of agreement exceeds chance. Scott proposed the following formula for taking the chance level into account:[13]

$$\pi = \frac{P_o - P_e}{1 - P_e}$$

where P_o is the observed percentage agreement and P_e is the percentage agreement expected by chance.

The cited example illustrates well why there should be concern about whether or not the agreement is greater than would be expected by chance. In the example, one would expect 50 percent agreement by chance. Thus, no coding skill is reflected in the results. Two chimpanzees might have done as well.

On the other hand, exceeding chance is not the only issue. If, instead of two categories, we have twenty, and the agreement is 50 percent, it obviously will be well above chance. Yet one can still challenge it as not being high enough to make the results of the study meaningful. There has been little agreement among content analysts as to what the minimum acceptable level of reliability is. Everyone would like to get it above 90 percent, but many content analysts are quick to point out that such levels are not attainable on the particular study they are involved with. We offer three suggestions by way of resolving this problem for the content analyst.

1. An estimate of reliability is necessary. It should be based on several samples of content from the material in the study.
2. A study must achieve reliability that exceeds the level that can be attributed to chance alone.
3. Achieving that level is not by itself enough. Absolute levels are difficult to prescribe, but the researcher needs to be realistic about the implications for the validity of his study of significant but relatively low reliability figures.

[13]William A. Scott, "Reliability of Content Analysis: The Case of Nominal Scale Coding," *Public Opinion Quarterly*, 19: 321–75 (Fall 1955).

9

Survey Research

George Comstock and Maxwell E. McCombs

The use of sample surveys for observing the social and behavioral characteristics, attitudes, values, and beliefs of large populations has a rather lengthy history, including at least occasional use in the nineteenth century by Karl Marx and Max Weber. But the real history of survey research as a major technique of data collection covers less than the last half century. It is these recent decades that have seen development of the scientific procedures for sample selection, questionnaire design, and measurement now widely used in communication research and other social science disciplines.

The primary characteristic of survey research that has made it such a widely used methodology is its *parsimony*. There are two important aspects to this parsimony. First, the use of representative samples rather than a census considerably reduces the logistical effort needed to make sound statements about the distribution of variables within a population. Prior to the use of sound representative samples, a hallmark of modern survey research, the alternatives were either a census, which except for certain rare and small populations is not feasible for anyone other than governments, or a catch-as-catch-can group of respondents who represent no one in particular.

But there is another equally important parsimony of effort in survey research. Once an interviewer has begun a dialogue—really an interrogation—with a respondent, there is considerable latitude in the number and kinds of questions that can be asked. In other words, it requires little more effort to collect dozens of facts from a respondent than to limit the interview to ascertaining eight or ten facts. This ability to collect a broad range of data means that a large number of hypotheses can be tested from a single set of data.

The other characteristics are implicit in the foregoing discussion of survey research. In practice, it is indirect observation, and the unit of analysis typically is an individual person. In theory, once a representative sample of individuals has been selected, clandestine observers could be posted to record their behavior, but this is rarely done. Typically, the observer approaches the respondent directly and requests an interview. In this interview the respondents furnish a variety of introspective and retrospective information about their own behavior. Hence, the data analyzed are based largely on self-report, not the direct observations of the researcher.

Although the emphasis has been on facts about an individual person, survey research has on occasion been applied to other units of analysis, such as families, neighborhoods, cities, nations, or mass media institutions. In those cases the research hypotheses concern the relationships among characteristics of these groups, rather than the characteristics of people.

Finally, while survey research is parsimonious in effort relative to the scope of data collected, it also encompasses a considerable methodological and substantive range. For example, survey data can be collected to approximate the logic of experimentation. As Chapter 13 points out, the spectrum of content analysis techniques can be applied to the responses to open-end survey questions, and surveys can be used to investigate a vast array of topics as disparate as politics, child rearing, consumer behavior, and use of the mass media. All these characteristics account for the broad appeal and wide use of survey research by scholars of mass communication.

INTERVIEWING

While the term "interview" may connote Hollywood, the White House, something granted, celebrities, or Andy Warhol, it is also the term for obtaining information from the persons drawn into a survey's sample. The information collected by survey cannot be better than the means employed; data poorly obtained will be impoverished of meaning and validity. The researcher makes a series of decisions that will determine the quality of information obtained. These decisions revolve around the mode of data collection, interviewer selection and training, interview techniques, and the reduction of nonresponse cases.

Mode of Data Collection

The three principal means of data collection are mail, telephone, and face-to-face interviews. Each has advantages and disadvantages;

the proper choice depends on the circumstances. The criterion is adequate information at the lowest possible cost. The survey is a means of buying knowledge about the public; we have made a bad buy if we get poor quality or pay more than necessary.

Mail questionnaire. The mail questionnaire is the least expensive of all means of obtaining information by survey. It is so inexpensive that anyone can attempt a mail survey, and it is surprising that more individuals and organizations do not take advantage of the remarkably cheap means of communication offered by the U.S. Postal Service. A sample of 200 costs no more beyond the mimeographing of the questionnaire and the drawing of the sample and the costs of envelopes and roundtrip postage.

Nevertheless, the mail "interview" is not the standard for survey research. It has several major weaknesses. Minor weaknesses include the limited optimal length of the questionnaire, since one cannot expect people to spend much time with an unsolicited intrusion, and the restriction of the sample to persons listed by address in some directory. Of course, there is no bar to attempting a weighty questionnaire or to asking the recipient to hand the questionnaire on to someone else in the household—a wife, the youngest male over eighteen, the oldest employed female—in accord with some predetermined ordering, but in both instances the risk of encouraging nonresponse is great.

The principal weakness of the mail interview is the absence of control once the questionnaires are placed in the mail above all, lack of control over who responds and what percentage respond. The limits on length and on flexibility in sampling are reflections of this; others include the inability to probe or to seek elaboration of responses, the lack of opportunity to check on accuracy, the absence of verification that the respondent is indeed the one intended, the loss of opportunity to encourage cooperation, and the inevitable imbalance of the group responding toward those able and willing to read, write, and reply to printed queries. These factors, products of that weakness of scant control, limit the usefulness of mail interviews to situations where the budget is severely limited, the population is identifiable in advance by individuals, the respondents are literate, and there is a high degree of interest in the topic that will ensure a substantial degree of cooperation. When circumstances are compatible with the mail survey, and it is reasonable to expect a sufficiently large return, its low cost strongly recommends it. If a true sample is required, however, the 30 to 60 percent response rates typical of mail surveys simply will not do.

Telephone interview. The telephone interview is much more expensive than the mail questionnaire. It typically is very limited in the amount that can be covered. It does provide greater flexibility in sampling, because the interviewer can seek out persons in the household that fit the requirements of the sample. It provides modest certainty that the party eventually queried is the one sought, since males and females, and at least the very old and the very young, betray their demography in their voices. The sample is limited to households with telephones; however, random dialing, which professional survey organizations can now automate, makes it possible to ignore directories. The several limits placed on the quantity that can be covered is a function of treating topics of low interest and of querying the general public. People are disinclined to chat at length with unfamiliar callers about their purchases, thoughts, and lives. Conversely, the telephone long has been the confidante of the journalist's typewriter; lengthy, probing, even harsh and abrasive inquiries are common. What this obviously illustrates is that with certain populations—those with interest and involvement in a topic—lengthier and elaborate telephone interviews are possible. Issues of community conflict over desegregation, fluoridation, property versus income taxation, or an ongoing election campaign may create widespread involvement conducive to fulsome telephone interviewing. A principal asset of the telephone interview is the speed with which data can be collected. Responses can be tallied as they are obtained. A second asset, akin to that of the mail interview, is that costs are relatively modest for geographically dispersed populations.

The telephone interview permits some flexibility in sampling of individuals, within the household, for the interviewer can ask if someone is available who fits prescribed characteristics. It also permits some opportunity to encourage response by promising to take no more than a few minutes. What the telephone interview provides that mail does not is the opportunity to probe and elaborate. The caller measuring awareness of "recreation facilities" can specify that he does not mean race tracks, ballparks, or discotheques but verdant greens available to all without charge; the mail questionnaire cannot expand on the original phrasing. Similarly, the caller can easily follow a reply with a new line of questioning contingent on the response; the questionnaire can do so only at the awkwardness of involved instructions directing the respondent as if he or she were completing a puzzle. This capability to probe and elaborate is the most significant of the various ways in which the telephone interview, compared to that by mail, increases control over the collection of information. It is this control that provides some hope that the information obtained will be of adequate quality.

The telephone interview, then, is recommended by its alacrity at collating information, modest cost, flexibility for sampling of individuals, and capability to probe and otherwise fit the questioning to the responses. Its principal weakness is the constraint on length of interview, a constraint that in a few circumstances may be dissolved by the passions of the population under scrutiny.

Face-to-face interview. The standard means of data collection by survey is the face-to-face interview. It is the most expensive. It imposes the greatest administrative burdens. Unless special and expensive arrangements are made, it is considerably slower than the telephone interview in amassing data ready for analysis. What it provides to a maximum degree is control over the collection of information. This is the justification for the expense of the face-to-face interview.

This high level of control is exemplified in three principal ways: sampling, coverage, and range of querying. The interviewer can actively sample in accord with the design and can reduce to a minimum the inclusion of unintended parties. Once geographic areas are specified, the interviewer can select, in accord with specified criteria, certain dwellings and, within them, certain parties to be interviewed. Unlike the telephone interviewer, the person on the scene is not restricted to parties with telephones. The interviewer will also be better able to apply those harmless manipulations of the salesman that encourage participation. The face-to-face interview typically also permits the coverage of a far wider range of material than either the mail or telephone interview. People do not become bored or impatient as quickly with another person as they do with a questionnaire or disembodied voice. The face-to-face interview thereby takes maximum advantage of the occasion to collect information.

These two advantages of superior sampling and coverage become even greater with the additional asset of the face-to-face interview: the increased range of querying that becomes possible. The interviewer cannot only probe, but can do so with greater sensitivity to facial expression, tone of voice, and gestures of uncertainty or confusion; the interviewer can alter the course of the interview in accord with responses, and can do so with the command of such backtracking and switching as only comes with personal interchange. What the interviewer can also do that is impossible in either the mail or telephone interview is use materials that require display or handling, such as photographs, drawings, graphs, and lists. By this means, the physical presence of the interviewer paradoxically makes possible greater exclusion from the collection of information. The interviewer need not commit the gaucherie of asking the respondent for income, education, or ethnic derivation; he or she can simply ask the respondent to check it off on a card. The interviewer can accurately determine recognition of television personalities by presenting photographs, or can inquire about the interpretation of symbols, instructions, slogans, and brand names by offering their replica. These various assets of face-to-face querying make such interviewing particularly appropriate with populations low in literacy and general knowledge. The face-to-face interview is the first resort when budget is no problem and there are doubts about the efficacy of mail and telephone interviewing; it may be the sole resort with such populations. In sum, the face-to-face interview offers, at high cost, quantity and quality of information. The high cost means that it is the first choice only when the other alternatives appear inadequate.

Choosing among the three. The first step in choosing the mode of data collection is to specify the information sought. This involves both the size and nature of the required sample and the questions to be answered. The second step is to estimate costs for those methods that may be considered candidates. Cost per respondent is the conventional metric for comparing samples of like size. In the typical situation there will be a conflict between apparent quality of information and cost. The survey practitioner often will have no option but a reasoned judgment as to the benefits and risks. The many advantages of the face-to-face interview, however, have made such surveys common and regular, and the practitioner may find it possible, precisely because they permit extended questioning, to attach his battery of items to an ongoing survey. Obviously, when national samples are sought, such piggybacking becomes the only practical means of obtaining information.

It would certainly be an error to assume that a face-to-face interview is necessary. For example, we might expect severe distortions of the sample, and thereby of the information provided, by telephone interviews of urban residents. Yet, in a rare situation in which results for telephone and face-to-face interviews could be compared, there were few differences that could not be attributed to sampling error rather than mode of survey.[1] The topic was crime, and neither for Cincinnati as a whole nor for a central city district did demographics, attitudes, or reports of crime differ markedly between the telephone and face-to-face interviews. This comparison offers the lesson that we should not assume that the dictates of logic necessarily will magnify in real life into differences that are meaningful.

Selection and Training of Interviewers

The telephone and face-to-face interview impose the necessity of recruiting and training interviewers. Professional polling organizations ordinarily have regular interviewers available throughout the country. However, the survey practitioner who is initiating a survey in a particular community may have to build his own interviewing staff. Interviewing is often casual employment; it is seldom a casual task. The implied conflict is real, for the problem facing the practitioner is the overnight conversion of neophytes into professionals. This is the burden that is assigned to training. There is always room in life for spontaneity and idiosyncrasy, but the survey is an occasion for their restraint. The principal means by which the practitioner can avoid chaos is uniformity in instruction and in its application. The interviewers must all receive identical instructions. This implies some formalization of training, so that repetitions do not vary in substance; a manual for interviewer study and referral will help. Questions asked by interviewers and their resolution should be recorded; ambiguities totally unforeseen typically flit back and forth like wasps, and it is a sad person who finds today that yesterday's solution cannot be recalled.

The demonstration of the conduct of an interview is desirable. What

[1]William R. Klecka and Alfred J. Tuchfarber, "Random Digit Dialing: A Comparison to Personal Surveys," *Public Opinion Quarterly,* 42: 105–14 (Spring 1978).

is far more important is the demonstration of the handling of obstreperous respondents, unanticipated replies, and other difficulties. The more accurately these can be predicted, and the more persuasive the model for their disposition, the less likely is disruption at their hands. Interviewers should be led through the questionnaire item by item. Ways of encouraging the recalcitrant should be suggested; the various set phrases that are the conventional courtesies of modern life—the supermarket checker's cheerfulness the most commonly encountered—should be supplied. Such precautions do not imply a lack of faith in the individual imagination, but simply ensure that it will not flag.

Interviewers should be required to practice their entire routine before embarking on the quest for respondents. In such practice, which should be incorporated in the training, the respondent ideally would be a person unfamiliar with the survey who does not differ from those to be sampled. Circumstances—living room, telephone, office—should be identical to those that will obtain in actuality. The message to be conveyed by the training is that the interview is to occur as closely as possible in the same fashion each time. These stipulations apply alike to telephone and face-to-face interviews.

Preparation does not terminate training. Any survey that continues beyond the first day requires a review of problems and a recapitulation of solutions and procedures. The initial experience with sampled individuals is almost certain to turn up unexpected events. The resolution of these surprises should be made part of the common knowledge of the interview staff. At the same time, such a reassessment offers the opportunity for praise and the reinforcement of desired behavior. Uniformity must not only be taught, but maintained. The reassessment thus emphasizes the applicability of what has been taught before, as well as the challenge of the unfamiliar. One logistical implication of the need for continuing training is a briefing session at the end of the first or beginning of the second day, and thereafter every few days for as long as the survey continues. A second is continued supervision.

The selection of interviewers is an art with only one vague rule: do not place the respondents at a disadvantage. It should be obvious that the information obtained is vulnerable to bias from the reaction of the respondent to attributes of the interviewer. These attributes include not only who and what the interviewer is, but what she or he does within the interview. The extensive literature on interview bias leads to the acceptance of three propositions: (1) interviews, although vulnerable, are often fairly resistant to serious bias; (2) bias is principally a function of the expectations of interviewer and respondent, and thus is sensitive to the social distance between the two; and (3) no set rule ensures the elimination of bias, because its foundation in a particular circumstance is often quite subtle.[2]

---

[2]Charles F. Cannell and Robert L. Kahn, "Interviewing," in Gardner Lindzey and Elliot Aronson, eds., *Handbook of Social Psychology*, vol. II (Reading, Mass.: Addison-Wesley Publishing Co., 1968); Carol H. Weiss, Laurie J. Bauman, and Theresa F. Rogers, *Respondent/Interviewer Interaction in the Research Interview: Abstracts* (Springfield, Va.: National Technical Information Service, 1971).

We should be skeptical of those who would discard a body of data because there is some reason to suspect bias. Frequently, suspected bias will not materialize. When it does, the magnitude may not be noteworthy even when statistically significant. Almost always, the likely direction of bias will be obvious so that the analyst will approach the data with caution.

Similarity between respondents in race, income, age, education, social class, sex, and religion generally decreases bias, for the respondent will not be tempted to conform to what is taken as an outsider's expectation, and the interviewer will be less likely to hold false expectations that distort what is said or recorded. The basis for this well-supported view is the reduction of a motive on either side to purposely or inadvertently falsify. The same basis inspires caution over too great similarity, for here too we might expect the interaction of the parties to constitute an unintended conspiracy. The phenomenon is documented in a survey of low-income mothers where similarity was associated with distortion of answers about voting, receipt of welfare, and children's school progress.[3] However, it takes very little insight to understand that peers may inspire puffery or pleas for sympathy.

Apart from adequate verbal skills, then, interviewers should be chosen who are not quite like their respondents yet not so socially distant as to create a theater of pretense. These stipulations obviously attain their full import only with face-to-face interviews. Nevertheless, even telephone interviewing requires some care that voice and inflection, however adequate by telephone operator standards, do not inspire striving in the respondent, and that interviewers do not presume too much simply from how the respondent sounds. The intent of these varied measures is to minimize the likelihood that the respondent will be motivated to mislead or will be misunderstood.

Techniques of Interviewing

The interview proceeds in four stages: introduction, query, probe and elaboration, and conclusion. The introduction is designed to gain cooperation. The conclusion should leave the respondent in an unvengeful state of mind. The two middle stages are the substance of the interview.

The introduction should state concisely the auspices and intent of the interview. This usually is confined to a statement of the sponsorship and the topic, often accompanied by an assurance of anonymity. Although brief, the statement in effect is a solicitation to grant an interview, and as such it should emphasize the businesslike, nonthreatening character of the enterprise and the importance of the individual's participation. In the mail survey, there is a temptation to make the statement lengthy because of the absence of conversational exchange. This temptation should be curtailed because lengthy explanations risk

[3]Carol H. Weiss, "Validity of Welfare Mothers' Interview Responses," *Public Opinion Quarterly*, 32: 622–33 (Winter 1968–69).

discard of the material before the questionnaire is even reached. In the telephone interview, usually a single sentence will suffice:

> This is National Consumer Surveys, and I would like to ask you six questions about recent purchases.

Even in the case of the face-to-face interview, the introduction should be brief, as exemplified by the script suggested by a national polling organization:

> Hello, I'm (*name of interviewer*) from the National Opinion Research Center. I'm working on a survey in this area and would like to get a few of *your* opinions about the community.

The telephone and face-to-face interviewer should be prepared to answer questions and alleviate anxieties, but should not in any way encourage preliminary conversation, for it only delays completion of the interview. Conversing in general about the survey also risks raising objections and doubts that the respondent would not have thought of otherwise.

The conclusion typically offers to answer questions, extends thanks, and courteously punctuates the termination of the interview. The respondent, if possible, should not be left chagrined over the experience. In the mail survey, the conclusion reemphasizes the importance of returning the questionnaire and restates the instructions for so doing.

The stages of query and probe and elaboration occur concurrently. The face-to-face interview, by the very nature of personal interaction as well as its typically more elaborate character, ordinarily imposes the greatest burden on the interviewer. In querying, the interviewer must follow the questionnaire or outline prepared in advance. It is in probing and seeking elaboration that the interviewer's skills will be maximally taxed. Certain homilies are obvious: establish rapport, avoid antagonism, speak clearly, display interest, ignore sexual innuendoes. Beyond this, the quality of the information obtained depends on the alertness of the interviewer in preventing the respondent's wandering from the question at hand. The interviewer must pay close attention to detect misinterpretations, must redirect the respondent to the question when necessary, and must rephrase and repeat to ensure that the reply is to the question asked. Such accuracy becomes particularly important when an interview is designed to "branch," depending on the previous response ("If *yes*, go to Q. 2b; if *no* or *don't know*, go to Q. 3."), for obviously the data obtained will hardly be useful if the branching is incorrect. The most common technique is to admit or feign confusion:

> Let me repeat the question to be sure I have this right.
> I think I have it. Could you say that again?

Besides guarding against the irrelevant and erroneous, the interviewer also must encourage the respondent. Here, numerous neutral but conversationally provocative phrases serve:

Hmm. Go on.

That's interesting.

Alright. Could you expand a little?

I see. Now let me ask you about something else.

The telephone and face-to-face interview both have features in common with the techniques of the journalist. It is relatively rare, however, that the survey will approximate the information goals of the journalist. Journalists seek to construct their stories, hopefully accurate as well as interesting, from a variety of sources. They will certainly occasionally seek quotations on the same issue from diverse, and possibly mutually hostile, persons, but the aim is to patch together an account with a yard here and a fragment there. The survey seeks the same information from everyone. The journalist who does not pursue an interesting intimation in an interview is incompetent or unimaginative. The survey interviewer who becomes distracted from the precise intent of the survey is irresponsible. The survey interviewer occasionally will want to record verbatim a poignant or pointed comment; the journalist enlivens his prose with such quotations. From the standpoint of interview creativity, journalism is *haute cuisine,* survey research, fast food.

Reducing Nonresponse

Nonresponse is of two kinds, sample and interview. The former represents failure of a party drawn into a sample to participate. The latter represents failure of a party interviewed to respond to a question. Both endanger the validity of a survey by diluting the representativeness of the responses.

There are four principal means by which nonresponse can be reduced. They are facilitation, encouragement, strategic search, and reopportunity. Facilitation means making participation as easy as possible. The most obvious example is the stamped, addressed envelope that is conventionally supplied for the return of a mail questionnaire. The underlying principle is broad: the avoidance of the perception by the respondent that the task is onerous and to be avoided. The brevity of introductions and of mail and telephone interviews are to the same end. Encouragement ranges between supplication and persuasion. The interviewer should not accept a "No" without a brief entreaty. Whether it is a question or the interview itself, the interviewer should attempt to win cooperation. Often, a personal appeal is decisive:

It would help me a great deal. It will only take 15 minutes.

I wish you'd help me. I'd be happy to tell you anything I can about the survey.

The importance of the survey and of the individual's participation should be stressed:

We want to represent the community accurately. I'd really like your views.

In many surveys, interviewers carry a certificate or other credentials attesting to their legitimacy, to be displayed only as needed. Interviewers may wish to reemphasize the anonymity of response, although, to the skeptical, it is obvious that anyone motivated to attach an identity to the responses could do so. Anonymity occurs not because it is technologically precluded by the procedures but because there is neither motive for nor the slightest interest in its violation among those who have the opportunity.

Strategic search simply means seeking out people when they are likely to be available. A telephone survey seeking male respondents would be ill-advised to schedule calling during the day; housewives may well be at home, but usually not working women. Weekend evenings, teenagers may be scarce. East Coast based calls to the West may be made between 9 P.M. and 1 A.M. to compensate for the time difference. Face-to-face interviews similarly must be scheduled to fit the likely presence of respondents.

Reopportunity means giving those unavailable or otherwise evasive a second chance. In the mail survey, this will amount to sending reminders or a second questionnaire. In the telephone and face-to-face interview, it will involve second and third calls or visits. When a party is unavailable, another call or visit conventionally is scheduled; when a respondent is uncooperative but does not flatly refuse, an attempt may be made to conduct the interview at another time:

> If this is inconvenient, may I telephone you again tomorrow at whatever time you would like?

> May I come back tomorrow for the interview? Just tell me what time.

For unavailable parties, three is considered the optimal number of repeated efforts. Fewer attempts risk the unnecessary omission of a selected respondent; more, and the likelihood of ever completing the interview becomes quite low.

The usual means of compensating for nonresponse is substituting persons with ostensibly similar characteristics. This is an imperfect if often the only possible measure. The reason is quite simple: those who for varying reasons refuse cooperation or are not available are very likely to differ in critical respects from those who prove willing substitutes. This stricture applies to interview as well as sample nonresponse, for a party edgy over a particular question may very well be atypical in that single regard.

DESIGNING QUESTIONS AND QUESTIONNAIRES

The design of questions and questionnaires is a well-developed craft. The product may vary from a single page of multiple-choice items to a thick document color coded by item, page, or section to expedite branching.

Framing the Questions

The appropriateness of a question is a function of its purpose. A confused and vague query is satisfactory if the intent is to elicit rambling on the subject. Unhappily, rambling is not often the goal, and questions must be scrutinized carefully and pretested to ensure that they serve their purpose.

There are two rules whose violation defeats the intent of most questions. The first is to use terms and language that will be understood without additional explanation. The second is to ask only one thing in a single question. They are violated so often that one must conclude that their simplicity is deceptive.

Language must be direct, concise, and comprehensible to the population to whom it is directed. One may only speculate on the interpretation that a person with less than a grade school education would place on this query:

> Charges of political chicanery are common in elections. Do you think much goes on?

Or

> Do you believe that probability sampling of the U.S. population produces valid results when used to predict future behavior?

The problem of being understood by the intended population is illustrated by the disclaimers that television toy advertisers are required to attach to television commercials. When children have been queried about their comprehension of the message, it turns out that the accepted phase, "Some assembly required," is far less often understood by young children than the more direct, "You have to put it together."[4] The advertiser, like the survey researcher, may understand what is meant, but not the persons to whom the message is directed. The toymaker courts ambiguity; the researcher shuns it.

The second rule is also violated by the last example, which is a "double-barreled" question: Does it ask about the representativeness of probability samples or about the capability of polls to predict future behavior? We do not know; we would have to ask the survey practitioner. We do know that the answer may reflect one or the other or both. In any case, it is certain to be ambiguous.

Whether questions and the answers they seek should be open or closed depends on the circumstances. The term *closed* simply means

---

[4]Diane E. Liebert and others, "Effects of Television Commercial Disclaimers on the Product Expectation of Children," *Journal of Communication,* 27: 118–24 (Winter 1977).

that alternatives are specific and limited. An open question that seeks an open answer is

What do you consider to be the greatest problem facing the nation today?

An open question can permit only certain alternatives:

When most people think of the problems facing the nation today, there is usually one they single out as most important. Is there a problem that you think stands out in this way?

_____ Yes   _____ No

A closed question can allow an open answer:

Many people think crime is the biggest problem in the cities today. Can you think of any steps to reduce crime that have been taken recently by officials in this city?

Perhaps the most usual form of all is the closed question that limits alternatives. Such structured items make the tasks of recording and tabulating replies easy.

How serious a problem do you think crime in the cities is today?
_____ Extremely serious.
_____ Somewhat serious.
_____ Not at all serious.
_____ No opinion.

The careful student will note immediately that this last example is seriously flawed by the alternatives offered. Unless we misperceive the public's mood, almost everyone will describe urban crime as "extremely" or "somewhat" serious; few will opt for "not at all." As a result, we would be unable to distinguish much among degrees of concern about crime, and could make only the most crude approximation of relating such concern to other variables.

Organizing the Questionnaire

The time and cost economies promised by items in which query and response are structured make it possible for a survey to cover a much larger range of issues and topics. Because of their advantages, they are deservedly used widely. However, they are not a sole solution. The other types of items have certain roles where they excel and where the structured query and response has limits and risks.

When query and response are both open, the respondent may voice any vaguely relevant opinion he or she cares to offer. Such an item can help establish rapport and can introduce the respondent to the general topic on which later questions will focus more specifically. The closed question that permits an open answer will direct the interview to the specific topic. The appendage of structured alternatives to an open question also will sharply focus the interview, and in addition will permit branching based on the reply. In the example, those who know of anticrime steps may be asked what they are and where they learned of them; those who do not might be asked if there are steps they advocate. Conversely, the unstructured item might terminate a topic:

> Those are all the questions I have on major problems. Are there any comments you would like to add?

As these examples suggest, the questionnaire, whether for mail, telephone, or face-to-face interview, typically will shift between the general and the specific as it guides the respondent through varied topics. Ordinarily, it will begin with the general, progressively narrow the focus, and then terminate the topic by a final, general query before advancing to a new topic.

The use of sets of items to measure a single dimension of attitude or behavior is common. A single item may be too simplistic, too limited in coverage, or too crude a gauge. The principal requirement for such scales and indexes is that the items measure the same thing. This is an empirical question that can be answered with finality only by analyzing responses to the items. Fortunately, there are numerous scales and indexes in the social science literature that have survived such scrutiny. They cover a myriad of topics—to give only a few examples, liberalism versus conservatism, use of community services, social status, and consumer optimism. The wise survey practitioner will search the literature before reinventing the wheel.[5]

The structured item is limited to topics where the range of options is known in advance. The circumstance it fits best is the distribution of the respondents between "not at all" or "none" and "extremely so" or "all," with as many intervening options as the investigator can invent. It is equally well suited to physical properties with finite limits, such as annual income or size of dwelling. It is less adaptable to topics where, by number, obscurity, or complexity, the alternatives elude categorization. Obviously, one may divide musical instruments into string, woodwind, and brass, but one had better be prepared to dispose of an oud.

The structured item also risks distorting public opinion. Alternatives may force respondents into a position they would not otherwise adopt. Similarly, the very posing of an issue may elicit opinion that will vary from what would be volunteered. For example, few people will mention television in connection with national problems. Yet, when asked specifically about television violence, or the intrusiveness of commercials, or the quality of programming, substantial proportions will give

---

[5]One of the best sources for capitalizing upon past research experience is John P. Robinson, J. G. Rusk, and K. B. Head, *Measures of Political Attitudes* (Ann Arbor: University of Michigan, Survey Research Center, Institute for Social Research, 1968).

their accord to responses highly critical of broadcasting.[6] The inclusion of "Don't know," "Don't care," and "No opinion," is a feeble solution, because it does not distinguish between issues of high priority to the respondents and those to which they will accord importance when brought to their attention. The latter clearly reside in a secondary universe, although not one necessarily unimportant. The meager solution, of course, is the use of both structured and unstructured items to contrast volunteered with elicited positions, the limiting of comparisons across time and population to items of the same character, and the candid qualifying of interpretations. Another is to follow each substantive question with a scaled question about the importance of the problem or the salience of an issue.

Pretesting

Pretesting is an odious term that derives from the notion that the true test is actual application; thus, a trial or shakedown can only be a "pretest." Unhappily, this misuse is ingrained in the jargon of social science, but should not distract us from the importance of the task.

The previously untried questionnaire should be subjected to a trial to eliminate possible ambiguities and errors. Obviously, a questionnaire that entirely repeats the past can omit this step.

The more common circumstances make a test of the questionnaire mandatory. Experience, or success with a different population, is no guarantee of present efficacy. For example, several Harvard researchers recently queried ethnically distinct samples about their television viewing. The questionnaire failed to elicit information from Puerto Ricans, although it had been thoroughly tested with white and black samples. In this case, accurate translation into Spanish and sympathetic interviewers failed to overcome differences in idiom and ways of thinking about the topic.[7]

The survey practitioner will be alert to meaning and syntax, clarity, elapsed time, and effects of the order of presentation. Ordinarily, it is desirable to move from the nonthreatening to the less comfortable, and from the simple to the complex. Ultimately, the concern is for reliability and validity. Reliability, of course, concerns the consistency of responses with variations in time, place, and interviewer; validity, the degree to which what is sought is actually reflected in the measurement. These concepts are discussed in greater detail at several points in this book. Neither can be completely freed from risk by simply trying out the questionnaire. However, both will be enhanced by ensuring that the questionnaire does not falter in practice.

---

[6]George Comstock and others, *Television and Human Behavior* (New York: Columbia University Press, 1978).

[7]Aimee Dorr, "Television and the Socialization of the Minority Child," paper presented at a symposium sponsored by the Center for Afro-American Studies, University of California, April, 1978.

SAMPLING RESPONDENTS

The conclusions that may be drawn from a survey are contingent on the nature of the sample. The flawless probability sample permits a description, with a specified margin of error, of the population represented, but may be inadequate for certain comparisons between components of that population. The nonprobability sample does not permit such description, but has important uses, which is fortunate, since it is often all that is available. The use of a sample for a purpose for which it is unsuited not only misrepresents the information it contains, but is an embarrassing revelation of the naivete of the survey practitioner.

Probability Versus Nonprobability Samples

A *census* is a tabulation of all the persons in a population. The *probability sample* is a portion of that population made up of persons each of whom had an equal chance of being drawn into the sample. This equal likelihood of inclusion ensures the represenativeness of the sample. The *nonprobability sample* is simply a set of persons chosen for scrutiny; it is sometimes called an "opportunity" or "convenience" sample, and its usefulness depends on the judiciousness applied to its selection.

The probability sample has two advantages. Its representativeness precludes bias, and the fact of equal opportunity for inclusion permits the precise calculation of the likely error of any measure. Its principal weakness is that it often will include too few members of groups of particular interest, simply because of their relative scarcity in the larger population. For example, national probability samples inevitably will contain too few representatives of ethnic minorities, professions, the quite rich or extremely poor, and many religious groups for more than the most crude analysis. They will appear in accord with their presence in the population as a whole, which is undeniably "representative," but the degree to which the small number of cases can reflect variations within this subpopulation will be severely limited. For example, a national sample of 1,200, recognized as adequate for estimating presidential voting preferences within accepted tolerances, will contain only about 120 blacks, and a comparison of whites and blacks of upper socioeconomic status will depend on the very few blacks with this attribute included in that number. When we contemplate adding to the variables of race and socioeconomic status a third, such as political affiliation, it can be readily perceived that the black sample within such subdivisions will be approaching the vanishing point and certainly will have left behind any possibility for reflecting those blacks in the larger population with such characteristics.

The solution is to devise a higher probability of inclusion for such groups, and apply statistical adjustments so that this "oversampling" does not distort results when values for the population as a whole are estimated. The result is a *stratified random sample*, which we will discuss

159

later. Those statistical adjustments in effect weight the responses of the varied subgroups so that the contribution of each to a measure offered as reflecting the population as a whole is equivalent to their presence in that population. For example, if we wish to compare the national black and white populations thoroughly, we might oversample the black population to produce black and white samples of equal size; we might even apply a different sampling rate to scarce groups within these populations, producing, perhaps, black and white samples of equal size equally divided among those of high, middle, and low socio-economic status; but when we combine the samples, we will wish to weight the responses of the subgroups to match the actual makeup of the country.

The nonprobability sample has the assets of convenience and modest cost. It is employed where probability designs are not feasible. However, an important qualification must be made. To the extent that a nonprobability sample avoids bias, it may be very useful. The avoidance of such bias depends on representative selection and sometimes the use of probability techniques.

Assume that we are interested in the media habits and political attitudes of black and white high school students, and that we cannot afford national probability samples. Fear of bias causes us to reject querying students simply where we find them. We might, based on the character of their neighborhoods, select schools roughly comparable socioeconomically that would provide black and white samples. Within the schools, we would avoid bias by either conducting a census or drawing probability samples. We would now be superbly prepared to discuss the media habits and political attitudes at these schools.

However, our concern is with more general black and white similarities and differences. We obviously cannot directly extrapolate our measures to the national high school population. What we can do is act with the reasonable expectation—but not certainty—that the pattern of relationships will be similar to that for the nation. By "relationships," we mean the way variables are associated within samples and the differences between samples. By "pattern," we emphasize that we refer to the direction of these relationships—greater or lesser, positive or inverse—and not the exact standing of a sample on any variable.

If we find that high grades among blacks are associated with more positive evaluations of schooling, but not among whites, we would seriously entertain the proposition that black and white students generally differ in this manner (a plausible explanation for such a finding is left to the imagination of the reader), but we would not take the proportion of blacks or whites holding a particular view as representing that proportion for the nation. Nonprobability samples can permit us to hazard, although with trepidation, that patterns are typical. The ability to do so is a function of avoiding bias in selecting a nonprobability sample.

Such tentative inferences based on nonprobability samples constitute hypotheses about the larger populations of interest but do not permit a test of such hypotheses. Our confidence in such hypotheses will increase or wane with additional evidence. Typically, such evidence will accrue from other nonprobability samples; far less often, a new probability sample will provide a direct test. As these circumstances imply, the conclusions drawn from probability and nonprobability samples have a different status. Probability samples provide conclusions that can be said with certainty to hold at least for the time of the survey; deviations in new probability samples may be interpreted as changes. Nonprobability samples provide no such surety; the applicability of their conclusions to the larger population, even as to patterns, is hazardous even for the time of the survey, and deviations in future nonprobability samples are ambiguous as to whether they represent change or reveal the peculiarity of the original sample.

The philosophical justification for nonprobability samples is the assumption that there are regularities in the relationships among human attributes. Thus, we will entertain the belief that differences among socioeconomic strata or ethnic groups will hold more widely, although we would not be willing to offer the exact measures obtained as estimates of such measures for the larger population. If we abandon this plausible assumption, we would have no choice but to rely only on probability samples or censuses.

Probability Sample Designs

Any sample that deviates from the principle of equal chance of selection from the first ten, fifteen, or forty names; for a sample of 1,000 thus attempt to simulate a lottery. Unhappily, true probability samples are seldom feasible. The *simple random sample* provides the standard but unhappily cannot always serve as the model. The alternative designs are treated as probability samples with the implicit qualification that they are imperfect attempts.

The purpose of the probability sample is to represent the larger population accurately. Obviously, a chance drawing creates precisely such a circumstance. The chance drawing is typically not possible because no list of all the members of the population is available. The alternative designs attempt to compensate.

The *systematic random sample* will use whatever list is available, such as a telephone book, registration list, or file. Every *n*th entry, such as every tenth, fifteenth, or fortieth, is chosen after an initial random selection from the first ten, fifteen, or forty names; for a sample of 1,000 from a listing of 27,000 we would draw every twenty-seventh entry from a random start. Even when a list covers the larger population, such sampling is more efficient than drawing names individually. Technically, however, the result is not a perfect probability sample because subsequent entries are determined by the initial selection, so that we do not have equal chance of inclusion in the sample once a random start has been drawn, but the somewhat different equal possibility of membership in one of the possible samples. What is more serious is the frequent circumstance that the roster only imperfectly represents the larger population. Thus, we do not sample potential voters with the telephone directory, but only those potential voters with listed telephones. We can discard the irrelevant who fall into such a sample—the under-age, foreign citizens—but we cannot add persons absent from the roster.

Random digit dialing, however, eliminates the imperfections in a telephone sample due to unlisted telephone numbers and new phone installations not yet published in the directory. The technique of random digit dialing begins with a pure random sample of telephone numbers. Of course, if all seven digit combinations were eligible to be drawn, a very large portion would be nonexistent telephone numbers, since only a few three-digit exchange numbers are in use in any particular locale; so the first three digits can be limited to those in use in the geographic area to be studied and a random sample of four-digit numbers drawn for each exchange in order to select specific telephones for the sample. Since the four-digit combinations are drawn entirely at random, usually using a computer with a random number generator, every telephone in each exchange used has an equal chance of being selected. Of course, some of the telephone numbers randomly created in this way are not in actual use. This means a certain amount of wasted interviewer effort, but at least every telephone number in actual use does have an equal chance of being selected. When households are being sampled, in some instances a large number of business phones can be eliminated because certain exchanges are assigned exclusively to such use. Furthermore, in a city with many different telephone exchanges, the number of telephone numbers randomly created for each exchange can be made proportional to the share of listings (or share of residential listings) in that exchange. With increased use of telephone interviewing in recent years, due among other factors to lower cost and very high telephone penetration in most areas, random digit dialing has been successfully used to create a pure random sample of telephones.

The sampling procedure of random-digit dialing increasingly is becoming part of a package that approaches the automation of survey research. It should be obvious that the use of computer terminals permits a telephone interviewer seeking prescribed responses—yes, no, multiple choice, or in conformity with previously selected categories—to enter responses directly into the data bank, bypassing handrecording and later transposition to the memory of a computer. Such a system becomes further automated, and, for the interviewer, simplified, when the questions to be asked are displayed on a televisionlike screen connected to the computer. Responsibility for the selection of questions varying in accord with previous answers—different things, for example, being asked of home owners than of renters or apartment dwellers—then becomes transferred from the fallible human to the (ostensibly) infallible and certainly tireless machine. Random-digit dialing advances such automation a further step by making it possible for the computer to generate the sample as calling occurs and in effect to undertake the tedious dialing itself. In such a system, the interviewer need only speak when called upon, and then only in accord with the stipulations of the computer, while that same computer selects the number to be called and calls it.

The *multistage area probability sample* deals with circumstances where no roster exists. We may first select states, within them counties, then smaller areas, then city blocks, and ultimately households. Within the household, we will select an individual. When the goal is to sample individuals, the inclusion of a state, county, or smaller area will vary with its population; the larger the population, the greater is the chance of inclusion. A common practical procedure is to list the candidate units with a cumulative tally of their populations and then select an *n*th individual, analogous to the procedure used with a roster. Thus, a sample of 1,000 from a state with 8 million would lead to the selection of every *8,000th* individual, and the inclusion of every county with 8,000 or more population at least once, while some with fewer persons might possibly be omitted. Households usually will be randomly selected within the surviving geographical units. Sometimes, the person who answers the door will be interviewed; in other cases, the design will advance priorities based on age, sex, or employment; in still other cases, the design may require that if a resident meets particular qualifications he or she be interviewed, in which case *callbacks* may be necessary.

In the construction of multistage samples, the selection of households in the final stage could be a pure random sampling or a systematic random sampling of the households in the area. But because either technique typically results in a highly dispersed pattern of interview assignments, many researchers randomly select a smaller number of points in each area and then systematically cluster a number of interviews in that area. For example, in a census tract where twenty interviews are to be conducted, only five actual locations might be randomly sampled and then some procedure devised for selecting four interview sites in each of those five vicinities. The procedure typically is some systematic sampling technique using the initially drawn location as a starting point for selecting the cluster. The principal arguments in favor of *cluster sampling* are its efficiency and lower per interview cost. The principal defect of cluster sampling is the greater homogeneity of the survey respondents, meaning that the variance of responses on the survey questions is reduced and the size of the sampling error tends to be underestimated.

Everything so far has concerned the sampling of persons (or other units) from some general population. But in some cases the researcher has a particular interest in some population subgroup or in the comparison of several subgroups. Now a random sample of the general population will include all the subgroups, but their exact representation will be subject to sampling error. The researcher can ensure that exactly the right number of persons from each subgroup is included by using a *stratified random sample*. That is, the population is divided into the appropriate subgroups (strata), and a random sample is drawn for each stratum. For example, a study of communication patterns among college students might stratify the student population according to year in school. In such a design there would be no sampling error on the stratification variable, year in school. This ensures tighter control in the analysis of other variables whose relationships may be contingent upon the stratification variable. Obviously, one does not casually use a stratified random sample. This strategy of sampling is justified by a theoretical or practical rationale for the selection of particular variables as the basis of stratification. However, when stratification is combined with random selection, we are assured of full control over the stratification variables and probability selection of all other potential sources of variation.

Quota sampling is a procedure that appears to ensure similar controls on the type of persons selected for interviewing. With this technique, one sets a quota for the number of persons of various types to be interviewed. To continue the example of a campus study, one could set quotas in terms of the number of freshman males, sophomore females, and so on, to be interviewed. The number of interviews in each quota could be made directly proportional to the share of such persons in the campus population. The basic idea of quota sampling is to balance the number of interviews across the entire population, but the appeal of this technique is specious, and it allows for a major methodological flaw.

First, there is the fundamental question of which variables are to be used in designing the quota. Class and sex seem obvious for a campus study, but what about type of residence or major field of study? In most instances, there is no clear rationale to guide the selection of variables used to define the quotas. And even in those rare instances when there is a rationale, assignment of quotas to interviewers does not guarantee real control over who actually is selected for an interview. Interviewers typically fill each quota with the most readily available members, thus introducing a major bias and source of nonrepresentativeness into the final sample of respondents.

The description of the behavior or opinions of the many from information obtained from a few is the purpose of sampling, but it works only when representativeness is assured. Probability samples ensure representativeness of persons. Nonprobability samples are useful to the extent that they can be used to test relationships. Factors that distort representativeness devalue a survey; at some point, it will cease to have currency at all. There is a curious paradox here. The relatively simple business of estimating parameters (characteristics) of a population requires the more sophisticated probability sample. But when the more sophisticated task of studying relationships within a population is undertaken, this may be carried out in some circumstances with a less sophisticated nonprobability sample.

Sampling Error

A major advantage of the probability sample is that it permits a precise statement of the likely error of any measure. Obviously, few samples will exactly match the characteristics of the population from which they are drawn. The probability sample makes possible a metric to account for such chance deviations.

Sampling error is the estimate of the range above and below the measure provided by the sample that will embrace the statistic for the actual population a specified, substantial portion of the time. For example, a sample measure of 40 percent might have a sampling error of 7 percent at the 0.95 level of confidence. This translates into the simpler statement that 95 out of 100 times the population figure would lie between 33 and 47 percent. The range on which we place such a probability of bracketing the population statistic is termed the confidence interval. As Chapter 4 makes clear, the confidence interval is a function of the estimated dispersion that would occur were there repeated sampling and the size of the sample, with the dispersion for the uncollected samples extrapolated from the dispersion of the sample measure itself. In the case of a percentage, we can calculate in advance a handy rule of thumb for a variety of sample sizes simply by using the estimated dispersion for 50 percent, for a 50–50 split in the sample produces the widest possible confidence interval. At worst, then, pending the calculation of the exact figure, we would conservatively overestimate the sampling error. As Chapter 4 also makes clear, size of population is irrelevant except in those rare cases when sample size begins to approach a significant portion of the total population; in such a rare case, the population size does affect sampling error. But in the more common instance, where population size is in the tens or hundreds of thousands and sample size in the hundreds, a smaller population reduces sampling error only minutely.

Validating the Sample

There are three types of sample validation: census, internal, and external. The intent of validation is to ensure that the sample represents the intended population. It is the evidence, beyond the compelling plausibility of the sample design, that the survey practitioner offers in behalf of the credibility of the obtained information.

Census validation involves matching characteristics of the sample with census figures. For example, the ethnic distribution and socioeconomic distribution of a sample might be compared with those reported in the most recent U.S. Census figures for the population from which the sample has been drawn. If sample and census distributions approximate each other, it is an indication that the sample is representative. However, the fact that the figures for a non-probability sample and the census are similar does not mean that the sample in question is the equivalent of a probability sample.

Internal validation means the application of sampling error. When we calculate the sampling error, we are determining the precision of our sample—that is, how close we can expect sample figures to be to population figures. Such validation cannot be applied to non-probability samples even if they do pass the test of census validation.

A special and sometimes puzzling case of census validation occurs in the matching of relationships within the sample against those presumably established. For example, political liberalism has "known" attitudinal and demographic correlates. Presence of such relationships heightens faith in sample representativeness. Their absence tests that faith. Our puzzle would be whether to treat the finding as a sampling anomaly—the representative deviation of an atypical population—or as a shift in those known relationships. Sample representativeness and lack of bias in sample selection favor one or the other of the latter two alternatives. There should never be a rush to such a conclusion, however, for the very principles that permit the calculation of sampling error guarantee that occasionally even a probability sample will deviate sharply from the population from which it was drawn.

CONCLUSION

We began by emphasizing the parsimony of the sample survey. We close by drawing attention to the concept responsible for that parsimony—representativeness. Narrowly, representativeness refers to the degree to which a sample reflects a larger population. However, the striving to be representative also marks every aspect of survey research—selecting the mode for data collection, designing questions and questionnaires, training of interviewers, reducing nonresponse, and the techniques of interviewing itself. We are made information poor, not rich, by a representative sample whose opinions or behavior are distorted in recording; a representative sample fails us when what we measure does not represent its character or beliefs. Representation of what the public thinks, does, and believes is the survey's justifying characteristic and the end toward which the procedures endowed with jargon are a means. As such, it is the criterion by which the success of those procedures constantly must be judged.

Statistical Designs in Survey Research

Serena E. Wade

As earlier chapters have repeatedly emphasized, there is no substitute for careful planning in the development of a statistical design to answer research questions. This is particularly true of studies for which data are gathered through survey methods. In the process of conceptualization, careful consideration must be given to the type of data needed to answer the research question(s), the levels of measurement for those data, and the types of statistical analyses permitted by the levels of measurement chosen. The last criterion is perhaps the most important, for it will govern the presentation of empirical evidence that describes and relates the variables of interest to the study. If there is no coordination between the research question(s) and the type of evidence to be presented, the researcher may find that the time and effort that have gone into data collection have been wasted or at least could have been better invested. ("If only I had thought of that before the survey went into the field. . . .")

Basic Decision Points

The choice of statistical design is much like the set of decisions involved in planning a cross-country automobile trip. At each highway intersection, a decision to turn left or right reflects the other alternative. Each decision in research (e.g., which questions to ask, which variables to measure) represents the selection of one option out of many that may be available. These decisions are inevitably influenced by time and money and affect the relationship of the decision maker and peers.

While the highway analogy to statistical design is not perfect, it does have several points of "good fit." First, the choice of a starting point and the main direction to follow parallel the definition of the problem and the major question(s) to be answered. Each destination to be included on the trip is analogous to a variable to be included in a statistical design. The roads selected for each destination require routing decisions comparable to the determination of the level of measurement for each variable in the statistical design. The final itinerary influences the enjoyment that results from the trip in the same way that the final statistical design (i.e., number of variables, level of measurement, statistical treatment) influences the depth and breadth of the analysis that may be used to answer the research question(s) and the contribution of the study to the field.

Remaining on the major highway may be the fastest way to reach your destination, but the most picturesque and enlightening features of the trip may be missed. Similarly, the researcher who creates a statistical design so that it can only answer, for example, "how many people are watching television at 7 P.M. on Sunday evenings," may have missed the most interesting explanations for that single statistic. The statistical design for survey analysis should reflect the thorough consideration of the complete research process, and the components of that design should be carefully selected in order to collect all the information required to answer the research question with predetermined accuracy and sensitivity.

Research Question and Design Requirements

While the nature of the research question will determine the survey design itself (i.e., descriptive, explanatory, longitudinal), the nature of that survey design will determine the appropriate type of statistical treatment. For example, if the design calls for the assessment of public preferences for news sources during a specified time period, the research question can be adequately answered by the presentation of a series of descriptive statistics—the proportions of the survey sample who prefer newspapers, television, magazines, and so on. If, on the other hand, the research question asks for the description of news source preferences for different population subgroups, then the survey design must include a number of additional variables (e.g., sex, age, and education level) that might explain those news preferences.

In a further extension of the inquiry into news source preferences, suppose the research question asks whether perceived gratifications from different news sources are more promising than general socioeconomic status in predicting an individual's news source preferences. This question requires that the survey design include the measurement of at least three variables (perceived gratification, socioeconomic status, preference). The corresponding statistical design must permit the interrelationship of these variables so that the relative effect of perceived gratifications and socioeconomic status on preferences can be assessed. Finally, a research question that asks whether there will be changes in preferences for news sources after the introduction of cable television in a community creates new survey design requirements with still different statistical requirements. Furthermore, if the research question asks whether cable television has *caused* changes in those preferences, the design must include consideration of criteria for determining causality. The corresponding statistical design must include measurement and statistical treatment of change over time and control statistically any explanations other than the introduction of cable television for any observed changes in news source preferences.

The preceding examples should illustrate a basic principle in statistical design for survey research: the interdependence of design and analysis requires thoughtful and comprehensive planning. The discussion of different statistical designs in this chapter will depend heavily on the reader's understanding of conceptual differences in levels of measurement for variables to be included in any statistical design. Measures that simply classify are generally called *categorical* variables; those that assume an underlying continuum are known as *continuous* variables. When the researcher assigns values to agree/disagree alternatives in attitude measures, for example, a continuous measure (a continuum of attitude intensity) is usually assumed. The most powerful statistical treatments require at least the approximation of continuous measures.

Summary

Regardless of the type of survey design, appropriate statistical representation depends on the level of measurement at which variables are conceptualized. To paraphrase the "Whorfian hypothesis," the researcher who is ill-prepared in statistical design and analysis cannot conceptualize a research study properly. Every research question makes different statistical demands, which, if ignored, can result in serious errors of analysis and interpretation. This chapter emphasizes the importance of a conceptualization that takes advantage of the most efficient statistical treatments at each measurement level.

The remaining sections of this chapter deal specifically with three types of statistical design and with appropriate strategies for analysis, using illustrative examples from current mass communication research literature.

DESCRIPTIVE STUDIES

Much survey research is basically descriptive. The epitome of the descriptive study is the presentation of an array of data whose whole purpose is the empirical representation of some phenomenon at one or more points in time, for example, a content analysis of the *New York Times* in 1907 and 1977. The data are presented in whatever form best describes the nature of the medium on a selected date or over a specified period. These "picture" studies focus mainly on frequency distributions of descriptive characteristics. Comparisons of distributions at different times are sometimes made. In terms of statistical design, "picture" studies are the least demanding, but they can provide some of the most fascinating data in mass communication research. Various content analysis strategies are treated in Chapter 8.

When the research design moves from pictures of mass communication to inquiry into the relationships between people and mass communication, however, the researcher is obliged not only to describe the survey results, but also to describe the survey sample and its relationship to the population from which it was drawn. The substantive findings almost always begin with simple frequency distributions of each variable and then proceed to more sophisticated statistical presentations.

Sample

The composition of the study sample is an important criterion in the assessment of the external validity of the study. Basic descriptive data about the sample include the following:

1. A definition of the population.
2. Specification of the selection method.
3. Sample size.
4. Comparative data (if available) to demonstrate the correspondence between sample and population characteristics.

This descriptive information is frequently buried in footnotes attached to the substantive research findings, tending to obscure the importance of these sampling data to the value of the research. If the findings appear to be important in their contribution to the development of some communication theory, for example, the quality of the sample may assure or destroy the value of that contribution.

While the above-cited data are often not included in discussions of statistical designs for survey research, the presentation of descriptive statistics for the study sample is a necessary condition for informed reader judgment regarding the results. If the sample size is inadequate or the demography is clearly unrepresentative, even the most sophisticated treatment of the data cannot survive these shortcomings. A simple frequency distribution of important sample characteristics is as important to the research as the level of measurement is to the statistical presentation of research findings.

Univariate Distributions (Marginals)

All survey research is designed so that univariate (one variable at a time) representation of the data is possible. Since they often appear only as "totals," they are also called "marginals." They simply count the number of cases for each value on one variable. In the majority of cases, the researcher uses these data only as checks on the sample and/ or starting points for more complex analyses of relationships between variables. There are several ways in which univariate analysis can be presented: individual responses, complete frequency distributions, classification by subgroup, and measures of central tendency.[1]

Suppose, for example, data reporting the average number of television viewing hours per weeknight were collected in a study, using an open-ended question for which the responses were in actual numbers of hours. Although reporting of individual responses is always possible (e.g., case 001 = 1, case 002 = 3, case 003 = 5), the data are not very useful in this form. Table 10–1 shows a more commonly used marginal distribution based on 100 responses. The frequencies have been converted to proportions, and the proportions may be converted to other data displays, if needed. Furthermore, responses may be grouped into meaningful subgroups using classification criteria that include all data, are mutually exclusive, and are exhaustive. The hours in Table 10–1 might be more economically presented in two classification groups, "1 to 3 hours (45%)" and "4 to 6 hours (55%)." The choice of classification criteria, the base for percentage computations, and the type of data display depend entirely on the purpose of the particular research. The statistical design should allow the maximum information required for meaningful analysis.

While marginal distributions for each variable in a study are indeed an important type of data to have available, typical research reports do not dwell at length on these basic descriptive statistics. The most common approach to the presentation of these data is a summary of measures of central tendency (mean, median, or mode) for continuous variables and the modal percentage for categorical variables. In a large study, where the statistical design calls for the association between variables considered two or more at a time, the first section of the study

Table 10–1   Frequency distribution of average weeknight television hours.

HOURS	p	Cum p
1	0.06	0.06
2	0.15	0.21
3	0.24	0.45
4	0.43	0.88
5	0.10	0.98
6	0.02	1.00

($N = 100$)

[1]Measures of dispersion (range, standard deviation, variance, etc.) are also used to describe the characteristics of the sample and the substantive research findings. However, their descriptive use is less common than their application in making inferences about population values and in tests of statistical significance.

results usually concentrates on a shorthand presentation of descriptive characteristics. For example, Baran, in a study that described how television and film affect sexual satisfaction, opened the results section with this paragraph:

> The 121 males and 86 females who completed the questionnaire consisted of 76 freshmen, 65 sophomores, 42 juniors, and 17 seniors (there were 7 special or other students). Their ages ranged from 17 to 26, with a mean age of 19.3 years. More than one half of the respondents were raised as Catholics (50.2%). 24.2% were raised as Protestants and 3.4% as Jews. 15.9% reported being raised in other religions while 2.9% were raised in no religion. Of the respondents, 44% still actively followed their religion, while the remainder did not.[2]

In a comparison of adult and youth mass media exposure, public affairs knowledge, and black militancy, Tan and Vaughn reported these marginal results for mass media use:

> *Mass Media Use:* Adult and youth samples reported moderate to heavy media exposure, particularly television viewing. Youths watched television on the average 4.9 hours a day; adults watched 4.4 hours a day. When asked to name their three favorite TV shows, 67.8% of the youth sample mentioned at least one black-oriented show (i.e., a show in which one or more of the leading characters is a black); only 26.2% of adults mentioned at least one black oriented show among their favorites.

> Both samples were fairly regular newspaper readers: 63.1% of the youth sample and 47.6% of adults reported reading at least one newspaper several days a week to every day, but only 16.7% of the youth sample and 27.9% of adults reported reading a black newspaper regularly.[3]

Marginals set the stage for a more penetrating look at the research data. For that reason, they are seldom reported in tabular form in professional journals (with the exception of "picture" studies, noted earlier). Mass communication research generally accepts the premise that a statistical design that describes human communication behavior by concentrating on univariate display is inadequate. If the nature of the research design and the type of data collected do not permit the causal explanation of differences between sample subgroups, the statistical design must at least permit the display of bivariate-to-multivariate distributions that describe those subgroup differences, and assess the significance of those differences using statistical treatments appropriate to the level of measurement.

Bivariate Distributions

The purpose of a descriptive bivariate distribution is the display of covariation and association between two variables. Bivariate distribu-

[2]Stanley J. Baran, "How TV and Film Portrayals Affect Sexual Satisfaction in College Students," *Journalism Quarterly*, 53: 468–73 (Autumn 1976), p. 472.

[3]Alexis Tan and Percy Vaughn, "Mass Media Exposure, Public Affairs Knowledge, and Black Militancy," *Journalism Quarterly*, 53: 271–79 (Summer 1976), p. 274.

tions typically appear in two forms, contingency tables and correlations. In a descriptive study design, the researcher frequently attempts to identify differences in one variable that may be associated with differences in a second or third variable in order to develop hypotheses for later explanatory testing. Whether the bivariate display is descriptive or explanatory is irrelevant to the statistical design. The statistical design seeks to present the covariation and association and to report on the probability that such covariation is either a function of random error or a true association between the covarying variables. Bivariate analyses have been, by far, the most common of all statistical presentations in mass communication research.

Contingency tables present bivariate analyses of variables whose level of measurement is categorical. The data entered into the cells of these tables should be the joint occurrences of single values on each of two variables. Schweitzer's study of young newspaper subscribers and nonsubscribers described their differences in major sources of information. His data, reported in part in Table 10–2, showed that subscribers found most of their information in newspapers.[4] Most nonsubscribers used television as their major news source. The inclusion of the chi square statistic testifies that these observed differences are not due to chance variation. Thus, Schweitzer has described the association between two variables in categorical form and has provided the statistical information needed to make correct inferences about that association. (Editor's note: "Categorical" data as used here is called "nominal scale" data elsewhere in this book.)

A contingency table may also present data for combinations of categorical and continuous variables in the form of mean scores for each subgroup. In a study that described dogmatism attributed to television characters, Leckenby assessed the differences in dogmatism scores assigned to television characters by respondents who were themselves high/low dogmatics. His results, reported in Table 10–3, showed that both high and low dogmatic respondents perceived Bunker and Jefferson in approximately the same ways, and that high dogmatics tended to attribute greater dogmatism to Welby and Kojak than did low dogmatics.[5] In this case, the data entries in the contingency table are mean

Table 10–2 Major news sources of young newspaper subscribers and nonsubscribers (in percent).

Source	Subscribers (N = 109)	Nonsubscribers (N = 83)
Television	42.2	54.2
Newspapers	45.0	22.9
Other	12.8	22.9
	$\chi^2 = 10.7$, df $= 2$, $p < 0.01$	

[4]John C. Schweitzer, "Comparison of Young Subscribers and Nonsubscribers to Newspapers," *Journalism Quarterly*, 53: 287–93 (Summer 1976), p. 291.

[5]John D. Leckenby, "Attributions of Dogmatism to TV Characters," *Journalism Quarterly*, 54: 14–19 (Spring 1977), p. 17.

Table 10–3 Mean attribution of dogmatism to four characters by low and high dogmatic respondents.

Characters	Low (N = 55)	High (N = 68)	t
Welby	38.5	45.2	4.43[a]
Jefferson	42.0	42.0	0.05
Kojak	37.3	41.2	3.20[a]
Bunker	46.3	46.7	0.39
All	41.0	43.8	1.67

[a]$p < .01$

dogmatism scores. The statistics are a series of independent t-tests between high and low dogmatic respondents.

The preceding examples use only two types of data with accompanying statistics. Other types of data require different statistics, a number of which are described in detail in Chapter 4. Bivariate distributions using contingency table formats nearly always have one variable in categorical form. This variable should be analogous to the "independent" variable in experimental design for purposes of statistical treatment only. Scores on the other variable in the bivariate analysis should be computed within the "independent" variable classifications. If both variables are categorical, the assignment of "independent" status depends on their relationship in the study.

Correlation

If both variables in a bivariate analysis are in continuous form, the use of various correlational techniques is appropriate. The most common measurement of association between two continuous variables is the Pearsonian product-moment correlation coefficient (r). In their inquiry into community newspaper content, Stone and Morrison selected numerous types of newspaper content and related those content types to the circulation of community newspapers. Selected results from their study are reported in Table 10–4 as correlations between content types and circulation.[6]

Correlation coefficients may also be presented in matrix form when more than two variables are related in a descriptive study. Tan and Vaughn have reported the relationship between various types of mass media use and public affairs knowledge (all measured as continuous variables) for black high school students (Table 10–5).[7]

[6]Gerald C. Stone and Janet Morrison, "Content As a Key to the Purpose of Community Newspapers," *Journalism Quarterly*, 53: 494–98 (Autumn 1976), p. 494.

Table 10–4 Correlation between circulation and specific types of newspaper content.

	Number of Pages	Total Column Inches	Local News, %	Feature, %	Local Photo, %
r	0.38[a]	0.50[a]	−0.13[b]	0.12	0.15[c]
No. of papers	251	251	251	169	241

[a]$p < 0.001$
[b]$p < 0.05$
[c]$p < 0.01$

Multivariate Descriptive Analyses

When the research design calls for the combined contribution of a number of variables to the variation in some communication behavior, the researcher would normally classify this type of study as explanatory rather than descriptive. The classification as explanatory is particularly appropriate when the research design attempts to establish a causal relationship between variables. Discussion of the statistical designs required for that type of research will be reserved for the next section of this chapter.

There are, however, descriptive studies where multivariate analyses are needed. These are often developmental research designs in which the contribution of various dimensions to the definition of a concept needs to be established. In this case, a common statistical counterpart of these designs is factor analysis. This analysis is generally considered to be a data reduction tool. In mass communication research, it is frequently used to select items to be included in measures of media characteristics or media behavior. Factor analysis is also one of several analytical tools used in the development of attitude scales. Presentation of factor analysis results is descriptive. Subgroup differences in factor

Table 10–5 Correlations between mass media use and public affairs knowledge, high school sample ($N = 257$).

	Newspaper Reading (N)	Magazine Reading (M)	Television Viewing (TV)	Public Affairs Knowledge (PA)
N	1.000	0.385[a]	0.0149	0.3407[a]
M		1.000	0.1405	0.291[a]
TV			1.000	0.048
PA				1.000

[a]$p < .001$

[7]Tan and Vaughn, "Mass Media Exposure," p. 494.

loadings can also be presented; these are comparable to subgroup classifications in bivariate analysis.[8]

In their inquiry into racial differences in family communication patterns (FCP), Allen and Chaffee looked at the applicability of the two dimensions (socio-orientation and concept-orientation) previously identified in the FCP measure. They performed the two factor analyses reported in Table 10–6.[9] The factor analysis results are displayed as factor loadings—the strength of association between each item and the underlying dimension of which the item may be a part. It is clear from the factor loadings for the FCP items that they fit black respondents rather badly. For white respondents, the two-factor solution explains 46 percent of the total variance, while only 27 percent of the total variance is explained for black respondents. The authors have used these descriptive data to suggest further inquiry into the appropriate number of FCP dimensions that will identify the communication behaviors in the black subculture.

Summary

Descriptive studies in mass communication research present empirical data that describe both the characteristics of the sample and the substantive results of the study. When the research design is restricted to media portraits, the information about the sample typically concentrates on the procedures used to select the issues of magazines or newspapers, nights of TV programs, and on the coding procedures used to classify content. When the research design includes the assessment of human communication behavior, the statistical design must also present data describing characteristics of the sample and its relationship to the population from which it was drawn.

Statistical designs for descriptive studies include univariate and bivariate statistical treatments and, in the special case of factor analysis and similar data reduction techniques, multivariate treatments. Univariate statistics include frequency distributions (also known as marginals), measures of central tendency (mean, median, mode), and, sometimes, measures of dispersion (range, variance, etc.). The type of statistical treatment should be appropriate to the level of measurement for each variable.

[8]Discriminant analysis is another descriptive multivariate procedure that produces a linear composite of several variables that maximally discriminate between groups of respondents. Variables have discriminant weights (analogous to factor loadings) that maximize between-group variance in the standard ANOVA interpretation. Results are frequently displayed in a figure with horizontal and vertical axes. The placement of the group means in this two-dimensional space graphically illustrates similarities and differences between respondent groups. Individual respondents may be classified into groups by generating discriminant scores.

[9]Richard L. Allen and Steven H. Chaffee, "Racial Differences in Family Communication Patterns," *Journalism Quarterly*, 54: 8–13 (Spring 1977), p. 11.

Table 10–6 Two-factor model factor analyses for each race.

Item	White respondents		Black respondents	
	I	II	I	II
a. Say that their ideas are correct and you shouldn't question them. (F)	−0.14	0.59	−0.31	−0.22
b. Answer your arguments by saying something like, "You'll know better when you grow up." (F)	0.06	0.67	−0.20	0.55
c. Say that you should give in on arguments rather than make people angry. (F)	0.01	0.49	−0.03	0.38
d. Tell you that you shouldn't argue with adults. (E)	0.12	0.82	−0.11	−0.45
e. Say that the best way to stay out of trouble is to keep away from it. (E)	0.08	0.56	−0.28	−0.25
f. Say that you should always look at both sides of an issue. (F)	0.77	0.16	0.25	0.02
g. Admit that children know more about some things than adults. (F)	0.63	−0.11	0.58	−0.04
h. Talk at home about things like politics and religion, where one person takes a different side from others. (F)	0.67	−0.10	0.50	−0.14
i. Emphasize that getting your ideas across is important even if others don't like it. (E)	0.68	−0.10	0.75	−0.16
j. Emphasize that every member of your family should have some say in family decisions. (E)	0.77	−0.17	0.64	0.13
Percent of total variance	25%	21%	19%	8%

Note: The first five items were taken from the socio dimension; the others were taken from the concept dimension based on previous surveys. Parenthetical (F) or (E) following each item indicates that the question asked about frequency of (F) or emphasis on (E) the behavior described in the item. Frequency items were preceded by the question: "How often did your parents . . ."; emphasis items were preceded by the question: "How much did your parents emphasize the following things in their family conversations?"

A typical descriptive study might include the content analysis and readership of two major news magazines. The research design seeks to describe both the makeup of the magazines and the persons who are reading them. The statistical design should reflect the intent of the research to identify major content categories and demographic characteristics of readers. The variables would typically include a set of content categories and the sex, education, and occupation of the readers of each magazine. Obviously, the research design might include other variables, but the inclusion of additional variables should be dictated by the research questions to be answered.

The statistical presentation would begin with the sampling data for the magazines and readers. Frequency distributions of basic sample characteristics should be available. Then frequency distributions of content categories for each magazine might follow. Finally, a set of contingency tables illustrating the differences in demographic characteristics for the readers of each magazine might conclude the necessary elements in the statistical design. The data in the contingency table might take the form of cell frequencies at each of several educational levels for readers of the two magazines, whose differences might be assessed using chi square or some other appropriate statistic. Or differences in average age of readers might be reported with means and *t*-tests for between-group differences. The design might include additional information about both the magazines themselves and about the readers (e.g., their attitudes toward advertising), but the research design per se only specifies the presentation of the information as described. That specification should serve as the major guide to the researcher in the development of the overall statistical design.

In descriptive studies, statistical designs for bivariate analyses include the use of contingency tables, with statistics appropriate to the cell entries, and correlations. The use of bivariate analyses in descriptive studies is focused on the description of differences between subgroups. While that description is a necessary condition for the explanation of variation due to subgroup differences, it is not a sufficient condition for the application of the logic associated with explanatory analyses.

Statistics appropriate to bivariate analyses are not sensitive to differences in research questions. They report associations and/or differences between groups. They report significance of those associations and differences whether the research design asks, "Does television viewing *cause* violent behavior?" or "What is the relationship between television viewing and violent behavior?" The researcher alone can make the distinction between association and causality. The statistical analysis should be approached with the clear intent to limit interpretations of descriptive study results to statements regarding observed differences. Explanations for those differences should be reserved for the study that includes sufficient explanatory framework for legitimate inferences about true relationships between variables.

EXPLANATORY STUDIES

When the research study begins with causal hypotheses to be tested or intends to explore the relationship between variables in some specifiable sequence, the bivariate distributions previously described for descriptive studies take on explanatory status. The statistical design is unaffected by this change in perspective, as long as the researcher limits the analysis to bivariate relationships. However, explanatory studies seldom restrict analyses to the consideration of only two variables at a time. Explanatory studies, by definition, require the elimination of alternative explanations for observed relationships between variables hypothesized as "cause" and "effect." And unlike the experimental design wherein the investigator can randomize or control these alternative explanations through features of the design per se, progress toward the establishment of causal relationships in survey research requires the elimination of these alternative explanations *after* the data are collected. The process of elimination, called elaboration by Kendall and Lazarsfeld,[10] involves the introduction of test variables into the analysis. These third variables are held constant through statistical procedures, and the original bivariate relationship is analyzed and reanalyzed while these controls are in effect.

At the beginning of this chapter, the criteria for causal inferences were briefly noted: covariation, time order (i.e., cause must precede effect in time), and control over alternative explanations. In any explanatory study, the statistical design begins with bivariate relationships that are statistically significant (i.e., the criterion of covariation is met). In these bivariate relationships, the designation of independent (predictor) and dependent (criterion) variables becomes important for explanatory studies. The predictor variables become the "cause" and the criterion variables the "effect" in explanatory statistical designs.

By logical reasoning, based on theory and/or previous research (e.g., frustration precedes and causes aggression) or on common sense (i.e., a respondent's sex precedes educational level), time order between variables is asserted. Time order is difficult to establish in cross-sectional survey research because all variables are normally measured at the same point in time. However, once the "cause" and "effect" are hypothesized, the statistical design in explanatory studies sets about the arduous task of eliminating alternative explanations for the observed bivariate relationship. If a test variable does, in fact, offer a better explanation for the bivariate relationship than would the hypothesized causal connection, then the *original relationship will change* when the test variable is held constant.

[10]Patricia L. Kendall and Paul F. Lazarsfeld, "Problems of Survey Analysis," in Robert K. Merton and Paul F. Lazarsfeld, eds., *Continuities in Social Research* (New York: Free Press, 1950).

The Elaboration Model

According to the elaboration model developed by Kendall and Lazarsfeld, there are three types of alternative explanations, each depending on (1) the time order relationship between the original variables in the analysis (*X* and *Y*) and the test variable (*T*) introduced as an alternative explanation fot the *XY* association, and (2) the impact of that test variable's introduction.

1. *Explanation:* If the test variable (*T*) precedes *XY* in time, is related to both *X* and *Y*, and the *XY* relationship is significantly reduced when *T* is held constant, the test variable is said to *explain* the original *XY* relationship. That is, the observed *XY* covariation exists only because that covariation is being produced by variations in *T*.

2. *Interpretation:* If the test variable (*T*) intervenes between *X* and *Y* in time, is related to both *X* and *Y*, and the *XY* relationship is significantly reduced when *T* is held constant, the test variable is said to *interpret* the original relationship. That is, the variation in *Y* is produced by *X*, but only when *T* is present as an intervening variable. The *XY* relationship is facilitated by *T*.

3. *Specification:* If the test variable (*T*) is related to *X* and *Y*, regardless of whether it precedes the *XY* relationship or intervenes between *X* and *Y* in time, and the *XY* relationship is significantly reduced *only* when *T* has a certain value, the third variable is said to *specify* the original *XY* relationship. That is, the variation in *Y* is produced by *X* only when *T* is present to a specified degree. The original *XY* relationship is true if and only if $T = c$, where c is a criterion specified in the analysis.

The general elaboration model can be expressed in the following formula:

$$XY = TX + TY + (xy{:}t_1) + (xy{:}t_2) + \cdots + (xy{:}t_n)$$

The *XY* relationship is the sum of the relationships between each variable and the test variable (*T*), plus the remaining (partial) *XY* relationships when *T* is held constant at any specific value.

When the variables in the explanatory study are conceptualized in categorical form, the statistical design for elaboration requires a series of bivariate contingency tables examining the relationship between *XY* when *T* is held constant. The analysis seeks to reproduce the strength of the original association when the variation in *T* is removed. In a hypothetical example using the elaboration model, suppose the research finds a strong relationship between respondent sex and major source of science information. Table 10–7 shows that men are more likely to use newspapers and magazines for their science information, while women rely more on television. This is the original *XY* relationship.

A review of previous research and other analyses using data from the same study also find a strong relationship between educational level (*T*) and media use (*TY*). Suppose the data also show that males, on the average, are better educated than females (*TX*). To draw appropriate conclusions about the validity of the original *XY* relationship, the contribution of education to media use should be established through

**Table 10-7 Major sources of science information for men and women.
(Hypothetical data)**

	Men (N = 462)	Women (N = 430)
(Y)	(X)	
Information source		
Newspapers and magazines	0.57	0.45
Television	0.43	0.55

the elaboration process. Since men are better educated and the better educated prefer print media, education offers a reasonable alternative explanation for the original XY relationship.

Elaboration proceeds at this point by prohibiting the covariation of education (T) with X or Y. Table 10-8 shows the partial XY relationships when education is held constant.

When education is held constant, differences in major source of information between men and women disappear. When respondents have a high school education or less, they prefer television. When educational level is higher, they prefer print. The original XY relationship is *spurious*. Education *interprets* the relationship between sex and preference for science information source. This is an example of interpretation, because educational level intervenes between a respondent's sex and media preferences. Male and female preferences for media sources are facilitated by educational level. It would be an example of explanation if the T variable had preceded X in time.

In a recent example of specification in the elaboration process, Dimmick investigated the relationship between family communication patterns and television program choice.[11] He asked adolescents in two age groups (twelve to fourteen and fifteen to seventeen) to identify their family's communication behavior using the FCP measures and their mode of conflict resolution when members of the family disagreed on the television program to be watched. Table 10-9 shows that the mode of conflict resolution in the four family types identified by the FCP was

**Table 10-8 Major sources of science information for men and women
at different educational levels. (Hypothetical data)**

	($XY:t_1$) High School or Less		($XY:t_2$) More than High School	
Information source	Men (N = 212)	Women (N = 267)	Men (N = 250)	Women (N = 163)
Papers and magazines	0.41	0.38	0.66	0.64
Television	0.59	0.62	0.34	0.36

[11]John Dimmick, "Family Communication and TV Program Choice," *Journalism Quarterly*, 53: 720–23 (Winter 1976).

Table 10–9 Family communication patterns and conflict resolution in disagreements about television program choice.

	Laissez-faire (N = 60)	Pluralistic (N = 59)	Protective (N = 50)	Consensual (N = 65)
Parent decides	0.43	0.22	0.50	0.40
No decision	0.12	0.10	0.10	0.08
Vote or compromise	0.45	0.68	0.40	0.52
	$\chi^2 = 14.26$, $df = 6$, $p < 0.05$			

Adapted from Dimmick, note 11, p. 722.

consistent with their emphasis on concept or socio-orientation.[12] The author states:

> More than two-thirds of the adolescents from pluralistic homes [high concept-orientation] report that voting or compromise-negotiation are the usual modes of arbitrating conflicts. Conversely, about two-thirds of the protective adolescents [high socio-orientation] reported that one of their parents . . . makes the program decisions or that no decision is made when the family disagrees.[13]

Conflict resolution in laissez-faire and consensual homes was similar.

At this point, Dimmick might have drawn the conclusion that the communication environment in the home influences the mode of resolving conflict over television program choices. However, earlier research had shown that socio-orientation was more common than concept orientation in homes of younger adolescents. The age of the adolescent, then, might present an alternative explanation for the relationship between communication environment and mode of conflict resolution. Dimmick analyzed the original XY relationship holding adolescent age constant (Table 10–10).

The elaborated analysis also permitted more refinement of the relationship between adolescent age and conflict resolution in different family types. In protective families, age of the adolescent made a difference in the mode of conflict resolution, with parent decision more common for younger than older adolescents. In pluralistic families, the relationship was reversed.

Again, the elaboration process shows that the original relationship is *spurious*. Adolescent age and family communication environment interact to produce the mode of conflict resolution. The elaboration *specifies* the conditions under which parental decision or compromise is most likely to occur.

[12]The FCP components are shown in Table 10–6. Concept orientation emphasizes self-expression and willingness to enter into controversy.
[13]Dimmick, "Family Communication," p. 723.

182

Table 10–10 Family communication patterns and methods of resolving conflict.

	Laissez-faire		Pluralistic		Protective		Consensual	
	12–14 years (N=27)	15–17 years (N=33)	12–14 years (N=22)	15–17 years (N=37)	12–14 years (N=29)	15–17 years (N=21)	12–14 years (N=36)	15–17 years (N=29)
Father or mother decides	50	38	19	24	55	42	41	38
No decision	12	12	5	14	14	6	5	12
Voting or compromise	38	50	76	62	31	52	54	50
	100%	100%	100%	100%	100%	100%	100%	100%

Note: Separate decisions by either parent and modes of compromise were combined in order to improve cell sizes for analysis.

Multiple Regression[14]

When variables in an explanatory study are conceptualized in continuous form, the original XY association is frequently expressed in terms of bivariate correlation (r).[15] The more general form of the relationship expressed by this measure of association is found in the linear equation

$$Y = bX + A$$

where Y is the dependent or criterion variable and X is the independent or predictor variable. The general linear equation permits the prediction of Y by the specification of the change in Y for each unit of change in X. The measure of rate of change is known as the regression coefficient (b). The remainder of the equation includes a constant, indicating the units of Y that must be added to place the predicted Y score accurately in relation to the average Y score.

The rate of change is a function of the degree of association between the XY variables, expressed by the formula

$$b_{yx} = r \frac{S_y}{S_x}$$

If the scores are expressed in deviation units, the standardized regression coefficient (B) is equivalent to the XY correlation (r) since $S_y = S_x = 1$. Also, when the scores are expressed in deviation units, the constant is eliminated, since the average deviation score for y then becomes zero.

When theory or prior research establishes the roles of several variables in the prediction of a criterion, the bivariate correlation between a single predictor and the criterion is no longer sufficient. The logic of the elaboration model requires specification of the contribution to variation in Y by X_1 and all other Xs that provide alternate explanations to a simple XY relationship. These additional Xs may be thought of as test variables, each of whose influences on Y may be assessed simultaneously using an expanded form of the general linear equation. Each X has its own rate of change, and that rate of change is independent of the contribution to Y made by any other X. In standard score form, the equation would be written

$$y = B_1 x_1 + B_2 x_2 + B_3 x_3 + \cdots + B_n x_n$$

[14]Multiple regression extends the formula for the bivariate Pearsonian product moment correlation coefficient ($Y = bX + A$) to include the simultaneous consideration of more than one predictor variable (X) in the computation of a criterion variable (Y). Multiple regression is frequently used in explanatory statistical designs in communication research. While it is not discussed in Chapter 4, its logic and assumptions may be learned from any introduction to statistics. And see note 17.

[15]Regression analyses do use variables in categorical form or dummy variables created from a series of discrete states. However, predictor variables in categorical form are less desirable than continuous variables because their contribution to variation in the criterion variable is almost always underestimated.

where each B is equivalent to the relationship between any XY, holding all other Xs constant. These *partial* regression coefficients are akin to the partial relationship of categorical variables when the test variable is held constant. The relative size of the partial regression coefficient is a significant indicator of the independent contribution of any X to Y.[16] The cumulative relationship between all Xs and the criterion Y is the multiple correlation coefficient R, which may be interpreted in precisely the same ways as the bivariate correlation r (see Chapter 4 for a discussion of r).[17]

In presenting this information, the researcher simultaneously investigates the importance of all X variables in accounting for variation in Y.[18] The multiple correlation coefficient represents the maximum correlation possible between the dependent variable (Y) and the linear combination of all independent variables (Xs). The minimal requirements of a statistical design that uses multiple regression include computation of the multiple correlation coefficient and either partial regression or partial correlation coefficients.

In two tests of media gratifications, Becker[19] entered several types of gratifications and avoidances into multiple regression equations, along with general public affairs variables that are common correlates of public affairs knowledge. In Becker's study, attention to Watergate hearings and perceptions of White House involvement were the dependent variables. Attention to the hearings was also an independent variable in the prediction of perceptions about presidential involvement. Table 10–11 reports separate regressions for young and old voters.

The multiple correlation for each dependent variable ranged from 0.25 to 0.50, using only the public affairs variables (Becker termed these "controls"). None of the gratifications and avoidances added significantly to the regression equation for young voters. The largest con-

---

[16]Partial correlation coefficients may also be computed in the multiple regression analysis. They represent the $X_n Y$ correlation when the influence of all other Xs is removed from *both* X_n and Y. Their interpretation differs from that of the partial regression coefficient in that they represent the association with the *remainder* of Y when all other associations have been removed.

[17]See Jacob Cohen and Patricia Cohen, *Applied Multiple Regression/Correlation Analysis for the Behavioral Sciences* (New York: John Wiley & Sons, Inc., 1970).

[18]The inclusion of large numbers of variables as predictors has both advantages and limitations, however. The presence of a fixed relationship between independent variables in multiple regression is called multicollinearity. When X_1 and X_2 are collinear, their simple correlation will be high (≥ 0.80) and X_2 will be superfluous when X_1 is in the regression equation. One recommended solution is to exclude the second independent variable from the equation: there is no effect on the prediction of Y and no change in regression coefficients associated with other variables. However, it is then impossible to isolate the separate influences of X_1 and X_2 on Y. The selection of which variables are to be included in a regression equation is a major problem in behavioral science. Where theory and previous research provide no guidance, the selection decision often becomes one of trial and error.

[19]Lee B. Becker, "Two Tests of Media Gratifications: Watergate and the 1974 Election," *Journalism Quarterly*, 53: 28–33, 87 (Spring 1976).

Table 10–11 Multiple correlation coefficients for variable blocks and standardized regression coefficients for individual predictor items: 1973 senate hearings study (Madison).

Dependent Variables	Controls					Gratifications					Avoidances		
	R	Party Affiliation	Public Affairs TV	Attention-hearings	R	Surveillance	Vote Guidance	Anticipated com.	Excitement	Reinforcement	Alienation	Partisanship	Relaxation
Young voters (n = 158)													
Attention to hearings	0.28[a]	0.21	0.13	—	0.37	0.08	−0.14	0.11	−0.04	0.00	−0.04	0.09	−0.08
White House involvement	0.47[a]	0.36	0.17	0.12	0.49	−0.05	−0.03	0.05	0.06	−0.02	0.00	0.07	−0.07
Older Voters (n = 125)													
Attention to hearings	0.25[a]	0.19	−0.11	—	0.43[a]	0.18	−0.02	−0.01	0.04	0.05	−0.03	0.13	−0.17
White House involvement	0.50[a]	0.44	−0.02	0.05	0.54	−0.10	0.14	0.00	0.12	0.04	0.02	0.02	−0.06

[a]Variables listed in this block make a significant contribution ($p < 0.05$); for the Gratifications and Avoidances multiple R, the test is for variance explained by that block controlling for variance explained by the Controls block. Entries for the individual control items and gratifications and avoidances are standardized regression coefficients for the final equation. The multiple R for the Gratifications and Avoidances block represents the final coefficient for the equation.

tributions were made by the vote guidance gratification for young voters. In fact, the greater the attention to the hearings, the smaller the vote guidance gratification. For older voters, the gratifications and avoidances nearly doubled the size of the multiple correlation coefficient for attention to the hearings. Surveillance and relaxation were the most important contributors to the variance in attention. No significant change was made in the multiple correlation for perceptions of White House involvement when gratifications were added to the regression equation.

Path Analysis

In multiple regression, the standardized regression coefficient is interpreted as the independent contribution of any X to variation in Y.[20] In research designs where the time order of the Xs can be established or inferred from theory or previous research, the appropriate statistical design uses path analysis. Path analysis requires the specification of independent and dependent variables, and is normally represented graphically by the presence of arrows denoting the direction of variable association and the strength of that association through the standardized regression coefficient (known in this procedure as the *path* coefficient). The research design specifies the causal path traveled by the dependent variable. The cumulative contribution of the squared path coefficients is the amount of variance attributable to the independent variables in a regression equation.

Previous discussion has indicated that the multiple correlation resulting from all independent variables included in a regression equation is the maximum linear correlation *possible* using those variables. However, path analysis seeks the explanation of 100 percent variance. Therefore, variables are arbitrarily added to the path diagram, representing the unexplained or residual variance after all the independent variables have been included in the equation. The combined contributions of variables included in the equation and residual (unknown) variables explain *all the variance* in the dependent variable. It is important to remember that the path coefficient for each variable represents the independent contribution of that variable with all preceding variables in the path held constant.

The final path diagram may include only a few of all the independent variables originally considered in the path analysis. Other variables may have been found to be inconsequential in tracing the path of the dependent variable through its hypothesized development.

In a recent use of path analysis, Bowes investigated the relationship of stereotyping and communication accuracy.[21] The positive and negative (polarization) dimensions of stereotyping, contact, and discussion

[20]The standardized regression coefficient is a *partial* regression coefficient, or the independent contribution of any X to Y, holding all other Xs constant. See note 16.

[21]John E. Bowes, "Stereotyping and Communication Accuracy," *Journalism Quarterly*, 54: 70–76 (Spring 1977).

with community agencies were related to familiarity with agency programs and accuracy of perceptions about regional development priorities. Data were collected in surveys of the general public, community leaders, and agency representatives. Figure 10–1 shows the path coefficients for significant variables in the analysis for leaders. The results showed that both general contact and discussion with agencies increased familiarity, but that general contact was negatively related to accuracy through the development of polarization.

Other Multivariate Techniques

An enormous variety of computer-based regression programs provides important options for the inclusion of variables in a multiple regression equation, depending on the purpose of the study.[22] In addition, techniques that assess the relationship between two or more linear combinations of variables (e.g., canonical correlation) are currently available to the researcher who has a large number of variables to include in analyses. Canonical correlation permits the development of a superconstruct, a canonical variate, by the weighted linear addition of component variables. A variate called SES, for example, might result from the appropriate linear combination of sex, education, occupation, income, and length of current residence. This variate might be correlated with another, called MEDIAUSE, which is the weighted combination of television hours, magazine subscriptions, daily newspaper

Figure 10–1 Path Coefficients among Information Sources, Stereotyping, Accuracy and Familarity for Community Leaders. Nonsignificant Paths Have Been Deleted ($n = 30$).

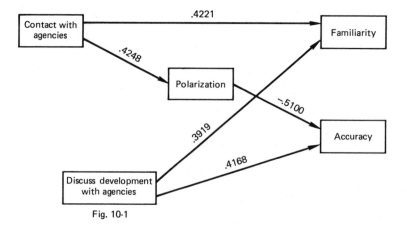

Fig. 10-1

[22]See Norman H. Nie and others, *Statistical Package for the Social Sciences*, for a discussion of the differences between standard and hierarchical inclusion.

reading, and books read per month. Canonical correlation combines data reduction strategies with techniques of statistical association.[23]

Finally, multivariate analysis techniques represent the epitome of simultaneous variable analyses. Combinations of independent variables and their interactions are used to explain differences in combinations of dependent variables and their interactions. Some foundation in matrix algebra is helpful for the development of a statistical design using these powerful statistical tools.[24]

The major difficulty with multivariate statistical techniques is always their interpretation. A significant association between the two canonical variates defined earlier, for instance, means that SES and MEDIAUSE covary in predictable ways. But it is obvious that these are "sets" of variables, and not all components in each set have equal strength within the set nor equal power of association across sets. The researcher is left with the knotty problem of trying to unravel both intraset and interset correlations. While modern statistical techniques and computer-based statistical packages provide enormously powerful analytic tools and save inestimable hours of computation drudgery, their application in a statistical design for survey research should be made with extreme care. Greater planning and foresight are required here than in analyses using only a few variables. There is danger that the statistical tail will de facto wag the theoretical dog.

Summary

In explanatory designs, the ultimate objective is to explain variation in the dependent variable. The establishment of a causal link is the sine qua non of this type of survey research. All the procedures described in the preceding pages are intended to reach the goal of explanation by removing alternative explanations for the hypothesized "true" relationship. The elaboration model presents the basic logic. The varying statistical techniques implement that logic by capitalizing on the different amounts of statistical power available when variables are conceptualized at different levels of measurement.

The researcher who begins with a priori hypotheses and proceeds to analyses that appear to establish causal relationships between variables in cross-sectional studies (data collected at a single point in time) remains at an interpretive disadvantage, even though the most sophisticated analysis techniques are at his or her disposal. There is no substitute for longitudinal survey data in causal arguments. Longitudinal studies offer the best opportunity to fulfill all the conditions for causal relations—covariation, time order, and control over alternative expla-

[23]For a discussion of canonical correlation, see Raymond B. Tucker and Lawrence J. Chase, "Canonical Correlation in Human Communication Research," *Human Communication Research*, 3: 86–96 (Fall 1976).

[24]For a comprehensive review of multivariate analysis texts, see Peter Monge and Patrick Day, "Multivariate Analysis in Communication Research," *Human Communication Research*, 2: 207–20 (Winter 1976).

nations. The application of statistical techniques suggested by the elaboration model to time-ordered data offer maximum analytical return for the extra effort and cost involved in the collection of longitudinal data.

LONGITUDINAL STUDIES

In survey research, the establishment of causal links between variables is usually very difficult. Even if the criteria of covariation and control over alternative explanations have been met, there is still a problem in the establishment of time order between hypothesized "cause" and "effect" when all data are collected at one point in time. The research design that can help to meet this remaining criterion in the causal argument is known as a longitudinal or panel study in which variables are measured on the same sample at a minimum of two points in time.[25] This minimum design parallels the pretest-posttest logic in laboratory experiments discussed in Chapter 11, but seldom includes a control group. Therefore, features of the statistical design are substituted in the longitudinal study for experimental design features that serve to rule out alternative explanations for the observed relationship.

Longitudinal research designs are used infrequently because they are extremely expensive, largely because respondents have an annoying mobility, and the researcher is forced to become a detective to assure the continuity of the sample. They also suffer from statistical problems, including regression toward the mean (or the tendency of extreme scores to "regress" toward the population mean with repeated measures) and multicollinearity (the indeterminate overlap in variables related to human characteristics). Statistical regression poses unique interpretation problems in longitudinal data because observed changes in variables over time may be artifactual, rather than real, due simply to the fact they have been measured more than once. There are few design measures that the survey researcher can introduce to prevent these problems, but awareness of their existence can lead to their consideration as alternative explanations for research results. Once these alternatives have been examined carefully by logical reasoning or statistical procedures, confidence in the "truth" of the observed relationships can be increased.

All the statistical design procedures appropriate to cross-sectional studies are equally appropriate to the longitudinal study. The statistical design must consider the representative characteristics of the sample, the marginal distributions, and the bivariate and multivariate relations of variables. The longitudinal study adds a time dimension to these sta-

---

[25]The panel study is to be distinguished here from the study of cohorts, or random samples from the same population at two points in time. Cohort studies, while superior to cross-sectional studies by virtue of their time-ordered data, do not present the same analysis advantages as panel data. Alternative explanations for observed relations between variables are better controlled in panel designs than in those employing cohorts.

tistical procedures that is absent from other types of survey research. With the same variables measured at two or more points in time, marginals-to-multivariate relationships are computable with respect to time and can serve both descriptive and explanatory objectives in the study. Moreover, in multiple regression or path analyses, the definite time order of variables serves to guide the order of variable inclusion in the regression equation and the direction of the links between variables in the path diagram.

A common statistical procedure found in the analysis of longitudinal data is cross-lagged correlation. In this procedure, the variables whose causal relationship is hypothesized are both measured at two points in time. If X is presumed to "cause" Y, then the relationship between X at $time_1$ and Y at $time_2$ (X_1Y_2) must be stronger than the reverse order (Y_1X_2).[26] If the X_1Y_2 relationship is significantly greater than Y_1X_2, the researcher has produced some empirical support for the direction of the causal link between X and Y.

Using cross-lagged correlation techniques, Atkin, Galloway, and Nayman[27] studied the relationship between news media exposure, political knowledge, and campaign interest. Students from two universities completed two questionnaires five weeks and one day before the 1972 presidential election. Four indexes of mass media exposure were constructed, and respondents were asked to specify their exposure to national and local political content. Data were also collected to indicate respondents' political knowledge and interest.

Figure 10–2 illustrates the relationships to be tested.[28] Using the procedure described, the relationship of interest was f (or X_1Y_2 in the notation of this chapter).

The Michigan results in Table 10–12 indicate a causal relationship between media exposure and political knowledge and political interest.[29] The results from Colorado indicate that knowledge and interest appear to precede exposure. The authors comment:

> In sum, the data presented here suggest that exposure, knowledge and interest are causally related. The results give limited support for the occurrence of two important cognitive outcomes of exposure that effects-oriented perspectives have not adequately examined. The investigation also demonstrates the potential utility of the panel design for detecting causality in analyses of political data.[30]

[26]The relative size of these partial relationships is assessed using the relationship between XY at $time_1$ and $time_2$ (i.e., the reliability of the measures themselves, X_1X_2 and Y_1Y_2, and their covariation at the same point in time, X_1Y_1 and X_2Y_2) as the estimate of the normal variation in this relationship. See Richard Rozelle and Donald Campbell, "More Plausible Rival Hypotheses in the Cross-Lagged Panel Correlation Technique," *Psychological Bulletin*, 71: 74–80 (1969).

[27]Charles K. Atkin, John Galloway, and Oguz Nayman, "News Media Exposure, Political Knowledge and Campaign Interest," *Journalism Quarterly*, 53: 231–37 (Summer 1976).

[28]Ibid., p. 234.

[29]Ibid., p. 235.

[30]Ibid., p. 237.

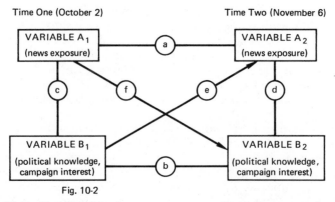

Time One (October 2)   Time Two (November 6)

Fig. 10-2

Figure 10–2   Relationship between news media exposure and political knowledge.

While the consistency of direction in the causal link between media exposure and political variables is unclear from these data, the longitudinal design provides considerably more information than its cross-sectional version would allow. The panel data permit the authors' interpretation that the three variables may operate in a causal spiral: exposure, to knowledge, to interest, to exposure, and so on. The point at which the spiral is entered, then, becomes important. Lacking empirical support from the cross-lagged correlation analyses, any such interpretation from correlations between variables at the same point in time would be sheer speculation.

Summary

The value of a longitudinal design lies in the presentation of data whose statistical procedures can provide appropriate empirical evi-

Table 10–12   Correlations between mass media exposure, political knowledge, and political interest.

	Knowledge			Interest		
	Exposur Knowled	Knowledge-Exposure		Exposure-Interest	Interest-Exposure	
			Base-line[a]			Base-line[a]
	(f)	(e)		(f)	(e)	
Michigan sample (N = 148)						
Overall exposure	0.33	0.27	0.24	0.29	0.26	0.23
National content	0.29	0.26	0.20	0.24	0.24	0.22
Local content	0.26	0.20	0.18	0.28	0.24	0.20
Colorado sample (N = 171)						
Overall exposure	0.18	0.28	0.19	0.21	0.31	0.23
National content	0.16	0.27	0.15	0.22	0.31	0.21
Local content	0.14	0.23	0.15	0.14	0.27	0.18

[a]For an explanation of the baseline, see footnote 26.

192

dence to establish causal relationships. While the cost of these designs is frequently prohibitive, their statistical advantages are many. All the statistical techniques available to cross-sectional designs are available to the longitudinal study. Time order in variables is also present. Whether the statistical design proceeds with cross-lagged correlation in a conventional bivariate analysis or a path diagram in multivariate analysis is left to the discretion of the researcher as she or he considers the research questions to be answered. In either case, the statistical design in a longitudinal study provides the best survey-based approximation to the controls of the experimental laboratory in fulfilling the criteria for causal inferences.

CONCLUSIONS

Intuition and energy applied to the development of statistical designs for survey research can yield handsome results. The examples provided in this chapter have demonstrated a variety of approaches to the analysis of survey data. The statistical designs have ranged from the minimal presentation of frequency distributions for categorical variables to the presentation of complex relations between variables indicated by path coefficients in a multivariate analysis. Each statistical design should be selected by the researcher because it is appropriate for the research question(s) to be answered by the collection of survey data. Each statistical design is limited by the measurement level of the variables involved. Strategically, however, each study can only follow the analytical procedure as far down the statistical road as the sophistication of the variables permits, a point also emphasized by Stamm in Chapter 9. In any study, the research question(s) and the level of measurement set the parameters of the statistical design.

Figure 10–3 shows the variety of analyses possible for descriptive and explanatory studies. As indicated earlier in this chapter, the researcher alone can make the distinction between the descriptive and explanatory research design. Except in the case where the causal relations between variables are clearly being explored (i.e., cross-lagged correlations or path analysis), the analysis procedures and statistical techniques are exactly the same for both types of study. It is just as meaningful to talk about statistical significance in a descriptive study as it is in the explanatory research mode. In the development of theory, descriptive studies should lead to explanatory research, but the statistics are oblivious to any difference in the theoretical underpinnings for the variables being analyzed.

On the other hand, an explanatory inquiry is obliged to present evidence of the degree to which a relationship between two or more variables can be expected by chance. An explanatory study is also obliged to present a statistical design that can rule out alternative explanations for a bivariate relationship or specify the contribution of multiple predictors in the variation of a criterion. A descriptive study *may* use sta-

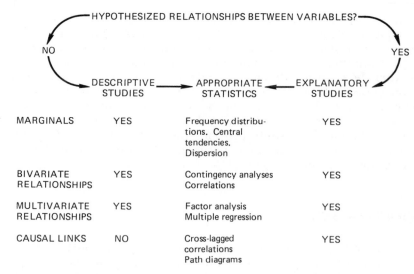

Fig. 10-3

Figure 10–3 Hypothesized relationships between variables.

tistical tools to describe "what is" and how often it might occur. The explanatory study *must* use statistical tools to help in the decision of "what must be" for the data to support any causal inferences.

The research question dictates the rigor of the accompanying statistical design. The level of measurement for each variable dictates the sensitivity of the information provided by the statistics employed. The researcher has important choices to make before the data are even collected. The importance of these decisions is often not recognized until it is too late.

To avoid some of the problems associated with the absence of statistical anticipation, the following steps are suggested:

1. *Plan the statistical design backward.* Once the research question is determined, establish the amount and type of evidence necessary to provide its answer. The answer criteria govern the statistical design.

2. *Use the most sensitive measures available for your variables.* This usually requires conceptualization at the interval level of measurement. The most powerful statistics are available when the data are in continuous form. Protect your statistical options. You can always "collapse" your variables to a lesser measurement level, if analyses require it, but you can never "expand" categorical variables into continua.

3. *If you are in doubt about the role of a variable in your survey design* (e.g., you consider a variable to have little explanatory power, but there are no guidelines from previous research), *measure it.* You can't lose. If it is not available as a component in your statistical treatment, it will always possess mysterious status as an alternative explanation for your results. If

you include the variable in your design, you can always exclude it from later analysis, but that exclusion will be based on empirical criteria, not on oversight.

4. *Be patient.* A good design requires long hours of concentrated preparation. The objective of this planning is the avoidance of fatal errors after the data have been collected.

The Controlled Experiment

Bruce H. Westley

The controlled experiment is, when carried out properly, probably the most powerful method of seeking answers to research questions available to the behavioral scientist. The simplest answer to the question "why?" is this: that the controlled experiment is our best—and very nearly only—way of finding out what causes what. As Weaver points out in Chapter 4, correlations permit causal inferences only under very special circumstances. Wade describes these conditions in Chapter 10.

One might wonder, however, how productive the method could be in a field in which media audiences are dispersed and only the generation of messages is centralized. But mass communication questions can be reduced to the requirements of the controlled experiment, and when that is not possible can be amenable to a sort of quasi-experiment that utilizes survey research in data gathering. The logic and requirements of the controlled experiment are discussed first. Quasi- and partial experiments are discussed later in this chapter.

As an example of a controlled experiment, an early one by Percy Tannenbaum will serve. As we have seen at various points in this book, nothing can happen until a question presents itself; in this case the question was "Do newspaper headlines have an effect upon the way newspaper readers perceive the story, even after reading the story? The question actually arose in a real-life setting, the copy desk of a newspaper on which the experimenter once worked. There he had noted that newspapers carrying identical wire service stories often topped them with very different headlines, so much so as to make them appear to be based on different facts.

Turning to the then sparse literature on headline effects, Tannenbaum found only three items, none of which shed much light on the question. Only one reported a controlled experiment on headline effects, and it did not deal with the relationship between headline reading and story reading.

So Tannenbaum devised two hypotheses, essentially based on newsroom wisdom, rather than more esoteric theory. They were "(1) Different headlines, presented with the same copy material, have different effects—that is they give rise to different impressions; (2) this effect of the headline is in reverse proportion to the extent to which [the story] is read." He proceeded ingeniously to "plant" differing versions of two student newspaper front-page stories. Three headlines were given to each of the test stories. In the case of a report of a murder trial, one headline suggested guilt, one suggested innocence, and one was meant to be neutral. In the other story, about various ways of accelerating college programs, one of three viewpoints was emphasized in the headlines. Both stories were fictitious.

Subject college students were assigned to treatments randomly and were instructed to read these front pages as they ordinarily would. The rationale given was a study of newspaper reading behavior of college students. Subjects were then given a readership test and, in the case of the trial story, a question about their impressions of guilt or innocence. The results showed that those who received the "guilty" headline tended to believe the accused was guilty; those who read the "innocent" headline tended to believe he was innocent. The neutral headline readers tended to give "no opinion" and fell neatly between the other groups in voting for guilt and innocence. (Still, "no opinion" was the most favored reply in all groups.) Significant differences were not obtained for the other story, although the results were in the predicted direction. A further test was run on the relationship between extent of reading and evidence of being influenced by the headline. For both stories these relationships were as predicted, and significantly so. Implications for the practice of journalism were discussed at length.[1]

While it is easy to fault this modest experiment, most elements of the controlled experiment are present. By taking measures immediately after the "manipulation" (reading differing versions of the front pages) and by randomly assigning students to "treatments" (headline versions), it was possible to say that the headline variations must have caused the response differences. But what makes this a "controlled" experiment? There were no "control groups." These matters will be

[1]See "The Effect of Headlines on the Interpretation of News Stories," *Journalism Quarterly*, 30: 189–97 (Spring 1953).

discussed more fully here and in a later chapter. But in this case the controls were statistical: random assignment to treatments. Additionally, the investigator controlled the environment within which the test was carried out, controlled the manipulation, and controlled the testing instrument. The control group is only one means of introducing sufficient structure into an experiment to assure that the hypothesis has an adequate test. The result was that the variance attributable to the relationship predicted (in one case of two) was sufficient to overcome the variance not attributable to the predicted relationship. The chi square test used in this case answers that question, although it must be said there are more powerful tests to the same purpose. We will return to the question of "accounting for variance."

We note in passing that this is an *after-only* design. That is, no measures were taken before the manipulation as a basis for comparison with the measures taken after the manipulation. As we shall see, there are problems with after-only designs. The short answer in this case is that there was no reason to expect anything but random variation in the answers to the same questions that might be given beforehand. (Therein lay the benefit of using entirely fictitious materials.) Besides, these questions make sense only after the manipulation. If both of these things are true, there is no reason to devise a before-after design. But the real proof is that the experiment worked. Significant differences were found. Greater refinement was not needed, given the investigation's purposes. The hypotheses were strong enough for the variance accounted for by the prediction to overcome the error variance.

Tannenbaum's experiment was more or less a *laboratory* experiment. But we also make use of other, often somewhat less rigorous, experimental designs, including the *field experiment*. The difference may be crudely shown to be a matter of locus. That is, the laboratory experiment is carried out on the experimenter's own turf; the subjects come to the laboratory. In the field experiment, the experimenter goes to the subjects' turf. In general, the physical controls available in the laboratory are greater than those to be found in the field. For that reason, statistical controls are often substituted for physical controls in the field.

However, the chapter title refers to the "controlled" experiment and assumes that the quality of any experiment must be judged on whether the controls were adequate, not whether they were obtained in the laboratory. The nature and extent of such controls depend on the hypotheses being tested and the measures utilized. For example, in the elaborate series of experiments on type formats reported by Luckiesh and Moss,[2] the manipulations, for example, small differences in type size, line length, leading, capitalization, screening, type family, and the like, were so weak that great pains had to be taken to control all other

[2]Matthew Luckiesh and Frank K. Moss, *Reading as a Visual Task* (New York: Van Nostrand Reinhold Co., 1944).

sources of variation. Individual subjects were seated inside a sphere to assure perfect control over lighting, for example.

As an instance of a field experiment we might take a massive study such as Feshbach and Singer's *Television and Aggression,* described by the authors as "the first work of its kind to take laboratory procedures into the field."[3] These experimenters went to seven schools to obtain measures and observations on junior high school boys ranging from 18 to 31 per school for a total of 625 subjects, a subject pool that for change measures reduced to 395 after absentees and illegible questionnaires had been excluded. Instead of making seven replications of these experiments, ns were combined across schools and school categories. Given the wide variation to be expected in such a range of schools, a design that permitted school to be a variant in an analysis of variance design would be preferable. But with ns varying that much, it is probably impractical. Altogether this was a massive field experiment, but one that nevertheless produced rather consistent results.

To turn to a more modest example, Dorothy Douglas, a University of Wisconsin M.A. candidate, wanted to test the effects of a multimedia information campaign in a county seat in south-central Wisconsin. Previous studies tended to show that such campaigns were usually ineffectual, and this had been blamed largely on what were called "chronic know-nothings" who would not be reached by the media, no matter how massive the effort. Douglas's campaign concerned knowledge of and attitudes toward mental retardation. The social invention for which this information was later used as a support was the creation of a "sheltered workshop" to serve the community's retardants.

Since awareness of the problem was gradually increasing nationally, it was necessary to go beyond a before-after test in community A. Otherwise, how could the experimenter be sure that any change from time 1 to time 2 was not the result of a local diffusion of a national trend? So a second community was identified as a control after its characteristics were compared and found similar on a number of parameters. Then information tests were administered in both communities both before and after the campaign was mounted in community A. Attitude measures were taken in both communities at time 2 only. The initial surveys were carried out by means of the usual survey methods, except that only "face-sheet" data were obtained by interviewers. The questionnaire itself was left to be filled out and mailed. The second questionnaire was mailed to those who responded to the first. The manipulation consisted in using all media and interpersonal channels exclusive to the experimental community: news stories in the county paper, announcements and discussions over the local radio station, store window displays on the main business street, speakers before local service clubs, and the like. Television was deliberately omitted, because television channels serving the area were the same for both com-

[3]Seymour Feshbach and Robert D. Singer, *Television and Aggression: An Experimental Field Study* (San Francisco: Jossey-Bass, 1971).

munities. Nor did anything reach regional newspapers serving both communities. Thus was "contamination" avoided.

This design enabled the experimenter to chart the spread of knowledge and the development of attitudes in the community on the basis of an information campaign that, it turned out, reached nearly every respondent. The experimenter was able to identify differences in the part played by the direct impact of the media versus the reinforcement provided by interpersonal communication.[4]

Readers of Chapters 9 and 10 might ask how this research differs from the *panel* study, which also surveys the same subjects at two or more times. The difference lies in the manipulation. Panel studies are designed to identify trends. Whatever happens between survey 1 and survey 2 is eligible to be considered a "cause" of the differences observed, which is another way of saying that such a study can deal with cause only speculatively except where special conditions are met, as in "cross-lagged correlation" (see Chapter 10). When Tannenbaum and Greenberg[5] sought to test for the effects of the great debates between candidates Kennedy and Nixon, they did not entirely control the manipulation—the first debate, for example—but they knew the debate would take place. So they obtained attitude measures from a sample of voting age adults beforehand, exacted a pledge to view the first debate, and left with the respondent a package containing further measures to be filled out immediately after the debate. It was a before-after experiment without control group, not a panel study, and the intervention of a media event was what made the difference, just as, in the Douglas study, it was a many-sided information campaign that constituted the manipulation. These may not qualify as fully controlled experiments, but they do meet the criteria for a field experiment.

This introduction to the use of the controlled experiment to test mass communication hypotheses is intended only to prepare the reader for the much more complex issues raised in the rest of this chapter and in Chapter 12.

THE LOGIC OF THE CONTROLLED EXPERIMENT

The controlled experiment may be defined as a procedure for testing cause-and-effect relationships within a setting that permits maximum control over extraneous variation and allows the experimenter to observe the effect of one variable on another in such a way as to demonstrate that no other variable could have produced the same effect

---

[4]Consult Dorothy F. Douglas, Bruce H. Westley, and Steven H. Chaffee, "An Information Campaign That Changed Community Attitudes," *Journalism Quarterly*, 47: 479–81, 492 (Autumn 1970).

[5]Reported in Sidney Kraus, ed., *The Great Debates* (Bloomington: Indiana University Press, 1962).

(or to test for the joint effect of two variables on a third). It is probably the most sophisticated means of testing causal propositions, as we have said, and particularly suits efforts to conduct "pure" research, that is, research which puts theoretically grounded propositions to direct test. How such propositions are generated from theory and how measures stand for concepts are discussed at length in Chapters 3 and 5.

As defined, the controlled experiment is a procedure or set of procedures structured in various ways to meet the requirements of a direct test of a hypothesis by observing the effect of one variable on another under controlled conditions. While the meaning of a "variable" is treated in earlier chapters, it is appropriate to remind ourselves that *variation* in *attributes* is what experimenters need if they are to test their propositions quantitatively. A concept in a theory becomes a construct in the testing process, and a construct must lend itself to measurement. A measured construct is what we mean by a variable. Behind the variable stands a hypothetical attribute. "Information seeker" is an attribute of a person. But information seeking cannot be observed directly. We must devise an instrument to measure it. But the point here is that operations are required to place the attribute on a continuum. We have to be sure that the attribute in fact *varies* (among human subjects). Thus with two *variables* we can test the effect of one on another by either varying one deliberately and observing its effect on the other or by measuring it before and after some manipulation.

"Manipulation" may sound chiropractic, but actually it is a crucial feature of the controlled experiment. The simplest way to show the effect of one variable on another is to measure an attribute at time 1, then inject a manipulation, and then measure the same attribute at time 2. As we shall see, it usually is not that simple; but for purposes of illustration, let us imagine testing the proposition that the more a persuasive communication arouses fear the less effective it will be persuasively. The manipulation in this case is the fear content of the message. Persuasion is measured by a set of attitudes *toward something*. In this case, let us imagine it is belief that speed is the principal cause of death on the highway.

Thus we assign subjects to treatments randomly, and in the treatments all receive the same message except that in one treatment a high fear message is added, in a second a medium level of fear is injected, and in a third a low fear level. Ideally, the experimenter should make the verbal message identical in all treatments and inject fear in another way, for example, visually only. But the point is that the fear induction is the manipulation, not the persuasive message that is constant in all treatments.

INFERRING CAUSE

What is there about an experiment that permits us to infer a causal connection between independent and dependent variables (that the independent variable caused the dependent variable to appear or change)? Common sense would suggest that we search for a single cause for each single event, and when we find it, we can say A causes B. But scientific endeavor does not assume single causes. Indeed, it searches for the *conditions* under which a particular phenomenon may be expected to occur. We say "may be expected" deliberately; at least in the behavioral sciences we demonstrate the *probability* that a phenomenon will occur when its conditions are present. We search for invariances in behavior, but what we find are never certainties. Our invariances are demonstrated in probability terms. When a set of conditions consistently (i.e., with a high degree of probability) produces the predicted results, we show that such a relationship, while not invariant, could not have been accounted for by chance. The best predictors are the ones that account for more variance in the dependent variable than any other set of predictors.

Rather than dealing with what causes what, then, we search for relative invariances in our data. Rather than seeking causes we search for *necessary* and *sufficient conditions*. If B can occur only in the presence of A, A is a necessary condition of B. If B occurs *whenever* A is present, A is both a necessary and a sufficient condition of B. At the very least, it is necessary to show (1) *concomitant variation* and (2) *precedence* to demonstrate causality. Concomitant variation means that B varies consistently with A. That is what correlation demonstrates. But in showing concomitant variation, we are only showing that two variables vary together. We need something more to tell whether a change in A *precedes* a change in B. So, when A and B vary together, and A precedes B in time (and the reverse is not also true), we have a basis for saying that A is causally related to B. Then, if we can be sure that A and only A produces B, we may say that B is a function of A. We are almost never in the happy position of saying that A is the sole cause of B.

The experiment, then, is advantageous for discovering causal relationships because the experiment permits control over the order of events. (Cross-lagged correlation permits causal inference because it, too, gives investigators control over time. However, they do not control the order of events; instead they make use of the existing order of events.)

But in demonstrating *a* causal relationship, we have not shown that A is *the* cause of B. Other variables that share concomitant variation with B when they precede B in time may also be shown to be causally related. The game becomes one of either showing that other explanations are spurious, for example that C's apparent causal relationship to B arises out of its correlation with A, or it may take the form of seeking out the *set* of conditions that most consistently produces change in B. If both A and C predict B and the two together predict B better than either alone, we have a basis for a finding of multiple causality. The game is played on the basis of what combination of conditions most consistently predicts the dependent variable. The combination that most parsimoniously accounts for variation in the dependent variable may be treated as the causal conditions of B (until some still more effective predictor is discovered).

But just as we may search for multiple causes in the experimental setting, the experiment permits us to control for extraneous or spurious variables. Control ideally means control over all other possible explanations. A well-designed experiment allows us to show that a set of conditions accounts for a large amount of the variance in the dependent variable and that no other causal agents could have accounted for that variance. In the sample survey we may be able to show that one variable is more strongly correlated with a second than are other variables in the survey. We may apply multiple regression, partial correlations, and other sophisticated multivariate techniques, but since all these variables are occurring together, we have no basis for inferring cause unless, in some fashion, we can show (or assume) that one preceded the other in time.

The laboratory experiment must be devised in a way to ensure that nothing but the independent variable or variables or an interaction between them could account for the behavior of the dependent variable, and partial and quasi-experiments may properly be called experiments only when they, too, meet these conditions. Campbell and Stanley call the former "internal" validity (internal to the design) and the latter "external" validity. (They found no designs that satisfy all questions of external validity.)[6]

To return to our example of the effects of fear on persuasion, so far we have described an after-only design (see Figure 11–1). But this design is rather obviously insufficient. How do we control for differences among subjects in prior attitudes? We have done so only by random assignment to treatments. If our manipulation is strong, our message persuasive, and our attitude measure reliable, we may be able to show a difference. But we do not know without before and after measures whether the message induced attitude change in the predicted direction, and we do not know whether the fear induction "took," that is, that it actually did create a degree of fear arousal. (If we also do not

Figure 11–1 Posttest-only design.

	Time 1 Induction	Time 2 Measure
Group 1	High-fear message	Attitudes 1
Group 2	Low-fear message	Attitudes 1

[6]See Donald T. Campbell and Julian C. Stanley, *Experimental and Quasi-Experimental Designs for Research* (Chicago: Rand McNally & Co., 1963), originally a chapter in N. L. Gage, ed., *Handbook of Research on Teaching* (Chicago: Rand McNally & Co., 1962), "the bible" of experimental research for years. A more recent version is Eugene J. Webb and Donald T. Campbell, "Experiments on Communication Effects," in Ithiel de Sola Pool and others, eds., *Handbook of Communication* (Chicago: Rand McNally & Co., 1973).

know whether our attitude measure is reliable and valid, it is time to start over, as previous chapters have emphasized.)

However, we may take certain additional steps. First, we can add a control group, which might watch a film unrelated (and it should be demonstrably unrelated) to the subject matter of the attitude test. This will tell us whether there was anything in the laboratory situation that the experimenter did not have under control that could have produced the effect we want to link to the manipulation alone. "Seeing a film," rather than the content of the particular film, might be producing the effect.

This leads us to a more nearly complete experimental design, which may be diagrammed as in Figure 11–2. This may be called a pretest-posttest or before-after design. With a separate test of the "take" of the fear induction, it would be even more elaborate; see Figure 11–3.

We still do not have a control group. Why should we? If the design allows us to see that there are no significant differences in the critical attitudes at time 1, that the three experimental groups experienced the fear induction as predicted (the high-fear message produced the strongest evidence of fear and the low-fear message the weakest), then what is the need for a control group? In effect, the three treatment groups are serving as controls on each other. This would be even more apparent if we had conceived the experiment differently: that our hypotheses allowed us to think not in terms of *how much* fear was induced but whether a fear manipulation was introduced at all. If our hypotheses required us to think in terms of the *amount* of fear induced by the message, then the three-group experiment would be essential. It would allow us to obtain the result that the highest fear condition produced the least attitude change and the least fear the greatest attitude change (the actual prediction in this hypothetical study, and in one very much like it carried out by Janis and Feshbach[7]). But if our prediction could be that the presence of fear nullified attitude change, then we could use the simpler design, and the no-fear treatment group would be the control.

However, there is another reason for introducing control groups in a before-after design. It relates to the question of possible unintended effects of the "before" measure itself. One advantage of after-only designs is that they eliminate the possibility that the preinduction mea-

Figure 11–2 Pretest-posttest design.

	Time 1 Pretest Measure	Time 2 Induction	Time 3 Posttest Measure
Group 1	Attitudes 1	High-fear message	Attitudes 2
Group 2	Attitudes 1	Medium-fear message	Attitudes 2
Group 3	Attitudes 1	Low-fear message	Attitudes 2

[7]Irving L. Janis and Seymour Feshbach, "Effects of Fear-Arousing Communications," *Journal of Abnormal and Social Psychology*, 48: 78–92 (1953).

sure may have an undesirable effect on the postinduction measure, especially when they are measuring the same thing to get a direct change measure, such as attitude change. Every experience may be presumed to have an effect. A potential effect of a base-line measure of attitude change is that the items that constitute the measure have a teaching effect. When the repeat measure is taken, we have no way of knowing whether the difference it shows results from having been exposed to the same items before or are a consequence of the content of the message. When we are testing for learning effects, such as "information gain," we are particularly subject to an inflation due to the first application of the same measure. But it may not be a learning effect; it could be a *sensitization* effect. The first application of the measure sensitizes subjects to what to look for in the persuasive message, for example.

There are some "practical" solutions, but they often are self-defeating. One is to allow a lot of time to pass between the before test and the manipulation and posttest, counting on memory loss. But the sensitization effect usually leads to *selective*, not random, memory loss. Another is to embed the pretest questions in another instrument in the hope that the connection between these items and those in the posttest will not be perceived. This can be helpful in reducing sensitization effects, but is fairly ineffective against test learning. Of course, many standardized tests offer equivalent forms with no items in common. But such tests are more often used to get a fix on stable attributes of individuals for use in stratification, for example, and are rarely useful as effects measures. We mostly devise our own effects measures and rarely go to the trouble of constructing equivalent forms of demonstrated reliablity.

A much more common solution to this problem is use of a control group to test for the effects on subjects of the pretest measure. And if more than one measure is introduced in advance of the posttest measure, two such groups may be indicated. For example, see Figure 11–4. (In this example and the next, we are acknowledging that there would be need for only two separate contacts with subjects, depicted as time 1 and time 2.)

What we are seeing is two tests of unintended measurement effects. Control 1 gives us the effect of the initial attitude measure on the second attitude measure. Control 2 gives us the influence of the measure testing the induction effect on the posttest measure. (Another version

Figure 11–3 Pretest-posttest design with induction test.

	Time 1 Pretest Measure	Time 2 Induction	Time 3 Induction Test	Time 4 Posttest Measure
Group 1	Attitude 1	High-fear message	Effect 1	Attitude 2
Group 2	Attitude 1	Medium-fear message	Effect 1	Attitude 2
Group 3	Attitude 1	Low-fear message	Effect 1	Attitude 2

would have both control groups take the pretest measure but only one of them the induction-effect measure, revealing in one case the effect of the pretest measure and in the other the combined effects of the two measures.)

More sophisticated readers will recognize that the preceding discussion raises more analytical problems, however, than it resolves. While it is true that each of these designs tends to provide solutions to the problem raised in each case, they often lead to "inelegant" solutions, to say the least, because they do not produce that single answer that we are seeking: does this investigation show evidence supportive of the hypothesis under test? A single yes-no answer is what we seek, and ideally such answer should be provided by a single test, usually a single analysis of variance (ANOVA). That is the elegant solution. When we have to go through a long series of such answers before getting to the crucial question, such solutions are inelegant.

Following the reasoning laid out so far, the last design presented would ask in the end whether group 1 posttest scores were significantly lower (on an algebraic scale) than the group 2 scores. Or it could test whether the time 1/time 2 *change* was significantly negative in group 1 while significantly positive in group 2. (That requires two separate answers.) But we could attribute this to the fear induction alone only as long as we found no significant effect of the pretest measure on the posttest attitude measure and no similar effect of the induction-test measure. Only then may we give credence to the "main effect." (This is not strictly true, since the effect of the pretest measure on the posttest, for example, would be only to decrease the chances of obtaining a significant main effect, in other words, contributes to a type II error, rather than a type I error. A type I error occurs when we reject the null hypothesis when it is actually true. A type II error occurs when we accept the null hypothesis when in fact it is false.)

All this is a reminder that there must be a close connection between the experimental design and the statistical design, or between what the experimenter does and what statistical test will provide the answer sought. This means either building a single design that will provide all the answers at once (e.g., a simple analysis of variance, which will yield one main effect) or a complex analysis of variance (yielding one or

Figure 11–4 Pretest-posttest design with controls for measurement effect and test of induction.

	Pretest Measure	Time 1 Induction	Induction Test	Time 2 Posttest Measure
Group 1	Attitude 1	Message + fear	Effect 1	Attitude 2
Group 2	Attitude 1	Message only	Effect 1	Attitude 2
Control 1	Attitude 1			Attitude 2
Control 2			Effect 1	Attitude 2

more main effects and all possible interactions). The separate tests mentioned may not fit a single ANOVA and may have to be dealt with during a preliminary series of tests partaking of the nature of a validation. For example, one such test might discover that the fear induction does consistently "take," and subsequent designs need not be cluttered with that measure. Another might discover that a before-after design is not needed because the attitude measure in question is distributed normally and yields trivial differences when taken before the induction and manipulation. Such preliminary tests can lead to a simplified analysis scheme (see Figure 11–5).

In this example group 2 is, in fact, a control group. Then why must we have three experimental groups (and no control group), as illustrated in the last previous example? As mentioned, it depends on what the hypotheses say. It is not the same to say the presence of fear inhibits attitude change in the direction advocated by the message and to say there is a linear and negative relationship between the amount of fear induced and the amount of attitude change that results. If a linear relationship is predicted, a linear relationship must be shown, and it cannot be shown without at least three points along the hypothetical "line" that constitutes the prediction. But in the present case we are predicting an effect, not a linear relationship.

SOURCES OF INVALIDITY

The need to control for the unknown effect of pretreatment measures, important as it may be, is one among many potential sources of invalidity that may reside in an experimental design. Campbell and Stanley[8] have listed an even dozen:

1. *History*, a problem for field experiments in particular: uncontrolled events occurring between initial and posttreatment measurements.

2. *Maturation* or what happens to a subject or a group or a community as a direct consequence of the passage of time.

3. *Testing*: as we have seen, the effect of taking a test on the scores of a subsequent test.

4. *Instrumentation*: an instrument in one set of hands may produce differ-

Figure 11–5   Pretest-posttest design with test for induction with internal control.

| | | Time 1 | | Time 2 |
	Pretest Measure	Induction	Induction Test	Posttest Measure
Group 1	Attitude 1	Message + fear	Effect 1	Attitude 2
Group 2	Attitude 1	Message only	Effect 1	Attitude 2

[8]Campbell and Stanley, *Experimental and Quasi-Experimental Designs*.

ent results in another. Such a scheme as "interaction process analysis" for observing group problem solving is a vulnerable example.

5. *Statistical regression* tends to reduce scores on a second testing when only extreme scores are used in constituting groups. "Regression (of extreme scores) toward the mean" is well known to measurement specialists.

6. *Bias in respondent selection* results when respondents are assigned to treatments or controls on any other basis than random assignment.

7. *Experimental mortality*, or the loss of subjects on some basis other than random deletion, often a problem in panel studies.

8. *Interaction between maturation and selection factors*, which arises only in certain quasi-experimental designs.

9. *Effects of testing*, both reactive and interactive. Reactive effects are effects on the dependent variable attributable to a premanipulation test; interactive effects relate to interactions between selection biases and the dependent variable. In such cases the testing or selection effects are said to "confound" the dependent variable, which means that the experimenter cannot know whether the results are owing to the predicted relationship or some uncontrolled cause.

10. *Uncontrolled interaction between selection biases and the dependent variable:* an example would be a failure to control sex differences in assigning subjects to treatments where sex is related to the behavior being predicted.

11. *The experimental arrangements are in some way unrelated to the general behavior being predicted* (in the real world); for example, the laboratory situation is so complex or artificial that the results bear no relationship to the order the experimenter wishes to discover.

12. *Confounding caused by multiple treatments* can arise, of course, only in particular designs that call for more than one treatment for a subject or group and the effects of the first are not successfully erased.

The first six of these attack the validity of the experiment. The last six raise questions about whether the results of an otherwise valid experiment may be generalized to human populations. In both cases these statements summarize points made in the rambling narrative that precedes them.

SOME EXPERIMENTAL DESIGNS

The three most widely accepted experimental designs are the pretest-posttest design with control group, the posttest-only design with control group, and the pretest-posttest design with additional control groups to deal with the effects of testing. All these have been mentioned in the preceding discussion.

In a nutshell, the pretest-posttest design with control group assigns subjects randomly to at least two groups, tests them at time 1, applies a manipulation to one but not the other, and then tests again.

The posttest-only design with control groups randomly assigns subjects to treatment and control groups, and tests after the manipulation but not before.

The four-group pretest-posttest design with controls, usually attributed to Solomon,[9] randomly assigns subjects to four groups, tests before and after the manipulation in one group, tests a second group at the same times but in the absence of the manipulation, tests after the manipulation (but not before) in a third, and tests a fourth group after only. This is the most elegant of the three most frequently used designs because it provides evidence not only that the experimental group gained significantly more than did the basic control group (the one not manipulated) in whatever direction the theory predicted, but that this gain could not be accounted for by an interaction between pretest experience and the manipulation. The problem, as we have seen, is that it is difficult to find a single analysis of variance that will test this interaction.

We have by no means exhausted the experimental designs available to us. The ones described here are perhaps the safest and the most straightforward. Much more complex designs are often needed, and an instance of this is given later in the detailed example. In addition, Chapter 12 explains some designs not included in this discussion.

We turn now to some special problems of the controlled experiment: how to assure randomness in the assignment of subjects to treatments and how to control order effects.

RANDOMIZATION IN ASSIGNMENT TO GROUPS

We think of the controlled experiment as being one conducted within the aseptic confines of a white-walled laboratory. But whether within a laboratory or in some real-life setting, the critical control is more often *randomization*. We must first recall that meeting assumptions required by the use of normative statistics requires that probability samples be used. In the sample survey this means that if we are to conduct a fair test of some hypothesis we must meet the requirements of a random sample.

The reasoning in the experiment is not the same as that of the sample survey, but both have one feature in common. It will be recalled (see Chapter 9) that the requirement of random selection is imposed on any sample of a carefully defined universe. This allows us to make inferences about what to expect if samples drawn under identical rules were endlessly repeated. The condition of random selection is critical to any use of probability-based statistics. In the laboratory we do not rely on sampling from a defined universe. We are not fooling ourselves

[9]R. L. Solomon, "An Extension of Control Group Design," *Psychological Bulletin*, 46: 137–50 (1949).

that the usual college sophomores used in such experiments are somehow a random selection from the human race. Instead, we treat them as *instances* of the human race, which, when randomly assigned to treatment groups, means that all characteristics not involved in the comparison—characteristics that, if they did vary uncontrollably between treatment and control groups, would affect the outcome—are controlled by random variation. This means that they are allowed to vary within such groups but are prevented by means of random (or stratified random) selection (explained later) from varying between groups and thus becoming sources of unpredicted and uncontrolled variance.

The experimenter prefers to make assignment to treatments from relatively homogeneous groups. This is another way of restricting uncontrolled variance. Making a random selection from a highly homogeneous group gets more mileage than the same system of selection applied to a highly heterogeneous group. College sophomores are a heterogeneous lot, but far more homogeneous than, say, the adult population of the nation.

If we were attempting to *estimate parameters* in that adult population (as we do in nationwide sample surveys), we would be foolish to sample college sophomores, obviously. But in the laboratory we are not estimating parameters in a defined population. Instead, we are carrying out controlled experiments that test for relationships between and among variables under conditions that permit us to make limited statements about what causes what. A second theory might say that we could account for more variance if age, for example, were treated as a variate rather than a controlled variable. But that would then be subject to the same sort of test. As a variable in an alternative theory, it can be tested in the same crucible: the laboratory experiment. If the second theory accounts for more variance in the dependent variable, then it takes its place (after replications, rarely on the basis of a single demonstration) as a superior theory.

Depending on group size and the fact that random selection *can* yield differences between groups by the accident of probability, we have an additional means of obtaining even stronger control over variables that may be especially risky sources of uncontrolled variation. On such variables we may *stratify before randomizing*. (The same is possible in designing a sample survey but is especially easy in the laboratory experiment.) If, for example, we are sampling from groups about equal in the distribution of men and women, and we are ignorant of or fear (but do not wish to vary deliberately) the possibility that sex may be a significant variable in the prediction under test, we can draw randomly from among the men and draw randomly from among the women, thus assuring that the experimental group has exactly the same sex composition as the group from which it was drawn. Often socioeconomic differences, even though there is no reason to hypothesize differences on that basis, are nevertheless carefully controlled to avoid their becoming artifacts (i.e., uncontrolled factors that may offer an alternative explanation of the outcome).

In studies using schoolchildren, we often group them by grade in school so that, for example, we can compare early, middle and later grades. But in combining, let us say, fifth, sixth, and seventh graders into a single treatment group, we would be wise to stratify before making random assignment to be sure that the three grades will be represented in the treatment group, for example, in exactly the way they are distributed in a control group.

Stratification should not be confused with *quota sampling*. In quota sampling we rely on a choice that bypasses probability altogether. In sample surveys this means the interviewer chooses respondents in a way to "fill a quota," the quota categories being variables that often confound surveys if not controlled. Needless to say, the assumption of randomness is violated and the survey team is left with no valid basis for using normative statistics. Stratification is an additional step beyond randomization, which, in effect relies upon probability selection to control for variables whose effects we do not know, but does not "leave to chance" the distribution in our samples of variables whose effect we either know or at least suspect.

It should be added that when we stratify before making random selection, we have the ideal distribution for purposes of studying the effect of the stratified variable, inasmuch as we may be sure of an ideal N: that the variable is equally distributed within groups. The same would apply to the use of such a variable as a covariate in covariance analysis or to use in testing for interactions not anticipated and thus not included in the original design. (See Chapter 4 for an explanation of interaction and Chapter 12 for an explanation of how covariance is used.)

CONTROLLING FOR ORDER EFFECTS

In the early days of mass communication research, a favorite study was one that tested for order effects, for example, in the ordering of arguments and their effects upon persuasion. However, the concern here is with controlling for unknown consequences in the ordering of tests and tasks in the experimental setting. We have already seen the experimenter's concern with the effects, for example, of pretesting. Solomon's wise solution was to use an additional control group to test for this unknown influence. With these examples in the background, it should not be surprising that experimenters are wary of the unknown consequences of the ordering of tests and tasks.

Where the ordering is arbitrary and not a meaningful element in the experiment, we can control for order effects by deliberate variation and randomization. We simply eliminate the possibility of order effects by giving half a group the tests or tasks in one order and the other half in the other order, while making sure that who gets what order is determined purely on the basis of random assignment. This permits us to test for order effects at the same time or to test for an interaction of order with some other variable, as long as the statistical design allows these tests to be made. Meanwhile, we have controlled the effect of order on the main result. Sometimes we can make a preliminary test for the existence of the effect and, finding none, eliminate it from the final analysis of variance. But the more elegant solution is to include order as a variate in a single analysis. The richness of our choices among ANOVA designs usually makes that possible if the planning includes taking account of the requirements of the chosen design.

A DETAILED EXAMPLE

Now that the logic of the true experiment has been discussed, let us run through an example step by step to show how that logic is applied. The instant case is a study carried out by Lionel C. Barrow and the author in the Television Laboratory of the University of Wisconsin. By one definition given previously, it was a "field" experiment in that the investigators carried it out on the turf of the subjects, not in the laboratory. The reader can determine whether or not it was a "true" (controlled) experiment in the sense that steps were taken to eliminate differences between groups owing to their being assembled in our different locations. The testing was done with two sixth grade classes in each of four schools.

The primary objective was to compare the effectiveness of radio and television versions of "Exploring the News," a weekly 15-minute program for the middle grades that had been on radio for many years and for several years on television. At that time a number of studies had suggested that television was the more effective medium. For that reason, the research hypothesis was that the television version should be superior to the radio version.

But we were also interested in using the same experiment to test another proposition: that television was more effective in teaching slow learners than fast learners. Several studies of film and television had reported such findings, although others had suggested the opposite. Our hypothesis was that the television version should produce higher information scores than radio for the lower-intelligence group and the radio version higher scores than television for the higher-intelligence group.

A third issue concerned the question whether television's supposed superiority over radio as a teaching instrument was due to that visual medium's ability to make visual themes more salient for sixth graders than is possible in radio. This required separating themes developed visually (in the television version) from those not developed visually, testing them for salience, and comparing their effects with those of the same themes in the radio version.

A fourth issue concerned the question whether class discussion is more effective when conducted before the program (sensitization) or after the program (reinforcement). This question, too, arose from ambiguous results from previous research. (It was included in the design and was reported,[10] but produced no consistent differences and is not discussed further here.)

A fifth issue concerned whether high information seekers benefited more than low information seekers from information programs such as these and whether that effect is influenced by the media differences. Our hypothesis was that the high information seekers should learn more and remember more (six to nine weeks later) in either medium, but there was no theory or previous work to predict an interaction with medium.

As to the first hypothesis (television versus radio), we had hard decisions to make as to how to treat their content equivalently while varying the medium. We considered two possibilities. The first was a "channel" comparison, which could be done any of three ways: use the audio from the television program as the radio version, thus favoring television; use the radio version as audio and point the cameras at the speakers, thus favoring radio; or produce a "simulcast," which would be more evenhanded but would not maximize the advantages of either medium. The second possibility was to instruct the script writers to make the most of both media while employing the same materials, which would, we thought, come closer to being a true "media" comparison. To be certain they did not differ significantly in their use of thematic material, a content analysis seminar was given the problem of identifying themes and counting their occurrence in the radio and television versions of the four news-background programs.

There were thus five independent variables [medium, programs, discussion (before versus after), thematic emphasis, and visual presentation]. Thematic emphasis was defined as the number of words devoted to the theme. Visual presentation identified the themes in the television version that were presented by supporting visuals, such as film clips, stills, and maps.[11]

There were also three mediating variables: intelligence, media use, and knowledge of news personalities. Intelligence test scores were obtained for all pupils who participated and were needed for the second major hypothesis. The media use and news knowledge scores were obtained as two ways of identifying our "information seekers." The correlations between them were low, but higher than their correlations with intelligence.

The major dependent variables were immediate recall (of factual in-

[10]Only in the complete report, *Exploring the News: A Comparative Study of the Teaching Effectiveness of Radio and Television*, Research Bulletin No. 12, Television Laboratory, University of Wisconsin, 1959.

[11]By accident, a visual theme crept into one radio version! The script called for "map scouts" to go to the front of the room and pull down a map of the Caribbean, which they presumably did.

formation in the programs), delayed recall (upon testing six weeks after the last program), and saliency (of themes). Immediate recall was measured by means of a twenty-four item multiple-choice information test (used after-only to avoid sensitization effects) administered by the classroom teachers. Delayed recall was measured with a thirty-two item test containing the eight "best" items in the tests for each of the programs, "best" being determined on the basis of item analysis (the ability of each item to predict the total scores). Saliency was measured by asking each pupil to write down immediately after each program everything remembered from the program. The *first* theme mentioned in each case was for each pupil scored as most salient.

Each program was devoted to a single recent event and presented in some depth. Because they were based on very recent events, there was no opportunity to pretest the information measures. Nevertheless, thematic analysis showed that, while radio used more words than television, as expected, there were no significant differences in thematic structure between the radio and television versions. This was determined by rank-order correlation (see Chapter 4).

To subject all this to analysis of variance with immediate test results as the dependent variable required a careful design, which was complicated by the fact of a 30-minute limit imposed by the schools on the entire activity. This meant that some groups received some after-program treatments not received by others. The after-treatment rotated design is shown as Figure 11–6. The large capital letters designate the four after-treatment patterns whose rotation assures that each of the four treatments is present once for all four schools and all four programs, the only difference being whether the recall test was based on the program just heard or seen (R_1) or an earlier program.

Figure 11–6 Experimental Design.

School	Class	Programs 1			Programs 2			Programs 3			Programs 4		
I	1	S	**A**	D	R_1	**D**	S	R_3	**C**	D	R_2	**B**	S
	2	D		S	S		R_1	D		R_3	S		R_2
II	3	R_1	**B**	S	S	**A**	D	R_2	**D**	S	R_1	**C**	D
	4	S		R_1	D		S	S		R_2	D		R_4
III	5	R_1	**C**	D	R_1	**B**	S	S	**A**	D	R_3	**D**	S
	6	D		R_1	S		R_1	D		S	S		R_3
IV	7	R_1	**D**	S	R_2	**C**	D	R_1	**B**	S	S	**A**	D
	8	S		R_1	D		R_2	S		R_1	D		S

S, saliency questionnaire.

D, discussion period.

R, recall test (subscript indicates program tested: R_1 is program 1, and so on.

Order effects were carefully removed by rotating the order of the after-program tasks. Thus discussion preceded the saliency test in one "classroom" and followed the test in the other (see the A blocks), preceded and followed the recall test in the C blocks. This balancing also applied to the order of the recall test and the saliency test (B blocks), and so on.

The 228 subjects were assigned to treatment groups randomly after a *double* stratification by verbal and nonverbal intelligence. The reason was, of course, the predicted interaction between intelligence scores and medium on information gain and the fact that our hypotheses were based on differences between verbal-only versus visual-verbal media. (The test employed provided verbal and nonverbal part scores.)

The radio and television versions were broadcast to the schools simultaneously and received in separate classrooms. The after-stratification random assignment was made by the investigators, but teachers shifted the subjects to their assigned classrooms. The delayed recall tests were administered in the home classrooms six weeks after the last program was presented, which meant that some of the material was 6 weeks old, some 7 weeks old, and so on.

Except for the discussion variable, the study turned out rather well. Our elaborate precautions to assure an ideal test of a number of hypotheses appeared to pay off, as did our hours of preparation time and time spent securing the cooperation of administrators, writers, producers and directors, a school system, four principles and eight teachers, and colleagues and students in the seminar. The saliency test produced significant differences as predicted. An unpredicted "emphasis" hypothesis was also found to contribute to salience (emphasis = number of words per theme). Television versions produced significantly greater immediate recall than did radio versions, but the same was not true of delayed recall.[12] Contrary to predictions, television was significantly more effective at the highest and lowest IQ levels but not at the medium IQ level, thus supporting both seemingly contradictory findings in previous research. However, these differences, too, washed out on delayed recall. There was some indication that verbal intelligence test subscores were contributing more (on this verbal learning task) than nonverbal intelligence in both media.[13]

The results of the "news seeking" study were that this attribute was unrelated to immediate recall but was significantly and positively related to delayed recall tests, a relationship that held for both of our measures of news seeking.[14] We had not had the subtlety to predict that the effect would be a delayed one, not an immediate one, but the

[12]Lionel Barrow and Bruce H. Westley, "Comparative Teaching Effectiveness of Radio and Television," *Audio-Visual Communication Review*, 7: 14–23 (1959).

[13]Lionel Barrow and Bruce H. Westley, "Intelligence and the Effectiveness of Radio and Television," *Audio-Visual Communication Review*, 7: 193–208 (1959).

[14]Bruce H. Westley and Lionel C. Barrow, Jr. "An Investigation of News Seeking Behavior," *Journalism Quarterly*, 36: 431–38 (Fall 1959).

outcome made more sense than the prediction. Such relationships are normally found, if at all, in immediate recall and wash out over time.

The design described here was more complicated partly because of constraints imposed as part of the price of obtaining subjects. It is not meant to be exemplary, but rather to illustrate the decisions made along the way and to underscore the practicality of what may seem to be purely theoretical concerns. This discussion is continued and expanded in Chapter 12, which emphasizes the statistical designs appropriate to experimentation.

Statistical Designs for Experimental Research

Hugh M. Culbertson

Experimentalists lead troubled lives. Their training stresses rigor but shows it to be an elusive, many-sided goal. They wind up feeling like the fabled Dutch boy who tries to protect his community from a flood. When he sticks a finger in one hole of the dike, the water threatens to break through elsewhere.

The "holes" number at least four: clarifying causal direction, control, generalizability, and precision. This chapter will center on these problems. We will note that, in some but not all cases, filling one "hole" tends to open others.

The first problem, clarifying causal direction, will get short shrift here partly because it is covered in Chapter 11. Manipulation of independent variables is basic to experimentation and is done largely to ensure that these variables have some "causal force."

We will begin by defining the remaining three "holes." Then we will discuss steps taken to fill each one. It will become clear that statistical procedures must be planned not as an afterthought but right along with conceptualization, hypotheses, sampling, instrument development, and data collection.

Now for brief definitions of the three basic goals of experimental design:

1. *Control:* ensuring that differences on a dependent variable that the re-

searcher attributes to an independent variable are not due to extraneous factors and thus remain when these factors are held constant.

2. *Precision:* reducing the error term or denominator of a statistic. This means cutting down on sources of variation among scores other than experimental manipulations.

3. *Generalizability:* determining the class of persons, situations, and tasks for which an observed relationship appears to be valid. There are really two sides to this, defining that class clearly and making it as large as possible. The latter facet has gotten much discussion, but the former is at least as important.

The three facets of generalizability merit further definition here. The first, centering on *persons,* has been called the Achilles' heel of experimentation. In a study of sixty-four recent communication experiments, more than 75 percent used college students, not a typical cross section of the total population.[1] Furthermore, another study has suggested that, even among students, those who volunteer for experiments differ significantly from those who do not.[2]

Generalizability as to *setting* and measured *behavior,* often called external validity, has gotten less attention than it deserves. Obviously, a subject *behaves* (or avoids behaving) in some specific *context* or setting. Equally obvious is that results are rather trivial unless they shed some light on other people carrying out other (usually somewhat different) behaviors in other settings.

Looking at settings, the author recently examined fifty-six experiments reported in communication-related journals from 1975 to 1977. Three fourths appeared to be done in classrooms or as class-related laboratory exercises.[3] Unfortunately, in a classroom students (at least, serious ones) tend to pay attention, take notes carefully, and think analytically. This could color results.

Orne has suggested that many subjects endure boredom and do weird things like saying dirty words partly because they feel science is good.[4] If that is true, one would expect efforts to guess hypotheses and help confirm them. In a related vein, other scholars have found subjects behaving so as to impress experimenters[5] or foul up research.[6]

[1]Charles M. Rossiter, "The Validity of Communication Experiments Using Human Subjects: A Review," *Human Communication Research,* 2: 197–206 (1976).

[2]R.L. Rosnow and J. M. Suls, "Reactive Effects of Pre-testing in Attitude Research," *Journal of Personality and Social Psychology,* 15: 338–43 (1970).

[3]Covered in this review were issues from Summer 1975 through Summer 1977 of six journals: *Communication Research, Human Communication Research, Journal of Broadcasting, Journal of Communication, Journalism Quarterly* and *Public Opinion Quarterly.*

[4]M. T. Orne, "On the Social Psychology of the Psychological Experiment: with Particular Reference to Demand Characteristics and Their Implications," *American Psychologist,* 17: 776–83 (1962).

[5]J. G. Adair and B. S. Schachter, "To Cooperate or to Look Good?: the Subjects' and the Experimenters' Perceptions of Each Others' Intentions," *Journal of Experimental Social Psychology,* 8: 74–5 (1972).

[6]J. Masling, "Role-related Behavior of the Subject and the Psychologist and Its Effect on Psychological Data," in D. Leving, ed., *Nebraska Symposium on Motivation* (Lincoln: University of Nebraska Press, 1966), pp. 67–103.

In gatekeeping studies, subjects have sometimes sorted pictures[7] and news leads[8] as to news value or level of interest. Such studies may lack generalizability because they fail to simulate the newsroom in at least two ways. The *setting* involves little of the deadline pressure and chaos found where a magazine or newspaper is coming together. And the *task* of ranking items does not include consideration of available space, specifying headlines or coping with the felt need for added space to clarify even an unimportant story.

Yet, as Chapter 11 indicates, all these matters can be controlled by the researcher if the design and procedures are carefully developed. We now turn to ways of achieving control.

CONTROL

Equivalence

The researcher checks before or after data collection to be sure experimental and control groups are similar as to the people in them, stimulus materials presented, and settings. No special statistical procedures are needed.

In a study of media learning, Helmreich reported evidence that treatment groups were similar as to sex, television viewing, radio listening, interest in and knowledge of subject matter dealt with, and intelligence.[9] Witt, comparing numbers with descriptive modifiers (lots, a high proportion, etc.) in science stories, checked to be sure different versions had nearly identical Flesch readability scores.[10] And Cohen focused on male candidates discussing only noncontroversial topics in a study comparing radio with television versions of campaign spots.[11]

Randomization

Randomization is a necessary part of experimental design as discussed in Chapter 11. We will explain it here with an example.

Assume we wish to determine the persuasive impact of words alone

[7]Malcolm S. MacLean, Jr., and Ann Li-an Kao, "Picture Selection: An Editorial Game," *Journalism Quarterly*, 40: 230–2 (1963).

[8]Hugh M. Culbertson, "Factors Influencing Coorientation Variables in News Judgment," paper presented to Theory and Methodology Division, Association for Education in Journalism, Ft. Collins. Colo., August 1973.

[9]Richard Helmreich, "Media-Specific Learning Effects: An Empirical Study of the Effects of Television and Radio," *Communication Research*, 3: 53–62 (1976).

[10]William Witt, "Effects of Quantification in Scientific Writing," *Journal of Communication*, 26: 67–9 (Winter 1976).

[11]Akiba A. Cohen, "Radio vs. TV: the Effect of the Medium," *Journal of Communication*, 26: 29–35 (Spring 1976).

and words accompanied by pictures. We design an experimental message without pictures and one with. Then we use a table of random numbers to assign one third of available persons to a control (no-message) group, one third to a words-only experimental group, and the remaining third to the words-plus-pictures treatment.

Random numbers can be used in assigning names in a roster to various treatments, in sending subjects to different locations (even where no roster exists), and in stacking test-booklet versions before handing them out to an intact group.

It is important to see how randomization figures in statistical analysis. Table 12–1 shows a one-way analysis of variance on data from the hypothetical words-and-pictures study. Between-group differences are reflected in the numerator of the F-ratio, within-group variance in the denominator.

Random assignment could place substantially more persuasible subjects (or persons agreeing with the message when they come to the experiment) in one group than in another. This is unlikely but conceivable, just as is getting nine or ten heads in ten flips of a true coin. Such an outcome could, it would seem, create differences attributed to the words and pictures but actually due to something else.

Statistical theory tells us, however, that such spurious factors are almost certain to add to *within* as well as *between-group* variance. Put another way, if subjects differ greatly as to persuasibility when entering the experiment, some gullible and some sales-resistant people are almost bound to fall within any given treatment group. This will increase the denominator of the F or t statistic, reducing the size of that statistic and making significance difficult to obtain.

This brings us to an important point. *A study that controls only via randomization is apt to have rather low precision* (unless, perhaps, a huge group of people is studied). Among the fifty-six recent communication experiments reviewed by the author, about 40 percent involved only randomization in statistical analysis.

Despite this, randomization is a must because it is the only way to control factors not identified and measured. Given the crude state of communication theory, we are bound to ignore many important variables. Thus randomization is a crucial "court of last resort" in control, even if carried out within subgroups already matched in some way.

A one-way analysis of variance relies solely on randomization (see Chapter 11). Table 12–1 gives such an analysis on our hypothetical data. Seeking to guard against false knowledge claims, we have set alpha at 1 percent. Alas, we have failed to achieve significance (the observed F is 4.83, less than the critical value of 5.49).

We feel blue until a colleague suggests an alternative. The literature implies high- and low-educated subjects may differ as to persuasibility. If so (and if we have collected data on education), we could do another analysis, *matching* for education to tighten control and increase precision. This would involve a third basic control technique.

Table 12–1 Mean attitude scores for control, pictures-plus-words, and pictures-only treatments (hypothetical data).

Control Scores	Pictures Only Scores	Pictures plus Words Scores	Total
4	3	8	
4	5	9	
6	6	10	
8	10	11	
8	11	12	
8	10	11	
9	10	11	
10	11	15	
11	12	15	
12	12	18	

$\Sigma X = 80$ $\Sigma X = 90$ $\Sigma X = 120$ $\Sigma X = 290$
$\Sigma X^2 = 706$ $\Sigma X^2 = 900$ $\Sigma X^2 = 1{,}526$ $\Sigma X^2 = 3{,}132$
$(\Sigma X)^2 = 6{,}400$ $(\Sigma X)^2 = 8{,}100$ $(\Sigma X)^2 = 14{,}400$ $(\Sigma X)^2 = 84{,}100$
$(\Sigma X)^2/10 = 640$ $(\Sigma X)^2/10 = 810$ $(\Sigma X)^2/10 = 1{,}440$ $(\Sigma X)^2/30 = 2{,}803.33$
$SS_w = 66$ $SS_w = 90$ $SS_w = 86$ $SS_w = 328.67$
$\bar{X} = 8$ $\bar{X} = 9$ $\bar{X} = 12$

$SS_{treatments} = 6{,}400/10 + 8{,}100/10 + 14{,}400/10 - 2{,}803.33 = 86.67$
$SS_{within} = 66 + 90 + 86 = 242$

ANOVA Table

Source of Variance	Sum of Squares	Degrees of Freedom	Mean Square	Observed F	$F_{0.990}$
Treatments	86.67	2	43.33	4.83	5.49
Within	242	27	8.96		

Matching

Matching resembles equivalence but goes beyond it in that we look at certain parts of the data set separately to be sure that, *within each part,* there is little or no difference on the variable(s) being controlled. There are really three approaches: matching of *subgroups,* matching of *individual subjects,* and the before-after or *repeated-measures* design. Each merits separate consideration.

Subgroup Matching. In the example, we divide each treatment group into high-educated and low-educated subjects, yielding the analysis in Table 12–2. The *F*-ratio jumps to 8.53, significant at the 1 percent level. Very happy, we may then call our colleague to say thanks for the advice.

What has happened? Comparing Tables 12–1 and 12–2, the between-group variance (and with it the numerator of our *F*-ratio) has remained the same in our reanalysis. The payoff has come in reducing

221

Table 12–2 **Mean attitude scores for control, picture-plus-words, and picture-only treatments, two education levels (hypothetical data).**

	Treatment		
	Control Scores	Pictures Only Scores	Pictures plus Words Scores
High-educated	4	3	8
	4	5	9
	6	6	10
	8	10	11
	8	11	12
	$\Sigma X = 30$	$\Sigma X = 35$	$\Sigma X = 50$
	$\Sigma X^2 = 196$	$\Sigma X^2 = 291$	$X^2 = 510$
	$(\Sigma X)^2 = 900$	$(\Sigma X)^2 = 1{,}225$	$\Sigma X^2 = 2{,}500$
	$(\Sigma X)^2/n = 180$	$(\Sigma X)^2/n = 245$	$(\Sigma X)^2/n = 500$
	$SS_w = 16$	$SS_w = 46$	$SS_w = 10$
	$\bar{X} = 6$	$\bar{X} = 7$	$\bar{X} = 10$
Low-educated	8	10	11
	9	10	11
	10	11	15
	11	12	15
	12	12	18
	$\Sigma X = 50$	$\Sigma X = 55$	$\Sigma X = 70$
	$\Sigma X^2 = 510$	$\Sigma X^2 = 609$	$\Sigma X^2 = 1{,}016$
	$(\Sigma X)^2 = 2{,}500$	$(\Sigma X)^2 = 3{,}025$	$(\Sigma X)^2 = 4{,}900$
	$(\Sigma X)^2/n = 500$	$(\Sigma X)^2/n = 605$	$(\Sigma X)^2/n = 980$
	$SS_w = 10$	$SS_w = 4$	$SS_w = 36$
	$\bar{X} = 10$	$\bar{X} = 11$	$\bar{X} = 14$

Computation of sums of squares:

$SS_{treatments} = 86.67$ (See computation in Table 12–1)

$SS_{ed} = (30 + 35 + 50)^2/15 + (50 + 55 + 70)^2/15 - (30 + 35 + 50 + 50 + 55 + 70)^2/30 = 120.00$

$SS_{total} = (196 + 291 + 510 + 510 + 609 + 1{,}016) - (30 + 35 + 50 + 50 + 55 + 70)^2/30 = 328.67$

$SS_{within} = 16 + 46 + 10 + 10 + 4 + 36 = 122$

$SS_{treatments \times education} = 328.67 - (86.67 + 120.00 + 122.00) = 0.00$

ANOVA Table

Source of Variance	Sum of Squares	Degrees of Freedom	Mean Square	Observed F	$F_{0.990}$	$F_{0.999}$
Treatments	86.67	2	43.33	8.53	5.61	9.34
Education	120.00	1	120.00	23.61	7.82	14.03
T × Ed	0	2	0	0.00	5.61	9.34
Within cells	122.00	24	5.08			

the error term of denominator (the mean square within declining from 8.96 in the simple-randomized version to only 5.08 with the factorial approach).

How was this possible? Basically, in moving to the second design, we have done three things:

1. Examined the impact of words and pictures among highly educated people alone.

2. Done the same with low-educated individuals viewed in isolation.

3. Come up with an average of the two effects, generally called a *main effect,* as an overall indication of message impact.

The key lies in the fact that we have examined the high-educated and low-educated separately. In light of that, *variance in attitude between the two cannot contribute to an observed difference between group means* (reflected in the numerator of our statistic). *Thus we are justified in removing such variance from the denominator,* and the analysis in Table 12–2 has done this. Variation between education levels is substantial and has been weeded out of the error term.

This last sentence is important. Subgroup matching aided control as well as precision *because the variable controlled* (education level) *correlated with the dependent variable* (attitude). Without such a correlation, matching would have helped very little, if at all.

Two unusual features of these data, introduced only for simplicity, deserve attention at this point.

First, the difference between treatments is identical as we move from the high-educated to low-educated people. In real life, one might expect words to have relatively great impact on the highly educated, pictures on the low-educated. Such a finding would be an *interaction effect.*

An interaction is important in at least two ways. It helps one assess generalizability, perhaps concluding that an effect holds with some but not all subjects or settings studied. And it may suggest that different relationships and processes hold with, say, high-educated and low-educated people. We will have more to say on interaction later.

Second, the number of subjects is the same (five) in each cell of Table 12–2. This is fortunate because the analysis assumes equal cell sizes.[12] An approximate F-test, focusing on cell means only, must be used if cell sizes differ.[13] A key point here is that, if the experimenter had manipulated education level or matched on it before collecting attitude data, he might have ensured that equal numbers fell in each cell. But it is clearly impossible to manipulate level of education in a free society. Furthermore, the researcher must "take what he can get" when

[12]In some analyses, equal cell *n*s through the table are considered unnecessary if one has proportional cell *n*s in moving down and across it. For example, a 40 percent high-education to 60 percent low-education ratio would be tolerable within the control group if this ratio also holds in each experimental group.

[13]Helen M. Walker and Joseph Lev, *Statistical Inference* (New York: Holt, Rinehart and Winston, 1953), pp. 381–2.

matching for education after data are collected. Randomly throwing out subjects to equalize cell size is a real, but costly, answer.

For most effective matching, we should have begun by obtaining level-of-education data on all subjects, identifying each one as high or low. Then we could have assigned persons to treatments *randomly and separately for the high- and low-educated subgroups.* This procedure would help ensure equal (or nearly equal) *n*s for all cells in the analysis. Also, it would have ensured rigorous control within education levels of variables not controlled by matching.

While helpful, subgroup matching is not the last word in precision and control. People in the high-education group may have degrees ranging from bachelor's through the doctorate. Likewise, the low-educated could include high school dropouts as well as college juniors. "Within-education-level" variance in the dependent variable (attitude) might affect comparisons and must remain in the error term.

Our next strategy, individual matching, provides one answer.

Individual Matching. In Table 12–3, a finer breakdown reveals three doctors, people with almost identical education. We randomly assign these three to the treatment groups and then do the same separately with three individuals who have only begun doctoral work, three who have earned the master's degree but nothing more, and so on.

The statistical analysis makes a separate comparison among treatments at each of ten education levels. As in subgroup matching, the overall or main effect represents an average of these individual comparisons. Here, however, we are able to delete from the error term variance among all ten education levels and not simply that between college graduates and nongraduates.

The error term must change as a result of all this. We cannot compute a within-cell mean square simply because there is but one score per cell. An error term is an estimate of variance, and a given score cannot vary from itself!

Fortunately, random error (i.e., variance stemming from extraneous factors that we control through random assignment to groups) largely determines the *interaction effect* (e.g., the extent to which the difference between picture and control conditions changes as we move from doctors through freshmen).[14] Thus, in individual matching, the interaction mean square is used as the error term.[15] This figure (or rather the sum of squares needed to compute it) can be determined by subtracting the between-treatments and between-education level sums of squares from the total sum of squares.[16]

[14]E. F. Lindquist, *Design and Analysis of Experiments in Psychology and Education* (Boston: Houghton Mifflin Co., 1956), p. 145.

[15]This assumes that observed interactions stem entirely from random error and are not systematic. While doubtless valid in many studies, this assumption merits careful study in any given case.

[16]Lindquist, *Design and Analysis*, p. 157.

Table 12–3 Mean attitude scores for control, pictures-plus-words, and pictures-only treatments at ten separate levels of education (hypothetical data).

Education Level	Control	Treatment Pictures Only	Pictures plus Words	ΣX	$(\Sigma X)^2$	$(\Sigma X)^2/3$
Ph.D.	4	3	8	15	225	75
Beyond M.A., no Ph.D.	4	5	9	18	324	108
M.A.	6	6	10	22	484	161.33
Some grad. study, no degree	8	10	11	29	841	280.33
B.A. only	8	11	12	31	961	320.33
Senior	8	10	11	29	841	280.33
Junior	9	10	11	30	900	300
Sophomore	10	11	15	36	1,296	432
Freshman	11	12	15	38	1,444	481.33
High school only	12	12	18	42	1,764	588 •

Column sum = 3,026.67

$SS_{treatments}$ = 86.67 (See computation in Table 12–1)
$SS_{education\ levels}$ = 3,026.67 − 2,803.33 = 223.34
SS_{total} = 328.67 (See computation in Table 12–1)
$SS_{treatments \times education}$ = 328.67 − (223.33 + 86.67) = 18.67

ANOVA Table

Source of Variance	Sum of Squares	Degrees of Freedom	Mean Square	Observed F	$F_{0.999}$
Treatments	86.67	2	43.33	41.79	10.39
Education levels	223.33	9	24.81	23.93	5.60
Treatments × education	18.67	18	1.04		

Returning to Table 12–3, the F-ratio for treatments has increased to 41.79 (compared with only 8.53 in Table 12–2). Why? The error term has declined from 5.08 in Table 12–2 to 1.04 in Table 12–3. It is now possible to reject the null hypothesis at $p < .001$ (compared with only $p < .01$ in the subgroup analysis). Individual matching has increased precision and permitted a conclusion warranting very high confidence.

In a common variant of individual matching, any given subject receives each possible treatment and "serves as his own control." We now turn to this case.

Repeated-Measures Design. To clarify, simply delete Ph.D. from Table 12–3 and insert "Subject 1, delete Beyond M.A." and insert "Subject 2," and so on. A given subject receives all three treatments, permitting a separate comparison for him or her alone. Thus all between-subject variation is removed from the error term. Statistical-analysis procedures are identical to those with individual matching.

While beautiful in theory, repeated-measures designs present practical problems similar to those with panel studies in survey research (but perhaps even more serious because experiments tend to be done over a short period). A given person must undergo each treatment separately and be tested on it prior to the next one. This takes time and patience. Furthermore, it introduces halo or consistency effects. Reading one version of an article seems very likely to affect later interpretation of other versions. Also, taking a test today could affect performance in retaking it tomorrow or next week.

It is important to note that more than one type of matching can be used in a study. There may, for example, be a repeated-measures comparison on one independent variable and subgroup matching on another. In such mixed designs, the error term will change from one test to another within the same ANOVA table. Lindquist,[17] Bruning and Kintz,[18] and Kirk[19] discuss these designs in some depth.

Table 12–2 involves two independent variables. A third or fourth can be introduced in a straightforward extension of the two-way case, but this takes many subjects (and with them, time and money).

For example, the hypothetical study reported in Table 12–4 analyzes factors affecting learning about news. Here three independent variables are used: story organization, medium, and class level. Each variable has four values. To ensure that one person receives each possible combination of treatments would require $4 \times 4 \times 4 = 64$ subjects. And if one introduces, say, five subjects per cell to permit greater precision as well as a test of interaction effects, $5 \times 64 = 320$ subjects would be needed. We can reduce this substantially (by 75 percent, from 64 to 16 with one subject per cell) by going to the next strategy: counterbalancing.

Counterbalancing

The analysis in Table 12–4 involves a Latin square design, the simplest case of counterbalancing. In assigning the sixteen subjects to treatment groups, one would complete these steps:

1. Using a table of random numbers, assign each freshman to one of the four media conditions (newspaper, radio, television, and magazine).

2. Again with random numbers, designate a given type of story organization (inverted pyramid, upright pyramid, equally important facts throughout, etc.) for each medium within the freshman row of the table.

[17]Ibid., pp. 254–316.

[18]James L. Bruning and B. L. Kintz, *Computational Handbook of Statistics* (Glenview, Ill.: Scott, Foresman & Co., 1968), pp. 54–83.

[19]Roger E. Kirk, *Experimental Design: Procedures for the Behavioral Sciences* (Belmont, Calif.: Brooks/Cole Publishing Co., 1968), pp. 319–83.

Table 12–4 Mean learning scores for newspaper, radio, television, and magazine consumers of different class levels and with different story formats.

Class Level	Treatment Newspaper	Radio	Television	Magazine	Row sums
Freshman	9 (B)	5 (C)	17 (A)	11 (D)	42
Sophomore	10 (D)	16 (A)	6 (C)	9 (B)	41
Junior	6 (C)	8 (B)	11 (D)	14 (A)	39
Senior	15 (A)	9 (D)	6 (B)	2 (C)	32
Column sums	40	38	40	36	Table sum = 154

A, inverted-pyramid format (sum of scores = 17 + 16 + 14 + 15 = 62)
B, upright-pyramid format (sum of scores = 9 + 9 + 8 + 6 = 32)
C, facts of equal importance throughout story (sum of scores = 5 + 6 + 6 + 2 = 19)
D, important and unimportant facts alternated (sum of scores = 11 + 10 + 11 + 9 = 41)

$SS_{medium} = 40^2/4 + 38^2/4 + 40^2/4 + 36^2/4 - 154^2/16 = 2.75$
$SS_{class} = 42^2/4 + 41^2/4 + 39^2/4 + 32^2/4 - 154^2/16 = 15.25$
$SS_{story\ structure} = 62^2/4 + 32^2/4 + 19^2/4 + 41^2/4 - 154^2/16 = 245.25$
$SS_{total} = 9^2 + 10^2 + 6^2 + 15^2 + 5^2 + 16^2 + 8^2 + 9^2 + 17^2 + 6^2 + 11^2 + 6^2 + 11^2 + 9^2 + 14^2 + 2^2 - 154^2/16 = 269.75$
$SS_{error} = 269.75 - (2.75 + 15.25 + 245.25) = 6.50$

ANOVA Table						
Source of Variance	Sum of Squares	Degrees of Freedom	Mean Square	Observed F	$F_{0.95}$	$F_{0.99}$
Medium	2.75	3	0.92	0.85	4.76	9.78
Class	15.25	3	5.08	4.69	4.76	9.78
Format	245.25	3	81.75	75.46	4.76	9.78
Error	6.50	6	1.08			

3. Repeat the process separately at each class level, but with the constraint that each medium and each class level, viewed separately, must contain all four story-organization types.

In comparing media, newspaper subjects get each of the four story formats. So do radio listeners, television viewers, and magazine readers. Thus any advantage gained from one or two of the story forms would hold equally for all media and should not affect intermedia comparisons. In like fashion, story forms should not influence comparisons among class levels.

Between-media and between-class sums of squares are computed just as are row and column sums of squares in the previous examples. To get the story-form sum of squares, add the scores for each version separately, square each sum, add the squared sums, and divide by $n = 4$. The error term is obtained by subtracting the medium, class-level, and story-structure sums of squares from the total sum of squares. (If more than one subject were used in each cell, the within-cell sum of squares might be the appropriate error term.)

In the data here, story structure makes the difference, not class level or medium. While it saves subjects (and with them, time and resources), counterbalancing has a major disadvantage. It does not permit a clear test of interaction effects.

Counterbalancing can be done to control for sequence effects where a subject receives several messages, tasks, or questionnaire items. As noted, early phases of an experimental procedure can affect those that come later.

More complex counterbalanced designs such as the Graeco-Latin square operate on the basic principles outlined here and can be studied in most research-design texts.

We now turn briefly to a final strategy: statistical control.

Statistical Control

Analysis of covariance is used quite often in experiments, partial correlation somewhat less often. Both mathematically extract variance in the dependent variable associated with a measured control variable. Thus both can aid precision.

As noted in Chapter 4, analysis of covariance (ANACOVA) permits control of factors not handled through randomization, a need sometimes found when dealing with intact groups. For example, separate versions of a film may be shown to school children in separate classrooms. It is desirable (and usually possible) to randomly assign children to rooms for the duration of such an experiment. But in some cases, time limitations, fear of disrupting classes, and other factors may force you to take classes as you find them. You can randomly assign treatments to classes, but not children to classes. A trigonometry class might get treatment A, a shop class treatment B, and English class treatment C, and so on.

Trigonometry may attract better students than shop, and you should work hard in arranging your study to avoid such gross inequities. Still, you cannot avoid them all (even within a given course, better students may tend to sign up for a hard but stimulating professor without your realizing it). ANACOVA can help control for such differences if you have data on academic potential or performance (perhaps IQ, SAT, or ACT scores) by adjusting scores in the dependent measure to weed out variance associated with ability.

ANACOVA is also used to control for pretest scores in some repeated-measures studies. This provides at least a partial solution to one control problem not handled by simply analyzing pre-post difference scores. A person who scores very high (or low) prior to a treatment has little room for scores to go up (or down). Thus pre-post difference scores can be affected by such a *ceiling* or *basement* effect termed "regression toward the mean" in Chapter 11.

The technique is not used often in communication, perhaps partly because it involves some worrisome assumptions. Most notable among these may be that the controlled and dependent variables relate linearly (i.e., in the same way throughout the range of values for each). For further discussion, see Kirk.[20]

It is important to note in closing this section that two or more (indeed, all) control strategies may fit in the same research design.

PRECISION

It has been noted that sole reliance on randomization tends to involve low precision (i.e., large error terms), while matching and statistical control can raise it. At least five other steps in designing a study can prove helpful. We now turn to these.

Analysis of Change Scores

In a repeated-measures study, one can subtract each subject's pretest score from his or her posttest score and treat the remainder as a single score in a one-way or *n*-way design. In this fashion, variance in pretest scores is directly "subtracted out" of variance in the scores analyzed.

While simple and fairly common, this procedure has some disadvantages noted earlier. Ceiling or basement effects may influence results when a person's pretest score is so high that it cannot go up much or so low that it cannot decline significantly. Also, merely completing a pretest can affect posttest responses.

Measuring "Pure" or Unidimensional Variables

Two researchers once manipulated source credibility by defining *Fortune* magazine as high, a certain woman movie-gossip columnist as low.[21] This assumed that credibility is a single, neat variable. However, later studies showed that, in assessing credibility, people evaluate several rather independent factors, including competency and trustworthiness.[22] *Fortune* and the columnist may both be seen as highly competent. If so, the scholars have really manipulated trustworthiness and not credibility as a whole.

This example focuses on a predictor variable, but the same concern

[20]Ibid., pp. 455–87.

[21]Carl I. Hovland and Walter Weiss, "The Influence of Source Credibility on Communication Effectiveness," *Public Opinion Quarterly*, 15: 635–50 (1951).

[22]James Lemert, "Components of Source 'Image': Hong Kong, Brazil, North America," *Journalism Quarterly*, 46: 306–13, 418 (1969); James C. McCroskey, Virginia P. Richmond, and John A. Daly, "The Development of a Measure of Perceived Homophily in Interpersonal Communication," *Human Communication Research*, 1: 323–32 (1975).

holds on the dependent side. One might set out to test learning with an index that also taps attitude. Variance in attitude, then, could contribute to variance among learning scores, increasing the error term.

As noted in Chapter 5, measurement techniques focus heavily on isolating sets of test items that measure a single variable. Multivariate techniques, on the other hand, analyze several variables as a group, taking into account how they interrelate. Such approaches are becoming more common as the field matures but lie beyond this discussion. The point here is that two variables should not be lumped together indiscriminately—without analyzing them separately to know whether and how they interrelate. Harris has written a useful text on multivariate techniques, many potentially important in experimentation.[23]

Careful Measurement

Chapter 5, among others, provides detail on this topic, but it is important to show here how measurement and statistical design work together. If instructions are unclear, people will interpret them differently. Within-group variance (hence a larger error term) is almost bound to result. Vague question wording and "double-barreled items" (lumping two basic ideas into one) can have the same effect.

In a related area, using several questions or behaviors to measure one concept will provide a more stable estimate and less error variance than will only one item or response. The reasoning here is similar to that noted later in choosing people. A sample of 1,000 is likely to resemble the population from which it is drawn more closely than would a sample of 100 or 10.

Our literature search revealed as few as one (often) and as many as ninety-three responses used to measure a given variable. Unfortunately, a subject will generally "sit still" for only a modest number of tasks or items. Therefore, measuring one concept with great care can reduce the number of concepts studied.

Increasing the Number of Observations

Various observers have noted, sometimes with a mild sneer, that any observed difference between two samples means, however small and trivial, will be significant if the n is large enough.[24] A glance at the basic independent-sample t-test formula shows why.

$$t = \frac{\bar{X}_1 - \bar{X}_2}{\sqrt{\dfrac{S_1^2}{n_1} + \dfrac{S_2^2}{n_2}}}$$

[23]Richard J. Harris, *A Primer of Multivariate Statistics* (New York: Academic Press, Inc., 1975).

[24]Jacob Cohen, "Some Statistical Issues in Psychological Research," in Benjamin B. Wolman, ed., *Handbook of Clinical Psychology* (New York: McGraw-Hill Book Co., 1965), pp. 95–121.

Increasing n_1 and n_2 boosts the size of the error term's denominator, reducing the overall error term. Thus, increasing the sample size may result in what were chance differences becoming statistically significant. However, in some instances when the sample size is increased, the difference between means also increases, and the difference remains a chance difference.

Studying Homogeneous Subjects

Experimenters have been chided for building a science of college sophomores with low generalizability.[25] However, enhanced precision is a silver lining in this cloud. Sophomores probably tend to be alike in many areas (at least when compared with the total population). And the more people are alike, the less apt they are to respond differently in research tasks. As a result, error terms are apt to be relatively low.

There are at least two ways to solve this puzzle and achieve fairly high generalizability as well as precision:

1. Matching in effect permits separate focus on two or more relatively homogeneous subgroups in a study. "Averaging" across subgroups can produce (in theory, at least) results that apply to all of them. Furthermore, interaction tests permit a check on generalizability—on where a finding holds and where it does not.

2. Replication with widely differing subjects can help. The author once conducted a study of artwork interpretation with high school students, neighborhood farm discussion groups, and college students.[26] Somewhat comparable results throughout suggested that something (albeit not much in this instance!) was happening with a variety of readers.

GENERALIZABILITY

It has been suggested that using homogeneous subjects can hamper generalizability, but that matching and replication can help it. Unfortunately, many experimentalists worry about this research goal but do little more. Two things may help explain this.

First, many studies seek to isolate effects of single variables operating one at a time and perhaps having only mild impact even then. Researchers thus feel compelled to create settings and tasks devoid of extraneous influences. For example, messages often deal with unknown and unimportant (to the subject) items such as the prime minister of a distant land.[27] Unfortunately, where such factors are present outside the laboratory, they may interact with independent variables so as to reduce, eliminate, or even reverse observed relationships.

[25]Rossiter, *Validity of Communication Experiments.*

[26]Hugh M. Culbertson, "The Effect of Art Work on Perceived Writer Stand," *Journalism Quarterly*, 46: 294–301 (1969).

[27]A. D. Annis and N. C. Meier, "The Induction of Opinion through Suggestions by Means of Planted Content," *Journal of Social Psychology*, 5: 65–81 (1934).

Second, in testing for such mild effects, researchers often create extreme values of independent variables. In one pioneering credibility study, the U.S. surgeon-general was pitted against a certain sophomore at Northwestern University.[28] Unfortunately, interpretation is hampered by the fact that sources of extremely high or low credibility may differ in ways quite unlike those at more moderate levels.

Hovland[29] noted a basic generalizability problem in early communication research. Effects tended to be stronger and more uniform in laboratory than in field studies, perhaps for several reasons. The laboratory setting produces a captive audience with little chance for "selective inattention," thereby almost ensuring that subjects will attend fairly carefully to messages (and perhaps note attributes manipulated by the researcher). Experiments look at immediate effects and do not often check their decay. Also, messages developed for laboratory use tend to be one-sided, enhancing impact because competing arguments are not made available as in naturalistic settings to "cancel them out."

In light of all this, some critics question the utility of experiments.[30] After all, what good are the confirmed relationships if they do not hold outside the laboratory?

Experimentalists counter by saying the laboratory per se may indeed have little direct practical import. But truth and practicality are different matters, and the conscientious scholar gives high priority to the former.[31] This forces her or him to:

1. Measure variables unidimensionally and with minimal error.

2. Clarify underlying processes by focusing on variables that intervene between presumed cause and measured effect. This need often forces one to measure such hard-to-get-at variables as eye movement, blood pressure, and palm sweating.

3. Look for mild relationships among variables. This becomes salient as the discipline matures and shows that communication phenomena result from many contributing factors, each making a little difference. It is often hoped that one or a few factors may eventually turn out to make most or all of the difference. However, such scientific "holy grails" have proved elusive.

4. Examine higher-order interaction effects. This means, for example, seeing how the relationship between variables 1 and 2 may change as variables 3, 4, and 5 assume all possible values.

[28]F. S. Haiman, "The Effects of Ethos in Public Speaking," *Speech Monographs,* 16: 192 (1949).

[29]Carl I. Hovland, "Reconciling Conflicting Results Derived from Experimental and Survey Studies of Attitude Change," in E. P. Hollander and Raymond G. Hunt, eds., *Current Perspectives in Social Psychology* (New York: Oxford University Press, 1963), pp. 378–89.

[30]Herbert Blumer, *Symbolic Interactionism: Perspective and Method* (Englewood Cliffs, N.J.: Prentice-Hall, Inc., 1969), pp. 24–7.

[31]Wayne N. Thompson, *Quantitative Research in Public Address and Communication* (New York: Random House, Inc., 1967), pp. 8–10.

Such needs in the research process point to (1) emphasis on precision, often requiring reduced generalizability in practice, and (2) complex and demanding (on subjects as well as researchers) measurement techniques and manipulations, which dictate the use of a limited range of subjects and settings.

It is common to assert further that relationships discovered with experimental rigor can be tested later in the field. While attractive in theory, this is seldom done in a systematic way. Only a few areas, such as the study of television and movie violence, have attracted both experimentalists and survey researchers in large numbers. Even there, studies in one camp seldom link up clearly with those in the other.[32]

Chapter 11 notes that field and quasi experiments can serve as a meeting ground for field and laboratory, combining the best of both. Also helpful in boosting external validity are unobtrusive measurement techniques that seek to control for various artifacts by ensuring that the subject does not know why, how, or perhaps even whether she or he is being tested. However, our survey of fifty-six recent experiments revealed few genuine field studies and still fewer "hidden measures."

Surprisingly little attention has been paid to two generalizability enhancing approaches to which we now turn.

Random Sampling of Respondents

Only four of the fifty-six experiments that we surveyed clearly used random sampling or a variant of it. This technique is often as basic to assessing subject generalizability as random assignment and manipulating are to control and clarifying causal direction.

Research may legitimately focus on specialized rather than general-population groups. Even then, however, rigor is needed to define the population about which one can talk. Sampling may be difficult, but it is seldom impossible. One can round up volunteers more easily than one can gain participation by sometimes reluctant persons chosen from a university or a city directory. Yet the latter can boost (or at least aid assessment of) generalizability.

Theoretic Analysis of Underlying Processes

Obviously, sampling of tasks and settings is often impossible. One simply cannot list a number of news-editing tasks or newsroom features and sample from these (though it may be possible to sample from questionnaire items, messages, and institutional settings). Thus theory that sheds light on underlying processes may be needed to help analyze generalizability. Such assessments are tentative when theory is incomplete or tentative, but they are better than nothing. For example:

[32]Douglass Cater and Stephen Strickland, *TV Violence and the Child: the Evolution and Fate of the Surgeon-General's Report* (New York: Russell Sage Foundation, 1975).

1. Small-group studies often define a leader as someone who contributes often and successfully in solving problems and winning games. Theory suggests such behavior may have little to do with leadership of, say, General Motors or Great Britain. Statesmen and other leaders of large institutions stress image management and human relations at least as much as logical or mathematical analysis.[33]

2. A good deal of evidence suggests people behave differently when moved from secure, quiet settings to those that are chaotic, unfamiliar, and anxiety laden.[34] In light of this, one needs to generalize with care from a classroom to a noisy, harried newsroom.

3. Developmental psychology suggested to one researcher that cross-media (print versus audio versus videotape) differences found with 12-year-olds would not hold among younger children.[35] As one grows older, one develops symbolic and reasoning skills needed to interpret cues in ways not previously possible.

4. Surlin and Kosak compared circular, square, and triangular visual elements in advertisements. They noted that circular items left more white space around the edges than did square artwork.[36] This raises an interesting question begging for conceptual analysis. Is the white space an extraneous factor or an inherent aspect of circularity? One must decide on the underlying process to which shape is related before really determining whether white space should be viewed as relevant.

This concludes the discussion of basic goals in experimental design. We now turn briefly to several issues that concern the experimentalist.

SOME IMPORTANT ISSUES

Power

In statistical testing, one can make two basic errors: *type 1* or *alpha,* rejecting a null hypothesis that is true, and *type 2* or *beta,* failing to reject a null hypothesis that, in fact, is false.

Other things being equal, setting a rigorous alpha level tends to increase the probability of beta error. Traditionally, discussion has focused on alpha, the probability of accepting false knowledge claims.

[33]Chris Argyris, *Behind the Front Page* (San Francisco: Jossey-Bass, Inc., 1974), pp. 238–68; Richard Neustadt, *Presidential Power* (New York: New American Library, Inc., 1964), pp. 88–106.

[34]James C. McCroskey and John A. Daly, "Teachers' Expectations of the Communication Apprehensive Child in the Elementary School," *Human Communication Research,* 3: 67–72 (Fall 1976); Harold M. Schroder, Michael J. Driver, and Siegfried Streufert, *Human Information Processing* (New York: Holt, Rinehart and Winston, Inc., 1967), pp. 29–41; Alvin Toffler, *Future Shock* (New York: Bantam Books, Inc., 1971), pp. 348–55.

[35]Caroline W. Meline, "Does the Medium Matter?" *Journal of Communication,* 26: 81–9 (Summer 1976).

[36]Stuart H. Surlin and Hermann H. Kosak, "The Effect of Graphic Design in Advertising on Reader Ratings," *Journalism Quarterly,* 52: 685–91 (1975).

In recent years, concern with beta error has increased.[37] For one thing, it has been argued that theory building and verification require separate approaches, and even tentative generalizations may warrant careful examination in the building process.[38] Second, in applied research, failing to detect an existing difference (for example, in the effect on juries of different approaches to pretrial publicity) may lead to dangerous practices or omissions.

Cohen has dealt extensively with the related concept of power. He defines a test's power in a given case as 1 minus the probability of beta error. Such error is said to depend on four factors: the predetermined alpha level, sample size, the error term, and the actual difference between population means.[39]

Alpha and sample size are, in theory, under the researcher's control. The error term can be estimated with some precision in a relatively small pretest. The actual difference between means is not known prior to a study. However, making some assumptions about differences large enough to warrant attention, Cohen has developed tables that permit one to estimate power in a study.[40]

Detailed treatment is not feasible here, but it is important to note that *power* relates closely to our research goal of *precision*.

Observed Effect Size

Many experimentalists report significance-test results and little else. Such data tell only the probability that the null hypothesis can be rejected safely (i.e., that a difference among groups does exist). As noted earlier, however, even very small differences can reach significance in a very precise study.

Katzer and Sodt[41] have argued that it is generally feasible to report size of effects in any one of three forms:

1. Actual differences among means. Ideally, this should involve computation of a confidence interval based on sampling error.[42]

2. Correlation measures, such as the product-moment correlation coefficient, the Spearman rank-correlation coefficient, and the contingency coefficient.

3. Measures of variance in one variable "accounted for" by variance in an-

[37]Jacob Cohen, "Some Statistical Issues"; Ivan Preston, "Choosing the Level of Significance in Communication Research," *Public Opinion Quarterly,* 31: 80–6 (1967).

[38]Barney G. Glaser and Anselm L. Strauss, *The Discovery of Grounded Theory: Strategies for Qualitative Research* (Chicago: Aldine Publishing Co., 1967), pp. 1–18.

[39]Jacob Cohen, "Some Statistical Issues," p. 96.

[40]Jacob Cohen, *Statistical Power Analysis for the Behavioral Sciences* (New York: Academic Press, Inc., 1969).

[41]Jeffrey Katzer and James Sodt, "An Analysis of the Use of Statistical Testing in Communication Research," *Journal of Communication,* 23: 251–65 (1973).

[42]Allen L. Edwards, *Experimental Design in Psychological Research* (New York: Holt, Rinehart and Winston, 1968), p. 87.

other. In practical terms, how much variance in a dependent variable would disappear when the independent factor is held constant? The eta^2 (η^2) statistic is often a help here. In ANOVA, this can be computed with the following formula (where F = the observed F-ratio, df_b = the degrees of freedom for the numerator, and df_w = the degrees of freedom for the denominator):

$$\text{Estimated } \eta^2 = \frac{df_b\,(F-1)}{df_b\,(F) + df_w}$$

If this procedure yields a value of 0.36, we can conclude that the independent variable accounts for 36 percent of variance in the dependent factor. However, such an estimate has clear meaning only where precision is fairly high. For further discussion, see Cohen[43] and Kirk.[44]

Selected Comparisons

In Tables 12–3 and 12–4, an F-test indicates an overall significant difference among three means (control group, pictures only, and pictures plus words). It is not clear, however, whether this difference holds for each possible pair of means. In the example, there are three such pairs, each with some possible substantive interest:

1. Pictures alone/control: a difference here indicates pictures have impact.
2. Pictures and words/control: this can establish that pictures and words in combination have impact (it is conceivable that, even if pictures alone make a difference, words might offset it!).
3. Pictures and words/pictures alone: adding words may or may not enhance the impact, if any, of pictures.

At first glance, it may seem appropriate to do three t-tests, one on each of the three comparisons. Statisticians see this as acceptable only where one has, *prior to the experiment,* advanced a separate hypothesis, buttressed by a separate and distinct theoretic rationale, for each of the three comparisons.

In the present example, this condition might well be met. Different theories are often applied to words and pictures. Kirk argues that one can legitimately compare two means in such a case even without first doing an overall F-test.[45]

In other cases, however, the researcher may predict one or more differences somewhere but rely on the data to tell where. This complicates testing. A t-test is designed for the case where two samples are chosen randomly. And in selected comparisons, one draws three or more samples, then seeks to compare two that may be the most or least different from each other.

The Scheffé test is simple and widely applicable in such a case. One computes a student's t value for a given comparison and derives a critical value (K) by substituting F into the following formula (where G =

[43]Jacob Cohen, "Some Statistical Issues," pp. 103–6.
[44]Kirk, *Experimental Design*, pp. 126–7, 134–5.
[45]Ibid., pp. 73–4.

the number of treatment groups, N = the total number of subjects or observations, and $F_{G-1, N-G}$ = the critical value of F for the ANOVA used for overall comparison):

$$K = \sqrt{(G - 1)F_{G-1, N-k}}$$

If the observed t exceeds this value, a given comparison is significant. The Scheffé test is relatively conservative,[46] and is usable where treatment-group ns are unequal. Also, it can be applied to a comparison involving one or more means averaged together (e.g., treatment A versus the average of treatments B and C).[47] Several texts deal with numerous approaches to the selected-comparison problem.[48]

A related concern deserves mention here. One lonely significant difference among, say, twenty nonsignificant ones may mean very little, because, given true null hypotheses throughout, one would expect an occasional significant difference purely by chance. Such "experiment-wide" error rates have gotten little attention from communication researchers. Kirk provides a good introduction.[49]

Manipulation Check

In an experiment, one manipulates the subject's environment. Unfortunately, a manipulation, like a medical inoculation, may not "take." In seeing if it does, a behavioristic psychologist is inclined to consult the *experimenter* and his colleagues,[50] while many other social scientists would want evidence from the *subjects* themselves.[51] Herein lies an important and fascinating debate, as noted in Chapter 2.

Philosophical arguments aside, the experimenter needs to use some judgment. For example, if he or she sees a piece of artwork as square or circular,[52] the subject is almost bound to see it that way.

In other cases, subjects need to be consulted because "beauty" is clearly in the eyes of the beholder. For example, *Pravda* is apt to seem more credible to Russians than to Americans, and it is necessary to check for such differences. For this reason, credibility researchers often use rating scales as a manipulation check.[53] Main-test or pretest subjects may provide the needed data.

[46]Ibid., p. 90.

[47]Gene V. Glass and Julian C. Stanley, *Statistical Methods in Education and Psychology* (Englewood Cliffs, N.J.: Prentice-Hall, Inc., 1970), p. 389.

[48]Kirk, *Experimental Design*, pp. 69–98; Glass and Stanley, *Statistical Methods*, pp. 381–97; Edwards, *Experimental Design*, pp. 130–53.

[49]Kirk, *op.cit.*, pp. 82–86.

[50]Robert S. Woodworth, *Contemporary Schools of Psychology* (New York: Ronald Press Co., 1948), pp. 68–94.

[51]Blumer, *Symbolic Interactionism*, pp. 1–60.

[52]Surlin and Kosak, "Effect of Graphic Design."

[53]Alexis S. Tan, "Exposure to Discrepant Information and Effect of Three Coping Modes," *Journalism Quarterly*, 52: 678–84 (1975); Tilden M. Counts, Jr., "The Influence of Message and Source on Selection of Statements by Reporters," *Journalism Quarterly*, 52: 443–9 (1975).

Other variables so treated have included perceived anxiety in communication,[54] relative dominance of people,[55] relevance of information to a topic,[56] the goodness or badness of news,[57] perceived intimacy,[58] level of power in personal relations,[59] and one's overall similarity to another person.[60]

To sum up, it is wise to analyze each independent variable and see if you can safely assume subjects will see it as you intend. If in doubt, add a few items as a check, usually late in the experimental procedure or in a pretest with a group of subjects not studied otherwise. These precautions are needed to avoid contaminating experimental responses. Chapter 11 discusses this further. Where an experimental manipulation requires presentation of varied stimuli, mean or median ratings will indicate overall perceptions of these stimuli on the attributes measured. Furthermore, a small variance or standard deviation among ratings may confirm high agreement among subjects, a comforting sign. Edwards provides a useful discussion of related measurement theory.[61]

CONCLUSION

The goals of control, precision, and generalizability seem basic to research design. This chapter will close by summarizing how some specific practices affect attainment of these goals. The reader who understands these points probably has a good handle on the goals themselves.

First, matching helps one look at varied individuals or groups separately, paving the way to generalizability. At the same time, matching on an appropriate attribute (i.e., one which correlates with the dependent measure) cuts the error term and aids precision.

Second, devising a measuring instrument free of error variance affords a real challenge. It will enhance precision if done successfully. Yet it may also hurt generalizability because only people with much academic training and reasoning ability may sit still for precise measuring procedures, which often require much skill and effort.

---

[54]McCroskey and Daly, "Teachers' Expectations."

[55]Joanne R. Cantor, "What Is Funny to Whom?: The Role of Gender," *Journal of Communication*, 26: 164–72 (Summer 1976).

[56]Edward M. Bodaken, "An Empirical Test of a Role Enactment Model of Persuasion," *Human Communication Research*, 2: 330–7 (1976).

[57]Shirley J. Gilbert and Gale G. Whiteneck, "Toward a Multidimensional Approach to the Study of Self-Disclosure," *Human Communication Research*, 2: 346–55 (1976).

[58]Ibid.

[59]Allen A. Turnbull, Lloyd Strickland, and Kelly G. Shaver, "Medium of Communication, Differential Power and Phasing of Concessions: Negotiating Success and Attributions to the Opponents," *Human Communication Research*, 2: 262–70 (1976).

[60]Charles R. Berger, "Proactive and Retroactive Attribution Processes in Interpersonal Communications," *Human Communication Research*, 2: 33–50 (1975).

[61]Allen L. Edwards, *Techniques of Attitude Scale Construction* (Englewood Cliffs, N.J.: Prentice-Hall, Inc., 1957), pp. 19–147.

Third, designing studies so as to minimize other influences and bring a sought-after effect into bold relief can hurt task-and-setting generalizability. Such outside factors may *qualitatively alter* (not simply drown out or reduce) experimental results when found to operate in natural settings.

Fourth, studying a homogeneous population should help precision by reducing error variance due to diverse subjects. However, unless buttressed by replication, such study will narrow the class of people to whom one can generalize. This latter point does not render research useless; it is often helpful to identify processes operating within narrow classes of people. However, and this point is often ignored in experimental practice, it is still important to *define clearly* the population about which one can talk.

The author would like to thank a superb instructor, Dr. David K. Berlo, for planting the seeds that grew into many ideas presented in this chapter. Dr. Berlo deserves much of the credit for any insights provided, but none of the blame for omissions or errors.

Secondary Analysis

Lee B. Becker

Secondary analysis is the reuse of social science data after they have been put aside by the researcher who gathered them. The reuse of the data can be by the original researcher or someone uninvolved in any way in the initial research project. The research questions examined in the secondary analysis can be related to the original research endeavor or quite distinct from it.

In a very real sense, then, secondary analysis is the use of available records, the records of other social scientists.[1] Because social scientists, particularly within the last 20 years, have been diligent in the preservation of some important records, data archives now exist that make the possibilities for secondary analysis quite astounding. The Roper Public Opinion Research Center contains records of sample surveys

---

[1] Many other kinds of records containing information of value to researchers exist. Governmental agencies, for example, gather and store massive amounts of information. Census data, birth, death, marriage, and similar records, and various health statistics are only a few examples. In general, such records differ from the records of social scientists in that they are less obtrusive. In other words, the person or organization providing the information is unaware that a researcher is observing. There are many social scientists in government, however, and the distinction is not always very clear. To be sure, Census data are usually thought of as social science archives. See Eugene J. Webb and others, *Unobstrusive Measures: Nonreactive Research in the Social Sciences* (Chicago: Rand McNally & Co., 1966) for a general discussion of the use of available records.

dating back through the 1930s. Literally thousands of data files are stored there.

ADVANTAGES OF SECONDARY ANALYSIS

Secondary analysis has a bad connotation for some researchers, particularly those unfamiliar with some of its potential. Students who do not have the resources for primary data gathering are sometimes encouraged to reuse existing data to complete course or degree requirements in the allotted time. It would be better to gather new data, these students are advised, but they may have to get by with secondary analysis.

To be sure, there is great value in gathering new data. Students learn most about the problems of design and measurement when they direct a project from beginning to end. And there are some very real problems with secondary analysis.

The secondary analyst is quite removed from the initial data-gathering procedures and consequently can be unaware of flaws and data limitations. Details of sample design and field operations, for example, are not always known. Peculiarities of data storage, including information on weighting or recoding of initial responses, may not be available. And because many of the archived data sets have been created by reputable organizations, some researchers may not be critical enough in their reuse. There is a tendency to think of archived data as "cleansed," as if aging makes them finer than they were when "put down."

The most serious limitation of secondary analysis, however, results from the fact that the primary researcher was unaware of the interest of the secondary analyst. While efforts are made by some organizations to anticipate future uses and plan for them, it is impossible to anticipate fully future research questions. The result is that archived data may not provide for an adequate test of the research questions of the secondary analyst. In such cases, the researcher has to weigh the advantages of secondary analysis and the advantages and disadvantages of new data-gathering operations.

The practical benefits of secondary analysis are rather obvious. Using data already gathered is cheaper and quicker than undertaking a second study. Most communication researchers lack the financial resources to field studies of the scope of many of those presently archived. Salaries for field workers have made survey interviewing extremely costly. The employment of coders for content analysis and supervisory personnel for laboratory work also is expensive. Payment of interview respondents or experimental subjects, when necessary, adds to costs.

Data archives, in addition to providing relatively inexpensive records for the researchers, also allow social scientists to save what good will exists in society for those situations in which it is necessary to gather new data. There is, to be sure, a real danger of "pollution" of the social environment by researchers. Most people probably have been contacted at least once by someone claiming to be a pollster, and many have participated in school or some other setting in some form of experiment. While there is evidence that the public is generally tolerant of such research (only 19 percent of those sampled in a Harris survey in 1976 said polls were an infringement of their right to privacy), it is impossible to know how long support will continue.[2]

Perhaps the greatest benefit of secondary analysis, however, results from its potential contribution to theory and substantive knowledge of the social processes. Sociologist Herbert Hyman, in his comprehensive text on secondary analysis, argues that existing data archives provide extensive opportunities for such contributions.[3] These data, for example, allow for an examination of important aspects of the past. The pollster can be thought of as a "contemporary historian," and the pollster's data are a rich source of information on opinion during important periods of our past.[4] These data also provide an opportunity to study social change in ways that are impossible in present-day primary analysis. Researchers would be forced to rely on retrospective reports by current respondents were it not for existing archives.

Secondary analysis of comparable data sets gathered in different countries or sections within a country also allows for comparative tests and consequent broadening of inferences. Because few researchers have the capability to field comparative studies, cross-cultural inferences are not often made from primary analysis. Similarly, secondary analysis allows researchers to replicate findings and in so doing enlarge on the original interpretation. Findings from one community or state, for example, can be tested with data gathered by a national organization. Or the findings can simply be replicated in another, somewhat different, setting.

Finally, Hyman argues, secondary analysis provides researchers with the impetus to elevate and enlarge their theories. Partly because secondary analysts seldom find perfect measures of needed concepts, they are forced to treat the measures as indicators of some general concept. In the process, they may change the level of abstraction, seeing the old concept as only a small component of some more abstract, and perhaps more important, social phenomenon.

EXISTING ARCHIVES

For rather obvious reasons, archives of experimental data are of less value to communication researchers than archives of survey data. Sec-

[2]The results, based on a Harris survey of late January 1976, were reported in the March 8 edition of the *Syracuse Herald-Journal.*
[3]Herbert Hyman, *Secondary Analysis of Sample Surveys* (New York: John Wiley & Sons, Inc., 1972).
[4]Paul F. Lazarsfeld, "The Historian and the Pollster," in Mirra Komarovsky, ed., *Common Frontiers of the Social Sciences* (New York: Free Press, 1957), pp. 242–62.

ondary analysts cannot add manipulated independent variables to experimental data sets and seldom have the opportunity to examine the effects of the manipulations on dependent variables other than those intended by the primary researcher. As a result, no major archive of experimental data from communication research exists.

The largest general archive of survey data is located at the Roper Public Opinion Research Center, an affiliate of Williams College, the University of Connecticut, and Yale University. Included are poll data of the American Institute of Public Opinion, better known as the Gallup Poll, Roper polls, as well as data from numerous other surveys conducted in this country and throughout the world. Questions from many of the polls housed in the Roper Center are indexed, and the index is stored on magnetic tape, so it is possible for researchers quickly to determine the locations of questions under a wide range of major or minor subject categories.

The Louis Harris Data Center at the Institute for Research in Social Science, University of North Carolina, Chapel Hill, houses data made available for secondary analysis by Louis Harris and Associates, Inc. Included are more than 200 national, state, and community studies conducted by the Harris organization since 1965. Topics covered by the studies range from voter preferences in elections to sports.

The Inter-University Consortium for Political Research at the University of Michigan has archived a general data collection with special emphasis on U.S. political surveys. Included are the data files from the election studies conducted every two years since 1948, except 1950. The 1974 file includes an unusually large number of questions on the communication behavior of respondents and can be linked to data derived from a large-scale content analysis of the mass media. Consortium holdings also include cross-national surveys and historical data of various sorts.

Numerous other archives of interest to communication researchers exist at universities around the country. The National Opinion Research Center of the University of Chicago, for example, has a general collection of the center's own surveys. Researchers may obtain data stored in many archives for the cost of duplication and mailing.

Summaries of recently published poll data, some of which are or will be archived, appear in "The Polls" section of *Public Opinion Quarterly,* *World Opinion Update,* published in Williamstown, Massachusetts, *Public Opinion,* published by the American Enterprise Institute, and the *Gallup Opinion Index,* published by the Gallup Organization.

TYPES OF SECONDARY ANALYSIS

Research projects relying on secondary analysis are of two general types. Many such projects follow the traditional model of research. A question is developed and shaped, perhaps with the assistance of some established theoretical perspective, into a hypothesis. The hypothesis is then subjected to empirical test with data having been collected by some other researchers. Were it not for the latter fact, that the data were not gathered by the persons performing the test, it would be impossible to distinguish this type of research project from any other.

 Many secondary analysis projects, however, are of a different sort. They begin when the researcher becomes aware of data already collected and is stimulated by some rather narrow, often descriptive, finding of the original researcher. A hypothesis is formulated, sometimes to explain that descriptive finding. Existing theory may be used to buttress the hypothesis, which is tested with the existing data set. In other words, existing data have given rise to the hypothesis and provided its empirical test.

For the most part, researchers do not report which of these descriptions best fits their research using secondary analysis. The reason is rather simple. The second situation, where an interesting data set stimulated the secondary analysis, seems more opportunistic, less programmatic, and less rigorous. That need not be the case. And it is probably true that more secondary analysis results from the fact that the data are available than from the formulation of research questions derived wholly independently of such data sets.

Because the process of conducting secondary analysis differs to some extent under these two types, we will discuss them separately here. No value judgment regarding their worth is being made.

Hypothesis-Then-Data Type of Secondary Analysis

The beginning stages in this type of secondary analysis are indistinguishable from those in primary analysis. The researcher develops a research problem, defines the concepts included in the problem statement, and formulates a hypothesis. At this point, however, the paths of the primary and secondary analyst diverge.

The primary analyst, having stated the hypothesis, attempts to enumerate the various ways of measuring each of the concepts included in the hypothesis. From this list of possible measures, the researcher then selects the measure or measures that best reflect the concept of concern. The feasibility of actually using the measure is then explored. The choice of a measure results from a weighing of its appropriateness and the likelihood that it can be taken.

The secondary analyst, on the other hand, does not have the luxury of selecting the best measure from a list of possible measures. Rather, he or she is constrained to select the best measure from those available, in other words, from those used by other researchers.

This process is illustrated fairly well by recounting some of the decisions made by Stroman and Becker in their secondary analysis examining racial differences in media use habits.[5] The general research problem arose from ambiguities in the previous literature regarding the exact nature of differences in the ways blacks and whites in this country use the mass media. Some research suggested they were the result of socioeconomic differences in the two population subgroups; other evidence indicated the differences were more deeply ingrained in the two subcultures.

In their search for existing data that would allow for a closer examination of these two positions, Stroman and Becker had two goals. First, they wanted to obtain as much diversity as possible in the types of media use measures included on the original questionnaire. Second, they wanted to obtain as large a sample of black respondents as possible to allow for a robust test of each position. They eventually settled on the 1974 University of Michigan Election Study, made available to them through the Inter-University Consortium for Political Research. The study included a wide range of questions on media that were asked of a relatively large number of black respondents.

The decision to use the 1974 Election Study, however, reshaped the original research question. Many of the questions included on the interview schedule had to do with the election or public affairs in general, so the analysis dealt with that subject matter. Because the schedule included questions on the gratifications audience members reported seeking from the political content of the media, the research question was expanded to examine differences in this aspect of media behavior.

The authors concluded that some real racial differences exist in key aspects of media behavior, and the differences are not entirely attributable to differences in social class. In some important respects, however, the two racial groups are quite similar. This is particularly true where gratifications sought from the political content of television are concerned. The conclusions, quite clearly, were influenced by the measures available for analysis. Those decisions on measurement had been made by the primary, not the secondary, analyst.

Data-Then-Hypothesis Type of Secondary Analysis

The secondary analysis project stemming from an existing data set has quite a distinct history from those for which the hypotheses are generated in the more traditional manner. The research endeavor begins when the secondary analyst stumbles on or is somehow made aware of an existing data set. The availability of the data set, rather

[5]The author is relying on research with which he has firsthand knowledge to accurately portray the different decisions made. See Carolyn A. Stroman and Lee B. Becker, "Racial Differences in Gratifications," *Journalism Quarterly*, 55: 767–71 (Winter 1978).

than some prior research problem, is responsible for the secondary analysis.

The problems encountered by the researcher in this second situation are quite distinct from those encountered in the more traditional approach. The problems are ones of operationalization, to be sure, but they have a different direction. Rather than asking whether existing measures adequately tap a concept of interest to the researcher, the secondary analyst working from the data is more likely to be consumed initially with identifying the concept measured by existing questions: the analyst is asking, What is it that is measured here?

Once the researcher has answered that question, or at least made some attempt at it, he or she can start to ask whether that concept is related to others measured in the data set. If the answer seems to be affirmative, the researcher has stumbled onto a hypothesis. If the hypothesis is of substantive interest, the secondary analysis may be warranted.

The secondary analysis by Becker, Beam, and Russial of the New England Daily Newspaper Survey data was of this second type.[6] It began when the authors became aware of the data set, which included evaluative essays of New England's daily newspapers written by trained critics, as well as large amounts of other data. It ended with empirical tests of a substantive hypothesis relating to correlates of press performance.

Through content analysis of the evaluative essays, the authors were able to derive performance scores for the approximately 100 newspapers included in the original study. Newspaper performance became the dependent variable in the analysis. The authors also sifted through the data reported for each newspaper to identify independent variables—factors that might be expected to be functionally related to performance. Measures were first grouped into two general headings: those measuring characteristics of the community served by the press, and those measuring characteristics of the news organization itself. After having made this distinction, the authors attempted to group and combine measures that seemed to tap similar concepts. Included in the community group were measures of market growth and newspaper competition. Examples of organizational measures were size of news staff and type of ownership.

The analysis showed that community factors measured were less important in understanding newspaper performance than organizational characteristics. As was true in the Stroman and Becker analysis, the conclusions were somewhat tentative because other measures not included by the primary analyst might have altered the empirical picture.

The process of naming variables, and defining them conceptually, is

---

[6]Lee B. Becker, Randy Beam, and John Russial, "Correlates of Daily Newspaper Performance in New England," *Journalism Quarterly*, 55: 100–108 (Spring 1978). The data originally appeared in Loren Ghiglione, ed., *Evaluating the Press: The New England Daily Newspaper Survey* (Southbridge, Mass.: Published by the editor, 1973).

probably the most challenging activity in the type of secondary analysis
that stems from existing data. Until that is done, however, it is not possible to formulate meaningful hypotheses. So it is the crucial step that
transforms what could be a "fishing expedition" using available data
into substantive theoretical research.

In naming and defining the measured variables, the secondary analyst also takes important steps toward elevating and enlarging existing
theories. As Hyman has argued, when researchers use measures created by others, they often break out of their own conceptual narrow-
ness and push toward higher levels of abstraction. The researcher is
forced to think "broadly and abstractly in order to find overarching
concepts or categories within which these varied specific entities can be
contained."[7] The result may well be better theory.

DESIGNS IN SECONDARY ANALYSIS

For the most part, researchers are restricted in the secondary analysis
to the designs of the primary analyst. This usually means a cross-
sectional design. There are two important exceptions, however.
Through use of more than one archived data set, researchers often can
perform trend and cohort analyses not otherwise possible. In this way,
secondary analysis can be used for rather sophisticated and theoretically important studies of change.

Trend and cohort analysis can be conducted by the primary analyst,
of course. But the existence of data archives increases the possibilities
for such analyses. For that reason, and because secondary analysis can
present some rather distinct problems in employing these designs, they
merit discussion here.

Trend Analysis

In its simplest form, trend analysis merely involves the laying side-by-
side of research results that are comparable except for the date of data
gathering. In this way, change in some criterion variable can be assessed. Although actually only a surrogate for some more substantive
factor, time becomes the independent variable in the analysis.

The Gallup data shown in Figure 13–1 are illustrative of the kinds
of data that are often used for this type of trend analysis.[8] They consist
of responses to a single item repeated on a large number of national
Gallup surveys over the 6-year span of the presidency of Richard

[7]Hyman, *Secondary Analysis*, pp. 23 and 24.

[8]Hyman would label this "semisecondary analysis" since it is reported by the organization that gathered the original data. It clearly fits under the broad definition of secondary analysis used in this chapter.

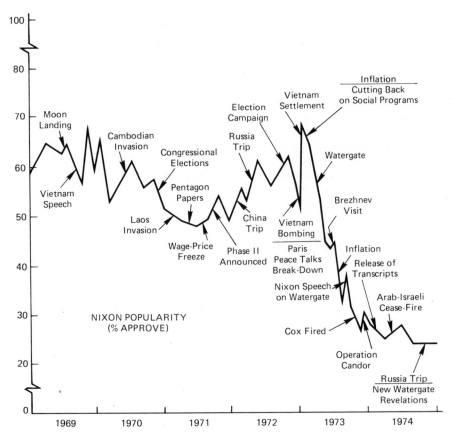

Figure 13–1 Trends in Popularity of Richard Nixon. From *The Gallup Opinion Index,* Report No. 111, September 1974.

Nixon. The question was designed to measure the electorate's approval of the incumbent president.[9]

The raw data merely show the high and low points of Nixon's popularity. That popularity was relatively stable during the first year and a half Nixon was in office. It dropped in 1971 and built again to a new high in 1973. At that time, it began to fall, almost without serious interruption, until the summer of 1974 when Nixon resigned in shame.

By coupling these raw data with an understanding of historical events, it is possible to get some rough indication of what might have been the cause of Nixon's loss of popularity. All presidents witness shifts in their support. Often the shifts seem quite unrelated to specific

[9]The exact question asked is, Do you approve or disapprove the job Nixon is doing as president?

presidential activities.[10] The drastic downturn in Nixon support as Watergate unraveled, however, would seem to be tied to that event. Nothing the president said or did during that time seemed to be able to pull him from the Watergate quagmire.

The difficulty with this kind of interpretation, however, is that it is impossible to argue with certainty that something other than the identified historical event produced the change in the criterion variable. While the drastic drop in 1973 and 1974 in Nixon support is easy to tie to such an event (Watergate clearly dominated the domestic and international scene during the period), other changes shown in Figure 13–1 are less easily explained. Did the Laos invasion in early 1971, for example, lead to a decrease in presidential popularity, or was Nixon's support on the wane as a result of other forces that preceded the invasion? Or perhaps it was a combination of factors, including the invasion, that produced the decrease in support.

At least two distinct solutions to this problem present themselves. The first is to attempt to disaggregate the trend. The second is to find correlates of it over a long period of time. Disaggregation of a trend is illustrated by a secondary analysis reported by Tichenor, Donohue, and Olien.[11] The researchers, using Gallup data, identified a general increase in the belief on the part of the public between 1949 and 1965 that man would reach the moon. The authors believed that this increase was due at least in part to discussion of the topic in the media during the period. If this was the case, those most likely to be in social environments facilitating this media effect should show a higher level of change in this belief than those in less facilitating environments. Using education as an indication of this type of environment, the researchers were able to disaggregate the trend and show that those with less formal education increased less in this belief than those with more formal education. The result was a better understanding of the overall trend in beliefs about man reaching the moon.

The second strategy, isolation of correlates of the shift in the criterion variable over time, is illustrated by a secondary analysis of data gathered by the National Opinion Research Center in the annual General Social Survey, an omnibus national survey conducted each spring since 1972.[12] The authors were able to show that changes in national evaluation of the press followed a pattern opposite that of evaluation of the executive branch of government, at least over the short period for which data were available. This finding was used to support the authors' inference that popular support of the press is dependent at least

[10]For a discussion of patterns in presidential popularity, see James S. Stimson, "Public Support for American Presidents: A Cyclical Model," *Public Opinion Quarterly*, 40: 1–21 (Spring 1976).

[11]P. J. Tichenor, G. A. Donohue, and C. N. Olien, "Mass Media Flow and Differential Growth in Knowledge," *Public Opinion Quarterly*, 34: 159–170 (Summer 1970).

[12]Lee B. Becker, Robin E. Cobbey, and Idowu A. Sobowale, "Public Support for the Press," *Journalism Quarterly*, 55: 421–430 (Autumn 1978).

in part on support of other institutions in the society with which the press is often in conflict.

In evaluating trends, of course, the possibility exists that the change observed in the criterion variable is not real, but rather an artifact resulting from sampling error, changes in the techniques of data gathering across the studies being analyzed, or changes in question wording. Problems of question wording will be dealt with later in this chapter. Suffice it to say at present that any variation in question wording poses a serious threat to an inference of real change, because, strictly, trend analysis assumes identical measurement across time.

Difficulties with sampling errors can be dealt with in a rather straightforward manner. Slight shifts in survey data are expected when they are derived from a sample of the population. Samples are estimates; as such, they contain error. By means of a simple difference of proportions test, however, it is possible to determine that shifts greater than 4 percent between any two data collection points in Figure 13–1 would be likely to occur by chance (or as the result of sampling) only one time in twenty.[13] Using a slightly more complicated procedure developed by Glenn, it is possible to evaluate the overall pattern of fluctuation due to sampling error in trends like those shown in the Gallup data in Figure 13–1.[14]

Changes in field or other techniques of data gathering are less easily overcome. The original researcher may have changed sample designs, altered field strategies, or obtained different overall return rates in the various studies the secondary analyst is using in the trend analysis. In the early years of the Gallup Poll, for example, the method of quota sampling used resulted in an underrepresentation of the less educated and lower-status members of the U.S. population. Changes in sample design were initiated around 1950 so that data gathered after that point do not have this bias. But trend analysis of the long series of Gallup polls is marred by this artifact.[15]

A final problem in trend analysis results from the fact that the lags between field dates are not always the ones the secondary analyst desires. Sometimes the spans between the field dates are not equal. In the

[13]See Chapter 4, this volume, as well as Herman J. Loether and Donald G. McTavish, *Inferential Statistics for Sociologists* (Boston: Allyn & Bacon, Inc., 1974) for a discussion of the difference of proportions test. Since national surveys, including those conducted by Gallup, are never simple random samples, the difference of proportions test, as well as other common statistical tests based on simple random sampling models, is not strictly applicable. It does provide, however, a rough guide in evaluating trends. See Norval D. Glenn, *Cohort Analysis* (Beverly Hills, Calif.: Sage Publications University Paper Series on Quantitative Applications in the Social Sciences, Series No. 07-001, 1977), particularly pages 41–45, for a detailed discussion of this problem.

[14]Norval D. Glenn, "Problems of Comparability in Trend Studies with Opinion Poll Data," *Public Opinion Quarterly*, 34: 82–91 (Spring 1970). For a more detailed discussion of measurement of change, including a discussion of time-series analysis appropriate for evaluating the comparability of trends in two variables, see Chester W. Harris, ed., *Problems in Measuring Change* (Madison: University of Wisconsin Press, 1963).

[15]See Glenn, "Problems of Comparability," for a discussion of this problem and a means of correcting for it.

Tichenor, Donohue, and Olien research, for example, four time points were used.[16] Five years elapsed between the first data point and the second, and between the second and the third. Between the third and final survey, however, 6 years elapsed. While it is doubtful this slight difference had any effect on the conclusions these researchers reached, there are other situations in which this might not be the case. At times large spans such as 5 years are completely inadequate to measure the type of change the secondary analyst is interested in studying.

Cohort Analysis

Cohort analysis refers to any study in which there are measures of some characteristic of one or more cohorts at two or more points in time.[17] A cohort is a population subgroup whose members have some particular experience or characteristic in common. Most often, cohorts are defined in terms of birth. The 1946–1950 birth cohort, for example, would consist of those individuals born during those 5 years. The cohort members have birth years in common.

Cohorts can be studied using panel designs, where the same persons are observed at more than one point in time. Or independently drawn samples of the various cohorts can be studied at more than one time point. The panel study allows for an examination of individual change. The independently drawn samples allow only for study of net change. This second type of cohort analysis can be seen as a subtype of trend analysis in which age is used to disaggregate the trend. Some of the problems that plague cohort analysis also affect other efforts at disaggregating trends.

Generally, researchers employ cohort analysis to test inferences about what have been labeled age effects, cohort effects, and period effects. *Age effects* are changes in the criterion variable attributable to the process of aging. For example, some have argued that individuals become more conservative as they get older for a number of psychological and social reasons. *Cohort effects* are those associated with cohort membership. To argue that individuals born during the Depression are different from those born before or after that period is to argue for cohort effects. *Period effects* are the result of influences within a given time span. For example, some have argued that the Watergate period produced a general drop in trust in government among all voters.[18]

Because a few researchers have the opportunity to gather data that allow for comparisons of cohorts across long periods, secondary anal-

---

[16]Tichenor, and others, "Mass Media Flow."

[17]Glenn, *Cohort Analysis.*

[18]In actuality, it seems cohort data alone cannot differentiate among these effects. In other words, most findings can be explained in more than one way. The nature of this discussion is beyond the scope of this chapter, and interested readers can consult Glenn, ibid., for more details.

ysis is commonly employed. These data, as might be expected, can present some problems.

Changes in study design, which restrict all trend analysis, can have particular importance for the cohort analyst. Because it is essential that cohorts remain identical across time, any changes that could produce fluctuation in small segments of the population (and consequently not be overly important in simple trend analysis) might jeopardize cohort analysis. Researchers need to be aware of these problems, which can be overcome to some extent by introduction of appropriate controls. For example, race or educational level of cohort members might be used as a control for differential mortality (or changes in cohort composition) across time.

The particular way the cohort-defining variable is measured and coded in the archived data set is of critical importance to the cohort analyst. If birth cohorts are being studied, age must be measured and coded finely and consistently. The secondary analyst, of course, must be able to reconstruct relevant cohorts at each date of data gathering. If age is coded into 10-year groups in one study and into 15-year groups in a second, use of the data will be difficult.

The final restriction (other than measurement problems, which is dealt with in the following section) resulting from use of archived data for cohort analysis has to do with the limited time span of the existing data. A most optimistic estimate is that, at present, a cohort could be studied only for about 40 years using existing data sets. A more realistic estimate is that change could be studied in a cohort for about half that time. The result is that it is not possible, at present, to follow cohort members from early adulthood through retirement and termination using archived data. But the archived data are probably richer in this regard than any other data sets available.

MEASUREMENT PROBLEMS

Difficulties of measurement are so pervasive they permeate the entire discussion of secondary analysis. The researcher using previously gathered data to test a hypothesis generated independently of the data must assess how well existing measures tap the concepts of concern. Most often the measures are imperfect, and the researcher must decide whether the analysis is worth the time and other resources it will consume, given the difficulties of measurement.

The secondary analysts employing trend and cohort designs must not only deal with these general problems of measurement but also with others that may result from noncomparability across the studies used. The primary analyst simply may have made a slight change in question wording or even response categories, which threatens the inference that the observed trend is a real one. Sometimes the change may be in use of a filter question, which results in changes in the sample across time. This problem sometimes can be dealt with through use of appropriate controls that make comparison groups comparable, but at a minimum this solution limits the generalizability of the findings. Sometimes, the difference in questions results not from changes in wording but rather from changes in what the words themselves mean. The term "liberal," for example, has taken on different meaning across time, as has the term "conservative." Questions using such words may seem comparable, and yet may artificially produce quite distinct responses across time.

The seriousness of this problem of question wording can be illustrated by a brief recounting of the controversy surrounding research that culminated in publication of *The Changing American Voter*.[19] The work was based on secondary analysis of the Michigan Voting Studies and reached the conclusion that, among other things, the American electorate had become more issue oriented during the 1960s and 1970s when compared with earlier periods. The critical turning point in this trend was the 1964 election. Critics have noted, however, that important question wording changes were introduced into the Michigan studies at precisely that point.[20] The result, these critics argue, is that the movement may not be real at all. The American electorate may not have changed. The way some important questions were asked did change.

There are few easy solutions to these problems of measurement. Researchers who have opted for secondary analysis, indeed all researchers, must confront such difficulties straightforwardly. If there is a solution, it probably rests in continued discussion of concepts and their operationalizations and replication of findings.

SECONDARY ANALYSIS AND ITS IMPLICATIONS

Communication researchers, as well as their colleagues in other disciplines, have been slow to recognize the value of secondary analysis. One result is that there has been relatively little research examining trends in key communication activities, such as mass media use, across time. The Roper analysis of trends in attitudes toward the media stands as a rare example of such research.[21] McCombs's economic anal-

---

[19]Norman H. Nie, Sidney Verba, and John R. Petrocik, *The Changing American Voter* (Cambridge, Mass.: Harvard University Press, 1976).

[20]George F. Bishop, Alfred J. Tuchfarber, and Robert W. Oldendick, "Change in the Structure of American Political Attitudes: The Nagging Question of Question Wording," *American Journal of Political Science*, 22: 250–69 (May 1978).

[21]Roper Organization, *Changing Public Attitudes Toward Television and Other Mass Media 1959–76* (New York: Television Information Office, 1977). Another example, on a much smaller scale, is Maxwell E. McCombs, "Negro Use of Television and Newspapers for Political Information, 1952–1964," *Journal of Broadcasting*, 12: 261–66 (Summer 1968). One of the difficulties in identifying communication trends is that little consistency on measurement of media habits exists in publicly available archives.

ysis of media consumption across time similarly has not been replicated or expanded upon despite its importance to the field.[22] There has been almost no research examining changes in relationships between variables, such as violence viewing and aggression among children, across time.

In addition, many data that should be archived are not. The vast amount of information gathered by newspapers in their now-routine polling projects has not been assembled and made available for secondary use.[23] In fact, there is no clearinghouse or archive handling the data gathered in recent years by communication researchers on the effects of violence viewing, Watergate, or the 1976 debates. For every data set saved, there are probably hundreds more slipping away.

Yet what is currently available in archives at the Roper Center, through the Michigan Consortium, or in Chapel Hill at the Harris Data Center is quite impressive. By contacting the primary researcher, persons interested in secondary analysis can probably gain access to much more. Tapping these data is important to the field.

---

[22]Maxwell E. McCombs, "Mass Media in the Marketplace," *Journalism Monographs*, No. 24, August 1972; Maxwell E. McCombs and Chaim H. Eyal, "Spending on Mass Media," *Journal of Communication*, 30:153–58 (Winter 1980). Some may argue that this is not secondary analysis since the data used were gathered by government agencies.

[23]There have been some efforts to include some major polls in the Gallup holdings.

14

Ethical Issues in Communication Research

Bradley S. Greenberg

This chapter fastens on basic issues in professional research conduct. It asks for self-examination and examination of those observable to you as to whether or not research is being carried out with due respect for the human participants in that research. As such, it is pertinent to virtually all research in which you rely on obtaining information from human subjects. The issues raised are germane to the several fields of social science.

Yet these issues have a peculiar symbiosis to communication research, as we shall point out, because several of the central issues are communication issues. They ask for an understanding of communication phenomena to which we have attended little in our theorizing or our research. For example, the concepts of informed consent, debriefing of human subjects after experimentation, or deception are communication processes about which we should know much, but apparently know little. If they are confusing to us, who are immersed daily in communication perspectives, think how much more difficult they must be for other social scientists, let alone biologists, ecologists, or pediatricians.

We will pose questions rather than answer them; we shall try to establish the parameters of concern—akin to providing the outside border for a puzzle and hoping that the 3,000 pieces remaining to fit inside can subsequently be aggregated.

This chapter is organized into two sections. The first is designed to inform about four issues: (1) the getting and giving of *informed consent,* (2) *deception,* (3) *debriefing,* and (4) the triad of *privacy, anonymity,* and *confidentiality* of research information.[1] The second section examines a set of professional roles faced by the social scientists in coping with those about them. It examines individual and institutional responses to questions about the ethical use of human subjects. As a preface to the first section, however, let us pinpoint the substance of this chapter with a series of illustrative examples. Consider the following:

1. As reported in a recent article in the *Journal of Communication,* subjects' self-esteem was lowered through alternative message manipulations, one using attacks on the individual subject's competence and another using attacks on his or her trustworthiness. It was determined that personal attacks on trustworthiness lower self-esteem more so and enhance the impact of persuasive messages.

2. In a recent SCA convention paper, experimenters burst into a series of experimental classrooms and announced that President Nixon had resigned. In a brief questionnaire, the researcher determined that "happiness" in that news was related to feelings of personal alienation, anomie, powerlessness, and interpersonal problems.

3. As reported in a text on organizational communication, the authors fed bogus calls into a student-run crisis information center over a three-week period to determine (1) reliability and validity of information given for identical problems, (2) responsiveness of the organization to information requests, and (3) the correspondence of information provided to staff people by trainers.

4. For a doctoral dissertation, the candidate obtained latent measures of homosexuality, and then, in concert with a local magazine distributor, mailed magazine subscription solicitations to the subjects. The available magazines included *Playboy, Playgirl,* and *Gay Guy.* The candidate examined the relationship between the latent measure of homosexuality and the manifest measure of magazine subscriptions actually bought or inquired about.

5. First-graders in an NIMH-sponsored research project were subjects for a television aggression experiment. Permission to ask the youngsters to participate came from the school principal. The youngsters were asked, "Would you like to watch some television?" Prior to watching, the teacher verbally assaulted the youngsters. The youngsters' interpersonal behavior in a postviewing task was the dependent variable.

6. In a medical school-communication department joint endeavor, terminally ill cancer patients were offered $100 for their next of kin if they would consent to complete a questionnaire describing the means by

[1]The preparation of the abstracts on these four topics was aided greatly by discussion with and concept papers prepared by several participants in a doctoral seminar. These included as co-instructor, Dean Erwin P. Bettinghaus, and four former students, Dr. John Hocking, now at the University of Georgia; D. Bruce Schreiman; Mark Steinberg, a staff researcher at the State of Michigan Office of Substance Abuse; and Dr. Barbara Walker, now at Florida State University.

which they were informed of their ailment, their subsequent communication behaviors with their relatives, and their information search behaviors about their condition.

All reasonable studies. Some rather interesting and inventive. All involved with human subjects. All at least partly fictitious for the purposes of this chapter, but not without real-life counterparts in the literature. And each study, in a different way, raises significant questions about proprieties involved in procedural or methodological decisions that were made.

This chapter asks communication scientists to consider more closely just what it is they do when they enter into a relationship with a human subject, and why they do it that way. Is anything fair game? Is deception the name of the game? What, if any, limits are there to what can be done and when it can be done in the name of communication theory and research?

Consider the following:

1. It has been a rare or nonexistent convention paper at SCA, ICA, or AEJ in the last five years that has addressed itself to the issue of scientist-subject relationships, and what is appropriate or inappropriate professional behavior with human subjects.

2. Not a single article in the *Journal of Communication, Speech Monographs, Journalism Quarterly,* or *Public Opinion Quarterly* in the recent past has addressed itself to such issues.

3. We know of no graduate training department in communication research and theory that formally trains its about-to-be scientists in the ethics of conducting research.

An assimilation of these facts might lead to the conclusion that the issue is trivial. Perhaps all communication scientists are imbued with a natural sense of ethical propriety that would inhibit any untoward behaviors. Or perhaps the issues have never come up or have been deliberately ignored. Yet, let us examine the types of issues pertinent to our fictitious studies.

For study 1, what assurances can we offer that the lowered self-esteem of the subjects will be restored through what are typically terse and mechanical debriefing techniques; for example, "We really didn't mean any of this." Is any debriefing done at all? What happens to the subject-scientist relationship or rapport as a function of tinkering with self-esteem?

For study 2, is deception the best alternative available to study these particular variables? Or is deception just the most frequently used practice and easiest to control? What does persistently lying to subjects do to the professional image of communication scientists? How will it affect the subjects the next time they believe themselves in a research situation?

Does study 3 involve an invasion of privacy to gather data? May social scientists go digging wherever they wish and in whatever fashion?

What will the volunteer workers think about the value of their time and contribution if they learn their hours were spent helping communication researchers who needed data instead of people who needed help? Is it justified not to tell them at all? Is withholding information likely to be more beneficial and, if so, how?

For study 4, if there is support for the operational hypothesis that latent homosexuals are more likely to subscribe to some magazines than others, shouldn't the scientist be concerned with the apparent reinforcement of that behavior stimulated by the research? What of creating a list of latent homosexuals and the problem of protecting that list? What of using that list for other than the original purposes?

Did study 5 involve informed consent from the first-graders? Could there be? What child would reject the opportunity to watch television, particularly in the middle of the school day? And what of the possible alteration of the teacher-student relationship if the teacher is a stooge for the communication researcher? What prevents long-term effects from the interaction of a massed dose of adult aggression, television aggression, and personal aggression, which a typical debriefing may not wipe out? What do we know about debriefing children?

Study 6 raises another aspect of the consent issue. If the project has a large enough budget to offer substantial incentives, is it okay to buy consent? Twenty dollars to an ADC mother will buy a lot of interview time. So will four packs of cigarettes to a prisoner or two pieces of bubble gum to a kingergarten child.

We are more skilled or at least more highly trained in research methods than in the definition of ethical issues. Many of the issues have little correlative data available to assist us in seeking resolutions. Questions about deceptive practices, debriefing modes, and risk to subjects have only begun to generate research interest.

A further purpose of this chapter is to argue that much of the research required in this area is straightforward communication research. Whether a subject has been properly informed about a research task before giving consent involves several communication issues: What amount of information, in what format, covering which task requirements is essential? Does the subject sufficiently understand such a message? The giving of consent requires the subject to return some information; that is, consent is a reciprocal communication activity. The debriefing of subjects who have participated in research tasks is another information-processing activity: What form of debriefing, if any, adequately debriefs? What message strategies for debriefing are best? The confidentiality of information involves information storage and retrieval and processing modes. We do not propose to reduce all ethical issues to communication questions, but we have been impressed by the extent to which communication components of these issues do exist, must be dealt with, and may lend themselves particularly to the substantive and theoretic bents of communication scientists.

INFORMED CONSENT

Let us examine first the operational definition of informed consent that has been proposed by a major federal agency:

Informed consent is the agreement obtained from the subject or from his authorized representative to the subject's participation in an activity. The basic elements of information necessary to such consent include:

1. A fair explanation of the procedures to be followed and their purposes, including identification of any procedures which are experimental;

2. A description of any attendant discomforts and risks reasonably to be expected;

3. A description of any benefits reasonably to be expected;

4. A disclosure of any appropriate alternative procedures that might be advantageous for the subject;

5. An offer to answer any inquiries concerning the procedures; and

6. An instruction that the person is free to withdraw his consent and to discontinue participation in the project or activity at any time without prejudice to the subject.

Although there is a substantial number of weasel words in these guidelines, their intent seems relatively clear. They call for a comprehensive explanation of just what it is that you propose to do to a person in order to obtain some data from that person. Furthermore, the informed consent guidelines quoted are from a medical model of research; the entire context of federal efforts in this area is geared to medical patient risk-taking.[2] But there are no separate guidelines for a nonmedical model, and therefore we are obliged to do the best we can with this set or to create a social science model.

The critical issue for the social scientist has to be, "How much information am I obliged to provide about my experiment in order to solicit the cooperation of participants?" Stated this way, it stipulates that such information shall precede any experimental or study procedures. Yet, still an open question in most research projects is the timing of the provision of this information. Those who have done research that employs deception as an experimental manipulation must face up to whether or not they can in any way describe or inform a subject about their deceptive practices in advance of engaging in them. Is it adequate, for example, in employing deceptive practices to inform a subject that "the research project in which we are about to engage will include deceptive practices for some of the participants. You may or may not be one of

---

[2]Risk taking is so complex an issue in itself that it is not dealt with in this chapter. The reader is referred to Mark Steinberg, "Risk of Harm to Subjects as a Variable in Social Research," paper presented at the Speech Communication Association annual conference, Chicago 1974, and *Ethical Principles in the Conduct of Research with Human Participants* (Washington, D.C.: Amer. Psych. Assoc., 1973).

the people to be deceived in this experiment, but we wish you to know that this may occur." Is this then a fair attempt to inform a subject about an experiment without providing complete information about the nature of deception and whether or not this particular individual will or will not be in a deceptive experimental treatment? At what point would "full" information sufficiently distort or destroy the experimental process?

How much information is enough information for the participant to be adequately informed to make a decision—give consent—about his or her willingness to participate in a project? Communication researchers might well wish to study the impact that the amount of information given about an experiment has on the study's dependent variables themselves. A second effort might be the effect of the amount of information given on the consent rate for participation.

Consent itself also has its associated ambiguities. More often, written consent is being demanded as proof of consent. This will make it very difficult in field survey situations if one would try to obtain written consent for home interviews at the same time that one is working very hard to obtain an agreement to participate. The classic picture of the door-to-door interviewer with a foot in the door need now be supplemented with a picture of the consent form in one hand and a questionnaire in the other. We do not tolerate interviewers fudging on question asking or answer recording; would we deal with fudging on consent getting as harshly? Escalating refusal rates is something with which we would have to contend.

In addition to being concerned with the general process of providing information to research participants, we might wish to think about gauging whether the information provided has been understood. The requirement for informing participants seems to carry with it some responsibility for assessing whether or not that information has been understood. It is not unreasonable then to consider including some cognitive items in our instruments that would assess the participant's understanding of the research project. I think of this as a parallel to our normal practice of including some items in our instruments that attempt to determine if the participants were able to "guess" the nature of the project in which they were participating, and questions that attempt to determine if the manipulation we were using took. Again we face a paradox. One of the sets of questions we normally include tries to find out if the participants could figure out what it was that was done to them. The informed consent process we have been describing suggests that they ought to be informed a good deal more about just what that is than is probably current practice by most of us. The judicious balance between the subject psyching out the experiment and the experimenter providing that information in advance clearly spotlights one of the substantial dilemmas between current practice and what research critics would propose.

Now let us turn from these kinds of questions to some problems that develop from questions of obtaining informed consent. Constraints revolve around a continuum of compliance or noncompliance intermingled with rewards or punishments. Many of our data-gathering operations are done with groups of individuals for whom compliance is either explicit or implied. The college classroom is of course the prime example of a situation in which individuals are expected to provide consent; some classrooms go further and demand student participation. Isn't the student sitting there saying to himself, "If I darn well don't participate in this study, somehow my instructor is going to find out and I am going to suffer as a result." Furthermore the pressure of peers participating can also yield a higher degree of coercion than most of us may wish to recognize. We probably overassess the degree of voluntarism that we have created in any intact group assembled in an authority-ridden context. How often have I walked into a classroom to collect data and indicated that my study has been sanctioned by the teacher and the principal of the school and that it has national importance. I am obviously trying to motivate participation and at the same time attempting to reduce the perceived level of voluntarism that remains available for the participant's decision-making process. It is not only the teacher-student situation that carries this kind of burden. It would be similar in the case of soliciting data from employees on the job.

Compounding this is the extent to which consent is obtained from some authority figure almost as a substitute for consent being obtained from a participating individual. For example, if one is doing research with a girl scout organization, one solicits consent from the troop leader; and if one is doing research with public schools, one solicits consent from the school administration. Is this an acceptable substitute for individual consent or only a precursor for obtaining consent from the individual participants?

Another issue is the extent to which a reward or incentive is being offered for participation above and beyond the incentive of personal pride in cooperating in what is described as an important research project. More and more, material rewards are being offered by researchers to obtain participation. There is the argument that the time of the participants is valuable and they should be compensated in some tangible fashion for the effort they have provided. This argument comes from an equity standpoint. Why should I only take something from the subjects and not give them something in return that is less esoteric than the incentive contained in my motivating message to them? Can't the participation of college students be rewarded by additional points toward a grade? Can't the participation of a girl scout organization be compensated for by the contribution of $50 for their next outing? Can't the participation of low-income respondents be compensated for by a $5 bill? All these rewards and others are identifiable in the research literature. But the ethical question is, can informed consent be obtained in situations where rewards are offered for participation? How will one know if participation has come because of the size of the reward in contrast to the individual's assessment of what will come from his or her participation? Perhaps informed consent should be sought and obtained, and after it is obtained, the participant be informed further that they will receive an incentive for their participation. I find it very difficult otherwise to separate the contamination of the offered reward from the informed consent decision-making process.

These questions tap some of the dimensions of the problems associated with informed consent. Clearly, informed consent as a concept bears some consideration by communication theorists as to its role and its parameters in our field. What could be more central to communication theory than the issues of providing adequate information, determining if that information is understood, assessing the strategies by which that information might be provided, and examining those situational variables that may impact most strongly on decisions that an individual must make after that individual has received such information. One can quickly generate a rather elaborate set of research propositions from the concepts involved in the process of obtaining informed consent.

DECEPTION

The question of using deception in the conduct of experimental research runs smack into the notion of informed consent. These tend to be contradictory. How can you obtain informed consent when deception is used in an experiment? Actually, that question is too imprecise. It ought to be, "Can *fully informed consent* be obtained when deception is used in an experiment?" If you take the position that informed consent exists along a continuum from some information to complete information, then it is still possible to slip in deception at earlier points on that continuum than the extreme of fully informed consent. Serious doubts have been raised about the use of deception in social research. Some deception critics who are very active social scientists themselves have taken the strong position that all deception research is wrong. Some who used deception practices in their earlier publications have vowed against using it any longer. Others maintain that it is a necessary tool for the conduct of some research and unnecessary for others. Typically, the question of the use of deception in communication research focuses on whether or not it is more important to avoid deceiving anyone, or to deceive a small number of subjects, however temporarily, with the expectation that many persons will benefit from the knowledge gained.

Let us summarize the major arguments of those who oppose the use of deception:

1. Deception takes away the subject's freedom to make a fully informed decision about participating in a given experiment. Given the typical superior status of experimenters to the subjects, they are likely to obtain con-

sent most of the time. Presumably not disclosing the deception to be involved in an experiment further enhances the experimenter's ability to obtain consent. What would the consent rate be if subjects were informed that they were about to be deceived, and the nature of the deception were disclosed?

2. The use of deception by social scientists institutionalizes deception. Using deception in social research transforms the subject into an object of manipulation, and that is demeaning to the human being involved. The dignity of human relationships is being subordinated to the desires of the experimenter.

3. By using deception, and developing or contributing to the development of an expectation about deception in subjects, we leave the subject with fewer qualms about deceiving the experimenter.

4. The public's attitude toward social research will be diminished as the public becomes aware of the use of deception in such research.

The counterarguments, those that advocate the acceptance of deception as an appropriate research tool, also merit identification:

1. Deception has long been used as a research instrument without any apparent negative results.

2. Deception may be the only way to obtain valid information in certain situations.

3. Any potential harm will be offset by the contribution of our research results to scientific knowledge.

Those are the major arguments that have been presented with regard to the use of deception in research. In an interesting experiment, Gallo and others[3] assessed the effects of deception in a conformity experiment. In the full information condition, subjects were informed that the experiment was about conformity and that they would be tested to see the extent to which they did conform to the judgment of others. In another condition the conformity nature of the experiment was completely masked. The results indicated that subject knowledge about being in a conformity experiment did not decrease their conformity at all. The authors speculated that "This type of response indicates that psychologists are disbelieved even in those rare situations in which they are caught telling the truth."

What is going on in an experiment is that the subjects themselves have a number of things at stake. They want to believe that their task performance is meaningful. Most are aware that they are only supposed to know as much about the experiment as they have been told and that internally hypothesizing about the parameters of the study might disqualify them or invalidate their data. Strickler and others[4]

---

[3]Philip S. Gallo, Jr., Shirley Smith, and Sandra Mumford, "Effects of Deceiving Subjects upon Experimental Results," *Journal of Social Psychology*, 89: 99–107 (February 1973).

[4]Lawrence J. Strickler, Samuel Messick, and Douglas N. Jackson, "Suspicion of Deception: Implications for Conformity Research," *Journal of Personality and Social Psychology*, 5: 379–89 (1967).

suggest that this results in a "pact of ignorance" between the subject and the experimenter. The subjects do not confess that they have some strong guesses about what is going on. At the same time the researcher is not interested in finding out what portion of his or her data may be useless. Strickler[5] found that only 24 percent of all studies using deceit provided data on how much subject suspicion of deception there was. Subjects may frequently not be deceived but behave as if they were. And if the same subject pool is used repeatedly, subjects ought to become more test-wise.

There is also the concurrent problem that participation in deception research by subjects, whether with beforehand or post hoc knowledge about the deception, may result in less favorable attitudes toward the results of such research. Cook and others[6] found that subjects who had participated in five deception experiments had less favorable attitudes toward experimental research than those who had participated in a single deception experiment.

If you take the position that deception in any form is improper, then you may have to argue that position in the context of colleagues who hold a more accepting view of deception. However, there are some guidelines that can be suggested for the latter as they begin to implement deceptive manipulated practices. Kelman[7] suggests that the researcher should evaluate (1) the significance of the proposed study, (2) the stage of the research effort, from preliminary pilot efforts to full-scale experimental data-gathering operations, (3) the possibility that alternative procedures such as role playing or field experiments may provide not only acceptable alternatives but more comprehensive alternatives, and (4) the "noxiousness" of the deception. Just how noxious the deception may be raises questions as to its intensity, its magnitude, the ability to counteract it after the experiment, and its possible impact on the self-esteem of the participants, let alone their consequent attitude toward the experimenter and social research in general.

Finally, if one were to take a more antiseptic than ethical issues approach to questions of deception, some interesting conceptual problems stand out. What are maximizing strategies for deceiving human beings? What messages, what themes, what symbol systems, can maximally deceive the given audience? Perhaps the most widely used content area for deception research in our own field has been on the effects of more or less credible information sources. When differing sources were attached to the same message, typically small but consistent differences in impact accrued. Another genre of research kept the source constant and altered the messages emanating from those

[5]Lawrence J. Strickler, "The True Deceiver," *Psychological Bulletin*, 68: 13–20 (July 1967).

[6]Thomas D. Cook and others, "Demand Characteristics and Three Conceptions of the Frequently Deceived Subject," *Journal of Personality and Social Psychology*, 14: 185–94 (March 1970).

[7]Herbert C. Kelman, "Human Use of Human Subjects: The Problem of Deception in Social Psychological Experiments," *Psychological Bulletin*, 67: 1–11 (January 1967).

sources; again, predicted results were obtained for purposes of studying in such heuristic areas as congruity theory and dissonance theory. Those have been classic deception situations in communication research. There is no doubt that the experimenters believed that the end knowledge obtained justified the mild deceptive practices used. Nevertheless, the issues regarding such practices have been articulated here only briefly, and the young scientist must begin to make his or her own decisions. There is of course the possibility that those decisions need not or should not be entirely self-made. An internal review body that could examine the significance of the proposed research, the noxiousness of the deception, and the need for deception could be useful in deciding research strategies.

DEBRIEFING

I doubt that any aspect of our research procedures is handled in a more cavalier fashion than the practice of debriefing research participants at the end of their participation. Presumably, debriefing contains a further explanation about the research effort in which the subjects have participated. Debriefing of course is partly a contradiction to the concept of fully informed consent obtained in advance of participation. If consent were fully informed, what would there be left to debrief a participant about? Therefore, our first ethical consideration has to take into account what it was that participants were not informed about before they consented to participate. And if we relate the question to the last section, the imperative for debriefing is maximum if we had also engaged in some form of deception.

The researcher must decide whether debriefing is at all necessary. In many situations involving nonobtrusive measurement, one would not argue for debriefing. It may be impossible if the researcher cannot identify those from whom nonobtrusive information was obtained. But it is more likely that the research we do brings us into a form of contact with participants that permits us to reidentify them if necessary for purposes of debriefing or taking second measures of our variables.

The most critical part of our present discussion is how effective debriefing is or can be. Debriefing is a communication subprocess; one is attempting to provide information to individuals in a way that will enable them to process and to integrate that information with whatever impact the experimental situation may have had on them before such information was available. We are guilty of knowing very little about how to create an effective debriefing, let alone the most effective debriefing.

The need for debriefing is easy to demonstrate. Take the classic research examining the effects of televised violence. Experimenters exposed young children to videotape examples of violence and then examined their postviewing behavior. This example contains no deception, but just what is the nature of postexperimental messages that will restore the prior passivity of the children or reduce the induced experimental aggression? The experimenter assumes that the aggression induced had at best a short-term impact. Just how far can that assumption go in terms of experimental manipulations? Now consider an example involving deception. A recent study used as the dependent variable the number of social dates accepted by female subjects in response to the request of male stooges. What is the residual effect on the young female subject after she is told, "It's only an experiment. The young men were carrying out orders to ask you out for a date." The importance of the debriefing in this second sample is apparent; the means by which that debriefing will be successful are not apparent. This second study could affect the self-esteem of subjects, and that may have negative consequences. Walster[8] and others manipulated the perceived sociability of experimental subjects. Half were told they were very high on sociability and half were told they were very low. All were given a thorough individual debriefing. After the debriefing, those subjects who had been told that they were stronger in sociability continued to rate themselves significantly higher on the sociability index than those who received an unfavorable report. This debriefing obviously did not eliminate the effects of the manipulation. Rather than criticize those researchers for their failure in debriefing, we should commend their courage in examining that aspect of the research process that lends credence to the proposition that the content and style of debriefing as an experimental procedure require stringent examination. It is our proposition that communication researchers ought to be more skilled than those in other conceptual study areas to cope with the informational and communication facets of debriefing. As yet we can identify no serious work in this area within our own field.

Worse still, we are typically sloppy in our approach to debriefing, although this is more supposition on my part than firm evidence. However, one is hard pressed when examining journal articles to find sufficient information on debriefing strategies used so as to capably evaluate their likely efficacy. It is not an uncommon practice in communication research to debrief subjects by handing out a mimeographed sheet of paper that purports to explain the research project. Sometimes this piece of paper is given to the class instructor to read; often that person is incapable of explaining beyond what it says on the sheet of paper, or fails to announce the information at all, or fails to distribute individual debriefing memos to participating subjects. Even more likely, in research with elementary school classrooms, is that some debriefing may be given to the school principal or school teacher but that the young children are already considered incapable of handling such additional information. Further, the issue of the relative effectiveness of an oral briefing of a group of subjects en masse as compared to a more personal one-on-one briefing is not known to us.

[8]Elaine Walster and others, "Effectiveness of Debriefing Following Deception Experiments," *Journal of Personality and Social Psychology*, 6: 371–80 (1967).

The case for offering debriefing is not all one sided. Campbell[9] suggests that there are arguments against debriefing:

> While debriefing has come to be a standard part of deception experiments in the laboratory, it has many ethical disadvantages. It is many times more of a comfort to the experimenter for his pain at deceiving than to the respondent who may learn in the process of his own gullibility, conformity, cruelty, or bias. It provides modeling and publicity for deceit and thus serves to debase language for the respondent as well as for the experimenter. It reduces the credibility of the laboratory and undermines the utility of deceit in future experiments.

It is a very interesting proposition to suggest that telling a subject what has been done to him or her may be more harmful than if they were not told. One can argue the merits of this proposition, but as yet no available evidence confirms or denies it. Consider this argument in the context of two experimental situations. In the first, you have identified and manipulated a group of subjects into believing that they are very popular with their classmates and have the potential for being even more popular. In the second, you have suggested to a group of young men that they have latent homosexual tendencies. Can one take the direction of the manipulation, place a value on it as socially constructive or socially destructive, and then determine where the debriefing will do more or less good? If so, perhaps you do not debrief in the first example and you do so in the second. It is such problematic situations as these that demand thorough discussion within our profession.

Another question relevant to debriefing is just when the debriefing can occur. The most common debriefing time is immediately after participation as a research subject. However, it is not uncommon that debriefing be delayed until all subjects have participated in an experiment. Sometimes this may be weeks or months after a particular subject has participated. Will the debriefing that takes place eight weeks after participation be as effective as the debriefing that takes place immediately? Are we mandated to do immediate debriefing? Can we trust subjects who are sworn to secrecy to fulfill that vow? Some evidence available suggests that subjects do remain still, and there is at least as much evidence that suggests they do not.

Hocking has posed several policy considerations relevant to debriefing that are useful in concluding this section.[10] He proposes that we consider guidelines for procedures to be used in debriefing research participants. Whether these guidelines are to be internally motivated or professionally sanctioned and codified remains open. Guidelines should deal with the questions of comprehensiveness of information,

[9]Donald T. Campbell, "Prospective: Artifact and Control," in Robert Rosenthal and R. L. Rosnow, eds., *Artifact in Behavioral Research* (New York: Academic Press, Inc., 1969).

[10]John Hocking, "Debriefing and Communication Research," paper presented at the Speech Communication Association Annual Conference, Chicago, 1974.

timing of the debriefing, and what information may be omitted. Hocking also asks whether more complete descriptions of debriefing procedures should be required in the methods section of journal articles, convention papers, and research reports. He makes a most interesting suggestion that the question of the effectiveness of a particular debriefing strategy be determined during the pilot stages of projects. Normally, pretesting occurs with small numbers of subjects prior to full-scale project activity. If that pretesting not only tested for measurement procedures and experimental manipulation but also included comprehensive debriefing, then the pilot-stage subjects could be assessed for any residual harmful effects of the experiment. If none was obtained, perhaps the debriefing procedures could be considered adequate. At least this suggestion raises the issue of debriefing to a position of prominence on the research agenda. Such status for debriefing has not been evident in our training nor in our consideration of research procedures.

PRIVACY

An interesting parallel can be made between the questions of privacy and confidentiality of social science data with the confidentiality journalists accord to their sources of information. There is a long-established tradition that journalists will choose to submit themselves to legal repercussions rather than reveal their sources of information. There is no such tradition with regard to the data that the researcher collects. One can start a consideration of privacy issues recognizing that the researcher stands in greater jeopardy as the holder of that information in its original form than does the journalist as the secondary source of perhaps the same information. We will not suggest that the communication researcher turn over his data to a journalist for safekeeping, but we do think the juxtaposition of the two situations provides reason for some thought and concern.

Privacy issues encompass three primary considerations. The first is the manner in which data are collected. The second is the content of the data. The third is control of the information or data after it has been assembled. In this section, we shall deal briefly with these three aspects of the privacy issue in order to suggest key considerations for research project directors.

The manner of data collection is basically the question as to whether or not the collector of data infringes significantly on the privacy of those individuals who provide the data points. Consider the form of data collection known as participant observation. There are classic studies in which investigators have become members of such social groupings as religious cults, political organizations, and campus organizations wherein their primary purpose was to observe behavior of nonresearch members of those organizations and to come away from that setting with sufficient information to prepare some kind of report.

Whereas this form of data collection had seldom been questioned before, it now is of sufficient concern to warrant a deeper analysis. Certainly, it is a method in which the investigator has neither revealed his true purpose for his presence nor informed anyone within that organization that he is there for a primary purpose that differs from that of the organization. Further, the investigator's information may clearly identify particular individuals being observed. A less blatant example, but suspect on the same grounds, would consist of telephone requests for information to an organization or set of individuals whose job requires the provision of that information. These might be telephone calls to the Internal Revenue Service, local crisis centers, or even to the local newspaper where the intent of the research is to determine the reliability of the information being offered over a period of time. This is another form of nonobtrusive data collection that places the investigators in a tenuous position in terms of potentially invading or at least scraping away at the privacy of the individuals or organization involved.

To the extent that data collection efforts such as these become known, it is possible to anticipate negative public and government response. It is of significant concern if social science becomes identified with activities that others might call snooping or prying, both lay terms for unnecessary invasion of privacy.

The investigator who proposes to use such means to collect data must bear in mind the potential repercussions of this type of activity. Clearly, a first step would be to gain acquiescence from the group or individuals who were to be studied. Perhaps it is reasonable to indicate that observation is going to occur in some form but without necessarily completely identifying that form. With no such arrangements, the questions of privacy and the invasion or evasion of that privacy are likely to continue to be sensitive considerations both in science and in the public.

A second area focuses on the content of data being collected and the sensitivity of those data. We certainly are familiar in recent days with the difficulties of collecting such information as race and sex. How much more sensitive it is when one is asking questions about illegal behaviors, abortions, the use of marijuana, how one is treated by one's parents, or the frequency of sexual activity with a marital partner. To the extent the data provide sensitive information and the investigator is interested in the sensitive data being valid, one must be concerned with the individual respondent's right of privacy about those data. This raises the question as to whether the data collection processes can guarantee anonymity to the individual or confidentiality. Anonymous data supposedly do not permit the identification of the individual from his or her responses. Then given no link between data and subject, the subject is presumably not at risk. However, truly anonymous data may be more rare than we are willing to admit. If one collects enough demographic indicators within the data set, some shrewd individual might well be able to piece together individual identifications. On the other hand, if we offer not anonymity but confidentiality, we are suggesting to the respondent that they trust us, that we will keep to ourselves the information believed to be sensitive as well as that which we believe is not sensitive. If one is doing panel analyses over time, it becomes mandatory that there be some means of identifying respondents from one time to another. Although we can create special codes for individuals to use over repeated time periods, similar possibilities occur for retracing the individual. The purpose of these guarantees or offers of either anonymity and/or confidentiality is to preserve the trust of the subject. Any belief on the subject's part that the researcher cannot keep the privacy promise would likely lead to less than complete responses, particularly with sensitive questions. That in itself makes an interesting research question—whether or not lack of trust in the researcher leads to even less valid responses for sensitive questions than for nonsensitive questions.

Another difficult point that the researcher should be cognizant of is asking one respondent questions about another person. To what extent is some form of permission necessary from the person being asked about? If I ask someone if his wife beats him, am I not tampering with the privacy of the other person?

The third consideration we would raise in this section deals with the control of information once it has been transformed into a data set and the uses to which those data are put. One thinks of that great data bank in the sky that contains all our biographical, financial, medical, cognitive, attitudinal, and behavioral facts. One sees computers around the world feeding into and getting from that great data bank a collection of information on which to base social and political decisions. I expect that the next successful disaster movie could be based on that conception. Nevertheless, for our purposes now, once we have a data set, how prone are we to make it generally available for secondary analyses to any who might ask for it without asking if doing that constitutes any form of privacy jeopardy? Are we not obligated to explain to research participants that the data they provide us may be used by others for quite different purposes than the purpose we are explaining to them at the time we attempt to obtain informed consent? We are not even taking into account unauthorized access, but focusing only on the possibility that authorized access can have a set of very different outcomes than those originally bargained for or agreed to. Clearly, by now the researcher must have made every effort to remove any chance of subject identification. That is a minimum condition for storing data in more public places.

Another issue deals with the duration of data storage. When we have collected data from individuals, are we suggesting that those data may be available permanently, or should finite time parameters be introduced? Clearly, the most suspect form of data storage would be to maintain the raw data either as questionnaires, interviews, recordings, or the like. This is an obvious threat to confidentiality, and we must quickly remove that possibility.

In determining who should access or have access to the data, should the subject have access to his or her own data? If we have granted the participants the opportunity to withdraw from the project, should the participants not also be given the opportunity to withdraw their data if perchance they should determine that it is not in their best interest or that it has been available for a sufficient period of time, or they have come to lose trust in the project? This could clearly occur in research projects with repeated measures over time. The normal attrition that is often fatal to such research could be exacerbated by subjects who say that they not only will no longer provide data but they wish to withdraw the data they have already provided. Who owns the data?

The concerned researcher will maintain close control of the data until such time as no subject can be identified from his or her responses. I have too often walked into a workroom and seen questionnaires lying about clearly identifying an individual by name or by address or by some other overt means. I have also seen instances in which individuals have picked up such questionnaires, thumbed through them, and then said, "Hey, I know that guy." Such occurrences ought not be permitted or tolerated; you would not be pleased if an instrument you had completed in confidence and signed were being routed on a buck slip to your colleagues.

In this section, we have attempted to identify and clarify a subset of the critical issues relevant to ethical considerations regarding privacy. This is not a comprehensive set; it would take far more than a chapter to deal with issues of privacy alone, let alone the other issues we have focused on. We have not proposed rules; rather we have opted to suggest alternatives for consideration. Now let us consider some mechanisms by which discussion of these ethical questions can be facilitated.

AM I MY COLLEAGUE'S KEEPER?

Any responsibilities I may have as a social scientist to analyze or to monitor the professional ethics of others who also go about doing research have seldom been enumerated. The American Psychological Association manual (1973) on ethics for psychologists devotes all its sections to self-examination of ethical practices. Perhaps because psychologists are more interested in individuals than in groups, this omission may be theoretically explicable. However, the same omission by the American Sociological Association in its ethical mandate to its members is less understandable. Professional discussion within the fraternity of communication scholars is overdue. If internal monitoring, which might range from professional codes or stated ethical principles to increased self-awareness, is preferable to outside regulation, the time for thought and activity is already delinquent. New proposed federal regulations and the large-scale changes in existing federal rules for human subject research require rapid professional response, or the opportunities for self-controlling procedures will be very limited.

Three questions will be examined in this section. (1) Am I responsible for the research practices of my colleagues in any fashion? To this, most of us would offer at least a restrained yes. (2) To what extent am I responsible? This will produce more variable responses. (3) Still another question would ask about the quality of my responsibility. In what ways am I responsible for how other communication scholars manage their human subjects?

To clarify these issues, let me mention a number of situations that vary in the ease with which one may seek to identify ethical responsibilities associated with membership in our community of scholars.

A common professional situation in which we have an opportunity to deal with the professional practices of others is when we are in the role of professional peer reviewer or monitor (e.g., as a reader of a journal manuscript or a research proposal that seeks funding). Surely, in the role of professional reviewer, anything read is fair game for review purposes. The anonymity usually associated with this role makes it easier to espouse any particular ethical stance that appears needed. To the extent scientists have been willing to monitor aggressively the ethical practices of their colleagues, whether with human subjects or not, it has been most common in this type of role.

A second situation that also permits a wide degree of authority is in managing the behaviors of students, at least our own graduate or undergraduate advisees. In these situations, there is little onus in suggesting that some practices they are considering may be questionable. We have few inhibitions in criticizing the behaviors of these junior professionals if we find them deviating from what we consider normative and/or acceptable practices with subjects.

A third situation is that of senior investigator with junior investigator, perhaps even senior professor with junior professor. This is a bit muddier in that the collegial association is closer to parity than any of the prior situations described. We are now talking about offering criticism, perhaps unsolicited criticism, to an individual whose privileges, benefits, and association with us probably extend beyond the professional into the social and/or personal realms. But what occurs if the roles are reversed? If either the students or research assistants in the prior situation or the junior colleagues in the current one observes us using practices they question, how free are they to become critics? The constraints on their expressing those concerns, because of some real or imagined repercussions, can severely restrain constructive growth in our recognition of questionable practices.

A fourth situation is that of senior investigator to senior investigator. In all the situations described, it would be easier for principal investigators to discuss, argue about, and make suggestions about theoretical issues, operational definitions, or data analytic techniques. It would be easier to manage discussion of those kinds of issues even in the reverse authority situation (e.g., students are expected and often praised for offering suggestions about research design or project operations). But suggesting to others that the practices they engage in when using human subjects may be unethical can be catastrophic to interpersonal and professional relationships.

Perhaps these examples are useful primarily in making the issue salient and in pointing out varying degrees of interpersonal difficulty in proposing to monitor others who do research or for others to monitor me. Professional scholars long ago adopted a mode of freedom of speech that in some fashion was reinterpreted as an unchallenged freedom of practices. However, external developments and concerns expressed by others no longer permit the exclusive use of self-imposed controls. There are now external controls to recognize.

Let us make apparent several disadvantages of intercollegial checks on research practices, other than where it has been formalized in the roles of manuscript reader, proposal reviewer, prospective employer, or student trainer. The more ticklish situations are those involving project or department colleagues. First, monitoring of subject practices may be taken to imply a mistrust or a distrust of the probable practices of a colleague. The review may be perceived by the receiver as saying, "Hey, he doesn't trust me in my work with human subjects, if he insists on being able to review what I do."

Or a reviewee may respond, "Hey, how come he's holier than I? What says that he can manage such a review system?" What is it about the ethical practices or posture of the reviewer that affords him the superior position in conducting reviews of others? Those reviewed may believe that their practices and their ethical postures are at least as good, if not better, than those being practiced or advocated by the collegial reviewer.

In this last statement, we used the term "superior" purposely. Anyone who assumes the role of critic on ethical issues or any other research issues may be labeled another boss in the research situation. And the last thing the practicing researcher wants is another self- or other-designated superior butting in on his research. The label superior may be an even more pejorative label if it is considered synonymous with censor. It is a very short step in a formalized review process from making suggestions about research practices to issuing orders about them.

Surely, these disadvantages must be considered as one proposes a means of overseeing the research practices of those among whom there is no clearly defined relational requirement for overseeing. At the same time, there are several advantages in advocating a shared professional responsibility in maintaining some form of peer review procedures in conducting research with humans. First, when we have been able to examine the relative acceptability of various research practices, we then could be looking at each other's work with mutually determined criteria. Perhaps one of our professional associations can create a minimal code of ethical standards and a minimal code of acceptable research operations, which implies mutually determined norms for examining adherence to those practices. Another advantage will be increased awareness among colleagues that such questions about research practices do arise. They should be concerned individually with such answers to these questions, and their professional associations are units through which such issues can be discussed collectively. Support for an individual's own beliefs by the posture of colleagues and/or of a professional organization would do well to bolster any particular position on research practices that may be advocated.

Another advantage in intercollegial action is that such issue recognition would make a sounding board available to all members of this profession. A sounding board could serve to suggest improvements in research strategies. It could possibly inhibit or deter potential improprieties before they occur. That is, if there were in my department, my college, or my association a group from whom I could request counsel either anonymously or openly about some potential research practices, this might be more acceptable than if I were engaged in only a post hoc research practices evaluation context.

This last point raises the question of timing in the practice of intercollegial review. In its simplest form it may be the question of pre- or postproject review. There are clear examples of both of these situations. The refereed article is a postproject review procedure. The research has been done, and if the practices are considered shoddy, they cannot be remedied. One must correct the experimenter through chastisement, rejection, or some sort of professional pillory. This may be the least advantageous time for the conduct of ethical reviews. If one were to seek a maximizing time for intervention, it could be that now mandated by the National Institutes of Health. Reviews of research practices are required at the institutional level before the proposals are submitted for federal funding. This stimulates a review of what colleagues propose to do well before they attempt to do them. Potential improprieties may be corrected or argued a priori.

A final advantage of collegial responsibilities might be in terms of converting or altering existing research practices to eliminate or at least minimize questions that relate to ethical difficulties. Perhaps the proposed deception could be altered in minor ways such that the practice is more acceptable than in its original form.

We have raised the specter of requiring or not requiring compliance with the outcome of a review process. An equally relevant question is whether the opportunity to seek or provide counsel for colleagues' work should be a mandatory or a voluntary activity. This is the issue of whether one *may* seek out a collegial review group or whether one *must* obtain clearance. The requirement by federal agencies for institutional clearances is clearly not voluntary. If one wants funding from such agencies, one must submit to review and accommodate the criticisms and suggestions made by a review panel. However, do not be misled by our resorting to examples that involve the seeking of federal funds. The same ethical issues exist for unfunded projects, for master's theses, for class projects, and for the full range of research efforts falling short of being mammoth projects. Questions about research practice propriety are not bound to the source of funds; they are constant issues for all levels of human subject research.

It is always more fun to give advice to others than to receive advice that one must implement or to be forced to seek advice if one had not seriously considered a need for advice. Yet the fact that most of our training in raising questions about the ethical aspects of our research practices is the result of nonsystematic learning should make it evident that we are rather naive about many of the central issues. Ethical practices are seldom emphasized among the set of operations we engage in to do research. The outline of a journal article into subdivisions of introduction, methods, findings, and discussion finds little place for a review of our practices. The typical caveat that subjects were informed at the end of the experiment and most expressed surprise may be an insufficient precaution in research situations.

What are some policy alternatives for intercollegial review? Alternative policies may be considered along two dimensions. One is an internal-external continuum. This would specify the group among whom review procedures would be implemented. The internal locus might be within a project staff or within the administrative unit of the principal investigator. External review processes would be those wherein a particular project is examined by a committee from outside one's department or at an intercollege or university level. The continuum from internal to external must be locally defined.

A second dimension to be considered in any policy would be the degree of voluntarism associated with the review. The extent to which one is submitting ideas or plans either voluntarily or involuntarily is important. Equally critical is whether the review body's comments are to be considered by the researcher or mandated to the researcher.

In a simple form, there might be a voluntary internal department clearance procedure wherein each investigator, from undergraduate student to senior faculty member, is asked to submit a statement of proposed research practices. This would go either to an anonymous or an identified body constituted by that department. This body may consist of those most capable in the planned research area. This internal, voluntary clearance would generate a review of practices for the investigator for whatever purposes he or she might wish. In this manner, counsel would be available from a group skilled in the appropriate areas. This review has the potential for a congenial relationship among the participants, where the counsel sought and the guidance given were voluntary. More rigorous review methods might choose to remove the degree of voluntarism either from the submission and/or from the results of the review process, but still retain the within-unit character of the review.

An alternative policy now in effect at many universities with regard to grants and contracts sought from federal agencies requires an a priori review by an institutional body. The funders will not make final judgments on project proposals until written approval for the proposed practices is received from the institution. This typically takes the form of an all-university committee reviewing the proposals for research by communication scholars. The practices being advocated are screened by engineers, English professors, mathematicians, and medical doctors, among other constituent members of such all-university bodies. It is not uncommon after such review to find requests for complete instrumentation or questionnaires, for written permission to conduct phone interviews from potential respondents, and a wide variety of misunderstandings from these review groups about the kind of research to be conducted by communication researchers. As one moves from an internal to an external review process, the burden on the researcher to justify her or his practices is more time consuming; the response must be far more elaborate.

Perhaps if an internal review process preceded the submission of a proposal to a university body, this might remove some of the difficulties found with the more eclectic interests and skills of an all-university committee. One might even argue successfully with some university administrations that this internal review process could substitute for the centralized review process.

We may believe that our personal practices are either beyond reproach or very close to it. At the same time, we are well aware of the increasing number of people who refer to themselves as communication scholars or scientists with highly variant credentials for claiming that title. We are also well aware of the variety of shoddy reports, papers, and studies that purport to be communication research. At this point, our major safeguards are the review panels of our journals and the hiring practices of our institutions. As more and more departments of varying backgrounds assume the label of communication department, the difficulties of maintaining professional identity may be compounded. So the issue of monitoring of research practices with human beings is related to a broad set of professionalization issues.

It is only one function of a review process to weed out unsatisfactory practices or practices that may raise more ethical concerns than the desired data would justify. One can posit some empirical, testable issues about a review process. For one, would not a policy of collegial overseeing result in better research procedures and therefore higher-quality research results? The kinds of suggestions made by colleagues attentive to our research interests and proposals could be useful ones. The process also might serve to inform our immediate colleagues about our research directions—an increasing problem in departments that are large in size and where intercollegial communication contacts are difficult to maintain. Research evaluations of our work by journal editors and grant readers also could become more favorable over the period of time in which we have been able to receive suggestions for alterations in procedures. A further testable consideration is whether the adoption of an internal review policy might reduce the instances of questionable research practices on our part. If the entirely internal review is not sufficient, then the number of questions raised by university committees should be much fewer if our submission already included the results of an internal monitoring process.

Perhaps the critical question is not whether there should be a review of research practices among colleagues. The most profitable use of our intellectual time and energy would be to determine what forms of review should be implemented. We can better be concerned with how extensive such a review process should be, the mandatory limits of that review, and the attendant research questions. We must be able to assure ourselves that the outcome of review practices will be generally beneficial to the community of scholars, the population of would-be scholars, the subjects of our research, the subjects in our research, and the larger community.

We are hard pressed to condone the extent to which the ethical issues raised in this chapter have been ignored not only by communication researchers but by their brothers and sisters in the social sciences. Because privacy as well as deception, debriefing, and informed consent have significant communication components in them, our one plea is that communication scientists approach these issues from the dual vantage points of (1) addressing their own practices with regard to these ethical areas and (2) concerning themselves with the concepts involved as areas available for a good deal of useful research.

15

The Logic of Historical Research

David Paul Nord and
Harold L. Nelson

WHAT IS HISTORY?

The nature of history has long puzzled philosophers and historians. Philosophers, who once thought history the queen of the sciences, have in the twentieth century hotly debated whether history is a kind of science at all or even a form of empirical inquiry. Though working historians have largely ignored the rising tide of analytical philosophy, they too have frequently discoursed on the question, "What is history?", usually in the form of ardent apologies for what they themselves do. Historians may not know philosophy, but they do know what they like. And the debates over such issues as specialization versus generalization, qualitative versus quantitative methods, narrative versus analytical explanations, and humanism versus social science have been lengthy and acrimonious.

The purpose of this chapter is not to resolve these issues on one side or the other but to suggest that most of them are nonproblems that need not be resolved at all. They are issues prompted by an unnecessarily restrictive view of what history is, or should be, a view that seems now to be fading. In recent years, social scientists and social science historians have become less strident in their criticisms of "traditional" history, while traditional historians have become more tolerant of social science theory and methods. This new era of good feelings should be especially helpful to journalism historians, who are (or should be) part of an interdisciplinary enterprise in the study of both the unique historical institutions of journalism and the broad social process of communication.

Some philosophers and many historians today would agree that perhaps the best way to describe history is to say it is simply the study of the past. As we shall see, the study of the past sometimes requires descriptive and explanatory schemes that are different from those usually employed in other disciplines. But as a form of logical inquiry or a form of knowledge, history is no different from the natural and social sciences.[1] History is an empirical study that uses various levels of generalization to describe, interpret, or explain collections of data. Scholars with strikingly different goals and methods work within this catchall category. All are historians.

The "pastness" of history led idealistic philosophers such as Collingwood and Dray[2] and relativist historians such as Becker and Beard[3] to suppose that history is essentially different from science. The scientist observes directly, while the historian confronts a lost past, an object of study that has completely disappeared. The problem with this view is not so much that it misunderstands history but that it misunderstands science.[4] Historians deal with incomplete, biased data; but so do scientists. No two experiments or surveys are ever exactly alike. Scientists also do not necessarily observe directly, but like historians they look for indicators of the unobservable. No living person has seen "George Washington," but neither has anyone seen an "attitude," a "cultural trait," or a "subatomic particle."

Murray Murphey makes this point rather well.[5] He argues that historical facts are very much like subatomic particles: they are theoretical constructs postulated to explain present data. In this sense, at least, historians act very much like scientists. They study the available evidence and form "theories" to explain it. The "theories" are not only the interpretations but are the facts themselves. For example, the concept "George Washington" is really a theoretical construct that historians offer to explain the existence of present data, such as documents, letters, statutes, memories, and Mount Vernon. The "theory" that George

[1]Murray Murphey, *Our Knowledge of the Historical Past* (Indianapolis: Bobbs-Merrill Co., Inc., 1973); Peter D. McClelland, *Causal Explanations and Model Building in History, Economics, and the New Economic History* (Ithaca, N.Y.: Cornell University Press, 1975).

[2]R. G. Collingwood, *The Idea of History* (New York: Oxford University Press, Inc., 1946); William Dray, *Laws and Explanation in History* (New York: Oxford University Press, Inc., 1957).

[3]Carl Becker, *Everyman His Own Historian* (New York: F. S. Crofts, 1935); Charles Beard, "Written History As an Act of Faith," *American Historical Review*, 39: 219–27 (1934).

[4]Arthur C. Danto, *Analytical Philosophy of History* (Cambridge, England: Cambridge University Press, 1965), pp. 110–11.

[5]Murphey, *Our Knowledge*, pp. 15–16.

Washington actually lived can be evaluated in the usual way—on whether it is plausible, parsimonious, heuristically useful, and so on. Thus, our knowledge of the past is based firmly on empirical evidence, but it must remain forever tentative in the way all theories are tentative.

This notion of history is admittedly incomplete. There is much more to most historiography than "establishing facts." The temporal flow of history, change over time, means that historians must not only try to make true statements about past events but must weigh the *consequences* of those events.[6] Describing the interconnection of events through time is what historians call interpretation or explanation, and it may take a form quite different from explanation in the sciences. Moreover, some historians are clearly more concerned about consequences and explanation than are others, and they go about their work in different ways. One historian, like a Marx or a Toynbee, might offer a grand theory of the rise and fall of civilizations; another, like a genealogist, might seek only to learn how to spell his great grandfather's name. Despite this diversity and the moral dimension of history (discussed in more detail below), all history is still basically a form of empirical inquiry that uses theoretical constructs to attempt to make true statements about the past. If this broad definition can be accepted, several troublesome issues of historiography need not trouble us at all.

One of the most persistent debates among historians has been about generalization. Do historians generalize? Should they generalize? As a philosophical problem, this issue is now dead or at least comatose. It now seems clear that all historians generalize, whether they want to or not.[7] The very words of the language of history are generalizations—war, nation, industry, the press. That this should ever have been an issue at all may surprise a social scientist, whose purpose most of the time is to generalize. The reason has to do with the goals of history. For many historians, the goal is not to generalize but to understand a particular event in a particular place and time. If generalization means stating general laws, in the scientific sense, historians are usually not interested. Today, however, most would agree that some generalization is inherent in any form of explanation or even description, even if the goal is particularistic. Different historians simply operate at different levels of generality.

Another controversy, which in a sense grew out of the issue of generalization, has been the debate over quantification in history. Many historians have attacked quantification as an especially vicious form of generalization. It destroys the rich variety of human experience by reducing people to numbers and artificial categories. This debate, too, now seems to have been over a nonproblem. All historians generalize, and quantitative generalities are not inherently different from linguistic ones. Quantification is merely a method for handling certain kinds

[6]Danto, *Analytical Philosophy*, p. 134; Murphey, *Our Knowledge*, p. 27.

[7]Consult Louis Gottschalk, ed., *Generalization in the Writing of History* (Chicago: University of Chicago Press, 1963).

of data in certain ways. Again, the goal of the historian and the nature of the data should dictate the method. Different historians use different methods.

Debate has also swirled around the issue of the appropriate form for historical explanation. Narration is the traditional form, though in recent decades historians have come to rely more on historical analysis, something like hypothesis testing and argumentation in the sciences. Both forms have had their proponents, though narration, because it is so characteristic of history, has received the most attention. The philosopher Arthur Danto argues that narrative explanation is the one thing that sets history apart from science.[8] Yet quite obviously historians do not always rely on narration.[9] In practice, they use narration or analysis depending on the specific problem at hand. Often they use both in a single work.[10] Again, the issue is related to generalization and to the goals of the historian. Narration is frequently more appropriate in explaining unique sequences; analysis is usually more helpful in generalizing about recurrent processes. Different historians use different forms of explanation.

In short, historians differ in method and approach depending upon their goals. Some are more interested in unique, particular events or sequences, some in general, recurrent processes. This is, of course, the familiar distinction between the idiographic (particularizing) and the nomothetic (generalizing), which derives from Dilthey and other followers of Kant. It is part of the positivist-idealist controversy now more than a century old.[11] What is new in recent years is the growing realization that for history (perhaps for all knowledge) the distinction is necessarily blurred. In practice, historians have never been completely idiographic, nor can they ever be completely nomothetic.[12] They move back and forth from the particular to the general, borrowing ideas and methods freely from any source available. This kind of theoretical and methodological pluralism has led, in the words of J. H. Hexter, to considerable "dis-ease" among analytical philosophers.[13] But historians themselves are increasingly at ease with it.

Though history as a whole is neither idiographic nor nomothetic, the distinction between the generalizing and the particularizing *goals* of different historians is a useful one and is one we make in this chapter. We will propose two ideal types that we will call, for want of better terms, the *humanist historian* and the *social science historian*. The humanist is interested primarily in unique events and sequences, seeks to understand an event by understanding its context in a particular place

[8]Danto, *Analytical Philosophy*, p. 111.

[9]Murphey, *Our Knowledge*, p. 124.

[10]J. H. Hexter, *Doing History* (Bloomington: Indiana University Press, 1971), pp. 40–41.

[11]Ronald H. Nash, ed., *Ideas of History*, vol. 2 (New York: E. P. Dutton, 1969).

[12]Robert F. Berkhofer, Jr., *A Behavioral Approach to Historical Analysis* (New York: Free Press, 1969), pp. 245–46.

[13]Hexter, *Doing History*, p. 73.

and time, must generalize and make comparisons, but is reluctant to generalize too broadly lest sight is lost of the rich variety of human history. The humanist may borrow ideas—even methods—from social science, but is not interested in contributing to social science theory. The mode of description and explanation is often, though not always, narration. The social science historian, on the other hand, is interested primarily in general processes, seeks to understand an event by grouping it with similar events, and ultimately hopes to construct generalizations and theories to explain classes of events without regard to space and time. Such historians often use social science theory and methods to help classify historical phenomena and hope to help build social theory. The mode of explanation may be narrative at times, but is more often similar to forms of scientific analysis.

Like all ideal types, these two tend unfairly to dichotomize what are essentially continuous variables. The distinction is useful, but unreal, in many ways. In practice, the work of historians is as varied as the past they write about. This is what makes the field of history a puzzle for philosophers, but an ever new adventure for historians.

HISTORY AND THE HUMANITIES

What Are The Humanities?

Humanists universally classify history as one of the humanities, along with literature, languages, and philosophy. It is not easy to find them agreeing on many other aspects of the subject. Even in this matter of what studies belong among the humanities, there are differences about including the fine arts.[14] Beyond the superficial problem of fields embraced by the humanities, in such matters as the concerns and importance of this sweeping realm of study and creation, ever more complex questions arise. "The humanities" is a difficult term, and the humanist learns to tolerate differences in all sorts of definition. (In fact, a somewhat different view may be found in Chapter 18.)

Defining the central concerns of the humanities, for example, and differentiating them from the social studies in particular becomes artificial and considerably a product of accident.[15] The interpretation of human values, ordinarily situated at the heart of the humanist's endeavor, and for generations claimed as a special province, has a place in science and social science as well.[16] No one suggests that dedication,

[14]Howard Mumford Jones, *One Great Society* (New York: Harcourt Brace Jovanovich, Inc., 1959), p. 11; Albert W. Levi, *The Humanities Today* (Bloomington: Indiana University Press, 1970), p. 16.

[15]John Higham, "The Schism in American Scholarship," *American Historical Review,* 72: 1–21 (January 1966), p. 20.

[16]Howard Mumford Jones, "The Humanities and the Common Reader," in Julian Harris, ed., *The Humanities: An Appraisal* (Madison: University of Wisconsin Press, 1962), p. 22; Levi, *Humanities Today,* p. 45.

commitment to honest reporting of findings, the elevation of the spirit through discovery, and many other values are not fostered in the study and practice of science. Few would allege that today's scientists are not concerned with the impact of their work on the human condition. It may be said, however, that the study of the humanities has at its core and as its overriding concern the illumination of what is "good" and what is "evil" in the entire experience of humanity. On a continuum of concern with values, then, humanistic study would crowd the upper end. "The whole race through its artists sets down the model of its aspirations," and this "suggests why the humanities claim a valuational priority against the sciences . . .".[17]

Distinctions between the sciences and the humanities are elaborated in the context of the humanities' widely presumed concern for the development, growth, and nurture of the individual human being. Through confrontation and immersion in the story of humanity and all its works, the humanities interpret for the individual the "galaxy of human acts and aspirations, the effect upon individuals of all types of experience throughout recorded time . . . , the range of individual choices in all environments."[18] The account of human beings in the past—their works, thoughts, impulses, examples—serves as model for the present. The liberal arts, closely associated with the humanities, were once called the liberating arts, in large part because "no one is ever free to do anything he cannot think of,"[19] and the human race needs to be informed of "ideas that diligence and brilliance have generated," because such ideas expand what the present generation can think of.[20]

Some humanists discern deep human needs in learning to know oneself and one's potentialities through contact with the web of achievement and disaster, of liberation and meanness, of elation and despair that the great stories and myths of the race offer.[21] Just as strong a theme for humanists who look inward is their belief that their realm teaches people how to live well, that acquaintance with the world of the humanities makes life worth living and is indispensable to its full enjoyment. This view asserts nothing about possible contributions of the humanities to the individual's capacity to solve problems, or to the race's solution of the constants of war, nationalism, cultural strife, or, indeed, man's inhumanity to man. Rather, it says the humanities serve human enjoyments such as dancing, reading, playing music, travel, languages, and story telling, and not with the intent or effect of curing

[17]Ibid.

[18]David H. Stevens, "What Are the Humanities?" in Robert E. Yahnke, ed., *A Time of Humanities* (Madison: University of Wisconsin Press, 1976), p. 121.

[19]Edwin J. Delattre, "The Humanities Can Irrigate Deserts," *Chronical of Higher Education*, Oct. 11, 1977, p. 32.

[20]American Historical Association "History and the Humanities," in Commission on the Humanities, *Report*, 1964, p. 108.

[21]Nathan M. Pusey, "The Centrality of Humanistic Study," in J. Harris, ed., *The Humanities*, p. 80.

illness. To think that the movers and shakers in America's conduct of the Vietnam War would have acted any differently had they been immersed from youth in the classics' accounts of strife and horror in the Greek myths is delusion: "Regardless of how pretty the parallels were, *it simply didn't matter.*"[22]

As humanists see their work coming to focus on the living individual human being, they are likely to take the individual human being of the past as model. "Not the scientific exploration of things, not the scientific examination of the behavior of groups of people, but the living, vivid acquaintance with the adventures of the human spirit . . ." fosters the fullest growth of human beings.[23] To look at the human heritage is to see it as "individual experience rather than as mass and generalization."[24]

The Historian as Humanist

The historian as humanist shares this outlook. We need true statements about the past not for the sake of establishing general laws that will embrace in grand explanation great reaches of the past and predict the future, but for the growth and development of the individual human being. "To widen our horizon, to make us see other points of view than those to which we are accustomed, is the greatest service that can be rendered by the historian. . . ."[25] History is valuable "for the conquest of parochialism, the parochialism of self, the parochialism of place, the parochialism of time . . . ," and it has a role as an area of knowledge that adds to the human being's poise and equilibrium.[26] The possibility always exists that history can provide perspective and wisdom to those who attend to it, and this may be the greatest of its contributions.[27] Shafer elaborates the same theme:

> There is much to be said for the view that the greatest function of historical study is as an addition to experience, tending to an appreciation of the existence in the past of the race of many confrontations with problems similar to our own. We see how recurrent are such problems as the necessity but the danger of resistance to tyranny, argument over the values and perils of freedom of expression, greed in the development of property, abuse of labor, the rivalry of culture groups, the competition of individuals for eminence and power, the lurking danger of demagoguery in free societies. This

[22]Pamela McCorduck, "An Introduction to the Humanities with Prof. Ptolemy," *Chronicle of Higher Education*, Feb. 9, 1976, p. 32.

[23]Pusey, "Centrality of Humanistic Study," pp. 80–81.

[24]Jones, *One Great Society*, p. 9.

[25]Morris R. Cohen, *The Meaning of Human History*, 2nd ed. (LaSalle, Ill.: Open Court Publishing Co., 1961), p. 28.

[26]Jacques Barzun, "History, Popular and Unpopular," in Joseph Strayer, ed., *The Interpretation of History* (Princeton, N.J.: Princeton University Press, 1943), p. 52. See also Gordon Wright, "History as a Moral Science," *American Historical Review*, 81: 1–11 (February 1976).

[27]David S. Landes and Charles Tilly, *History as Social Science* (Englewood Cliffs, N.J.: Prentice-Hall, Inc., 1971), p. 19; AHA, *Report*, 1964, p. 112.

broadening of experience promotes sophistication and judgment in the contemplation of public decisions, and tends both to the reduction of parochialism or insularity, and to steadiness in consideration of grand decisions by elimination of the supposition that all current problems are uniquely terrible in the history of man.[28]

For some humanist historians, the product of their craft may have a cumulative impact, a social impact, reaching many individuals and through the many reaching society. History becomes the social memory, storing past experience of the group, the people, the race, for comparison with the present.[29] Even for social planners, some hold, history can at least provide necessary warnings in extraordinary circumstances, not telling us what to do but rather some things we ought not to do.[30] Humanists in the historian's craft, then, while rejecting those who see grand designs and overriding causal factors reaching through the past and present into the future, such as Marx, Buckle, Spengler, and Toynbee, yet may see history helping the race, not to foretell, but to meet the future.[31]

Although unpersuaded that generalizations of great sweep about the past will help us predict, that laws of human behavior can be made from the story of the past, the humanist historian who denies that generalizations of any kind about the past are possible has become a rarity.[32] All historians generalize in some ways, even if the constants, similarities, and regularities that they find in the past are of low level.[33] If debate on the problem of generalization exists, it is cloistered.

The Unique and Particular

Yet the unique, the particular, continues to impress humanists, though they know that the universal will also appear with the unique in each product of study.[34] Much as they may find helpfulness in the hypothesis testing and the quantification of their historical brethren inclined toward the social sciences, they remain unconvinced that the historian's work can or should turn away from the unique and particular event of the past, for it is close acquaintance with that kind of event that most importantly contributes to the growth of the individual. In

---

[28]R. J. Shafer, *A Guide to Historical Method* (Homewood, Ill.: Dorsey Press, 1974), p. 14.

[29]G. J. Renier, *History, Its Purpose and Method* (Boston: Beacon Press, 1950), p. 19. See also Carl Degler, "Remaking American History," *Journal of American History*, 67: 7–25 (June 1980).

[30]W. B. Gallie, *Philosophy and the Historical Understanding* (London: Chatto & Windus, 1964), p. 127; Howard Beale, "What Historians Have Said About the Causes of the Civil War," in Committee on Historiography, *Theory and Practice in Historical Study*, Social Science Research Council Bulletin 54 (New York: SSRC, 1946), p. 92.

[31]Quoting Carl Becker, in AHA, *Report*, 1964, p. 196.

[32]David Hackett Fischer, *Historians' Fallacies* (New York: Harper & Row, Inc., 1970), p. 95.

[33]Gottschalk, *Generalization;* Allan Nevins, *The Gateway to History*, rev. ed. (Garden City, New York: Doubleday & Co., Inc., 1962), p. 334.

[34]Fischer, *Historians' Fallacies*, p. 97; Nevins, *Gateway*, p. 334.

addition, humanists are likely to hold that other factors compel them to this focus: complexity, responsibility, and interest.

The complexity of the past is inordinate, infinite. And the surviving record of the past, immense as it is and ever more swollen with the mushrooming of twentieth-century collectors' capacities, can in this view give us only partial, incomplete data for attempting to establish laws of human behavior. However we may classify facts and measure dimensions of the past, far too much must escape us to find large, indisputable patterns. Great events from nation to nation (the example given is ordinarily revolutions) unquestionably have similarities for which there is good reason to search; but in the complexities of the individual events, it is their differences that impress the humanist historian. The constants of revolution furnish "analogous situations," which may guide the search for regularities, but revolutions differ and constant elements from one to another provide no proof of laws in history.[35]

If complexity is a barrier to broad generalizations in the view of humanists, they add that their responsibility to the human beings in history requires that they treat them as individuals, not as statistics. This is not to say that averages, norms, and aggregates are unimportant in history, but that historical research commonly encounters persons as persons, and these persons must be characterized or the historian is refusing to deal faithfully with the past.[36] One may indeed choose a characteristic of a group of persons, sum its instances of appearance, and find means and tendencies; but to avoid the uniqueness of individuals is to dehumanize. And as with persons, so with events: responsibility to the historical process requires that events in which important changes in human affairs are deeply implicated be treated individually, in their singular contexts of time and place.[37] Futhermore, for the living to do justice to the dead should matter to the living. It is important to historians "to do justice to any man that they humanly encounter in the record of the past. Not to be concerned with justice to one or many so encountered is to diminish not their human stature but ours."[38]

As for the way in which interest conducts the humanist historian to his or her focus, it is the contention that it is the concrete, particular event that is most interesting about the human past, for historians as well as for readers. The elements peculiar to each revolution, their diversity and differences, make the study and writing of history fascinating for both.[39] In this context, complexity within the individual event or person becomes a positive attribute that can and should be dis-

---

[35]Jacques Barzun, *Clio and the Doctors: Psych-History, Quanto-History, and History* (Chicago: University of Chicago Press, 1974), p. 123; Committee on Historiography, *Theory and Practice*, p. 137.

[36]Hexter, *Doing History*, p. 52.

[37]Landes and Tilley, *History as Social Science*, pp. 10–11; Gertrude Himmelfarb, "The 'New' History," *Commentary*, June 1975, p. 73.

[38]Hexter, *Doing History*, p. 132.

[39]Nevins, *Gateway*, pp. 334–6.

cerned and dealt with, its analysis serving as a source of intellectual pleasure and stimulation for writer and reader.[40] Readers seek that which has engrossed the historian in leading them into the past—meeting its intricacies of human relationships, of forces, of resolutions.

The Story as Explanation

As developed by humanist historians, adequate explanations of the past are not those that conform to a general law or formula as in science. Particular historical events or cases are not, to them, results of the requirements of such laws. They deny that the criteria of the sciences alone are appropriate to explaining past or present. In making true statements about the past, and in finding connections among facts, humanists have contributed understanding about the past for centuries, and explanatory adequacy has been achieved without reference to the deductivist model.[41] Writer and reader alike base explanations on experience. Accounts are intelligible because they are congruent with experience, and to readers a matter is intelligible if congruency is strong enough to lead them to accept the unfamiliar and bring it into a picture that is, for each of them, enlarged.[42] This is not to say, of course, that every explanation is correct.

The overarching concept of narrative or story as providing historical explanation is probably common to all humanist historians. Yet the precise nature of how narrative performs this explanation is little discussed and is more likely to engage the epistemologist than the historian. Danto finds that what has to be explained by the historian is the connection between the beginning and end events in a change, that when we demand an explanation of some event we are in fact referring to a change.[43] Gallie reasons that historical understanding is the exercise of the capacity to follow a story, and that explanations by the historian are interruptions in the story, interruptions injected as aids to help readers follow further when their vision begins to blur or their credulity is taxed.[44]

Mink argues that historians' insistence that their work provides perspective is partly their claim that historical understanding of an event requires that one know the consequences as well as the antecedents of the event, the "after" as well as the "before." In responding to the question frequently posed to the historian, "And then what happened?", the historian contributes understanding with a narrative an-

[40]Gallie, *Philosophy*, pp. 83–6; Landes and Tilley, *History as Social Science*, p. 10.

[41]Hexter, *Doing History*, pp. 30–34; Gallie, *Philosophy*, p. 105.

[42]Barzun, *Clio*, p. 65; Sir Isaiah Berlin, "The Concept of Scientific History," in William H. Dray, ed., *Philosophical Analysis and History* (New York: Harper & Row, Inc., 1961), p. 34.

[43]Danto, *Analytical Philosophy*, pp. 141, 233, 246; Lawrence Stone, "The Revival of a Narrative: Reflections on a New Old History," *Past and Present*, 85: 3–24 (November 1979).

[44]Gallie, *Philosophy*, p. 105.

swer, which may be called a sequential explanation. This is not to suggest, however, that it is the only explanation possible of the particular event or that it answers the quite different question, "Why did it happen?"[45]

Hexter's view, that a mode of explanation is valid only in relation to what particular inquirers seek to know, is related to Mink's. The appropriate explanatory response to the often-asked "how" question, "How did it come about that . . . ?", is a story or narrative. The general laws of science are here of no use, for a general law cannot tell a story: How it happened that President Theodore Roosevelt came to order the prosecution of Joseph Pulitzer for criminal libel and was squelched by Judge Anderson; how days of debate and doubt among reporters, editors, and management of the *New York Times* led finally to the decision to print the Pentagon Papers; how newspapers' content changed with new tools for fact gathering in the decades before the Civil War. The inquirer here is likely to be asking the historian for description, for something that shades almost imperceptibly out of explanation into "confrontation with the riches of the event itself, a sense of vicarious participation in a great happening. . . ."[46] And if some do not choose to call this "explanation," it nevertheless is indispensable to understanding the past as it was.[47]

Moreover, it is arbitrary to say that the only appropriate response of the historian in giving readers access to what he knows is something termed "explanation." Historians may be asked simply for a statement of the facts of past experience. Or, again, "explanation" in the scientific sense is not what the historian sets out to provide when he or she tries to help readers "to follow the movement and to sense the tempo of events; to grasp and do justice to the motives of men; to discern the imperatives that move men to action . . . ; to recognize the impact on the course of events of an accident . . . ; and to be aware of what the participants in a struggle conceived the stakes to be."[48]

As the narrative form brings understanding, so it may seize and hold readers through its depiction of change, through the building tension and excitement of unfolding events, through the development of character and the probing of human relations. The narrative form thus encourages people to read history, contributes to widespread interest in the past, and provides general access to the story of the past for large audiences, which are essentials, the humanist holds, for history's duty and well-being.[49] Narrative history's strength, then, includes its inherent capacities for attracting a general, literate audience to whatever it has to say.

As the humanist's account of the past uses its advantages as story, it

[45]Louis O. Mink, "The Autonomy of Historical Understanding," in Dray, *Philosophical Analysis*, p. 172.

[46]Hexter, *Doing History*, pp. 42–3; see also Dray, *Laws*, p. 157.

[47]Hexter, *Doing History*, p. 43.

[48]Ibid., p. 25. See also Renier, *History, Its Purpose*, p. 23.

[49]Barzun, *Clio*, p. 105.

also employs a language different from that of the sciences. In Hexter's words, it is the ordinary discourse of educated persons, frequently evocative and connotative, not denotative like the universal rhetoric of natural science. The social sciences, in pursuing the elusive goal of a value-free vocabulary similar to that of the natural sciences, meet insurmountable difficulties, while the humanist historian knows that the rhetoric that must be used in writing of human beings and in keeping Clio accessible to the public is inevitably value laden. To bring readers into close contact with events and persons long past and dead, the use of evocative language is inescapable. It is "the appropriate rhetoric of history, when historians try to tell what it was like to have been Another."[50] Without these words, the characterization of groups, individuals, or events is impoverished and trivialized, the historian's capacities for judgment and interpretation short-circuited, the handling of such abstractions as obligation, responsibility, and conscience hedged.

HISTORY AND SOCIAL SCIENCE

Social science theory and method have found their way into history in recent years in two ways. First, historians have borrowed ideas and techniques from the social sciences to answer traditional historical questions. Second, a few social scientists and historians have begun to try to use historical data to test and develop social science theory. These are two essentially different enterprises; the second is social science, the first is not. The failure to recognize the difference has led to some exaggerated claims for "social scientific history" and has contributed to the bootless debate between humanists and social scientists over what history "really is."

Social Science—On Loan

By far the greater proportion of what has been proclaimed social science history in recent years has been of the former type: history that simply uses social science theory and methods to make traditional historical generalizations and to answer traditional historical questions. This has hardly been a revolution that has changed history into a social science.[51] Historians have always borrowed ideas from other disciplines and have always prided themselves on their methodological pluralism. Though the practitioners of this sort of history have been fond of calling their work "the new history," it has rarely been new in either goal or final product.

[50]Hexter, *Doing History*, p. 131; Berlin in Dray, *Philosophical Analysis*, pp. 43–4.
[51]Jerome Clubb and Allan G. Bogue, "History, Quantification, and the Social Sciences," *American Behavioral Scientist*, 21: 167–85 (November/December 1977), p. 170 ff; Michael Kammen, "The Historian's Vocation and the State of the Discipline in the United States," in Michael Kammen, ed., *The Past Before Us* (Ithaca: Cornell University Press, 1980), pp. 29–30.

Despite that disclaimer, however, it is fair to say that the impact on historiography of this borrowing of social science theory and method has been great.[52] First, historians have learned from the social sciences some new ways to think systematically about research design. Second, social science theories have suggested new approaches for research in fields such as economic, urban, and political history, and have helped to create largely new fields of study in social history and historical demography. Third, and perhaps most striking, historians have learned to use sophisticated quantitative methods borrowed from the social sciences, which have opened up whole new sources of historical data.

The contribution of the social sciences to research design has been something of a retooling of a traditional strategy in historical research: comparison. Though some people have argued over the years that comparative history is either imprudent or impossible, most historians have long recognized that comparison is not only useful but is inherent in even the lowest-level generalization.[53] Social science methodology, however, has taught historians to be more rigorous in setting up and carrying out comparative studies, with close attention to careful definition of terms and precise specification of underlying assumptions. Historians have often been lax in this regard, and many historiographic debates have turned on little more than semantic confusion. Obviously, we have to be clear on what we are talking about before we can compare one thing to another. Social science also taught the historian the value of unbiased, scientific sampling procedures and the need for control groups in comparison.[54]

Though many of the specific research designs used by social scientists are inappropriate for the study of the past, the systematic process of reasoning that social scientists employ can be and has been an invaluable guide for comparative history. One part of the methodological literature that deserves to have more impact on history than it has had is the literature on quasi-experimental designs, which are quite similar to what a comparative historian tries to do.[55] For example, historians

[52]Lawrence Stone, "History and the Social Sciences in the Twentieth Century," in Charles F. Delzell, ed., *The Future of History* (Nashville, Tenn.: Vanderbilt University Press, 1977); J. Morgan Kousser, "Quantitative Social-Scientific History," in Kammen, *Past Before Us.*

[53]Berkhofer, *Behavioral Approach,* p. 261. See also C. Vann Woodward, ed., *The Comparative Approach to American History* (New York: Basic Books, 1968); and George M. Frederickson, "Comparative History," in Kammen, *Past Before Us.*

[54]Stone, "History and the Social Sciences," p. 16.

[55]J. David Singer, "The Historical Experiment as a Research Strategy in the Study of World Politics," *Social Science History,* 2: 1–22 (Fall, 1977). On the comparative method in political science see Robert T. Holt and John E. Turner, *The Methodology of Comparative Research* (New York: Free Press, 1970), and Adam Przeworski and Henry Teune, *The Logic of Comparative Social Inquiry* (New York: John Wiley & Sons, 1970). On quasi-experimental designs see Donald T. Campbell and Julian C. Stanley, *Experimental and Quasi-Experimental Designs for Research* (Chicago: Rand McNally & Co., 1963), and James A. Caporaso and Leslie L. Roos, Jr., *Quasi-Experimental Approaches: Testing Theory and Evaluating Policy* (Evanston: Northwestern University Press, 1973).

have tested Frederick Jackson Turner's ideas about the impact of the frontier on democratic institutions by comparing the American case with other countries that have had similar frontier experiences, such as Canada, Australia, Argentina, and Brazil. If the institutional development in these frontier societies was quite different, it would seem rather risky to call the frontier (the "experimental treatment," so to speak) the cause.[56]

Social science theory also has had a great impact on historical scholarship in recent years, guiding historians into new lines of research. Again, this is certainly not altogether new. The "Scientific" historians of the nineteenth century were profoundly influenced by the evolutionary doctrines of social Darwinism and the general spirit of scientific inquiry. In the early decades of the twentieth century, the practitioners of what was then called "the new history," led by James Harvey Robinson, Frederick Jackson Turner, and Charles Beard, enthusiastically embraced the new social sciences and the new social theories.[57] But in the 1920s and 1930s, historians drifted away from this alliance, just as social scientists had earlier abandoned history. Thus, the revival of interest among historians in social science since the 1950s seems like a more radical change than it really is. On the other hand, this most recent alliance between history and social science probably has been more profound, more productive, and more permanent than any similar alliance of the past.

The earliest and most thorough change has come in economic history.[58] Here the traditional emphasis on entrepreneurs and institutions has virtually disappeared, replaced by studies of economic growth and income distribution, studies that are based on neoclassical market theory, mathematical models, and quantitative data.[59] Similarly, urban history has shifted from a narrow focus on city administration and institutions to the study of the broad social and economic processes of urbanization. In the 1960s and early 1970s, historians borrowed ideas of class and social stratification from sociology to conduct trail-break-

[56]David Harry Miller and Jerome O. Steffen, eds., *The Frontier: Comparative Studies* (Norman: University of Oklahoma Press, 1977); Richard Hofstadter and Seymour Martin Lipset, eds., *Turner and the Sociology of the Frontier* (New York: Basic Books, 1968). This approach has also been taken increasingly by historians of slavery. See for example David Brion Davis, *The Problem of Slavery in Western Culture* (Ithaca: Cornell University Press, 1966); Carl Degler, *Neither Black Nor White: Slavery and Race Relations in Brazil and the United States* (New York: Macmillan, 1971).

[57]John Higham and others, *History* (Englewood Cliffs, N.J.: Prentice-Hall, Inc., 1965), pp. 113–14.

[58]Douglass C. North, "The New Economic History After Twenty Years," *American Behavioral Scientist*, 21: 187–206 (November/December, 1977); Stanley L. Engerman, "Recent Developments in American Economic History," *Social Science History*, 2: 72–89 (Fall, 1977).

[59]Peter Temin, ed., *The New Economic History: Selected Readings* (New York: Penguin Books, 1973); Jeffrey G. Williamson, *Late Nineteenth-Century American Development: A General Equilibrium History* (Cambridge, England: Cambridge University Press, 1974). See also the *Journal of Economic History*.

ing studies of social mobility in nineteenth-century cities.[60] More recently, urban historians have used concepts and models from economics, geography, and demography to begin for the first time the systematic study of how cities have grown.[61] Meanwhile, historians of past politics and government have increasingly employed models of voting behavior and methods of voting analysis developed by political scientists. These studies have led to significant new insights into the ethnic and cultural basis for popular voting behavior[62] and into the behavior of legislative bodies.[63] Other traditional areas are also transformed by the new links with social science.

In several areas, social science disciplines have suggested whole new fields for historical study. Two notable examples are historical demography and history of the family. Historians have, of course, always been interested in past populations, but only in the last few decades have they begun to use demographic theory and method systematically to study historical fertility rates, migration, and other population

[60]See, e.g., Stephan Thernstrom and Richard Sennett, eds., *Nineteenth-Century Cities: Essays in the New Urban History* (New Haven, Conn.: Yale University Press, 1969); Peter Knights, *The Plain People of Boston, 1830–1860: A Study in City Growth* (New York: Oxford University Press, 1971); Stephan Thernstrom, *The Other Bostonians: Poverty and Progress in the American Metropolis, 1880–1970* (Cambridge, Mass.: Harvard University Press, 1973); Michael B. Katz, *The People of Hamilton, Canada West* (Cambridge: Harvard University Press, 1975).

[61]For example, David Ward, *Cities and Immigrants: A Geography of Change in Nineteenth Century America* (New York: Oxford University Press, 1971); Sam Bass Warner, Jr., *The Urban Wilderness* (New York: Harper & Row, Inc., 1972), Allan R. Pred, *Urban Growth and the Circulation of Information: The United States System of Cities, 1790–1840* (Cambridge, Mass.: Harvard University Press, 1973); Leo Schnore, ed., *The New Urban History: Quantitative Explorations by American Historians* (Princeton, N.J.: Princeton University Press, 1974); Don Harrison Doyle, *The Social Order of a Frontier Community: Jacksonville, Illinois, 1825–70* (Urbana: University of Illinois Press, 1978); J. Rogers Hollingsworth and Ellen Jane Hollingsworth, *Dimensions in Urban History* (Madison: University of Wisconsin Press, 1979). The literature is reviewed in Michael Frisch, "American Urban History as an Example of Recent Historiography," *History & Theory*, 18: 350–77 (1979). See also the *Journal of Urban History*.

[62]For example, Paul Kleppner, *The Cross of Culture: A Social Analysis of Midwestern Politics* (New York: Oxford University Press, 1970); Richard J. Jensen, *The Winning of the Midwest: Social and Political Conflict, 1888–1896* (Chicago: University of Chicago Press, 1971); R. L. McCormick, "Ethno-Cultural Interpretations of Nineteenth-Century American Voting Behavior," *Political Science Quarterly*, 89: 351–77 (June, 1974). Paul Kleppner, *The Third Electoral System, 1853–1892* (Chapel Hill: University of North Carolina Press, 1979); Melvyn Hammarberg, *The Indiana Voter* (Chicago: University of Chicago Press, 1977); Joel Silbey and others, eds., *The History of American Electoral Behavior* (Princeton: Princeton University Press, 1978). Some of this literature is reviewed in Allan Bogue, "The New Political History in the 1970s," in Kammen, *The Past Before Us*.

[63]Allan G. Bogue, J. M. Clubb, R. McKibbin, and S. A. Traugott, "Members of the House of Representatives and the Processes of Modernization, 1789–1960," *Journal of American History*, 63: 275–302 (September 1976); William O. Aydelotte, ed., *The History of Parliamentary Behavior* (Princeton, N.J.: Princeton University Press, 1977); Clubb and Traugott, "Partisan Cleavage and Cohesion in the House of Representatives, 1861–1974," *Journal of Interdisciplinary History*, 7: 375–401 (Winter 1977).

changes.[64] Historians have been particularly interested in using demographic variables in broad studies of economic and social change.[65] A central concern of demographic history, the family, has turned into a separate subfield of study and is currently in an explosive phase of development. Here historians have borrowed from several social science disciplines to help explain changes in kinship ties and family structure, sex roles and sexual relations, marriage arrangements, and child rearing customs.[66]

Though concepts and perspectives borrowed from the social sciences have had a great impact on history, the greatest influence has probably been in the area of quantitative methods. In fact, for many historians, and social scientists, too, quantification is what social science is all about. This is, of course, not true, and confusion on this point has led to needless misunderstandings. Nevertheless, quantitative methods have radically changed the way many historians go about their work.

Though the recent flush of quantification has been inspired by the social sciences, quantification in history is not new. Implicit quantification has always pervaded every historical work, disguised by such words as "more" or "less," "increasing" or "decreasing." Some historians would go so far as to argue that *all* generalizations are implicitly quantitative.[67] But beyond this, historians have in the past been leaders in the use of explicitly quantitative methods. In fact, quantification was important in historical analysis before it became important in social science.[68] Before the turn of the century, Frederick Jackson Turner and his students were using statistical mapping and collective biography techniques to study correlations between voting behavior and a variety of economic, social, political, and geographical variables. After World War I, quantitative history lost favor for several reasons. The growing availability of manuscript and archival materials, not readily quantifiable, reduced the historian's need to depend on purely statistical rec-

[64]Maris A. Vinovskis, "Recent Trends in American Historical Demography: Some Methodological and Conceptual Considerations," *Annual Review of Sociology*, 4: 603–27 (1978). See also the classic of historical demography, E. A. Wrigley, *Population and History* (New York: McGraw-Hill Book Co., 1969).

[65]Allan N. Sharlin, "Historical Demography as History and Demography," *American Behavioral Scientist*, 21: 245–62 (November/December 1977).

[66]For example, Charles E. Rosenberg, ed., *The Family in History* (Philadelphia: University of Pennsylvania Press, 1975); Tamara K. Hareven, ed., *Transitions: The Family and Life Course in Historical Perspective* (New York: Academic Press, 1978); Tamara K. Hareven and Maris A. Vinovskis, eds., *Family and Population in Nineteenth-Century America* (Princeton: Princeton University Press, 1978); Louise A. Tilly and Joan W. Scott, *Women, Work, and Family* (New York: Holt, Rinehart & Winston, 1978); Carl Degler, *At Odds: Women and the Family in America from the Revolution to the Present* (New York: Oxford University Press, 1980). See also the *Journal of Family History*.

[67]William O. Aydelotte, *Quantification in History* (Reading, Mass.: Addison-Wesley Publishing Co., Inc., 1971), p. 4.

[68]Charles W. Dollar and Richard J. Jensen, *Historian's Guide to Statistics* (New York: Holt, Rinehart & Winston, 1971); Robert P. Swierenga, ed., *Quantification in American History: Theory and Research* (New York: Atheneum Publishers, 1970).

ords. New fields such as diplomatic and intellectual history, in which quantification seemed less useful, became more popular. And, perhaps most important, the followers of Turner were often sadly negligent in adopting new statistical techniques and in communicating with each other about methodological problems. The flame of quantification was kept burning, however, by a small group of historians working mainly in the realm of agricultural history.[69]

In the 1960s and 1970s, this small flame touched off an explosion. The "lust to quantify," as one historian called it,[70] pervaded nearly every subfield of history, and the computer card became as common as the note card in the arsenal of the historian. In general, this excitement over quantification was highly productive. Historians learned to use, carefully and systematically, source materials that had seemed intractable before: manuscript censuses, parish and baptismal registers, city directories and biographical dictionaries, ward and precinct voting records, factory inspection reports, routine business and mercantile data, large archives of newspapers, and so on. Without formal sampling procedures, statistical methods, and computer analysis, many of these records would have remained forever baffling. Today, economic history, urban history, demographic history, in fact almost all histories that propose to speak about the behavior of masses of men and women, depend heavily on quantitative methods.

By the early 1970s, social science research design, theory, and quantitative methods had helped to create a whole new body of historical scholarship. And those who called themselves social science historians looked upon it and saw that it was good.[71] It became standard practice for books in the new mold to begin with a preachy introduction, extolling the virtues of the new systematic history and dismissing older studies as little more than speculation and gossip.[72] Of course, the older generation of humanistic historians, such as Schlesinger, Bridenbaugh, and Barzun, complained.[73] But much of this early criticism focused too much on quantification, thus obscuring the real differences between history and social science and the real difficulties of forging a link between the two.

---

[69]Dollar and Jensen, *Historian's Guide.*

[70]Stone, *History and the Social Sciences,* p. 30

[71]Don Karl Rowney and James Q. Graham, Jr., *Quantitative History* (Homewood, Ill.: Dorsey Press, 1969); Swierenga, *Quantification;* Dollar and Jensen, *Historians Guide;* Edward Shorter, *The Historian and the Computer: A Practical Guide* (Englewood Cliffs, N.J.: Prentice-Hall, Inc., 1971); Landes and Tilley, *History as Social Science;* Aydelotte, *Quantification;* William O. Aydelotte, Allan G. Bogue, and James Q. Graham, eds., *The Dimensions of Quantitative Research in History* (Princeton, N.J.: Princeton University Press, 1972).

[72]For example, Kleppner, *Cross of Culture.*

[73]Arthur Schlesinger, Jr., "The Humanist Looks at Empirical Social Research," *American Sociological Review,* 27: 768–71 (December 1962); Carl Bridenbaugh, "The Great Mutation," *American Historical Review,* 68: 315–31 (January 1963); Barzun, *Clio.*

A Touch of Humility

Today the hubris of the early 1970s is something of an embarrass-ment for historians genuinely interested in both history and social sci-ence. A new humility has come in two different forms. First, it has be-come increasingly clear that traditional, humanistic history, a discipline of context and of uniqueness of time and space, is far from passé. Quite the contrary. Even social scientists have been discovering the need for bringing contextual and historical variables into their studies. Thus, many historians, quantifiers included, are today reasserting his-tory's traditional concern for the rich variety of human experience. Second, it has also become clear that the practitioners of the various "new" histories have failed to be social scientific. They have borrowed ideas and methods, but have scarcely begun the task of building social theory in history. Thus, while some historians today still assert their commitment to make history social scientific, this new effort is without the former brag and bluster, without, in fact, a firm faith in their ulti-mate success.

The first brand of humility has been exhibited by none other than Robert Fogel, one of the founding fathers of the new economic his-tory. While still an avid promoter of quantification, Fogel has come to believe that history is primarily a humanistic discipline. He says that the writing of *Time on the Cross* (1974) (and presumably some of the controversy that followed) taught him and co-author Stanley Enger-man that historical synthesis transcends social science:

> We have come to recognize that history is, and very likely will remain, pri-marily a humanistic discipline. We now believe that the issue raised by his-torical quantifiers is not whether history can be transformed into social sci-ence but the realm of usefulness of social-science methods in a humanistic discipline.[74]

Another pioneer in the imaginative use of quantitative data, Lawrence Stone, has also lately reaffirmed history's essentially humanistic char-acter: "It deals with a *particular* problem and a *particular* set of actors at a *particular* time in a *particular* place."[75] Stone urges historians to pick and choose ideas from the social sciences to suit their own purposes. This is not the time for historians to ally themselves unthinkingly with the social sciences, almost all of which are in turmoil themselves over their own shaky claims to scientific validity. "It might be time," Stone suggests, "for the historical rats to leave rather than scramble aboard

---

[74]"The Limits of Quantitative Methods in History," *American Historical Review*, 80: 329–50 (April 1975); see also Gilbert Shapiro, "Prospects for a Scientific Social History," *Journal of Social History*, 10: 196–204 (Winter, 1976).

[75] "History and the Social Sciences," in Delzell, *Future of History*, p. 28; Kammen, "His-torian's Vocation," in Kammen, *Past Before Us*, pp. 32–33.

the social scientific ship which seems to be leaking and undergoing major repair."[76]

The arguments of Fogel and Stone in these essays are not very different from the arguments of a traditional humanist historian such as J. H. Hexter.[77] Hexter is not opposed to quantification or to the use of social science theory. He is opposed to subordinating history to social science. "What historians badly need," he says, "is not an impossible grand strategy but a quite possible small bag of tricks that will direct their attention to social-science knowledge that they can use on the record of the past."[78] The impact of social science on history has not yet been revolutionary; it has indeed been largely a borrowed bag of tricks. And in recent years those historians who rely on social science and those who do not have come increasingly to understand how much common ground they share.

A Theory-Free Science?

Some historians are still determined to make their discipline, or at least their little corner of it, as social scientific as possible. They hope to build gradually a social theory based on historical data. They hope to be social scientists who work in history rather than historians who merely borrow ideas and methods from social science. Like their humanist colleagues, these scholars have been critical of the new histories of the 1960s and 1970s, but their criticism is that this recent work has lacked a theoretical base, that it has not been social science. They believe that historical studies can become more social scientific. But whether history can ever become a full-fledged social science now seems a much more open and troubling question than it did ten years ago.

The new histories, despite the aura of social science, have so far been only consumers, not producers, of theory.[79] The new political historians, for example, have used reference-group theory to explain the voting behavior of segments of the American electorate. Here, the effect has been to particularize rather than generalize a social theory—a standard approach for history, but the opposite of social science.[80] Similarly, the new urban history has so far produced mostly a series of ever more detailed case studies and has yet to generate useful gener-

---

[76]Stone, "History and the Social Sciences," in Delzell, *Future of History*, p. 29.

[77]*Doing History*, and *The History Primer* (New York: Basic Books, Inc., 1971). See also Aydelotte, *Quantification*.

[78]*Doing History*, p. 113.

[79]Clubb and Bogue, *History, Quantification*, pp. 175–6; J. Rogers Hollingsworth, "Some Problems in Theory Construction for Historical Analysis," *Historical Methods Newsletter*, 7: 225–44 (June 1974).

[80]Allan G. Bogue, J. M. Clubb, and W. H. Flanigan, "The New Political History," *American Behavioral Scientist*, 21: 201–26 (November/December 1977), p. 204.

alizations about the processes of social mobility or urbanization.[81] It has been largely "bare-bones empiricism."[82] The new economic history has been inflexibly wedded to neoclassical market theory, which assumes away so many crucial nonmarket variables that "it is not surprising that the new economic historians have contributed little to our understanding of economic growth."[83]

Though somewhat disappointed over recent efforts, some of these critics believe that history can become more social scientific, that it can become "a means to test, refine, and develop scientific theories of human behavior."[84] They argue that the data of history may be fragmentary and biased, but are not fundamentally different from the data of social science or even physical sciences such as astronomy or geology. What sets a social science historian apart from humanist colleagues is the goal. The goal is to build general theories rather than to use general theories to explain specific events.[85]

The logic of this kind of historical analysis is no different from any other behavioral science. The first step is to specify variable concepts and then to begin to suggest and test theoretical linkages.[86] Though the ultimate goal is the formulation of lawlike propositions without regard to time or space, middle-range theory may be no more than tentative models of relationships in specific times and places. This is very much what historians already do. But for the social scientist, this model-building stage has a different final goal: theory that is neither time nor space bound.

The methods of the social science historian are also essentially no different from those of other behavioral scientists. Historians refine their theoretical models by testing hypotheses derived from them. Since they are interested in general and recurrent phenomena, they often will use quantitative or aggregate data and statistical analysis rather than narrative explanation. But this is not a fundamental difference between social science and humanistic history. Like all social scientists, the historian may rely on case studies, narration, and nonquantitative data when useful or necessary. In fact, social science history may frequently read much like humanistic history. But always the goal

---

[81] Fogel, "The Limits of Quantitative Methods in History," p. 334; Frisch, "American Urban History," pp: 364–65.

[82] John B. Sharpless and Sam Bass Warner, Jr., "Urban History," *American Behavioral Scientist,* 21: 221–44 (November/December 1977), p. 224.

[83] North, "New Economic History," p. 194; David S. Landes, "On Avoiding Babel," *Journal of Economic History,* 38: 3–12 (March 1978).

[84] Clubb and Bogue, *History, Quantification,* p. 178; Kousser, "Quantitative Social Scientific History," in Kammen, *Past Before Us.* See also the journal *Social Science History.*

[85] Ibid., Hollingsworth, "Some Problems."

[86] Ibid., Jerald Hage, *Techniques and Problems of Theory Construction in Sociology* (New York: John Wiley & Sons, Inc., 1972); Arthur Stinchcombe, *Theoretical Methods in Social History* (New York: Academic Press, 1978).

is to develop general theory rather than to explain specific historical situations.

The value of social science history is becoming increasingly apparent. Social scientists are finally beginning to recognize (remember, actually) that many social processes are greatly affected by changes over time and are only obscured by cross-sectional data analysis. Longitudinal panel studies, natural experimentation over time, and historical data analysis are all tools of growing importance in the social sciences. While historians have been using social science theories and methods to do traditional history, social scientists, particularly economists, demographers, and political scientists, have been using history in their work. In fact, there is some indication that much of the best work in social science history is now being done in social science departments other than history.[87]

Despite the obvious value of history to social science, the fact that so little successful social science history has been done is no mere accident. Using historical data to test social theory is at best extremely difficult, at worst even impossible. Historical data are not intrinsically different from the data of social science; the data difficulties are of the same kind, but are much more severe for history. According to Murray Murphey, the historian must solve five data problems if she or he hopes to confirm lawlike statements in the manner of the social scientist: the problems of quantity, aggregation, sampling, informant bias, and measurement.[88] Only the first two are likely to be solved soon, through the sophisticated use of computer analysis. Sampling from unknown or incomplete populations, informant bias of unknown direction and degree, and the general problem of measurement (constructing indexes of past social change) are all problems, Murphey says, that are not likely to be solved for history. Thus, he concludes that "present methods for confirming general hypotheses regarding past populations cannot meet the standards which now prevail in the social sciences."[89]

Social science historians are somewhat less pessimistic than Murphey, though most are properly humble in the face of such difficulties. They say, first, that social science is not much better off than history in the area of data collection and measurement.[90] And they argue that history can and should at least begin to try to solve these problems, recognizing that there may be real limitations on how much knowledge can ever be gleaned from the past. Consequently, theory building in history must necessarily remain a modest enterprise for some time to come. But the social sciences have not been very successful in building

---

[87]Clubb and Bogue, *History, Quantification*, p. 185.
[88]*Our Knowledge*, pp. 155–6.
[89]Ibid., p. 201.
[90]Clubb and Bogue, *History, Quantification*, p. 179.

testable theory, either.[91] The important thing is that the goal remain the building of general theories of human behavior, though that goal may lie forever out of reach.

In summary, social science theory and method have to date been used largely as tools for traditional history. Genuine social science history is a modest affair, barely underway and scarcely able to displace humanistic history as a reliable guide to the past. To explain human history is an awesome challenge that requires the services of both humanist and social scientist. Though their goals and tools may differ, they are both, while in this service, historians.

JOURNALISM HISTORY

Journalism history has been almost thoroughly in the humanist vein, concerned with limited historical questions bound by space and time. Though ordinarily working within schools whose names include the word "communication," most journalism historians have not joined the effort to build communication theory. They have been much less interested in the social process of communication than in the detailed stories of certain American individuals and institutions that have, at some time in the past, communicated.

The old sacred scripture of journalism history, like holy writ in most fields, is hagiography. The saints are James Gordon Bennett, Joseph Pulitzer, William Randolph Hearst, Adolph Ochs, and others in the heavenly company that has helped to make American journalism the glorious, progressive, and just institution it is today. The best of this literature, such as Frank Luther Mott's encyclopedic chronicles and W. A. Swanberg's sweeping biographies, is good and useful history.[92] Willard G. Bleyer, Edwin Emery, Robert Rutland, John Tebbel, and others have also contributed in useful ways to the general history of journalism in America.[93] But this literature has largely been institutional history and biography. To the extent that these traditional histories have had theoretical foundation, it has been discernible as a

[91]Hollingsworth, "Some Problems," p. 225.

[92]Mott, *American Journalism*, 3rd ed. (New York: Macmillan, Inc., 1962); *A History of American Magazines* in 5 vols. (Cambridge, Mass.: Harvard University Press, 1957–1968). Swanberg, *Citizen Hearst* (New York: Charles Scribner's Sons, 1961), and *Pulitzer* (New York: Charles Scribner's Sons, 1967).

[93]Bleyer, *Main Currents in the History of American Journalism* (Boston: Houghton Mifflin Co., 1927); Emery (originally Emery and Henry Ladd Smith, 1954, most recently Emery and Michael Emery),*The Press and America*, 4th ed. (Englewood Cliffs, N.J.: Prentice-Hall, Inc., 1978); Rutland, *The Newsmongers: Journalism in the Life of the Nation, 1690–1972* (New York: Dial Press, 1973); Tebbel, *The Media in America* (New York: Thomas Y. Crowell Co., Inc., 1974).

somewhat vague faith in progress, a faith adhered to by declining numbers of historians in this and other fields.[94]

Some journalism history has been good traditional history, stating problems clearly and developing limited but illuminating explanatory themes. Perhaps the most exemplary work has been the history of freedom of the press. Leonard Levy carefully set the stage for what has been a productive debate over the status of seditious libel and press freedom in colonial America.[95] Frederick S. Siebert's classic study of freedom of the press in England inspired several careful studies of the impact of social and economic variables on press control, and did so in the social scientific context of testing propositions about relationships between freedom and control unrestricted by time and place.[96] Other examples of good traditional journalism history are Theodore Peterson's study of the relationship between advertising and twentieth-century magazines, Bernard Weisberger's sociological perspective on the American newspaperman, and Anthony Smith's international history of the newspaper.[97] A trend in journalism history in the last few years has been an increasing emphasis on women and minorities.[98] This literature has also helped, though on a very modest scale so far, to break the traditional focus on great men and great institutions.

The impact of social science on journalism history has been slight, limited largely to a sometime pursuit of rigor through the use of hypothesis testing, quantitative content analysis, and statistics. In content analysis, journalism historians have decades more experience than their colleagues in other subfields of history. But, ironically, the wide-

---

[94]James W. Carey, "The Problem of Journalism History," *Journalism History*, 1: 3–5, 27 (Spring 1974); Joseph B. McKerns, "The Limits of Progressive Journalism History," *Journalism History*, 4: 88–92 (Autumn 1977). The standard literature of journalism history is reviewed in John D. Stevens and Hazel Dicken Garcia, *Communication History* (Beverly Hills, Calif.: Sage Publications, 1980), chapter 1.

[95]*Legacy of Suppression* (Cambridge, Mass.: Harvard University Press, 1960). See also Dwight L. Teeter, "Press Freedom and the Public Printing: Pennsylvania, 1775–83," *Journalism Quarterly*, 45: 445–51 (Autumn 1968); Mary Ann Yodelis, "Courts, Counting House and Streets: Attempts at Press Control, 1763–1775," *Journalism History*, 1: 11–15 (Spring 1974); Gerald J. Baldasty, "Flirting with Social Science: Methodology and Virginia Newspapers, 1785–86," *Journalism History*, 1: 86–88 (Autumn 1974).

[96]Siebert, *Freedom of the Press in England, 1476–1776* (Urbana: University of Illinois Press, 1952); Donald L. Shaw and Stephan W. Brauer, "Press Freedom and War Constraints: Case-Testing Siebert's Proposition II," *Journalism Quarterly*, 46: 233–54 (Summer 1969); John D. Stevens, "Freedom of Expression: New Dimensions," in Ronald T. Farrar and Stevens, eds., *Mass Media and the National Experience* (New York: Harper & Row, Inc., 1971); Stevens, "Press and Community Toleration: Wisconsin in World War I," *Journalism History*, 46: 255–59 (Summer 1969).

[97]Theodore Peterson, *Magazines in the Twentieth Century*, 2nd. ed. (Urbana: University of Illinois Press, 1964); Bernard Weisberger, *The American Newspaperman* (Chicago: University of Chicago Press, 1961); Anthony Smith, *The Newspaper: An International History* (London: Thames and Hudson, 1979).

[98]For example, Marion Marzolf, *Up from the Footnote: A History of Women Journalists* (New York: Hastings House, Inc., 1977); the special issues of *Journalism History* 1 (Winter 1974–75), 3 (Winter 1976–77), 4 (Summer 1977), and 6 (Summer 1979).

spread use of this tool has probably made journalism history less social scientific, less interested in generalization. The rising flood of M.A. and even Ph.D. theses that report "what the press said about this or that" are often methodologically sound, but are devoid of theoretical value. They represent what Lee Benson has aptly called "brute empiricism."[99] One of the few areas where social theory has been borrowed to help explain journalism history has been media economics. But the best historical work here has not been done by journalism historians, but by sociologists, economists, and communication researchers.[100] Some of the most interesting research in journalism history in recent years has been in what might be called the sociology of the journalist and advertising practitioner. The work of Michael Schudson stands out, but others are working in this field, too.[101]

The lack of interest in social science, or even in systematic generalization, in journalism history may seem somewhat odd in view of the fact that the journalism historian usually works in what has become a predominantly social science milieu. Journalism historians have found little use for the communication models and perspectives developed by their social science colleagues. The journalism historian's separateness, however, is really not surprising. Most of the practitioners in this field do not have backgrounds in social science or in history, but in journalism, and no field is more atheoretical, more particularistic, more devoted to the simple story than journalism. But more important than personal predilection is the split in the journalism and communication field itself. Research on journalism and research on communication are overlapping but distinctly different enterprises, even though much communication research emanates from journalism. Journalism involves communication, but it is also a social, economic, and political institution with an important and unique history. Journalism historians would surely be remiss if they were to limit themselves to the study of the communication aspect of journalism and ignore the infinite variety of journalism history. Yet they are also remiss when they fail to participate in the creation of a science of communication.

[99]"An Approach to the Scientific Study of Past Public Opinion," *Public Opinion Quarterly*, 31: 522–67 (Winter 1968).

[100]Alfred M. Lee, *The Daily Newspaper in America* (New York: Macmillan, Inc., 1947); Melvin L. DeFleur and Sandra Ball-Rokeach, *Theories of Mass Communication*, 2nd ed. (New York: David McKay Co., Inc., 1970); Maxwell E. McCombs, "Mass Media in the Marketplace," *Journalism Monographs* No. 24 (August 1977); Bruce Owen, *Economics and Freedom of Expression: Media Structure and the First Amendment* (Cambridge: Bollinger Publishers, 1975).

[101]Michael Schudsen, *Urban Growth* (New York: Basic Books, Inc., 1978); Clifford G. Christians, Quentin J. Schultze, and Norman H. Sims, "Community, Epistemology and Mass Media Ethics," *Journalism History*, 5: 38–41, 65–67 (Summer 1978); Quentin J. Schultze, "The Quest for Professional Advertising Education Before 1917," paper presented to the Association for Education in Journalism, annual convention, Boston, August, 1980; Ted Curtis Smythe, "The Reporter, 1880–1900: Working Conditions and Their Influence on the News," *Journalism History*, 7: 1–10 (Spring, 1980).

What we are suggesting here, of course, is that there is not only room but need for all kinds of historians. This has been a theme throughout this chapter. It seems especially important for a field such as journalism research, which has an interest in specific historical institutions as well as an interest in a broad social process. The important thing is for the historian to understand what his goal is and what is the best way to achieve it. Journalism history clearly needs both the humanist and the social scientist.

A couple of useful suggestions have been made recently for improving humanistic journalism history. Several writers have urged journalism historians to break away from the ideology of progressive history.[102] Journalism historians need to be much more aware of interpretative developments in other areas of history, particularly in studies of analogous social institutions. Several commentators on journalism history in recent years have urged more attention to the cultural function of journalism and more appreciation of the place of journalism in a cultural milieu.[103] This suggests the need for a closer alliance with American studies, social and economic history, and cultural anthropology, though the links in this alliance have yet to be forged.

Humanist journalism history could also be improved, as other forms of history have been, by borrowing more freely from the social sciences, both theory and method. For example, though the media are large formal organizations, little use has been made by journalism historians of organization theory. Though the media have been important forces for socialization, little use has been made of socialization theory from political science and sociology. Though the media were intimately involved in the professional and bureaucratic revolution around the turn of the century, historians are only beginning to look at theories of management and professionalization. Though the media after the 1880s developed into large-scale economic institutions, little attention has been paid to economic theory or models of business organization. The list could be continued. Similarly, journalism history could profit from borrowing methodology, not just methods, from the social sciences. Though many studies now use content analysis, few are based upon well-constructed, systematic comparative designs.

While improving their traditional humanistic history of the people and institutions of journalism, journalism historians should also begin to explore the role of history in the developing social science of com-

[102]Ronald Farrar, "Mass Communication History: A Myriad of Approaches," in Farrar and Stevens, *Mass Media*, pp. 1–13; James W. Carey, "Problem of Journalism"; Joseph P. McKerns, "Limits of Progessive."

[103]Carey, "Problem of Journalism," pp. 3–5; Marion Marzolf, "American Studies—Ideas for Media Historians," and Jean Ward, "Interdisciplinary Research and Journalism Historians," both in *Journalism History*, 5: 13–19 (Spring, 1978); Stevens and Garcia, *Communication History*, chapter 3.

[104]Harold A. Innis, *The Bias of Communication* (Toronto: University of Toronto Press, 1951); Marshall McLuhan, *Understanding Media* (New York: McGraw-Hill Book Co., 1964).

munication. The only real attempts to build theory in communication history have been the grand schemes of Harold Innis and Marshall McLuhan[104] and the ideal types of Fred S. Siebert, Theodore B. Peterson, and Wilbur Schramm.[105] To make communication history more social scientific, however, we would need to begin on a much more modest scale, specifying variable concepts and suggesting tentative testable theoretical linkages.[106] This kind of history would seek to make general statements about human communication, not to explain unique historical events. History would merely be the realm in which such statements are tested.

The value of such a social science history of communication would be enormous, for many important attributes and effects of communication can only be studied over long stretches of time. They are, in a word, historical. Urban geographers, for example, have already been able to explain much about the growth and government of nineteenth-century cities in terms of communication and information costs.[107] It seems clear that urbanization itself is at heart a communication process.[108]

Another example of the importance of history to communication studies is in the area of political interest group activity. It appears that interest groups use their control of information to influence government regulatory bodies in ways that can only be sorted out over long periods of time.[109]

Both of these examples suggest the importance of historical studies to a general understanding of the effects of communication constraints on social change. Other examples could be cited as well, but very little of this historical communication research is being done in schools of journalism. Clearly, communication studies need history. Important communication processes, involving economic, political, and other forms of social change, move so slowly that they can only be studied over broad sweeps of time.

The data problems facing this kind of communication history are

---

[105]*Four Theories of the Press* (Urbana: University of Illinois Press, 1956). See also Garth S. Jowett, "Toward a History of Communication," *Journalism History*, 2: 34–37 (Summer 1975). Jowett has been a strong advocate for both theory borrowing and theory building in communication history. For example, "Communication in History: An Initial Theoretical Approach," *Canadian Journal of Information Science*, 1: 5–13 (1976).

[106]David P. Nord, "First Steps Toward a Theory of Press Control," *Journalism History*, 4: 9–13 (Spring 1977).

[107]Richard L. Meier, *A Communication Theory of Urban Growth* (Cambridge, Mass.: MIT Press, 1962); Pred, *Urban Growth;* Seymour Mandelbaum, *Boss Tweed's New York* (New York: John Wiley & Sons, Inc., 1965).

[108]Sharpless and Warner, "Urban History," p. 237. For example of an attempt to explain the interplay of new forms of mass communication with the urban political system in the late nineteenth century, see David Paul Nord, *Newspapers and New Politics: Midwestern Municipal Reform, 1890–1900* (Ann Arbor: UMI Research Press, 1981).

[109]David P. Nord, "The FCC and Educational Broadcasting," *Journal of Broadcasting,* 22: 321–338 (Summer 1978).

enormous, perhaps insurmountable. Communication is ephemeral in the extreme. Studies must depend on the written record, even though nonwritten communication has probably always been more important in human affairs. And even the written record is incomplete, biased, and a poor reflection of what people actually said or meant to say. But because of the difficulties, it has been all too easy for communication researchers simply to ignore history and for historians to ignore communication. No real effort has yet been made to explore the limits of communication history. We really do not know whether the limits lie in the paucity of the data or the poverty of our own imaginations.

Journalism historians will never become, nor should they become, exclusively social scientists, interested in the past only as a place to conduct longitudinal tests of communication theory. Though they work within a largely social science community, they will remain as much interested in the unique characteristics of specific journalism institutions as they are in the process of communication.

In this respect, journalism history is analogous to the history of science or the history of education, and journalism historians could learn much from these subfields of history. Historians of education, for example, frequently work in schools of education, and their interests range from the study of past educational institutions to the study of the social process of education. Like journalism history, education history was once largely the chronicle of great men and great institutions. Today, some of the most exciting work in American history is being done in the history of education.[110] These historians, borrowing from sociology, classical and Marxist economics, and theories of educational policy, have begun to tell the story of American education as a cultural institution for socialization and social control. They have begun to make it clear that to understand the economics, politics, and sociology of education is to understand much about the origins of modern America.

Journalism is not unlike nor less important than education; it is both a complex institution and a pervasive social process. To understand it fully, a wide-ranging vision and a broad research commitment are required. Both the humanist and the social scientist will find steady employment. But the work of the two, it can be hoped, will begin to overlap more than it has in the past. If journalism historians will at last recognize the value of social science, and communication scientists the value of history, we may finally be able to give to journalism the kind of history it deserves.

[110]For example, Michael B. Katz, ed., *Education in American History: Readings on the Social Issues* (New York: Praeger, 1973); Katz, *Class, Bureaucracy, and the Schools*, 2nd ed. (New York: Praeger Publishers, Inc., 1975); David B. Tyack, *The One Best System: A History of Urban Education* (Cambridge: Harvard University Press, 1974); Samuel Bowles and Herbert Gintis, *Schooling in Capitalist America* (New York: Basic Books, 1976); Harvey J. Graff, *The Literacy Myth: Literacy and Social Structure in the Nineteenth-Century City* (New York: Academic Press, 1979).

The Method of History

MaryAnn Yodelis Smith

Most historians probably would agree with J. H. Hexter's comment that "History stands sorely in need of a pedagogic equivalent of *The Joy of Cooking*,"[1] and communications historians undoubtedly would endorse that sentiment even more strongly. Because journalists generally are comparative neophytes to historical method, debates between quantifiers and nonquantifiers merely have added to the methodological confusion. The time has come for communications historians to put aside their semantic analyses of method and continue the process of researching and writing respected communication history.

The point is developed in more detail in Chapter 15, but the issue of quantification in history raises a false dichotomy. The focus of the methodological discussion should not be on whether the historian may properly use quantitative methods, but on whether historians will indulge in impressionistic research and the subsequent necessarily empty rhetoric or whether communication historians will discipline themselves to the rigor of empirical study. Only from the latter will come some limited, but nonetheless, reliable generalizations. This kind of historian indeed may only use varying degrees of sophisticated statis-

[1]J. H. Hexter, *Doing History* (Bloomington: Indiana University Press, 1971), p. 14.

tics borrowed from the behaviorist to synthesize "a highly selective account of a postulated past reality."[2]

Empirical history is merely the application of system and rigor to the study of the past. On the other hand, the impressionistic or scissors-and-paste historian industriously labors over notes about an event or person, shuffles them into topical areas, adds the literary polish of transitional phrases, and tacks a summary at the end. But that historian has failed to ask the crucial question: to what end is this note taking directed? Of this approach, which serves neither history nor communications, Allen Nevins suggested that ideal history is a balance of scientific elements and literary skill.[3] The question, then, is not whether one will choose quantification or nonquantification, but whether one will succumb to random note taking instead of applying system and rigor to data gathering. The choice is between impressionistic and empirical history.

Because of its complexity (and even frightening implications), the term empirical, or scientific, history perhaps requires further explanation. The empirical historian fully recognizes that a systematic account of relationships among events and/or persons is only *a* history of communications and not *the* history of communications. Unlike researchers in disciplines where a complete data base is available, the communications historian recognizes the limitations of the data and seeks a "*verisimilitude* rather than *objective* truth."[4] Of the events in an era, only some are remembered, fewer are recorded, and only a small portion of those recorded ever survive to be studied systematically by researchers. With this in mind, historian David Fischer defined an empirical historian as one "who asks an open-ended question about past events and answers it with selected facts which are arranged in the form of an explanatory paradigm. These questions and answers are fitted to each other by a complex process of mutual adjustment."[5] The explanatory paradigm, of course, takes different forms—narrative, statistical explanation—but always consists of a reasoned, systematic examination of surviving recorded happenings, written in a spirit of critical inquiry seeking the whole truth.[6] To accomplish this, the empirical historian must read an immense amount of general history, theories of human behavior, and communication theory.[7] Communications historians cannot afford to be labeled those who write without fear and without re-

---

[2]Robert F. Berkhofer, Jr., *A Behavioral Approach to Historical Analysis* (New York: The Free Press, 1969), p. 23.

[3]Ray Allen Billington, ed., *Allen Nevins on History* (New York: Charles Scribner's Sons, Inc., 1975), p. 140.

[4]Louis Gottschalk, *Understanding History* (New York: Alfred A. Knopf, 1950), p. 140.

[5]David H. Fischer, *Historians' Fallacies* (New York: Harper & Row, Inc., 1970), p. xv.

[6]Billington, *Allen Nevins*, p. 39; Fischer, *Historians' Fallacies*, pp. xv-xxii.

[7]See Hexter, *Doing History*, p. 9, and Murray G. Murphey, *Our Knowledge of the Historical Past* (New York: Bobbs-Merrill Co., Inc., 1973), p. 121, for example.

search.[8] This essay, then, as an introduction to the method of empirical communication history, reviews the process of question formulation, the nature of historical evidence, and systems of data analysis.

FORMULATING THE RESEARCH QUESTION

For want of a research question, many noble attempts at writing history have failed. This perhaps is one of the most difficult tasks of the historian; yet, it is one treated casually and superficially by novices in history. Fischer described research questions as "the engines of intellect, the cerebral machines which convert energy to motion, and curiosity to controlled inquiry."[9] Significant research questions are best formulated after immersion and guided entry into historical data. That process is described briefly next.

The first requisite for asking questions is a thorough knowledge of general history and communications history. A wise and revered American historian, Merrill M. Jensen, often admonished those in his research seminar that "The trouble with most journalists is that they don't know any history!" Because this general knowledge is so significant, the most practical approach to question framing for the historian is saturation in historical readings and immersion in communication history data. Communications historian Harold L. Nelson noted that immersion begins when individual interest leads a researcher to seek materials about a general communications subject.[10] The historian, then, fortified by a general understanding of events, immerses himself or herself in a general topic like sensationalism in the nineteenth century. As the immersion process begins, the historian might ask the journalist's traditional *who, what, when, where, why, how* questions to guide the data search. In this way, the historian generally limits the area of immersion (to prevent drowning) by arbitrary, but helpful, geographical, biographical, chronological, functional, or occupational boundaries.[11] To continue our example, because even sensationalism in the nineteenth century is too broad a topic, the historian might limit that to a specific geographical area or to a class of publications. These are flexible limitations as the process of question forming continues.

In essence, then, immersion parallels the literature search of the social scientist, and there are several common sources that are good starting points for the pursuit of evidence. A visit to the card catalog of any nearby library would be first on the list. Electronic search, which by and large has been generated by university libraries, has just begun to be utilized in history and perhaps is most functional for the legal his-

---

[8]Carl Becker undoubtedly used the expression first; since then, it has been applied to those writing impressionistic history.

[9]Fischer, *Historians' Fallacies,* p. 3.

[10]Harold L. Nelson, "Guides to Morasses in Historical Research," *The Journalism Educator* reprint, vol. 19, no. 2. Spring 1964, pp. 38–42.

[11]Gottschalk, *Understanding History,* pp. 62–3.

torian. In addition, the researcher should check a number of standard bibliographic references on American history;[12] the *Harvard Guide to American History*[13] is indispensable. Periodical indexes, newspaper indexes, and reference works like *The Newspaper and the Historian*[14] are useful. There are many published guides to government documents and manuscript collections, as well as guides to constitutions, statutes, and case law. The careful researcher will not overlook oral history collections like that at Columbia University, collections of broadcast tapes, or materials in the Prints and Photographs Division of the Library of Congress.[15] The bibliography compiled from these reference aids will constitute only a small part of the final bibliography as the historian continues to find new clues to primary sources.

After immersion and consideration of the breadth of data available in a general area of interest, the researcher focuses on a more specific part of the data in a process called guided entry. The immersion and guided entry phases of research are not totally separable.[16] In the process of guided entry, the historian further delimits the data to be studied and the process of general question forming begins. A thorough knowledge of general communications history and a strong foundation in communication theory again permit the historian to conceptualize the research problem more easily and to formulate specific questions more precisely.

Remember that question forming is the most critical part of the task. Unlike researchers in other social science disciplines, historians cannot properly begin by formulating a research hypothesis before the immersion process narrows into guided entry because, for historians, the existence of an adequate data base is a prime factor in question forming.[17] Further, because of the very nature of historical data—its incompleteness—the historical question ought to be a neutral one, receptive to both yes and no answers.[18] By starting with a declarative hypothesis, the historian might find the temptation too great to select data only on one side of the question.

Questions that produce an analysis of relationships among historical variables will contribute most to communication history. A question must be, first of all, worth asking. The researcher may have discovered

---

[12]Wood Gray, *Historian's Handbook* (Boston: Houghton Mifflin Co., 1964) has an excellent bibliographical reference section; also see Homer C. Hockett, *The Critical Method in Historical Research and Writing* (New York: Macmillan, Inc., 1955), pp. 265–95.

[13]Cambridge, Mass.: Belknap Press of Harvard University Press, 1954.

[14]Lucy Maynard Salmon, *The Newspaper and the Historian* (New York: Oxford University Press, 1923).

[15]For other visual collections, see R. Smith Schuneman, "Photographic Communication: An Evolving Historical Discipline," in Ronald T. Farrar and John D. Stevens, eds., *Mass Media and the National Experience* (New York: Harper & Row, Inc., 1971), pp. 152–58.

[16]Nelson, "Guides to Morasses," p. 38.

[17]Murphey, *Our Knowledge*, p. 149.

[18]Nelson, "Guides to Morasses," p. 39.

a new data base that is substantial and significant and deserves to be analyzed. Or an existing data base may be found that will yield a significant reinterpretation of written history that is both valid and demonstrable.[19] All terms in the historical research question must be capable of being operationally defined. In the past, this perhaps has been a more common procedure for the behaviorist; however, the historian cannot slight this vital part of the research process. The operational definition describes the specific operation the historian performs to discover the presence or absence of the attribute being studied. In a sense, the operational definition establishes categories or classifications. For example, an historian might ask whether, in a certain time period and geographic area, there was a relationship between newspaper advertising income and political content of the newspaper. The operational definition of advertising might be the annual gross advertising income reported on institutional balance sheets or it might be represented by another economic indicator like the annual average number of columns of advertising.

Also, the language of the question ought to be explicit and precise. Questions should not be based on unproved assumptions. For example, because H. V. Kaltenborn was the most important commentator during World War II, what are the relationships between his rhetorical techniques and those used by television anchorpersons in the 1970s? Not every historian would agree with the assumption about Kaltenborn's standing. In addition, the historical research question should be open ended in that it dictates the kinds of facts to be observed in responding to the question without dictating the solution or the analysis to be offered in the response.[20] Therefore, the researcher would discard a hypothesis stating that improved technology caused the sensationalist press. Many other conditions, in addition to technology, may have spurred sensationalism.

Finally, the research question ought to be flexible enough that it can be refined as the study progresses. Often, researchers begin with a cluster of questions generated by hunches obtained from the immersion and guided entry process. As the operational definitions take shape, the questions themselves can be refined at various stages of the study. In short, communications historians should conceive questions with imagination and honesty to define clearly the relationships being observed within certain parameters of time and place in history. Although questions asked by early communication historians on a purely descriptive level—who were the first newspaper publishers in Montana?—served a necessary and laudable function of providing a data base for today's scholars, communications history has progressed to relational questions, exploring the complexities of communication history through the centuries.

---

[19]Gray, *Historian's Handbook,* p. 10.
[20]Fischer, *Historians' Fallacies,* p. 38.

AUTHENTICATING THE DATA

Although the existence of a data base has to be confirmed before the research question may be formulated, there are many more aspects of the nature of historical evidence to examine here. More than one historian has used the analogy of the historian and the detective[21] as the work of locating and analyzing primary source material for its authenticity and credibility progresses. Also, some secondary source material can be of value to the researcher, provided it is used selectively and properly.

The historian works by accretion of evidence from primary sources, and there is no substitute for painstaking culling of those sources. A primary source basically is eyewitness testimony. A primary source, then, is a person or thing (tape recorder, camera) present at the events and a narrator of those events. It is not necessary that a primary source be original, except in the sense that it is firsthand testimony. For example, a primary source may well be a copy of the original manuscripts containing the eyewitness testimony.[22] Some historians categorize primary sources as records and relics. Records are differentiated from relics in that records are intentional eyewitness testimony. This suggests that the motivation for the record keeping must be examined, as well as the content. Intentional eyewitness testimony indeed may function to obscure the interpretation of an historical event. Most records take the form of written documents, but records may be oral or works of art, including film. Relics, on the other hand, although also eyewitness accounts, were recorded for purposes other than to form a data base for future historians. Most relics, like financial records of businesses, have in recent years been well preserved because institutions have provided procedures for retaining such historical evidence. Language and customs of a region and artifacts like tools and machinery also are classified as relics.[23] Obviously, some institutional records, such as government documents, may have been generated from mixed motives: to facilitate the daily workings of government but also to leave a historical record favorable toward some particular power group. The essential requirement for the historian is that the evidence come substantially from primary sources and that the historian analyze such evidence for its authenticity and credibility.

Establishing authenticity becomes more difficult with the passage of time. An authentic document is the product of the eyewitness, not a forgery. The historian should first try to establish the date of the document and determine whether the materials (ink, paper, type of film)

[21]Robin W. Winks, ed., *The Historian as Detective* (New York: Harper & Row, Inc., 1970); Jacques Barzun and Henry F. Graff, *The Modern Researcher* (New York: Harcourt Brace Jovanovich Inc., 1970), p. 63; Gray, *Historian's Handbook*, p. 57; Edward Hallett Carr, *What Is History?* (New York: Random House, Inc., 1961).

[22]Gottschalk, *Understanding History*, pp. 53–4.

[23]Barzun and Graff, *Modern Researcher*, p. 148, for example, use this classification of primary sources.

were available at that time. Handwriting can be matched with the primary source's handwriting on documents already verified. The source's style of writing should be analyzed, and the historian should ask whether the views expressed in the document are in harmony with other recorded views of the source. Anachronistic references to events in the document should also be searched out. Further, the document should have come from a line of well-authenticated, reputable owners, or it should have been found where it logically ought to have been (in a government document warehouse, the attic of a house where the source once lived, in a relative's possession).[24] In other words, authentic documents do not spring up like lilies of the field! Although the researcher today can expect that the authenticity of documents found in established depositories already has been verified, the serious historian cannot proceed blithely down the research path without asking some of these questions again.

Once data have been authenticated, the more difficult work of establishing the credibility of the evidence begins. The historian must ask how much of the authentic evidence is credible and to what degree.[25] Recently, the so-called radical historians have stressed that researchers can no more write the history of the American revolution from the papers of George Washington than they can trace the history of Watergate solely from the memoirs of Richard M. Nixon. Letters particularly are susceptible to failing credibility tests because, as Nevins commented, "some people change their personality when they pick up the pen."[26] Louis Gottschalk wrote that credible testimony "is not *that it is actually what happened,* but that it is *as close to what actually happened as we can learn from a critical examination of the best available sources.*"[27] Spontaneous and intimate personal letters and photographs generally are rated high in credibility, as are personal notebooks, written and tape-recorded diaries, interoffice memoranda, and artifacts. The primary source producing the best evidence from the historian's point of view is the eyewitness with expertise in an area, but one who lacks bias and motives of self-interest. Again, this is a crucial point for the researcher to remember because not all that was said about a person or event was recorded, and much of what was recorded has not survived. Further distinguishing marks of credible evidence include the witness's physical proximity to the described events, as well as the proximity of time of testimony to the event. For example, memoirs present reflections rather than reports. Because of the timely factor, newspapers, magazines and broadcast tapes are good primary sources; nevertheless, these sources must also be treated with caution. The researcher should consider the tone of the news medium and how that affects reporting

[24]Gottschalk, *Understanding History*, pp. 122–3; Paul M. Angle, "The Case of the Man in Love: Forgery, Impure and Simple," in Winks, *Historian as Detective*, p. 128.

[25]Gottschalk, *Understanding History*, p. 27.

[26]Billington, p. 229.

[27]Gottschalk, *Understanding History*, p. 139.

(the progressive, crusader newspaper, for example, projects a news bias), the news medium's general adherence to reasonably acceptable standards of ethical and professional journalism, and the degree to which the publisher controls the newsroom.[28] Robin Winks commented that "newspapers are not only the products of fallible men; they are the products of fallible men under pressure, and they are owned, on occasion, by men who would use them for their, or even their advertisers', purposes."[29] Further characteristics of credible testimony include published eyewitness accounts that reflect unfavorably on the eyewitness or contradict the eyewitness's earlier stated expectations, as well as eyewitness comments on events incidental to the main topic of discussion.[30]

A particular caution in weighing credibility of evidence is the effect of language. Like any cultural phenomenon, language changes over time, and modern meanings cannot be imposed on words used two hundred, or even ten, years ago. Experienced historians suggest that the meaning of a word be inferred from the use of the term in context if that meaning makes sense in all contexts in which the word appears in testimony of that time period.[31] Research experience, of course, adds incrementally to a historian's tested methods of assessing the credibility of evidence. The suggestions here are not meant to be exhaustive.

It bears repetition that primary documents must be studied in context. As Berkhofer noted, documents tell us what an actor did, not necessarily what he or she thought; indeed, subjective documents may intentionally obscure what the actor did. Berkhofer distinguished between behavioral evidence and ideational evidence that reflects the thought of the actor or primary source.[32] Carr agreed that "no document can tell us more than what the author of the document thought—what he thought had happened, what he thought ought to happen or would happen, or perhaps only what he wanted others to think he thought, or even only what he himself thought he thought."[33] For this reason, the historian studies an incident both from the view of the participant primary source and the observer of the primary source who comments on the symbolic and nonsymbolic behavior of the primary source.[34] Nevins cautioned, however, that circumstantial evidence should be used with care and considered inferior to direct evidence. The historian needs to consider carefully the deceptive possibilities of circumstantial evidence.[35] Such complexities of interpreting evidence

[28]Billington, p. 209.

[29]Winks, *Historian as Detective*, p. 193.

[30]Gottschalk, *Understanding History*, pp. 161–4, 90–109; Billington, 198; Winks, *Historian as Detective*, p. 509.

[31]Murphey, *Our Knowledge*, pp. 53–5; Winks, *Historian as Detective*, p. 188.

[32]Berkhofer, *Behavioral Approach*, p. 17.

[33]Carr, *What Is History?*, p. 16.

[34]Berkhofer, *Behavioral Approach*, pp. 42–5.

[35]Billington, p. 224.

do not baffle the empirical historian because formulating a precise research question aids in the systematic review of all possible sources of response.

Indeed, the consensus among some historians is that all evidence must be clearly established by the testimony of independent witnesses.[36] Imagination and creativity will lead the researcher to verify data, not only from manuscript files of libraries, but from personal and business check stubs, receipts, company records, tax records, legal records like wills and affidavits, letters and reminiscences of associates of the primary source, and even cemeteries. The historian needs to publicize this kind of search for evidence; in the early 1970s a researcher was led to an attic trunk stuffed with documentary evidence, heretofore untouched, about D. W. Griffith, the film maker. Even investigating how data were destroyed tells the historian where there was bias and perhaps the extent of the missing data. It is a tragedy to find a five-year gap in some institution's records because of flash flood, but it may be a record of bias to find a five-day gap in a politician's tape-recorded diary, for example. The historian's judgment is the key factor in this process. Admittedly, it is somewhat subjective, lacking the experimental certainty of the behaviorist, but because of this the historian's goal is no more than "verisimilitude with regard to a perished past."[37]

As a final note, evidence must be affirmative. Because of the possibilities of destruction and natural loss of evidence, negative evidence used to support a hypothesis or answer a research question is no evidence at all.[38] For example, because only one complete circulation list from a colonial publisher is known to have survived, a historian cannot write that circulation lists generally were not common. Perseverance through the morass of data is the only answer to most of the historian's problems. Experimental research may be completed in months; the historian's work, by its nature, takes years. It is far better for a historian to forego writing than to write after a less than complete search for primary sources.

This is not to say, however, that the wheel must be reinvented each time a historian takes pen in hand. Secondary sources indeed have a place in historical research. These sources can be useful in establishing the historical context for the research problem. Historians often look to secondary sources for research questions and hypotheses that might be tested. Frederick Siebert's two propositions on the relationship between government and the news media, for example, would provide a research question for a contemporary historian.[39] But it took primary

[36]Carl Becker, quoted in Winks, *Historian as Detective*, p. 14; Gottschalk, *Understanding History*, pp. 166–7.

[37]Ibid., p. 47.

[38]Fischer, *Historians' Fallacies*, p. 62.

[39]See Frederick S. Siebert, *Freedom of the Press in England 1476–1776* (Urbana: University of Illinois Press, 1952); Donald L. Shaw and Stephen W. Brauer, "Press Freedom and War Constraints: Case Testing Siebert's Proposition II," *Journalism Quarterly*, 46: 243–54 (Summer 1969).

sources to answer it. Secondary sources, of course, can be invaluable in the immersion process, providing leads to both bibliography and evidence. At times, when a primary source has been destroyed, the secondary source reporting the eyewitness testimony may have to be used. In such cases, the historian needs to question whether the eyewitness testimony might have been reported inaccurately.[40]

Finally, the techniques for recording evidence will be mentioned briefly. If the responses to the research question call for quantitative analysis, then reference should be made to the appropriate chapters in this text. If documentary analysis will predominate or if the quantitative operations will not utilize a computer, then traditional note taking will suffice. A full bibliographic reference must accompany every shred of evidence, including that which is tape recorded. While many historians prefer a folded sheet of typing paper because of the surface space it affords, its compactness in filing, and its economy, some prefer cards, either computer cards or file cards, because of the flexibility possible. With cards, you can quickly rearrange the material into any particular grouping such as date or region.

Imagination will lead the historian to various other refinements in data recording, such as photographing rare documents or taking oral notes on a tape recorder. The important aspects of any system are accuracy, completeness, and permanency. After locating and recording sources of authentic and credible evidence, however, the historian's task has just begun.

SELECTING ANALYTICAL STRATEGIES

Decision making on data analysis is not entirely separable from the gathering of evidence because the kind of analysis affects the form of the data gathered. The arbitrary separation here is made only for ease in discussion. Decisions on data analysis are made in response to the research question. Without a research question in hand, the scissors-and-paste historian essentially cuts and pastes together all the testimony to be found about some group of events—an impossible task because there is no selection of relevant evidence—and hopes there is enough for a book.[41] On the other hand, a biased research question may result in what Alfred H. Kelly called law-office history: "selection of data favorable to the position being advanced without regard to or concern for contradictory data or proper evaluation of the relevance of the data proffered."[42] When the research question was formulated and the data base surveyed generally, the decision should have been made whether the historian uses the more traditional documentary

---

[40]Gottschalk, *Understanding History*, pp. 115, 165–7.
[41]See also, R. C. Collingwood, "Who Killed John Doe," in Winks, *Historian as Detective*, pp. 55–7.
[42]"Clio and the Court: An Illicit Love Affair," 1965 *Supreme Court Review*, p. 122.

analysis or quantitative analysis or both. Ideally, multiple measures are used; this reduces uncertainty in interpreting results when the historian reaches the same general conclusions through several measures. Those who would isolate themselves from either the traditional documentary analysis or quantitative analysis have little to learn from one another and little to offer in their own historical analysis. As Dollar and Jensen wrote, a dichotomy between quantitative and qualitative data is largely a false one. "Almost any attribute that people, events, or institutions possess can be quantified in one way or another. When the data are of poor quality because of loss, etc., quantification won't work, but hardly anything else will either."[43] The historian cannot afford to say with W. H. Auden, "Thou shalt not sit with statisticians, nor commit a social science." On the other hand, it would be a mistake to believe that because of the recent impetus given to quantitative history, all significant history is written in that way. Historians can use social science methods as a tool only if they have mastered historiography first. In considering data analysis, then, the historian must consider the nature of historical reasoning, the documentary approach to data analysis and its advantages with incomplete data, the applicability of quantitative methods, forms of data presentation, and literary style.

In contrast to the traditional view that the historian's method is inductive,[44] it seems more practical to take Fischer's view of the historical reasoning process. He wrote, "It consists neither in inductive reasoning from the particular to the general, nor in deductive reasoning from the general to the particular. Instead, it is a process of *adductive* reasoning in the simple sense of adducing answers to specific questions, so that a satisfactory explanatory 'fit' is obtained."[45] Adduction permits the historian to respond to a research question with multiple measures. It allows the historian to find the relationship between the ideation and behavior of the primary source.[46] For example, one might compile statistics on the behavior of the primary source, as well as analyze the ideas he or she expressed in writing. In studying the partisan press, the historian needs the quantitative data describing published propaganda, as well as a documentary analysis of the ideas therein.

To arrive at a verisimilitude of the past, the historian applies traditional documentary analysis to evidence too skimpy to permit quantification. The historian also applies traditional documentary analysis to parts of quantified evidence to enhance and illuminate the historical record. In the course of extracting the credible material from the authentic data, the historian notes the primary source's interpretation of the situation, as well as the source's behavior in the situation. The historian's analysis includes reports on the feedback to the primary source, noting whether the feedback was the intended result of the

[43]Charles M. Dollar and Richard J. Jensen, *Historian's Guide to Statistics* (New York: Holt, Rinehart and Winston, Inc., 1971).

[44]Billington, p. 234.

[45]Fischer, *Historians' Fallacies*, p. 1.

[46]Berkhofer, *Behavioral Approach*, p. 20.

source's activity or whether it disagreed with the source's aims. The historian also defines other observers' views of the situation and traces the anticipated and unanticipated consequences of the source's activity, noting relationships among those views and the primary source's ideational and behavioral aspects, as well as the feedback.[47] This information then is organized in meaningful fashion, depending on the structure of the research question. What results is verisimilitude, a reconstruction of relationships among variables at a particular place during a particular time. Two cautions should be exercised by the historian: (1) evidence should be interpreted in terms of the postulated past time; and (2) while relying on general behavior theory or group behavior theory to analyze the primary source's ideational and behavioral activity, as well as the observers', the historian should not fall into the excesses of some psychohistorians (psychoanalysis is properly practiced on a living, communicating subject).[48] Nevertheless, as Nevins suggested, historical research needs to be "ventilated, then, by fresh perspectives and new interpretations even more than by additional data."[49] For example, communication historians might fruitfully consider cultural interpretations of history.

Quantification complements this traditional documentary method of analysis. While Fischer points out the fallacy of misplaced precision in empirical statements[50] (when using microfilm, it makes little sense to measure column space in sixteenths of an inch), some variables are best counted. For example, rigor and precision can be injected into a study by using a historical standard by which to measure press coverage of an event.[51] The historian also can apply the statistician's basic understanding of conceptualization and theory building, various measurement tools, data processing, and statistical analysis, particularly content analysis techniques. This text deals with these procedures fully. The historian's problems of sampling, reliability, and validity are much the same as the behavioral scientist's. The historian particularly may be troubled by an incomplete data base; however, statistical techniques are being developed to correct for this. For example, the historian generally should not infer individual behavior from aggregate behavior, but there are some statistical tests under certain data conditions that permit some such inference. Data relating to deviance usually can be used by the historian because it refers to a small number of cases. Further, historians can use sampling methods to deal with incomplete data when there is incomplete data on some or all members of the population or when there is aggregate data for some or all members of the

[47]Ibid., 73; Gottschalk, *Understanding History*, p. 28.
[48]See Kenneth S. Lynn, "History's Reckless Psychologizing," *Chronicle of Higher Education*, January 16, 1978, p. 48.
[49]Billington, p. 95.
[50]Fischer, *Historians' Fallacies*, p. 61.
[51]L. John Martin and Harold L. Nelson, "The Historical Standard in Analyzing Press Performance," *Journalism Quarterly*, 33: 456–66 (Fall 1956).

population.[52] Finally, content analysis has become almost indispensable to the communications historian. It permits systematic and objective classification of communication content into categories according to specified characteristics so that inferences can be made from the data.[53] In brief, quantification techniques can be studied to inject rigor and system into traditional documentary analysis, and, when the data base permits, such techniques can be used to make more reliable generalizations.[54]

Most historians admit to some generalization whether the method employed was traditional documentary examination of evidence or a quantitative technique. Although William O. Aydelotte suggested that generalizations are implicitly quantitative in character,[55] historians do suggest that A occurred antecedent to or concurrent with B, that A and B were similar in behavioral or ideational characteristics, that B acknowledged A's influence, or even that other causes for B's actions can be eliminated.[56] Unlike the social scientist studying contemporary communication behavior, the historian cannot predict on the basis of such generalizations, because the historian's legitimate inferences are incapable of being tested by means of the null hypothesis. Yet every historian makes some leap of faith between evidence and generalization. The resulting inferences are valuable as long as the reader has a full description of how that leap was made. The one exception would be the case study where little generalization, if any, is possible; the case study, however, has only limited value as a pretest for further research. In making that leap of faith, the historian generally does not establish the substantial certainty required by a court of law, but the historian does show high probability. High probability means "the balance of chances that, given such and such evidence, the event it records happened in a certain way; or, in other cases, that a supposed event did not in fact take place."[57] In the traditional documentary approach to history, the historian is the judge of what constitutes high probability; in a quantitative approach, this is indicated in advance and tested statistically. In either case, the reader should be able to accept or reject the judgment made by the historian from the evidence presented. Because historical inference is a matter of judgment, many historians are loathe to use the word "cause" in their analyses. Causal explanations, however, may be suggested by the historian who remembers there are

[52]For further comment, see John Higham, *Writing American History* (Bloomington: Indiana University Press, 1970), 39; Murphey, *Our Knowledge*, pp. 156–70, 200.

[53]Ole R. Holsti, *Content Analysis for the Social Sciences and Humanities* (Reading, Mass.: Addison-Wesley Publishing Co., 1969), p. 25.

[54]Robert K. Thorp, "Behavioral Concepts and Tools: The Historian as Quantifier," Farrar and Stevens, *Mass Media*, p. 187; Robert P. Swierenga, *Quantification in American History: Theory and Research* (New York: Atheneum Publishers, 1970), p. xx.

[55]Ibid., p. 7.

[56]Fischer, *Historians' Fallacies*, has an excellent chapter on generalization.

[57]Barzun and Graff, *Modern Researcher*, p. 155; also see Billington, p. 196.

many causes of historical phenomena. Again, difficulties in dealing with causal antecedents of historical events can be controlled in the question-forming process when operational definitions are explicated.[58] Certainly, the historian can generalize with a smaller leap of faith if there are complete data on all the population, but that is rarely the case.[59] Finally, it ought to be reemphasized that even when historical generalizations cannot be stated with absolute certainty, they are not without value. Arthur Schlesinger, Jr., wrote:

> Even historians who are skeptical of attempts to discern a final and systematic order in history acknowledge the existence of a variety of uniformities and recurrences. There can be no question that generalisations about the past, defective as they may be, are possible and that they can strengthen the capacity of statesmen to deal with the future.[60]

Using either or both documentary and quantitative analysis, historians use several forms of report and data presentation. All reports should reflect the rigor and precision applied to the data, without, however, losing the literary quality of the report. When the historian deals with a limited range of data in response to a research question, the report may take the form of a case study or biography.[61] When the relationships delineated in response to the research question are much broader, the report may become an article, a series, a monograph, or book. The historian at times may analyze and critique the work of other historians. Also, the documentary approach has value for the social scientist in the process of literature review.

Whatever the form of the report or data presentation, there are common structural qualities. These perhaps are best summarized by a journalism professor who steadfastly maintains that the structure of good writing is simple: You tell 'em what you are gonna tell 'em; you tell 'em; and then you tell 'em what you told 'em! That is, all historical reports should begin with a conceptualization of the problem and a clear statement of the research question, followed by a literature survey appropriately integrated into the narrative and an explanation of the research method, full and precise presentation of evidence responsive to the research question, and finally, the generalizations in response to the research question. The exercise of some rigor in presentation of evidence, as noted, does not preclude the inclusion of anecdotal material where relevant. Rigorous, systematic history does not have to be dull history. And, surely, communications history should be written in the best literary style.

[58]See Fischer, *Historians' Fallacies*, pp. 164–86.
[59]Murphey, *Our Knowledge*, p. 201.
[60]Winks, *Historian as Detective*, p. 525.
[61]Nevins, the journalist and historian, suggested strongly that an excessive dependence on biography distorts history. Billington, p. 179.

AN INTEGRATED DISCIPLINE

More and more, the work of communications historians is being recognized for its significance and value in understanding general history. The time has come, however, for those whose vision does not extend beyond documentary analysis and for those whose practice does not reach beyond statistical analysis to understand the necessity for an integrated discipline of empirical history. Mass communication history has been ill served by impressionistic history, which was neither communication nor history. Documentary and quantitative analysis merely are systems—complementary systems at that—of gathering and classifying evidence responsive to significant historical questions. Although the authors of Chapter 18 appear to dispute this, it seems to me that the energy expended in scrapping over the false dichotomy between quantitative and qualitative analysis might better be directed toward producing significant, empirical communications history so that once contemporary communicators have been apprised more clearly and accurately from whence they have come, they may better plan where they are going!

17

Legal Research in Mass Communication

Donald M. Gillmor and
Everette E. Dennis

To the student learning the traditions and tools of communication re-search, legal research in mass communication may seem at first to pre-sent a conceptual puzzle. Law, like history, is an area of *substantive knowledge,* but legal scholarship is also linked to specific *legal research methodologies.* Confusion increases when you realize that studies of legal issues and problems in mass communication (or in other fields, for that matter) also lend themselves to a variety of other methodological ap-proaches. The methods of history, philosophy, sociology, and other disciplines have been applied to the law for many years.

It is important, therefore, to distinguish substantive legal topics that might interest researchers in various fields using differing scholarly methods from the methods of legal scholarship that have a direction and purpose of their own. At the same time, it is imperative that sub-stantive legal issues and problems of interest to mass communication researchers be put in the context of the law generally.

When it comes to substantive legal topics, historians might want to know something of the evolution of libel law in the English courts; phi-losophers might want information about the reasoning process of judges in making particular legal interpretations; sociologists might be interested in the influence of the law on social class; and political sci-entists might explore the relationship between election returns and ju-dicial decisions. In carrying out these studies the scholarly investigator will use whatever research methodology is appropriate to the problem. These might include the historical method, linguistic analysis, participant observation, survey research, content analysis, experimental design, and other approaches. Researchers will conduct their work in accordance with the standards and norms of their scholarly disciplines. The result of this research might be a better understanding of law and legal institutions, but this is not legal research per se.

Legal research methodology for the student of mass communication falls into a number of general areas. First, there is traditional legal research, which involves an exhaustive examination of legal materials in a law library setting; second, there is empirical and behavioral legal research, which employs the methods of social science while recognizing the unique circumstances and problems of law. Both approaches will be examined.

Another consideration for the student of mass communication law is *context*. Most mass communication researchers are not fully grounded in all areas of law, nor are they generally concerned with them. Yet, from time to time it is necessary to understand the context of a communication law problem that has its origins in earlier legal areas unrelated to communication law.

For example, one of the authors of this chapter, in a study of the Pentagon Papers, found it necessary to explore rather obscure reaches of the ancient law of trover and conversion in order to understand the concept of information as property in the public sector.[1]

Areas of law of greatest interest to mass communication researchers have been (1) *torts*, especially libel, privacy, and unfair competition; (2) *criminal law*, affecting sedition, criminal libel, contempt, and journalist's privilege; (3) *personal property*, including copyright, trademark, and commercial speech; (4) *constitutional law*, freedom of speech and press and guarantees of liberty under due process of law; (5) *legal procedure*, the enforcement of substantive rights, and free press and fair trial; and (6) *administrative law*, the regulation of broadcast and advertising communication. Important as these topics are, they are not the whole of U.S. law. So it is that communication law researchers must put their work in the overall context of law lest they be left with juridical fragments.

Frederick S. Siebert, a notable communication scholar, put the point well in a 1949 essay:

> Research in the field of legal problems of communication, like research in other areas of the social sciences, cannot be sharply segregated either as to subject matter or as to methods. Almost every research project in the broad

[1]Everette E. Dennis, "Leaked Information as Property: Vulnerability of the Press to Criminal Prosecution," 20 *St. Louis University Law Journal* 610 (Spring 1976); "Purloined Information as Property: A New First Amendment Challenge," *Journalism Quarterly*, 50: 456–62, 474 (Autumn 1973); "Purloined Papers or Information as Property: A Study of Press-Government Relations," unpublished Ph.D. dissertation, University of Minnesota, 1974.

areas of communications involves economic, political or social as well as legal problems, and in many cases it is impossible to separate the strictly legal from other aspects. To add to the complications involved in any attempt to segregate the legal aspects is the modern tendency of legal research to branch out into the social sciences and to utilize the findings of those areas in the solution of juridical questions.[2]

THE STATUS OF COMMUNICATION LAW RESEARCH

Although one of the oldest areas of communication research, legal studies in schools and departments of journalism have been modest in number. Central to a sustained interest over the years has been the need for current information on law as it applies to the press. At a time when there was less public interest in issues of press law, journalism educators provided colleagues with careful, though sometimes narrowly focused, updates on current cases and their effects.

Doctoral dissertations and master's theses in journalism and mass communication add to the literature, as do occasional articles in the major communication journals. From time to time historical treatises and textbooks on mass communication law appear. A few communication researchers publish in the law reviews. Fortunately for the field, scholars in other fields (law, political science, and history, for example) have provided a substantial yield of communication law studies and theorizing on freedom of expression.[3] Notable exceptions to the overall paucity of legal literature in journalism education are the works of Siebert (legal history)[4] and Gerald (constitutional law and the press),[5] both of whom held journalism appointments.

Articles on legal research methodology in mass communication have been included in two books on communication research since 1975,[6] the first such entries since the 1949 Siebert article.[7] Several doctoral

---

[1]Frederick S. Siebert, *Freedom of the Press in England, 1476–1776* (Urbana: University of Illinois Press, 1952).

Louisiana University Press, 1949), p. 26.

[3]Zechariah Chafee, Jr., *Free Speech in the United States* (Cambridge, Mass.: Harvard University Press, 1954); Alexander Meiklejohn, *Political Freedom: The Constitutional Powers of the People* (New York: Harper & Row, Inc., 1948), reissued by Oxford University Press in 1965; Leonard W. Levy, *Freedom of Speech and Press in Early American History: Legacy of Suppression* (Cambridge, Mass.: Harvard University Press, 1960; New York: Harper Torchbook & Row, Inc., 1963); Thomas I. Emerson, *Toward a General Theory of the First Amendment* (New York: Random House, Inc., 1963), and *The System of Freedom of Expression* (New York: Random House, Inc., 1970, Vintage Books, 1971).

[4]Frederick S. Siebert, *Freedom of the Press in England, 1476–1776* Urbana: University of Illinois Press, 1952).

[5]J. Edward Gerald, *The Press and the Constitution* (Minneapolis: University of Minnesota Press, 1948).

[6]Donald M. Gillmor and Everette E. Dennis, "Legal Research and Judicial Communication," in Steven H. Chaffee, ed., *Political Communication*, Sage Annual Reviews of Communication Research (Beverly Hills, Calif.: Sage Publishing Co., 1975), pp. 283–305; and the present chapter.

[7]Siebert, "Research in Legal Problems."

programs in mass communication have strong communication law components. The Law Division of the Association for Education in Journalism, formed in 1973, has encouraged legal scholarship through an active papers competition. While the communication law field does not yet have its own journal, there is every sign of a new vitality that may change the productivity pattern of research in the field. Media law teachers have established important connections with the Mass Communication Law Section of the Association of American Law Schools and with the Communications Bar section of the Practising Law Institute.

WHAT IS LEGAL RESEARCH?

For those conversant with scientific method, a first encounter with traditional legal research may be disappointing. Sometimes law review articles will unabashedly advocate a position based on normative assumptions. Other legal research will seem tediously encyclopedic and pedantic.

Legal research, however, serves several explicit functions, including,

clarifying the law through analysis of procedure, precedent and doctrine; reforming old laws and creating new ones; providing a better understanding of how law operates in society; and furnishing materials for legal education.[8]

These are somewhat distinctive and differing purposes. Many, if not most, legal researchers would like their research to have an impact on the law itself. It is considered a mark of considerable prestige for a piece of legal scholarship to be cited in a court decision as secondary authority for a new interpretation of the law. Of course, not all legal scholarship finds its way into judicial opinions, but with that as a kind of ultimate goal, the role of the legal scholar is different from that of a researcher who is satisfied simply to observe, analyze, and explain. The observation-analysis role is more common to the social scientist engaged in empirical and behavioral legal research.

Legal research of the traditional, documentary mode is largely adversarial. The legal researcher sets down a provocative proposition and marshals evidence to support its plausibility, and that evidence may come from opinions for the court, dissenting opinions, legislative histories, constitutional interpretation, and legal commentaries.

THE TOOLS OF LEGAL RESEARCH

Cases, statutes, and constitutions are the primary stuff of the law. If you cannot retrieve and read them, you are forever doomed to secondary sources; someone else will have read and interpreted them for you.

---

[8]"How Does the Law Change," *Research News*, Office of Research Administration (Ann Arbor, University of Michigan, February 1971), p. 4.

Many campuses will not have law school libraries. There are alternatives. Metropolitan counties often have substantial law libraries in their courthouses or government centers. State capitols usually house law libraries. In addition, general libraries, political science departments, and private law firms may be able to assist you.

A new and invaluable resource for college, school, or department is the Bureau of National Affairs *Media Law Reporter* (Med. L. Rptr.). On an almost weekly basis it reports all cases having a bearing on journalism and communication law. Issues include news notes, occasional bibliographies, Supreme Court schedules or dockets, and special reports (e.g., a 1977 report on the federal Freedom of Information Act). The heart of its content is the presentation of complete decisions covering the broadest spectrum of mass communication law. Subscriptions are $283 per year.

An older and more general alternative is *United States Law Week* (USLW) at $291 per year. It comes in two parts, one providing Supreme Court opinions shortly after they are rendered, the other federal statutes, administrative agency rulings, and significant lower-court decisions.

If you have access to a law library, you have at your fingertips an ingenious, if primitive, information retrieval system, much of which is now, or soon will be, computerized and thereby accessible in less laborious ways.

Abbreviations used in the following section are part of a *Uniform System of Citation* used in all legal writing and reporting and designed for precise communication and for brevity.

Remember that constitutions, legislative enactments, and court decisions of the jurisdiction involved are primary authorities. Treatises, law reviews, the *Restatements* of the American Law Institute, for example, are secondary sources. Annotations, encyclopedias, loose-leaf services, dictionaries, and Reporters may be cited as persuasive authority; digests, citators, and indexes may not.

A very first step in legal research might be to find the words, the legal vocabulary of your problem. Any one of a number of law dictionaries would serve this purpose (*Black's, Ballentine's*). Assuming some legal knowledge of your topic, you might prefer to begin with a resource that demonstrates how state and federal courts have construed your concept. Such a work is *Words and Phrases,* an alphabetical list of words and phrases followed by abstracts of judicial decisions using them. Pocket parts or supplements inside the back cover keep this and many other legal publications up to date. Do not overlook them.

Legal encyclopedias: notably *Corpus Juris Secundum* (CJS) and *American Jurisprudence 2d* (Am. Jur. 2d) provide yet wider sweeps of legal issues and principles. Use their general index volumes and, again, do not forget the updating pocket supplements. *American Jurisprudence 2d* will reference you to *American Law Reports* (ALR, ALR 2d, ALR 3d, and ALR Fed.), which contains brief essays or annotations on significant legal topics suggested by the approximately 10 percent of state and federal appellate court decisions this service considers leading cases. A good annotation may discuss all previously reported decisions on your topic. There are topical *Digests* to the first two series and a *Quick Index* for ALR 3d. ALR and ALR 2d are updated by a *Blue Book* and a *Later Case Service*, respectively, ALR 3d and ALR Fed. by pocket supplements.

By now you have encountered a good many *case* citations and, in West Publishing Company's *Words and Phrases* and *Corpus Juris Secundum, Key Numbers.*

First, the *cases*. All reported state cases can be found in West's National Reporter System. For example, *James v. Gannett Co., Inc. 335 N.E. 2d 834 (N.Y. 1976)*, a citation to a libel case, provides the following information and in this order: names of plaintiff and defendant, volume number of Reporter series in which the case is found, the Reporter series itself, the page number, state, and year of decision. All case citations provide this kind of information.

N.E. stands for *North Eastern Reporter, 2d* for the series. *North Eastern* reports the cases of Illinois, Indiana, Massachusetts, New York, and Ohio. The remaining states are grouped within *A.2d (Atlantic), N.W.2d (North Western), P.2d (Pacific), S.E. 2d (South Eastern), S.W.2d (South Western),* and *So.2d (Southern).* There are additional Reporters for New York and California, e.g., *N.Y.S. (New York Supplements),* and *Cal. Rptr. California Reporter).*

Federal District Court decisions are found in *F. Supp. (Federal Supplement)* and are reported as follows: *Sheppard v. Maxwell, 231 F. Supp. 37 (S.D. Ohio 1964).* S.D. stands for Southern District.

Circuit Court of Appeals decisions are found in *F.* and *F.2d (Federal Reporter)* and are reported as follows: *Sheppard v. Maxwell, 346 F.2d 707 (6th Cir. 1965).*

United States Supreme Court decisions are found in three parallel reporters, one official, published by the Court itself *(U.S.),* another a West Publishing Company series *(S.Ct.),* and yet another, this one annotated, a Lawyers Cooperative Publishing Company series *(L.Ed.2d).* S.Ct. is an abbreviation for Supreme Court; *L.Ed.* is an abbreviation for Lawyers Edition. A complete citation for a Supreme Court decision would be *Sheppard v. Maxwell, 384 U.S. 333, 86 S.Ct. 1507, 16 L.Ed.2d 600 (1966).*

Summaries of lawyers' written briefs are found in *L.Ed.2d.* Complete briefs can sometimes be obtained from law libraries or from the law firms on either side of a case. You should, however, be sure to determine the price or set a maximum price when you order. Addresses of law libraries and law firms can be found in a legal directory called *Martindale Hubbell. St. C. Reporter* is part of the West Key Number System.

Cases, of course, can be cited as persuasive authority. But it is important in reading cases to learn to distinguish between what a court rules and what it says in passing *(dicta),* for example, concurring opinions. *Dicta,* of course, can influence future decisions.

The next task is to find aids that will lead quickly to all the cases in point. For this purpose we use *digests, indexes,* and *citators.* A digest is a case finder or an index to the law. One of the best-known digests is West's *American Digest System,* which cumulates all reported state and federal cases in 10-year segments or decennials, the most recent being the *Eighth Decennial Digest, 1966–1976.* Current cases are found in the *General Digest* and organized around the Key Number System.

Key Numbers represent principles or points of law. Once having found one or more Key Numbers relating to your problem, you should be able to find all the relevant cases in the *American Digest System.* There are specialized and regional digests, such as *Modern Federal Practice,* covering all reported federal cases since 1939, as well as the overarching *General Digest.* The latter has a *Descriptive Word Index* to help you get started. A *Cumulative Table of Key Numbers* will tell you which volumes of the set have digest material relating to the key numbers you have.

One specialized digest is Lawyers Cooperative's *U.S. Supreme Court Reports Digest.* Volume 16 is an index. A separate index to annotations covers the annotations in *L.Ed.2d* and *ALR.*

Citators trace the life history of a case, a statute, or an administrative ruling. Has it been modified, reversed, affirmed, superseded, criticized, distinguished, explained, limited, overruled, or questioned? What have attorneys general and law review writers said about a case? Is it still good authority? Has a statute been amended, appealed, or declared unconstitutional? How has it been treated by courts and periodical commentators? There are *Shepard's Citations* for every state, each region of West's National Reporter System, for lower federal courts and the U.S. Supreme Court, for federal administrative agencies, for state and federal constitutions, the U.S. and various state codes, municipal ordinances, labor law, and for the law reviews. Now to statutes.

If you know approximately when a statute or an amendment to a statute was passed, it can often be located in *U.S. Code, Congressional and Administrative News.* From it one can construct the legislative histories of federal statutes and review congressional committee reports. *United States Code Annotated* (U.S.C.A.) is the best place to go for federal law, updated by pocket parts. Annotations include summaries of court decisions interpreting the laws, texts of the Constitution and their interpretation, opinions of attorneys general, and, occasionally, citations to law reviews or other secondary sources. There are indexed, annotated codes for most states (or see *Shepard's State Citations*). Usually, as in U.S.C.A., each title of a code will have a specific index. U.S.C.A. has a four-volume general index as well.

United States Code Congressional Service reports on the status of all pending legislation and publishes the full text of bills enacted, together with their legislative histories. Of notable interest for some research purposes are the positions of various interest groups in relation to a bill.

Rules and regulations of the federal administrative agencies, organized by subject matter, are found in the *Code of Federal Regulations,* supplemented by the daily *Federal Register.* The latter includes official notices of each rulemaking and other proceedings to be conducted by agencies such as the Federal Communications Commission (FCC). In the rulemaking process, FCC dockets or files, unfortunately located in Washington, D.C., often contain primary evidence in support of one regulatory position or another.[9] The *Congressional Information Service* monthly index provides much of the raw material of the legislative process.

The *United States Congressional Record* provides an edited transcript of congressional debates. It has a *Daily Digest*. See also the Commerce Clearing House (CCH) *Congressional Index*.

One of the many loose-leaf services necessary to the study of administrative law is *Pike and Fischer Radio Regulation* (R.R. and R.R.2d). This is the most comprehensive source of FCC decisions and regulations, and statutes and court decisions pertaining to broadcasting and cable television.[10] The key to using *Pike and Fischer* expeditiously is to begin with the volume titled *Finding Aids*, which includes a Master Index to the paragraph numbers by which all materials are ordered. The *Current Service* volumes (currently six of them) contain up-to-date versions of laws and regulations and any pending proposals for change. The three *Digest* volumes contain subject-matter digests of FCC and court actions and decisions; the *Cases* volumes (now in Volume 43) contain full texts. Index paragraphs in *Pike and Fischer* are referenced to sections of the amended Communications Act of 1934 and to the Code of Federal Regulations.

If you do not find what you want in the *Federal Register*, the official *FCC Annual Reports, Broadcasting Yearbook, Television Factbook,* or *Pike and Fischer,* call the FCC's public information officer and specify what you are looking for.

After you have a *Pike and Fischer* citation, you can use Shepard's *United States Administrative Citations* to find all subsequent citations to that FCC action. *Broadcasting* magazine will keep you posted on pending FCC actions. *Trade Regulation Reporter* (CCH) provides a like service for advertising communication and the work of the Federal Trade Commission (FTC). *Advertising Age* is the most useful counterpart trade publication. *Broadcasting* and *Advertising Age* are indexed in *Business Periodicals Index,* and *Broadcasting* has published its own comprehensive index for the years 1972 to 1976.

There is a *U.S. Catalog of Government Publications* and a *State Checklist of Government Documents.* The *U.S. Catalog* is a monthly compilation of

---

[9]Erwin G. Krasnow and G. Gail Crotts, "Inside the FCC: An Information Searchers Guide, *Public Telecommunications Review,* 5: 49–56 (July/August 1975).

[10]Don R. LeDuc, "Broadcast Legal Documentation: A Fourth-Dimensional Guide," *Journal of Broadcasting,* 17: 131–45 (Spring 1973); Joseph M. Foley, "Broadcast Regulation Research: A Primer for Non-Lawyers," *Journal of Broadcasting,* 17: 147–57 (Spring 1973). See also Henry Fischer, "Uses of Pike & Fischer," *Broadcast Monographs No. 1, Issues in Broadcast Regulation,* pp. 134–38 (1974); Russell Eagen, "How A Broadcast Attorney Researches Law," *Broadcast Monographs No. 1, Issues in Broadcast Regulation,* pp. 139–43 (1974).

all federal executive, legislative, and administrative documents open to the public. It has a cumulative annual index.

When primary research is completed, it is time to survey the *Index to Legal Periodicals* to see what others have written about your topic. Some advise beginning legal research with the *Index* in order to survey the boundaries of a topic. It is tempting, however, to rely too heavily on these secondary sources at too early a stage. There is also an *Index to Foreign Legal Periodicals* and a new (Jan. 1, 1980) *Legal Resource Index* on microfilm and a less comprehensive paper edition counterpart, *Current Law Index*.

Books or textbooks on legal topics are called treatises, and a library's holdings are indexed in its card catalogue. A *hornbook* is a single-volume summary of a field of law. A *nutshell* is an even more drastic summary. There are a number of legal bibliographies, among them *Harvard Law School Library* and *Current Publications in Legal and Related Fields*.

The American Law Institute's *Restatements of the Law* are attempts to reorganize, simplify, and move case law toward comprehensible codes. Begin with the *General Index to the Restatement of the Law*.

For legal style and citation forms, see *A Uniform System of Citation* published by the Harvard Law Review Association, and sometimes referred to as the Harvard Blue Book. Any standard text on legal research and writing will provide similar information.[11]

TYPES OF LEGAL RESEARCH IN MASS COMMUNICATION

We have indicated that several explicit functions are performed by legal research generally. These also apply to legal research in mass communication.

Some research clarifies the law, and offers explanation through an analysis of procedure, precedent, and doctrine. Pember, in his important book *Privacy and the Press*, used historical analysis and a synthesis of leading cases affecting the press to clarify the law of privacy.[12] In such works as the American Law Institute's *Restatement of the Law of Torts, 2d*, an effort is made to codify and otherwise make sense out of court decisions in libel law.[13]

---

[11]Morris L. Cohen, *How to Find the Law*, 7th ed. (St. Paul, Minn.: West Publishing Co., 1976); Morris L. Cohen, *Legal Research in a Nutshell*, 3rd ed. (St. Paul, Minn.: West Publishing Co., 1978); J. Myron Jacobstein and Roy M. Mersky, *Fundamentals of Legal Research* (Mineola, N.Y.: Foundation Press, 1977); J. Myron Jacobstein and Roy M. Mersky, *Legal Research Illustrated* (Mineola, N.Y.: Foundation Press, 1977); Miles O. Price and Harry Bitner, *Effective Legal Research*, 3rd ed. (Boston: Little, Brown & Co., 1969); William R. Roalfe, ed., *How to Find the Law* (St. Paul, Minn.: West Publishing Co., 1965); James A. Sprowl, *A Manual for Computer-Assisted Legal Research* (Chicago: American Bar Foundation, 1976).

[12]Don R. Pember, *Privacy and the Press* (Seattle: University of Washington Press, 1972).

[13]Restatement of the Law of Torts, 2d.

Some legal research tries to reform old laws and suggest changes in the law. Law professors Jerome Barron and Benno Schmidt, Jr., have pushed and pulled the concept of "access to the press." Barron, in a landmark law review article and in his book, *Freedom of the Press for Whom?*,[14] calls for a "realistic" reinterpretation of the First Amendment so as to accommodate the freedom to have access to the major media in order to express one's opinions where they will matter. Barron lost a decisive battle for his proposed changes in the law before the U.S. Supreme Court in the case of *Miami Herald Publishing Co. v. Tornillo* (1974).[15]

Evaluating Barron's proposal in an access context that includes the broadcast media and a consideration of antitrust laws, Schmidt opts for journalistic responsibility through such vehicles as press councils and journalism reviews.[16]

Research may be conducted to provide a better understanding of how law operates on society. Levy's *Freedom of Speech and Press in Early American History: Legacy of Suppression*[17] deals with the social and political effects of constitutional interpretations of the crime of seditious libel in the formative years of the American republic. The endurance of the crime of sedition in the American experience is the chilling theme of this revisionist history.

Preston's *The Great American Blow-Up*[18] is a legal analysis of the social effects of false and deceptive advertising (puffery) and of the inability of the courts and regulatory agencies to deal with it. Most of the empirical and behavioral studies discussed later in this chapter also fall under the general heading of "social effects."

Research may analyze the political and social processes that shape our communications laws. Here the focus is not on the effect of the law on society; rather, it is on the effect of society upon the law. Krasnow and Longley's *The Politics of Broadcast Regulation*[19] is a perceptive analysis of how formal legal institutions, such as the FCC, congress and the courts, interact in social and political terms with citizen groups and the communications industry lobby to create and enforce broadcasting law.

Research may furnish materials for legal and journalistic education in mass communication. Here we think of two kinds of textbooks that provide the basis for mass communication law courses. These include the hornbooks that synthesize and present in easily understood categories the

---

[14]Jerome A. Barron, *Freedom of the Press for Whom?* (Bloomington: Indiana University Press, 1973).

[15]*Miami Herald Publishing Co. v. Tornillo,* 418 U.S. 241 (1974).

[16]Benno C. Schmidt, Jr., *Freedom of the Press vs. Public Access* (New York: Praeger Publishers, Inc., 1976).

[17]Levy, *Freedom of Speech.*

[18]Ivan Preston, *The Great American Blow-Up* (Madison: University of Wisconsin Press, 1975).

[19]Erwin G. Krasnow and Lawrence D. Longley, *The Politics of Broadcast Regulation,* 2d ed. (New York: St. Martin's Press, Inc. 1978). See also Barry Cole and Mal Oettinger, *The Reluctant Regulators: The FCC and the Broadcast Audience* (Reading, Mass.: Addison-Wesley Publishing Co., 1978).

law of mass communication. Examples are the works of Harold Nelson and Dwight Teeter, William Francois, and Donald Pember.[20] Another kind of text is the casebook that presents a series of analytical comments and questions integrated with edited selections of leading cases. The best known casebooks are by Gillmor and Barron, Franklin and, for the electronic media, Ginsburg, Jones, and Kahn.[21]

Beyond the general materials of mass communication law there are programmed instruction materials in libel law, treatises on advertising, and broadcast law and regulation. Communication law research also focuses on news media coverage of courts and the law. A major work on news coverage of the U.S. Supreme Court is Grey's *The Supreme Court and the News Media*.[22] Studies are underway on the coverage of state and local courts. In addition, educators have prepared material on legal process coverage for reporting textbooks. All this is legal research in mass communication for teaching purposes.

EMPIRICAL AND BEHAVIORAL LEGAL RESEARCH IN MASS COMMUNICATION

Sir Henry Finch observed in his *Discourses on Law* in 1627 that "the sparkes of all the Sciences of the World are raked up in the ashes of the Law."[23] If Sir Henry intended to convey the idea that law, like other realms of human thought and action, is amenable to a variety of mental disciplines, he was prophetic. That is where we are today.

Methodologies applicable to the study of legal questions have been called traditional, empirical, and behavioral. Yet the most insistent advocates of each recognize the inevitable overlap. The traditional legal material retrieval system we have described depends for its logic upon words and numbers; thus the relative ease of its computability. Methodologies diverge, however, when their adherents are pressed to define what they mean by "theory." For the traditionalist, theory may be

---

[20]Harold L. Nelson and Dwight L. Teeter, *Law of Mass Communication*, 2nd ed. (Mineola, N.Y.: Foundation Press, 1973); Don R. Pember, *Mass Media Law* (Dubuque, Iowa: William C. Brown Company, Publishers, 1977); William E. Francois, *Mass Media Law and Regulation*, 2d ed. (Columbus, Ohio: Grid, Inc., 1978).

[21]Donald M. Gillmor and Jerome A. Barron, *Mass Communication Law: Cases and Comment*, 3rd ed. (St. Paul, Minn.: West Publishing Co., 1979); Marc A. Franklin, *Mass Media Law: Cases and Materials* (Mineola, N.Y.: Foundation Press, 1977); Marc A. Franklin, *The First Amendment and the Fourth Estate* (Mineola, N.Y.: Foundation Press, 1977); William K. Jones, *Cases and Materials on Electronic Mass Media* (Mineola, N.Y.: Foundation Press, 1976); Frank J. Kahn, ed., *Documents of American Broadcasting*, 3d ed. (Englewood Cliffs, N.J.: Prentice-Hall, Inc., 1978). Douglas H. Ginsberg, *Regulation of Broadcasting* (St. Paul, Minn.: West Publishing Co., 1979). Unlike the other words listed here, Kahn presents texts in unedited form and offers limited analysis or commentary.

[22]David L. Grey, *The Supreme Court and the News Media* (Evanston, Ill.: Northwestern University Press, 1968).

[23]Quoted by Edgar A. Jones, Jr., in Foreword to Layman E. Allen and Mary E. Caldwell, eds., *Communication Sciences and the Law: Reflections from the Jurimetrics Conference* (Indianapolis: Bobbs-Merrill Co., Inc., 1965), p. ix.

no more than a preference for a particular ordering of values, a model of action that can be applied generally and with feeling to a set of everyday occurrences. Oliver Wendell Holmes' "clear and present danger" test, Thomas Emerson's "speech/action" dichotomy, and the Burger court's doctrine of judicial restraint are such models, lending themselves to the logical process of analogy, discrimination, and deduction.

Behavioral theory is presented as something grander. It relegates to itself the power of prediction, but perhaps not its invention. Holmes, in his 1897 address to the Massachusetts Bar, "The Path of the Law," had already staked a claim to prediction:

> The object of our study, then, is prediction, the prediction of the incidence of the public force through the instrumentality of the courts. . . . The prophecies of what the courts will do in fact, and nothing more pretentious, are what I mean by the law.[24]

Legal sociologist Aubert believes it important to understand the characteristics of traditional legal research that set it apart from scientific thinking. They are:

(1) Scientific approaches tend to emphasize, often to the exclusion of everything else, that aspect of a phenomenon which is general. Judicial opinions, and also legal theory, tend . . . to stress the unique aspects of the case. . . .

(2) The web of relationships which legal thought throws over the facts of life is not a causal or functional one. Legal thinking, legislation, and judicial decision-making are (only) peripherally touched by schemes of thought in terms of means and ends. . . .

(3) Legal thinking is characterized by absence of probabilism, both with respect to law and with respect to facts. Events have taken place or they have not taken place. A law is either valid or invalid. . . .

(4) Legal thinking is heavily oriented to the past. . . .

(5) Law is a comparison process. . . . The legal consequences, in the terminology of the law, are not those factual consequences expected to follow a certain action. . . .

(6) Legal thinking is dichotomous. Rights or duties are either present or absent. . . .[25]

The goal of legal scholarship in mass communication is not always knowledge for the sake of knowledge; it is often an applied knowledge in keeping with the lawyer's adversarial purpose. Political behavioralist S. Sidney Ulmer writes:

[24]Oliver Wendell Holmes, Jr., "The Path of the Law," in Ephraim London, ed., *The Law as Literature* (New York: Simon & Schuster, Inc., 1960), pp. 614, 617.

[25]Vilhelm Aubert, "Researches in the Sociology of Law," *American Behavioral Scientist,* 7: 17 (December 1963).

In choosing among hypotheses concerning historical fact, the lawyer seeks victory not truth. The adversary process repels evidence as do delays in litigation. In making decisions the judge recognizes (1) that the case must be decided one way or another, whether or not the evidence is sufficient for a scientific conclusion; (2) that judicial fact-finders are not bound by rules of consistency; and (3) that facts may be bent by the judicial process to serve an ulterior purpose.[26]

It is perhaps unfortunate that much legal scholarship methodologically parallels the opinions of judges. The mass communication researcher, less wedded to the judiciary than the legal scholar, has an opportunity to make more scientific applications and to develop a more disinterested scholarship. Unfortunately, however, the communication scholar gets caught up in another kind of adversarial system and often becomes an advocate for the press and the communication industry; he or she looks for the effects of law on the absolute command of the First Amendment that "Congress shall make no law, abridging freedom of speech or of the press. . . ."

But it is overstatement to say, as Schubert does in the introduction to his landmark, *Judicial Behavior,* that "the traditional approach is interested in neither the descriptive politics of judicial action (i.e., the facts) nor the development of a systematic theory of judicial decision-making (through the use of scientific theory and methods)."[27] The aversion is not that strong, and such methodology may simply not be appropriate to some kinds of research. Often the legal scholar works with the singular instance, that is, the individual case. A new court decision is regarded as a landmark and the law changes. That singular instance can be related historically to earlier cases and to external influences that may have brought it about. But does this lead to theoretical formulation?

"Theory" in mass communication studies generally implies a set of related and highly abstract statements from which propositions testable by scientific measurement can be drawn, and upon which explanations and predictions about human behavior can be based. Theoretical models in legal research are different since they must accommodate changes in the law created by case adjudication and statute. This difficult task is compounded by the fact that "theory" in law, according to *Black's Law Dictionary,* is explicitly defined as "facts on which the right of action is claimed to exist." When a judge asks the question, "On what theory?" he wants to know the basis of liability or the grounds of defense. From Mill to Mieklejohn to Emerson, First Amendment claims have issued from theoretical frameworks that validate the asking of these questions. To lack a persuasive theory of freedom of expression is to lack any explanation for individual cases.

[26]S. Sidney Ulmer, "Scientific Method and Judicial Process," *American Behavioral Scientist,* 7: 22 (December 1963).

[27]Glendon Schubert, ed., *Judicial Behavior* (Chicago: Rand McNally & Company, 1964), p. 3.

Drawing too rigid a line between traditional and empirical methodologies, however, can be misleading. Traditional legal methodologies, it is true, are qualitative, their outcomes sometimes inexplicable, even unique—but not always. Scientific methodologies are quantitative, their outcomes lawful and noncontradictory—but not always.

Basic steps in the empirical test of generalizations might be (1) reviewing the relevant literature, (2) deciding upon testable hypotheses, (3) setting up a research design, (4) collecting and analyzing data, (5) testing the hypotheses with the data collected, and (6) offering conclusions and explanations for one's findings.

The traditional researcher, though in a less formal and systematic way, follows the same procedure. But again there are differences. If the trial is substituted for, say, the experimental research design, the difference becomes dramatic. The trial can never be repeated or replicated. It can only happen once. The legal hypothesis can be retested in an appeal, and often is, but the appeal process is finite. In principle the retesting and reformulation of hypotheses in science may continue endlessly. The legal scholar, however, unlike the trial lawyer, can enjoy some of the experimentalist's theoretical opportunities.

The application of social science methods to the study of mass communication law and other legal problems is of relatively recent origin, and there is a paucity of literature. The new approach is an outgrowth of scholarly trends in jurisprudence and political science away from natural law toward positivism (legal realism, political jurisprudence, and judicial behavioralism). Legal realists, including Holmes, Roscoe Pound, Llewellyn, Frank, and Olivecrona,[28] reacted negatively to traditional legal philosophy and the self-contained structure of legal research. They saw the judiciary as an integral element of contemporary social life, amenable to systematic observation and analysis.

Motivated by the legal realists, a number of political scientists and legal scholars observed that traditional legal research, relying on the exhaustive reading of cases and statutes, focused only on an intrinsic aspect of the law: the law is what the courts and the legislatures say it is, nothing less, nothing more. But thoughtful observers knew that extrinsic factors like politics and elections also influenced the court and the law, although these influences were seldom acknowledged in the decisions of courts or in the opinions of individual justices. This concern led to a school of political jurisprudence that included the study

[28]Holmes, "The Path of the Law," 10 *Harvard Law Review* 457 (1897), and Mark DeWolfe Howe, ed., *The Common Law* (Cambridge, Mass.: Belknap Press of Harvard University Press, 1963); Roscoe Pound, "The Need of a Sociological Jurisprudence," 19 *The Green Bag* 607 (October 1907) and *An Introduction to the Philosophy of Law*, rev. ed. (New Haven, Conn.: Yale University Press, 1954); Karl N. Llewellyn, "Some Realism About Realism," 44 *Harvard Law Review* 1222 (1931) and *The Bramble Bush* (New York: Oceana Publications, Inc., 1951); Jerome Frank, *Law and the Modern Mind* (New York: Coward McCann & Geoghegan Inc., 1949) and *Courts on Trial: Myth and Reality in American Justice* (Princeton, N.J.: Princeton University Press, 1950); Karl Olivecrona, *Law as Facts*, 2d ed. (London: Stevens, 1971).

of judicial lobbying, the political functions of judges, and constitutional politics.[29]

Political jurisprudence concerns itself largely with the impact of politics on judicial institutions. Judicial behavioralism looks more closely at the behavior of individual judges, blocs of judges (liberal versus conservative, for example), and the courts generally. Using theoretical models created by social psychologists to study individual and group behavior, a number of political scientists began to analyze judicial behavior in order to explain and predict what courts were doing and would do.[30]

Again it is important not to overlook the overlap in methodologies. Courts, of course, have not been oblivious to social science techniques. Indeed, legal empiricism may have begun with the *Brandeis Brief* in 1908,[31] a legal argument based on sociopsychological data. And scientific data collection was advocated by Loevinger, a former Federal Communications Commissioner, jurist, and law professor, in a system he called "jurimetrics." All other jurisprudence, said Loevinger, is

> based upon speculation, supposition and superstition; it is concerned with meaningless questions; and, after more than two thousand years, jurisprudence has not yet offered a useful answer to any question or a workable technique for attacking any problem.[32]

Judicial behavioralism is designed to take the scholar beyond any one court decision or line of cases into an examination of patterned behavior. It might also look at judges in attitudinal terms or explore ethnic and religious variables in their decisions. Ulmer points out some of the virtues of the behavioral approach in legal research:

> It is both pertinent and instructive to study the interpersonal relationships and behavior patterns of the members of a collegial court. By doing so, we recognize what legal analysis ignores, namely, that the law, the courts and the judges are something more than mere abstractions. The nature of the endowments, outlooks and attitudes which judges bring to the discharge

[29]See for example, Arthur A. North, *The Supreme Court: Judicial Process and Judicial Politics* (Englewood Cliffs, N.J.: Prentice-Hall, Inc., 1966); James Eisenstein, *Politics and the Legal Process* (New York: Harper & Row, Inc., 1973); and Samuel Krislov, *The Supreme Court and Political Freedom* (New York: Free Press, 1968).

[30]Stuart Nagel, *The Legal Process from a Behavioral Perspective* (Homewood, Ill.: Dorsey Press, 1969); Glendon Schubert, ed., *Judicial Behavior*, and *The Judicial Mind: Attitudes and Ideologies of Supreme Court Justices, 1946–63* (Evanston, Ill.: Northwestern University Press, 1965), and *The Judicial Mind Revisited, Psychometric Analysis of Supreme Court Ideology* (New York: Oxford University Press, 1974); S. Sidney Ulmer, ed., *Introductory Readings in Political Behavior* (Chicago: Rand McNally & Company, 1961).

[31]See *Muller* v. *Oregon*, 208 U.S. 412 (1908), wherein Louis Brandeis, then an attorney, furnished the Court with what for its time was overwhelming social scientific documentation of the deleterious effect of long periods of work on working women.

[32]Lee Loevinger, "Jurimetrics: The Next Step Forward," 33 *Minnesota Law Review* 455 (1949).

of their duties may be revealed in the identification of individual behavior patterns. The discrepancies among these patterns in turn, reflect the differences among the actors.[33]

EXAMPLES OF NONTRADITIONAL METHODS IN COMMUNICATION LAW STUDIES

Judicial behavioralism moves away from the factual web of particular cases and their idiosyncratic nuances and moves toward generalization. Space will permit only a few examples of empirical and behavioral studies from mass communication.

Thomas A. Schwartz, a journalism professor at South Dakota State University, did pioneering work in a master's thesis, "A Study of the Relationship Between the Ideological Tendencies of United States Supreme Court Justices and Their Voting Behavior in Selected Cases Affecting the Press, 1946–74." Schwartz tested three hypotheses:

(1) Basic attitudes of Supreme Court justices contribute to their voting behavior.

(2) Basic attitudes of Supreme Court justices toward civil liberties contribute to their voting behavior in civil liberties cases.

(3) Basic attitudes of Supreme Court justices toward press issues contribute to their voting behavior in press cases.[34]

Schwartz used judicial behavioralism in this mass communication law study. The Supreme Court case was his unit of analysis. He drew his data from all nonunanimous cases decided on their merits by the Supreme Court between October 1946 and February 1974 and two subsamples of civil liberties and economic cases. Units of measurement included Supreme Court justices, "courts" formed by the justices, ideological outcomes of cases, press favorableness of outcomes, and votes of individual justices. Schwartz was able to use a data package collected by the American Political Science Association and to computerize his work.

Patterning his study on the work of Schubert, Schwartz replicated tests of justices' attitudes using factor analysis. His conclusions:

(1) Supreme Court justices tend to form blocs; (2) In all cases in civil liberties cases these blocs can be identified as liberalism, conservatism, moderation, neutralism, and independence; (3) In cases affecting freedom of the press, these blocs normally can be identified as favorable-

---

[33]S. Sidney Ulmer, "The Analysis of Behavior Patterns on the United States Supreme Court," *Journal of Politics*, 22: 630 (1960).

[34]Thomas A. Schwartz, "A Study of the Relationship Between the Ideological Tendencies of United States Supreme Court Justices and Their Voting Behavior in Selected Cases Affecting the Press, 1946–1974," unpublished master's thesis, South Dakota State University, 1977, p. 16.

ness, unfavorableness, and neutralism.[35] More important perhaps were the implications of his work for the study of mass communication law:

(1) The establishment of the existence of distinct voting blocs in First Amendment cases can facilitate study of Supreme Court justices' attitudes toward a system of free expression.

(2) Since justices do vote in blocs in First Amendment cases, mass communication law researchers can have more confidence in describing the attributes of blocs and in explaining First Amendment freedoms.

(3) Explication of Supreme Court bloc arrangements in such areas as economic and civil liberties adjudication is well developed. Comparisons between those arrangements and First Amendment bloc arrangements could be worthwhile.[36]

In 1977, Gaziano, a graduate student at the University of Minnesota, became interested in the relationship between Supreme Court decisions and public opinion about freedom of expression for deviant political groups. Relying on a sociopsychological model of judicial behavior—the higher the tension and the greater the uncertainty, the more likely the group to seek a dominant outside referent such as public opinion—Gaziano stated the hypothesis:

(1) Decisions of the Supreme Court on freedom of expression for deviant political groups are related to public opinion on this issue.

Data fitting her research design were available in Court decisions and poll results over her stipulated 34-year period, and she found support for her hypothesis.[37]

Although the data do not account for judicial *behavior,* they do provide for an empirical test of at least a significant statistical relationship. If empirical studies, then, do not permit us to predict judicial behavior, they begin to explain it, and they help to reveal the nature of the rules of law. As has been noted, these rules are expressed in constitutions, statutes, ordinances, regulations, judicial opinions, and scholarly writings. And these are systematically preserved and catalogued. The traditional study of law is more than hunch and hope, and it lends itself to rational analysis in a number of modes.

Other mass communication law studies include Robbins' examination of the uses of social science data in deciding First Amendment decisions,[38] Anderson's empirical investigation of social responsibility the-

---

[35]Ibid., p. 240.

[36]Ibid., p. 241.

[37]Cecilie Gaziano, "Relationships Between Public Opinion and Supreme Court Decisions, Was Mr. Dooly Right?" *Communication Research,* 5: 131 (April 1978).

[38]Jan C. Robbins, "Deciding First Amendment Cases: Part I," and "Deciding First Amendment Cases: Part II, Evidence," *Journalism Quarterly,* 49: 263–70, 569–78 (Summer and Autumn 1972); see also Robbins, "Social Science Information and First Amendment Freedoms: An Aid to Supreme Court Decision-Making," unpublished Ph.D. dissertation, University of Minnesota, 1970.

ory,[39] and Holim's look at a conflict between two professions—lawyers and journalists.[40]

These studies, and others that could be cited, were careful to take into consideration linkages between and among court cases, as well as that long march of the law sometimes called the "dead hand of precedent" or *stare decisis*. The point is this: one does not "sample" cases in the sense of drawing a random sample. Conventional sampling procedure could be disastrous in legal studies if employed without real knowledge of all the cases in a particular area of the law.

No doubt, the authors suggested in an earlier book chapter,[41] there are many paths one might follow in searching for a research model. The creative researcher will find one best suited to his or her own needs. However, some considerations are immediately evident. For legal scholarship to become part of the totality of communication research it must:

(1) Consider the systematic, step-by-step procedures of the scientific method from problem formulation to hypothesis development, methodological strategy, data collection and analysis, and discussion of findings.

(2) Frame hypotheses that move away from normative, adversarial positions and are instead based on a preponderance of evidence growing out of a complete review of the relevant literature.

(3) Present the often-important dissenting views of judges in their full historical context so that they can be understood as part of the fabric of judicial behavior and not simply as exercises in legal reasoning (it is here that the distinction must be made between holdings and dicta).

(4) Make efforts to temper normative assumptions when analyzing the admittedly normative behavior of jurists. That is, while recognizing the value-laden quality of court decisions, the communication researcher should nonetheless seek systematic and value-free modes for dissecting and discussing them and their implications.[42]

PUBLICATION OUTLETS FOR RESEARCH IN MASS COMMUNICATION LAW

Scholars seeking publication in this field have a wide variety of outlets from which to choose. These include the periodicals of journalism and mass communication and the numerous law reviews and journals. To date there is no single scholarly journal devoted to research in mass communication law, but there are such magazines.

Two factors may determine where the scholar will publish: (1) form

[39]H. A. Anderson, "An Empirical Investigation of What SR Theory Means," *Journalism Quarterly*, 55: 33 (Spring 1978).

[40]Kim Holim, "Free Press and Fair Trial: An Attitudinal Study of Lawyers and Journalists in a Conflict Between Two Professions," unpublished Ph.D. dissertation, Southern Illinois University, 1972.

[41]Gillmor and Dennis, *Legal Research*.

[42]Ibid., p. 299.

and style of the research paper and (2) the audience one desires to reach. Most journalism and mass communication publications do not want traditional law review articles with their length, heavy documentation, and adversarial tone. They simply would not fit. By the same token, brief analytical papers without detailed backgrounding and exhaustive precedential referencing will not make it in the law reviews.

The scholar's purpose in doing legal research may be varied, but inevitably one hopes that one's work will be read. By whom is the question. If one wants to become part of the standard legal literature, be indexed in the *Index to Legal Periodicals,* and included in *Shepard's Citations* periodical references, the legal periodicals are one's outlet. However, legal periodicals are parochial in their nonlibrary circulations and not likely to be well read by persons in mass communication law, unless your article is discovered as part of a specific search. If one wishes to be read by the journalism community, the mass communication periodicals are the primary outlet.

Communication Journals

Publications like *Journalism Quarterly, Journal of Broadcasting,* and the *Journal of Communication* are interested in short (usually under fifteen typewritten pages) scholarly studies of communication law subjects. The *Journal of Communication* tends to be more topical and sometimes presents thematic issues. *Journalism Quarterly* will take a wider range of articles, from short historical studies to empirical analyses. Behavioral studies can find an audience in *Communication Research* and *Public Opinion Quarterly.* Short articles with broad implications for the media and society might be directed to *Mass Comm Review.* Legal historical work on a wide range of communication topics is sought by *Journalism History.* Lengthy legal articles, sometimes growing out of dissertation research, are occasionally published in *Journalism Monographs.* An article on a topic close to mass communication law teaching might find an eager audience in the pages of *Journalism Educator.* Articles of very current importance and written in the traditional magazine style can be submitted to a variety of publications, including *Columbia Journalism Review, The Quill, Nieman Reports, The Masthead, Grassroots Editor,* and many more. Industry or trade publications such as *Editor & Publisher, Broadcasting, Advertising Age, Publisher's Auxiliary,* and *Public Relations Quarterly* are good markets for short news articles about current cases and their implications. For a number of years William Francois of Drake University's School of Journalism wrote a regular column on communication law for *Writer's Digest.*

Useful listings of communication publications are found in the *Aspen Handbook on the Media*: 1977 to 1979 edition (William L. Rivers, Wallace Thompson, and Michael J. Nyham, eds., Praeger Publishers, New York, 1978).

Legal Periodicals

There are a significantly greater number of legal periodicals than there are communication publications. Legal periodicals are published mainly by law schools, but also by professional associations, groups of legal specialists, and commercial legal publishers. *Index to Legal Periodicals* is the *Reader's Guide* of the law field. Included in it are most American legal periodicals, both scholarly and professional. Articles about the law in more general circulation publications, as has been indicated, are indexed in *Legal Resource Index* and *Current Law Index,* international materials in the *Index to Foreign Legal Periodicals.*

The major publication outlet for the serious legal scholar who wishes to reach a legally minded audience is the law reviews, published mainly by an elite corps of third-year law students. These are *student* publications only in a technical sense. They feature articles by important legal scholars, judges, political scientists, and others. Nearly every law school has a law review, and most are general publications interested in a broad spectrum of legal topics. As one might expect, some give special attention to proximate federal circuit courts or the special legal problems of a region. But, for the most part, the law reviews are not parochial in content. An article on the Freedom of Information Act, for example, would be of interest to a wide variety of law reviews.

Like most publications, law reviews have a pecking order. The Harvard, Yale, Columbia, Michigan, Chicago, and Stanford law schools have the most prestigious law reviews, although there are at least twenty other highly rated law reviews.[43]

Content differs from review to review, but two types of content constitute the prevailing pattern. There are (1) *articles* and (2) *comments* or *notes.* Articles are substantive legal studies, usually well documented in nearly exhaustive, and exhausting, footnotes chronicling the judicial and legislative histories of particular cases, statutes, and legal concepts. Articles often begin with a hypothesis or proposition offered forcefully in an introductory section. This is followed by supporting units set off by subheads, a conclusion, and a discussion of implications. Legal scholars are the main contributors, but other disciplines may be represented as well. A number of communication law scholars publish regularly in the law reviews.

Comments are briefer treatments of legal issues and frequently focus on recent cases, putting them in context and analyzing their meanings. Most comments are written by the law review staff, although outside comments are welcomed.

A few law reviews favor review essays on current books and recruit outside specialists for this purpose.

The neophyte legal scholar may be overwhelmed by the number of law reviews in a law library. How is one chosen for publication pur-

---

[43]A. S. Miller, "The Law Journals," *Change,* 5: 64–66 (Winter 1973–1974).

poses? The *Index to Legal Periodicals* is a place to start. It will tell you where recent articles on your topic have been published. It will help you decide when to query an editor. By looking under headings such as freedom of expression, freedom of the press, or specific media headings, one can begin to detect the editorial patterns of particular law reviews.

There is some specialization in the law reviews. Some emphasize public law, others administrative law or property law. One should look carefully at a particular review before submitting an article.

Another possible publication outlet, but less varied in its approach, is the professional legal journal. Virtually every state and major metropolitan bar association has one. Some are scholarly, others newsy. For topics with a particular state or jurisdictional bias, these are outlets to consider.

There are a number of quasi-popular legal publications such as *Juris Doctor, Student Lawyer,* and *Case and Comment.* They prefer the more typical magazine article, and so the usual principles of magazine article submission apply.

For empirical studies, publications like *Law and Society* are appropriate, as are some of the journals of political science and sociology. Examine these for their contents and their methodological approaches, as well as their lead time for publication, before submitting.

Another form of publication is presentation of a paper at an academic meeting. Such a meeting is the annual convention of the Association for Education in Journalism. Legal research papers, depending upon topic and methodology, might be delivered to any of a number of Association divisional meetings (e.g., law, mass communication and society, history, radio and television journalism, advertising, newspaper, or theory and methodology).

There are obviously many possibilities for publication of mass communication law research. It is not always easy to locate the most responsive journals, and the author may have to make several submissions (one at a time) before finding a "market" for his or her research. Submissions to law reviews are most promising early in the academic year since a new law review staff has just taken over and it is eager for material. By mid-year the same review may be booked up for its remaining issues, and its staff will have no authority over next year's publication.

CONCLUSION

As the student delves into legal research, it will become clear that this mode of communication study requires a good grounding in legal reasoning and judicial decision making. As has been suggested, it will be necessary for the rigorous scholar to set stringent personal standards so as to avoid the usual pitfalls of law research with its normative bias. Mass communication law scholars sometimes see themselves more as defenders of the faith (the First Amendment) than as disinterested investigators.

The student of mass communication law must break new ground while taking advantage of a legacy of both documentary and behavioral-empirical research that provides a richness in hypotheses and method. In so doing, the contributions that he or she can make to the understanding of freedom of expression are large indeed.

18

The Logic and Aims
of Qualitative Research

Clifford G. Christians and
James W. Carey

Most American students think of the social sciences as woven from the same cloth as the natural sciences. The social sciences are said to share certain aspirations with physics, chemistry, and biology: to develop laws that hold irrespective of time and place, to explain phenomena through causal and functional models, to describe relationships among phenomena in essentially statistical and probabilistic terms, and to make controlled experiments the ideal methods of investigation.

However, it often comes as a surprise to American students to discover that this "social science as natural science" view is not so widely accepted outside the United States. Particularly in Europe, the subject matter of the social sciences is distinctively different from the natural sciences, thus creating a set of philosophical and methodological problems of a radically peculiar kind. There is considerable disagreement, of course, as to just what this distinctiveness entails, but the conclusion is the same: that there is no warrant for believing that the social sciences should imitate the natural sciences in form or method or that they will ever achieve the same success.

This conclusion was not concocted yesterday. One of the great initiators of this view was the eighteenth-century Neapolitan philosopher, Giambattista Vico.[1] For Vico the social sciences belonged with the hu-

---

[1] Giambattista Vico, *The New Science of G. Vico*, translated by T. G. Bergin and M. H. Fisch (Ithaca, N.Y.: Cornell University Press, 1948).

manities as part of a coherent group of studies. The social sciences were not dedicated, in his view, to studying natural objects or organic processes nor to elucidating physical laws or organic functions (though such laws and functions act as constraints on human action). Instead, the social sciences possessed for Vico a common task with the humanities: the explanation of how people create what is distinctively human—civilizations and cultures. In Vico's view the social sciences were scientific in the sense that they aimed at systematic knowledge, but they were oriented toward a human enterprise that has no analogy in the physical and biological world and therefore requires a distinctive mode of explanation.

For Vico, the world of nature, because it was created by God, must always remain somewhat a mystery, our knowledge of it as outsiders always shot through with uncertainty.[2] Civilizations and cultures, however, are human creations, things we ourselves bring into existence and maintain. Therefore, the world of man and society is more accessible to us than the world of nature, and our knowledge of it potentially more reliable.[3] It follows, then, that a major part of our task is to clarify systematically what we and others already know, or potentially know, of the social world based solely upon our ordinary immersion in this world. From this perspective, every man is a social scientist.

In other words, following the tradition of Vico, what we are here calling qualitative research is an attempt to offer an alternative to a natural science model of the social sciences, communications in particular. In fact, much of the work of many seminal figures in the social sciences may be seen as part of this tradition: Marx, Weber, Freud, James, Dewey, Tocqueville. At the empirical level such research originated with Frederick LePlay's provocative study of kinship patterns in nineteenth-century Europe.[4] Wilhelm Dilthey's seminal work and Max Weber's protean essays written between 1903 and 1917 are also basic.[5] In American sociology the "Chicago School" introduced qualitative research early in the century: the W. I. Thomas and Florian Znaniecki classic, for example,[6] field research in the 1920s inspired by Robert E.

---

[2]That it was God's creation was self-evident to a man of the eighteenth century. In an age of skepticism, many are uneasy viewing nature as part of the handiwork of any God. But however nature is seen, it cannot be taken as a human product or creation.

[3]This is why the more rapid progress of the physical sciences is something of an illusion. We knew much more about humans and their products and processes than we knew about nature prior to the institutionalization of science. The physical sciences came a long way because they had a long way to come.

[4]*Les Ouvriers Europeéns*, 6 vols., 2nd ed. (Tours: A. Mame et fils, 1877–1879); *La réforme sociale*, 3 vols., 3rd ed. (Tours: A. Mame et fils, 1887).

[5]Collected as *The Methodology of the Social Sciences*, Edward Shils and Henry Finch, eds. (New York: Free Press, 1949).

[6]*The Polish Peasant in Europe and America*, 5 vols. (Chicago: University of Chicago Press, 1918–1920). For the most complete description of the views that informed his methodology, see Florian Znaniecki, *The Method of Sociology* (New York: Farrar and Rinehart, 1934). His best work on the philosophical foundations of sociological inquiry is *Cultural Science* (Urbana: University of Illinois Press, 1952).

Park and Ernest W. Burgess, and influential pieces of naturalistic observation by Anderson, Sutherland, Zorbaugh, and Whyte.[7]

The attempt to develop an alternative tradition has taken many forms and is known by quite different labels in different countries: *les sciences humaine, Geisteswissenschaften*, critical theory, interpretive social science, hermeneutics, cultural science, or, in the general terms we have chosen, qualitative studies. These names point to important differences of outlook: differences in philosophical orientation, national tradition, research priorities, and ideological stances. We do not attempt here to sort out these differences but rather to merge them uncritically. We wish to present some of the intellectual dilemmas that concern these alternative traditions. We wish in particular to outline their underlying logic. Following this we suggest four criteria that guide this style of research. Thus we locate our essay in a middle range between the poles of epistemology (theory of knowledge) and technique. We do not systematically confront those questions pertaining to phenomenology (description of phenomena) as a philosophical enterprise or introduce a set of operational procedures.[8] Obviously, many concrete methods have been inspired by the guidelines contained here: symbolic interactionism, aspects of American studies, ethnomethodology, humanistic sociology, cultural hermeneutics, for example. We shall not deal with the many difficult and contentious problems in the philosophy and methodology of the social sciences that qualitative studies raise. Instead we wish to present this mode of investigation in a wide-ranging sense, noting it has long been nurtured in the humanities, has been brought into social sciences by the major figures mentioned previously, and recently has witnessed a resurgence of interest.[9] We intend then to outline an alternative tradition of social research, provide some guides to its major concepts and problems, make suggestions for further reading and reflection, and offer some notes concerning research procedure. Our concern is to bring this universe of explanation known as qualitative studies solidly into communication scholarship and introduce media students to the significant literature.

[7]Nels Anderson, *The American Hobo* (Leiden: Brill, 1975); Edwin H. Sutherland, *The Professional Thief* (Chicago: University of Chicago Press, 1939); William F. Whyte, *Street Corner Society*, 2nd ed. (Chicago: University of Chicago Press, 1955); Harvey W. Zorbaugh, *Gold Coast and Slum* (Chicago: University of Chicago Press, 1929). This approach has been further developed by Robert Redfield, Everett Hughes, Alvin Gouldner, Arthur Vidich, Herbert Gans, Howard Becker, Jack Douglas, and Erving Goffman.

[8]While we do not present an encyclopedia of fieldwork, we do recommend Robert Bogdan and Steven J. Taylor for an outline of procedures, *Introduction to Qualitative Research Methods* (New York: John Wiley & Sons, Inc., 1975). Severyn Bruyn's exhaustive work also provides specific suggestions, "Methodological Procedures," *The Human Perspective in Sociology: The Methodology of Participant Observation* (Englewood Cliffs, N.J.: Prentice-Hall, Inc., 1966), pp. 198–254.

[9]For good summaries of the contemporary scene, see Bruyn, *Human Perspective in Sociology*, and William Filstead, ed., *Qualitative Methodology: Firsthand Involvement with the Social World* (Chicago: Markham Publishing Co., 1970). Many of Howard Becker's writings deal with qualitative methodology; see his *Sociological Work* (Chicago: Aldine Publishing Co., 1970).

TWO MISCONCEPTIONS

Before proceeding further, let us eliminate two misconceptions. The first is that qualitative studies are opposed to statistics, mathematics, counting—indeed everything that might be called quantitative. This is to reduce, in other words, intellectual matters to the simple choice of "to count or not to count." But this is not the real issue, at least in the minds of the present writers. Counting, even the more elaborated forms of counting, are among the most extraordinary and indispensable tools invented by humans. No one can get by very long in scholarly research without such tools, and simple arguments about quantifying versus nonquantifying distort and even obscure the real intellectual problems. We do have reservations about certain forms of statistical accounting, but these arise because of assumptions contained in statistics concerning the meaning of norms and the "normal distribution of phenomena." On these matters, more later. The simple point here is that qualitative studies do not rule out arithmetic.

The second problem is more difficult because it is more subtle; it concerns the assumption that qualitative studies is simply another name for historical research. There is truth here and that is what makes this problem so subtle. Qualitative studies do move close to conventional forms of historical analysis. However, there is a real difficulty. In recent years students of communications have tended to divide the intellectual field into two domains, history and theory. The terms have been made mutually exclusive so that doing history precludes a contribution to communication theory. This division of domains has suited certain academic interests, but it has obscured some genuine problems.

Qualitative studies start from the assumption that any adequate theory of communication will be historical in a dual sense: it will be grounded in the knowledge of what communication has been and how it has become what it is, and its theoretical propositions will be designed to account for this historical and comparative variation and not its presumed universal or contemporary form. If communication theory must be historical, then communication history must be theoretical, as we have seen in Chapter 15 and expanded in Chapter 16. Such history must, in other words, go beyond the mere collection of historical fact and attempt to provide explanations. But qualitative studies differ from historical work in one critical way. They are concerned not only with the explanation of past events but with contemporary phenomena as well. Qualitative studies emulate historical explanation as method, not history as subject.

As we have already tried to make clear, the inverse of qualitative studies is that version of social science (or history) philosophically known as positivism and methodologically known as empiricism. This model has been both powerful and enslaving. In fact, it was such a model that Sir Isaiah Berlin had in mind:

The history of thought and culture is, as Hegel showed with great brilliance, a changing pattern of great liberating ideas which inevitably turn into suffocating straightjackets, and so stimulate their own destruction by new emancipating and at the same time enslaving conceptions. The first step to understanding of men is the bringing to consciousness of the model or models that dominate and penetrate their thought and action. Like all attempts to make men aware of the categories in which they think, it is a difficult and sometimes painful activity, likely to produce deeply disquieting results. The second task is to analyze the model itself, and this commits the analyst to accepting or modifying or rejecting it and in the last case to providing a more adequate one in its stead.[10]

Here Berlin points out a general task of qualitative studies—to make us aware of the categories in which we think and to analyze and critique such models. Qualitative studies are a self-conscious attempt to restore the critical and liberating function to intellectual investigation. They do not view the social sciences as a natural science of society, but as a distinctive science of the human. They do not view society as a body of contingent and neutral facts to be charted but as an active creation of its members. They do not view social science as "objective" in the ordinary and simple understanding of that term, but as an active intervention in social life with claims and purposes of its own.

If qualitative studies aim at restoring the critical and liberating spirit to scientific investigation, a question immediately follows: what is it that qualitative studies investigate? What is the object of study and the form of understanding?

Qualitative studies start from the assumption that in studying humans we are examining a creative process whereby people produce and maintain forms of life and society and systems of meaning and value. This creative activity is grounded in the ability to build cultural forms from symbols that express this will to live and assert meaning. To study this creative process is our first obligation, and our methodology must not reduce and dehumanize it in the very act of studying it. Such creativity is unique to the human species, and to this distinctive aspect we must pay circumspect attention. In Berger's useful phrase, our research must not treat a person as a puppet on a string or a prisoner, rather than as a live actor on a stage who constantly improvises as the drama unfolds.[11]

Humans live by interpretations. They do not merely react or respond but rather live by interpreting experience through the agency of culture. This is as true of the microscopic forms of human interaction (conversation and gatherings) as it is of the most macroscopic forms of

[10]Isaiah Berlin, "Does Political Theory Still Exist?" in Peter Laslett and W. G. Runciman, eds., *Philosophy, Politics, and Society: Second Series* (Oxford: Basil Blackwell, 1962), p. 19.

[11]Peter Berger, *Introduction to Sociology: A Humanistic Perspective* (Garden City, N.Y.: Doubleday & Co., Inc., 1963), chs. 6, 8.

human initiative (the attempt to build religious systems of ultimate meaning and significance). It is, then, to this attempt at recovering the fact of human agency—the ways persons live by intentions, purposes, and values—that qualitative studies are dedicated. Thus we do not ask "how do the media affect us" (could we figure that out if we wanted to?), but "what are the interpretations of meaning and value created in the media and what is their relation to the rest of life?"

Again, humans live by making interpretations. We are born into an intelligible, an interpreted world, and we struggle to use these interpretations creatively for making sense of our lives and the lives of those around us.[12] The task of social science, the basic task of qualitative studies, is to study these interpretations, that is, to interpret these interpretations so that we may better understand the meanings that people use to guide their activities.

FOUR CRITERIA

To make these concerns somewhat more concrete, we suggest four criteria by which competent qualitative studies can be judged: naturalistic observation, contextualization, maximized comparisons, and sensitized concepts. These four aims distinguish this mode of inquiry from other research styles. We separate out these elements for analytical purposes only, reiterating all the while that the kind of investigation described in this chapter is an ongoing, essentially dialectical process and not a series of discrete stages.

Naturalistic Observation

The qualitative approach, which puts human interpretation at the core, emphasizes naturalistic observation as the way of determining those interpretations. Observers, from this perspective, must pitch their tents among the natives, must enter the situation so deeply that they can recreate in imagination and experience the thoughts and sentiments of the observed.[13] In this regard, Florian Znaniecki introduced

---

[12]When someone explains why the fish are not biting, he theorizes. See Nicholas Wolterstorff, *Reason Within the Bounds of Religion* (Grand Rapids, Mich.: Wm. B. Eerdmans Publishing Co., 1976), pp. 59–66, for several examples of theorizing as a natural everyday activity. As Stephen E. Toulmin observed, in understanding each other's behavior we always name and classify: *The Philosophy of Science* (London: Hutchinson's University Library, 1953) and *Foresight and Understanding* (Bloomington: Indiana University Press, 1961).

[13]Charles H. Cooley called it "sympathetic introspection," putting oneself into "intimate contact with various sorts of persons and allowing them to awaken in oneself a life similar to their own"; in *Social Organization* (New York: Charles Scribner's Sons, Inc., 1909), p. 7. He elaborates: "Sympathy in the sense of compassion is a specific emotion or sentiment, and has nothing necessarily in common with sympathy in the sense of communion." *Sociological Theory and Social Research* (New York: Holt, Rinehart and Winston, Inc., 1930), p. 102. Obviously, research immersion refers to the latter.

his famous label, "the human coefficient," arguing that data always belong to somebody, that they are constructed *in vivo* and must be recovered accordingly.[14]

As good anthropologists, effective researchers learn a "foreign language" thoroughly enough to have it condition their thinking.[15] Vocabulary provides worthwhile clues to the way people define their situation; words indicate levels of trust, the nature of cohesiveness, status categories, authority structures, and personal bias.[16] Through patient attention to social nuance, the investigator can begin to think in the language of those being studied. As Park noted about himself, "I expect that I have actually covered more ground, tramping about in cities in different parts of the world, than any other living man."[17] His purpose was not merely observing and cataloging externals, but familiarizing himself with the inside meaning.

Symbolic activity is recognized as central to our personal and social experience, symbols and symbolic patterns the irreducible sociocultural data of qualitative research. Getting an insider's view takes it for granted that to understand someone's thought one needs to think with

[14]Florian Znaniecki, *Method of Sociology*, pp. 36 ff. For example, in the debate over whether cable media can mature into a full service communication network, the perception of municipal and FCC officials must be clearly determined. If city politicians only view cable television as a one-way tool for informing citizens, not as a two-way avenue for everyone's participation, and if FCC commissioners assume cable to be a noncompetitive extension of existing broadcasting, it is naive to believe that a mighty multiband system will ever result. Robert E. Jacobson documents the truncated outlook of city officials by interviews and participation in their meetings, *Municipal Control of Cable Communications* (New York: Praeger Publishers, Inc., 1977).

[15]Rosalie Wax develops that analogy further: "The fieldworker begins 'outside' the interaction, confronting behaviors he finds bewildering and inexplicable; the actors are oriented to a world of meanings that the observer does not grasp. With a strange language, at first all is mumbo-jumbo; then patterns begin to emerge, and the student proceeds from halting discourse to the fluency of one increasingly at home in the language and situation. Likewise, the fieldworker finds initially that he does not understand the meanings of the actions of a strange people, and then gradually he comes to be able to categorize people (or relationships) and events." *Doing Fieldwork: Warnings and Advice* (Chicago: University of Chicago Press, 1971), pp. 12–13.

[16]For studies that take vocabulary seriously as insight into group assumptions, see Samuel Wallace, *Skid Row as a Way of Life* (New York: Harper & Row, Inc., 1968); Rose Giallombardo, *Society of Women: A Study of a Women's Prison* (New York: John Wiley & Sons, Inc., 1966); Ned Polsky, *Hustlers, Beats and Others* (Garden City, N.Y.: Doubleday & Co., Inc., 1969); and such Tom Wolfe studies as *The Pump House Gang, Radical Chic and Mau-Mauing the Flak Catchers*, and *The Electric Kool-Aid Acid Test*. Howard S. Becker and Blanche Geer discuss the importance of learning the language in "Participant Observation and Interviewing: A Comparison," *Human Organization*, 16: 28–32 (1957). As Robert Redfield has noted, we must be careful that our descriptions match native perceptions since we can call clothes "rags" or "costumes." *Tepoztlan: A Mexican Village* (Chicago: University of Chicago Press, 1930). Edward T. Hall and William F. Whyte stress accuracy also, even to catching the tone of voice correctly; "Intercultural Communication: A Guide to Men of Action," *Human Organization*, 19: 7 (Spring 1960).

[17]Robert E. Park, *Race and Culture* (New York: Free Press, 1950), p. viii.

the same symbols. The social scientist must study the human spirit as expressed through symbolic imagery. "The Chicago School" taught us that social feelings (attitudes and sentiments) and life-style are most fully expressed in actual situations, and must be recovered unobtrusively through participant observation, from personal documents, and by open-ended interviewing.[18] To get inside the realm of lived experience, the natural processes of communication are especially valuable (such as correspondence, eyewitness accounts, songs, jokes, folklore, memoranda, diaries, ceremonies, citizen group reports, sermons), and methods must be avoided that disrupt the social process and thereby skew our vision.

The investigator has a "peeping Tom" curiosity about humanity's many affairs, including a semiotician's fascination with all the varied human vistas expressed in symbols—verbal, nonverbal, and graphic.[19] All of them are useful not to verify hypotheses but as sources for understanding meaning, for interpreting the mental content from which these expressions spring. As Charles Kuralt demonstrates in his fascination with local subcultures, the researcher learns confidence and freedom with regard to symbolic sources, examining them all in order to gauge preoccupations and prevalent values. Researchers emphasizing the insider's view will, in Rosalie Wax's terms, "learn new languages, play various roles, take on obligations . . . live inside or outside a community, or, as Groucho Marx once put it, 'wrestle with anyone in the house,' if they think this will help them find out what they want to know."[20] Qualitative research in its best form seeks through naturalistic observation to set up a poetic resonance with the native interpretation. In the process of studying human meanings as they come to expression in various communicative forms, the researcher gains a feeling for the

[18]These three mainstays of the qualitative approach (participant observation, personal documents, open-ended interviewing) are outlined in detail by Bogdan and Taylor, *Introduction to Qualitative Methods*, chs. 2–5. Thus Thomas and Znaniecki rely heavily on all manner of private and public personalia—letters, agency accounts, life histories, memoirs, and court records.

[19]Had the scope and space of this book permitted, a separate chapter on textual criticism would be valuable since documentation research has an indentifiable shape as an academic pursuit. However, we are implying in this essay that much literary criticism naively makes print the cornerstone, whereas we take the linguistically more adequate view that oral forms are basic and must flavor our attitude toward other symbolic forms such as print and electronic. Literary criticism of the nonstatic kind is not inconsistent with the approach we advocate here, only rooted in a nonsociological tradition. As Wilhelm Dilthey made no sharp distinction between social activity and written documents, as Clifford Geertz called culture "an acted document," and as Barney Glaser and Anselm Strauss in *Discovery of Grounded Theory*, Chapter 7 (Chicago: Aldine Publishing Co., 1967) compare listening to books with listening to dialogue, so do we. Certainly, Geertz believes that ethnography and textual criticism are similar in that both "conventionalized graphs" and "transient behavior" may be "foreign, faded, full of ellipses, incoherencies, suspicious emendations, and tendentious commentaries." See "Thick Description," in his *The Interpretation of Culture* (New York: Basic Books, Inc., 1973), p. 10.

[20]Wax, *Doing Fieldwork*, p. 5.

central symbols around which a culture is organized and pursues every clue to help evaluate them.[21]

Contextualization

Contextualization is a second phase in the investigative process. Researchers attempting to bring out all the distinctive elements of the case being studied must become masters of context.[22] Because symbols carry meaning invested by the situation, environments become crucial for proper understanding. A description is meaningful to the degree we can grasp the various arenas in which things stand.[23] In this view, meaning is not determined by statistical indexes of external behavior, but by context.

Swinging a baseball bat on a playing field or at home against my family changes the meaning of this activity completely. Differences between a twitch of the eyelid and a wink are clarified contextually. A parent grunting on hands and knees is understandable in the context of playing a game with the children. A stone marking a boundary and a stone leaving an assailant's hand are two different expressions conditioned by context. Say "adultery" and this verbal symbol can be understood as "pleasant," a "crime," or a "sin" depending on cultural frame.[24] In an analysis of ethical decision making among media professionals, we cannot overlook the fact that broadcasters work within the Federal Communications Act while print journalists have no similar restrictions.[25] Contexts must be made explicit whenever behavior is not routine or commonplace and certainly whenever events seem puzzling or paradoxical. Conventional inquiry, by contrast, screens out uncontrolled variation and therefore favors the laboratory as the supreme context-free environment. Qualitative research seeks instances in

[21]Which symbol sets are most definitive varies significantly among cultures. Adequate interpretive research locates such symbols accurately. Thus Jerome Mintz astutely settles on folktales as the key to unlocking Hasidic culture in Brooklyn's Williamsburg in *Legends of the Hasidim* (Chicago: University of Chicago Press, 1974). His research demonstrates vividly how these oral accounts, collected in their natural state, "present a rounded portrait and contain the full scope of Hasidism" (pp. 2–3).

[22]In fact, naturalistic inquiry has been defined with context explicitly in mind as "the investigation of phenomena within and in relation to their naturally occurring contexts," in Edwin P. Willems and Harold L. Rausch, *Naturalistic Viewpoints in Psychological Research* (New York: Holt, Rinehart and Winston, Inc., 1969), p. 3.

[23]"Indexical expressions" is Harold Garfinkel's term inherited from Charles S. Peirce and means that "meanings are determined by the contextual elements of time, place, situation, and the knowledge that is taken for granted about the persons involved." See Jack D. Douglas, *Understanding Everyday Life* (Chicago: Aldine Publishing Co., 1970), p. 38.

[24]For more examples of the manner in which context determines meaning, see Harold Garfinkel, *Studies in Ethnomethodology* (Englewood Cliffs, N.J.: Prentice-Hall, Inc., 1967), pp. 11 ff.

[25]Research conducted at the College of Communications, University of Illinois-Urbana, supported by the McCormick Foundation.

which the phenomena can be observed naturally rather than arranging for them to happen under contrived conditions.

Expressions usually occur in several contexts simultaneously, conceptual structures commonly knotted into and superimposed upon one another in peculiar ways. Cultural life is intricate and emotionally complex, symbols requiring a multitude of nuances for their proper exegesis.[26] Exploring one context usually exposes another, and the richness of particular events is uncovered only as single situations are fit within their multiple contexts. That people act so differently in a private setting than they do in a social setting indicates how important it is to determine context precisely. Any significant event is surrounded by a web of connections that in some ultimate sense touch the whole of mankind and history.

Each of these concentric circles has instrinsic value, but the best interpretive research always returns to the most concrete, immediately circumscribed boundaries within which the activity was first expressed. Investigation properly begins and ends with the immediate intersections of observer and observed. The significance that a detail receives from the whole must emerge first from the event itself. Thus the interpretive process is not mysterious flashes of lightning as much as intimate submersion into actual traditions, beliefs, languages, and practices.[27]

However, for all the necessity of immediate contextualization, awareness of intrinsic place in the wider culture is a further epistemological condition of understanding and not just a theoretical ideal. Meaningfulness implies relevant linkages among various units on a broader scale, these connections being another term for cultural contexts and likewise an arena for our research. Manifold individual forms could not be measured unless there were some interconnectedness. Cultures are systems, that is, coherent units with a characteristic form. Therefore, taking those systems seriously is an important element in developing context. T. S. Eliot contrasts "material organization and spiritual organism."[28] Working from this latter metaphor, that is, giving priority to the organism's connective tissue, opens up interesting vistas for inquiry. If the world is dynamic and not a static system, if life

[26]Claude Levi-Strauss makes that clear in *The Raw and the Cooked*, trans. J. Weightman and D. Weightman (New York: Harper & Row, Inc., 1969), p. 341.

[27]Rosalie Wax develops that notion in more detail: "Understanding does not refer to a mysterious empathy between human beings. Nor does it refer to an intuitive or rationalistic ascription of motivations. Instead, it is a social phenomenon—a phenomenon of *shared* meanings. Thus a fieldworker who approaches a strange people soon perceives that this people are saying and doing things which they understand but he does not understand. One of the strangers may make a particular gesture, whereupon all the other strangers laugh. They share in the understanding of what the gesture means, but the fieldworker does not. When he does share it, he begins to 'understand.' He possesses a part of the insider's view" (*Doing Fieldwork*, pp. 10–11).

[28]*Notes Towards the Definition of Culture* (New York: Harcourt Brace Jovanovich, Inc., 1949), p. 197.

is the fundamental fact that must form the starting point, then contextual wholes become essential to our intellectual enterprise. In a profound sense, human behavior is a total reality and isolating certain aspects may be done provisionally, but it always involves great dangers of distortion.

We make an appeal for sociologically spacious study here. The texture of a cultural system at large, the *Zeitgeist* of an era, must be understood for an immediate event to be appraised accurately. Jacques Ellul's analysis of propaganda receives much of its strength from his placing it "within the context of civilization."[29] To best "pass judgment," "assign magnitude," "make distinctions," and "assess connectedness," one must finally be macroscopic.[30] A communication network exists only to the extent that an underlying code is essentially the same for all. Without culturally pervasive themes, a society could not demonstrate such categories of meaning as insult, delicateness, pride, vulgarity, and offense. While skeptical of any Hegelian attempt to consider patterns as the unfolding of absolute spirit, we may not assume the opposite either—that we live in a welter of unconnected facts without rhyme. For Rickman, "it is a matter of empirical facts and not of metaphysical speculation that we touch life in terms of patterns, connections and relationships which constitute for us the meaning of our experiences and indeed of our lives."[31] Man creates science, art, religion, cities, laws, and institutions. All these are meaningful contexts that need clarification for behavior to be intelligible, for us to understand what people intend and the reasons they have for their actions.

Qualitative research does not set brick upon brick and painstakingly construct the larger building. Certainly, the wider cultural context may be construed in that fashion—as when we study the shout, the brandished fists, a distorted face, and then realize that all can be classified as socially designated ways for expressing anger. But we are really talking here about the opposite movement, from large to small, of which, once again, knowing a foreign language is analogous. Fluency in language is a precondition for competent understanding of explicit actions and events, the necessary framework for preventing total misconceptions. So-called facts achieve significance only within a comprehensive context that allows extraction of the human content.

Immediate and wider contexts are obvious boundaries, but historical contexts deserve attention also. In C. Wright Mills' descriptive phrase, "history is the shank of social study," and interpretive research, as we argued, simply cannot succeed without penetrating the historical setting. Human interpretations emerge in time-space, and locating events squarely within their historical sequence is a radically different orien-

---

[29]*Propaganda*, trans. Konrad Kellen (New York: Alfred A. Knopf, Inc., 1965), p. xvii.

[30]These are Jacques Barzun's terms in "Cultural History," *The Varieties of History*, Fritz Stern, ed. (New York: World Publishing, 1956), pp. 394–5.

[31]H. P. Rickman, "Introduction," in Wilhelm Dilthey, *Pattern and Meaning in History* (New York: Harper & Row, Inc., 1961), p. 30.

tation than the "dull little padding known as 'sketching in the historical background' with which our studies of society are often prefaced."[32] The interpretive approach avoids the static at every point. It catches hold of the ambulation of history. Qualitative research self-consciously avoids the assumption that the problem or social group under study is an autonomous creation arising by spontaneous combustion and challenges the ahistorical bias of empiricism. We chart our own course as humans, but always over seas and continents where voyagers have gone before.

The world in which we live is in essence a temporal sequence manifesting recurrent qualities. It consists of a series of individual events that follow one another in a time relationship. Culture has continuity; it lives on in a way individual events do not. Therefore, the interpretive mode deals in large part with the modifications, the new combinations, the rearrangements of ideas and feelings in the present moment. In contrast to synchronic approaches, research from this viewpoint recognizes the emergent property of human life so that two visits to Moscow, though seemingly identical in every respect, are never considered the same because the second occurrence is always conditioned by the first.

Qualitative research, serious about establishing historical frameworks, assumes that every event and image are historically concrete. For Mills, "What Marx called 'the principle of historical specificity' suggests that any given society is to be understood in terms of the specific period in which it exists."[33] Every occasion has a historically singular location that gives it uniqueness. Thus Cicero's orations, rooted in oral culture and formulaic memory, bear no resemblance to political speeches or sermons that depend on rote memory and written text. Likewise, if one places video cassettes in historical context, one washes away all rhetoric about its revolutionary character. As television emerges out of radio's womb, so video cassettes are conditioned by television's structure to the point where they too become no more than a promoter of standardized products anchored in an advertising base.[34]

New events flow from past events, and even though similar themes emerge they acquire new meanings. Unless we live into historical contexts, we do not realize that Weber's objectivity, for example, refers to liberation from political power (i.e., freedom from the *Reich* and *Kaiser's* interference) and not to raw neutrality. Without a historical anchor we overlook stages of development, we misjudge whether events are in their incubation period or denouement, whether in the affective domain, for instance, what was once interesting has now become boring. History corrects our exaggerations also, reminding us through

[32]C. Wright Mills, *The Sociological Imagination* (New York: Oxford University Press, Inc., 1959), pp. 143, 154.

[33]Ibid., p. 149.

[34]With the same diachronic contextuality, James W. Carey and John J. Quirk orient technology to its historical development in the United States in "The Mythos of the Electronic Revolution," *American Scholar*, Summer-Spring, 1970, pp. 219–41, 395–424.

Whitehead, for example, that modern science, for all its vaunted dominance, is actually rooted in the weaker side of Greek philosophy. C. Wright Mills, to cite another case of taking one's bearing from history, describes the massness of our society in terms of the amount of time we speak and listen. He could not phrase it in this way without knowledge of nonindustrial societies where the listening-speaking balance is maintained.[35]

Contextualization is a vital dimension of interpretive studies. While extraordinarily complex, this guideline calls our attention to immediate, wider cultural, and historical contexts if we are to interpret human interpretation accurately.

Maximized Comparisons

"Maximize the comparisons" is Glaser and Strauss's way of describing another dimension of the interpretive process.[36] Obviously, this does not simply mean the testing of hypotheses under varying conditions, as typically done in empirical science and in the new scientific history. It refers instead to a judicious choosing of several comparison groups, not for the purpose of testing the null hypothesis, but to improve the substance and explanatory power of our interpretations.

Comparative analysis has often meant cross-cultural studies among various nation states. We refer instead to an advanced form of this strategy embracing comparative units of any size and configuration. Comparative analysis requires carefully selected cases, without any claim to knowledge of the whole field or that random sampling was strictly satisfied.[37] The overall aim of qualitative studies is well rounded and parsimonious explanation. Matching different examples serves that end by clarifying gross features and making conceptual categories more precise.

In keeping with qualitative assumptions, the researcher does not normally select statistical aggregates as the comparison group (such as millionaires, voters over 65, people with IQs above 140, what Daniel Boorstin calls "everywhere communities"), but more natural socially identifiable settings. Thus Louis Wirth compares a Chicago ghetto with those in Europe in order to distinguish their features.[38] Warner compares a modern New England community with a primitive Australian one in order to highlight the similarities in ritual.[39] Social scientists contributing most to qualitative research use intact settings within which

[35]*The Power Elite* (New York: Oxford University Press, 1959), ch. 13.

[36]Glaser and Strauss, *Grounded Theory*, ch. 5. See also Barney Glaser, "The Constant Comparative Method of Qualitative Analysis," *Social Problems*, 12: 436–45 (1965).

[37]Glaser and Strauss present an entire chapter on concrete guidelines for selecting comparative cases wisely (*Grounded Theory*, ch. 3, pp. 45–78).

[38]*The Ghetto*, rev. ed. (Chicago: University of Chicago Press, 1962).

[39]W. Lloyd Warner and Paul S. Lunt, *The Social Life of a Modern Community* (New Haven, Conn.: Yale University Press, 1941).

social life occurs—hospitals, prisons, residential neighborhoods, schools, regions of poverty and affluence, airplanes, parks, factories, streets, sidewalks, and ethnic enclaves—as their primary resource. All the while they do not wish to "lose touch with the hard surfaces of life." The process of writing about status, death, ethnicity, and revolution is really one of outlining "particular attempts by particular peoples to place these things in some sort of comprehensible, meaningful frame."[40] Insofar as status, for example, is a powerful factor in the interpretive structure of communication, this idea must not only be theoretically clarified, but it must be studied in terms of its concrete manifestations in the relations of social workers and their poor clients, in the operative principles of television drama, in the relations between news sources and journalists—comparing all such concrete instances where humans meet through the agency of communication.

Nor do you typically select a single variable and look for this one narrowly sliced indicator in all conceivable situations. Clifford Geertz, for instance, does not isolate the economic process, but examines economic development by comparing two towns in Indonesia, focusing on the constellation of socioeconomic patterns that characterize each.[41] In a similar fashion—with cable television, for example—we can compare various types of systems already in operation, describing them on a city-wide basis rather than isolating one factor such as public channel use.

We should not be misunderstood here. The qualitative mode predisposes research toward comparison in terms of social wholes. However, while keeping an expansive cultural outlook, one can select simultaneously features of that larger environment for more in-depth analysis. Erving Goffman does this successfully when he focuses on stigmas, developing a conceptual scheme out of all the studies of this phenomenon that had accumulated.[42] One can certainly choose a factor such as two-wayness and compare Martin Buber's I-Thou as it comes to expression among the Hasidim of Brooklyn's Williamsburg with the two-way capability of modern cable. In every case, however, the concern is not merely to isolate one abstract element, but to discover "underlying regularities in the natural structure of the social world."[43]

Comparison can also be of the internalized type—meshing one's own experience into the research process. E. E. Evans-Pritchard's famous theory of magic emerged out of a vast series of internal comparisons. Evans-Pritchard studied only Azande society, but in the process of describing its witchcraft and sorcery he wove in extraordinary detail that he had assimilated from years of observing alternative groups and

---

[40]Geertz, "Thick Description," p. 30.

[41]*Peddlers and Princes* (Chicago: University of Chicago Press, 1963).

[42]*Stigma* (Englewood Cliffs, N.J.: Prentice-Hall, Inc., 1963).

[43]Jesse G. Delia, "Constructivism and the Study of Human Communication," *Quarterly Journal of Speech*, 63: 78 (Feb. 1977).

other locations.[44] Robert Park's imaginative studies also rest on implicit comparison. His concepts of marginality and the race relations cycle are built from relevant materials assimilated by him as he traveled the globe and are rooted in compulsive reading.

In addition to the virtually automatic connections that any capable scholar makes, comparisons across history are unusually important too. John Dewey, for example, when evaluating democracy's prospects in the 1920s, instinctively flavored his conclusions with democratic styles of the small town American frontier and in the ancient Athenian city-state.[45] Marshall McLuhan can be put into fruitful perspective by comparing him with his forerunner, Harold Innis, and other academics who make the media central to an understanding of culture.[46] A generative way of confronting contemporary pornography is to compare its exploitative treatment today with the healthy attitude toward genitalia as symbols of life in ancient art. Durkheim understood organic solidarity only vis-á-vis an earlier form of mechanical solidarity, and many other equally famous distinctions are historically rooted: Cooley's primary and secondary groups, Tönnies's community and society, Weber's status and class, Becker's sacred and secular. Lewis Mumford contrasts the rigidities and objectivation of the mechanized world view with poetic and vitalistic qualities in an organic one.

In addition to situational and historical comparisons, an even more sophisticated comparative mode originated with Max Weber, that of ideal typing. This sociological procedure tries to recover something of the spirit of an older religious culture and turn it into a methodological instrument. Among the most famous examples is Weber's *The Protestant Ethic and the Spirit of Capitalism* (New York: Scribner and Son, 1930), in which Weber built two ideal types—protestantism and capitalism—and used such ideal or purified forms to examine the deviation of actual societies from them. Tocqueville's great study, *Democracy in America*, is another well-known work based on this form of analysis. Tocqueville created two ideal forms of social organization: aristocracy and democracy. He then showed the absence of the aristocratic type in American life and the presence of the ideal type of democracy in the peculiar conditions of America. Through imaginative use of such ideal types, qualitative research is more than an uncommitted, antiseptic study of "what is." Each richly interpretive type can be deployed as a device for assessing the direction of contemporary history so that in the service of reason and freedom men and women might better grasp the implicit values governing their lives.

In all this we are aware of the typical complaint that comparison

[44]Edward E. Evans-Pritchard, *Witchcraft, Oracles and Magic Among the Azande* (New York: Oxford University Press, Inc., 1937).

[45]*The Public and Its Problems* (Chicago: Swallow Press, Inc., [1929] 1954).

[46]James W. Carey, "Harold Adams Innis and Marshall McLuhan," *Antioch Review*, 21: 5–39 (Spring 1967).

may only yield impressionistic data, accumulate circumstantial evidence, and violate statistical procedures for assuring representativeness. However, our purposes differ in qualitative research, so that we are continually building a cumulative perspective that makes the interpretation more penetrating and coherent.[47] We need all the varieties of human society—cross-cultural and historical—to set the questions properly and avoid flatness in description. Our goal is not abstract truth but meaning-specific insight through continuing comparative analysis. And to do that well demands attention to a multiplicity of moments and locales.

Making fruitful correlations and contrasts involves natural social groups, a host of comparative detail assimilated into the observer's frame of reference, making connections across history, and comparing actualities with ideal types. Taken together, such comparisons help ensure that our explanations will be well rounded and our conceptual categories precise.

Sensitized Concepts

Qualitative research does not simply emphasize immersion, contextualizing, and comparisons. Establishing sensitized concepts is another dimension of the research process, that is, formulating categories that are meaningful to the people themselves, yet sufficiently powerful to explain large domains of social experience. Interpretive research seeks to capture original meanings validly, yet explicate them on a level that gives the results maximum impact. Naturalistic generalizations combine a scientific need for precision with the necessity to represent complex culture accurately. Glaser and Strauss correctly argue for vigorously analytical grounded theories so aptly stated that they can be grasped through experience.[48]

Our terminology here takes its inspiration from Herbert Blumer's useful distinction between sensitizing and definitive concepts.[49] Quantitative research traditionally produces lawlike abstractions through fixed procedures designed to isolate concepts so that IQ, for example, becomes the operational definition of intelligence. We introduce a different device for ordering empirical instances—expressions that develop an insightful picture, which distinctively convey the meaning of a series of events.

Concepts are the gateway to the world, the point of reference by

---

[47]Erving Goffman's *The Presentation of Self in Everyday Life* (Garden City, N.Y.: Doubleday & Co., Inc., 1959) is evidence that these objectives can be met. Certainly all the new concepts he introduces and the stimulating nature of his study indicates that comparative work can "build toward saturation."

[48]*Grounded Theory*, ch. 1.

[49]Herbert Blumer, "What is Wrong with Social Theory?" *American Sociological Review*, 19: 3–10 (Feb. 1954). See also his *Symbolic Interactionism: Perspective and Method* (Englewood Cliffs, N.J.: Prentice-Hall, Inc., 1969).

which research proceeds.[50] If too vague, they hinder our coming to grips with salient issues, and if wrongly formulated, they obstruct relevant problems from our investigation and foster misunderstanding or lead to oversimplification. Science agrees on the significance of conceptual clarity and the need for fruitful interplay between theorizing and empirical data. The question here revolves around the nature of conceptualization itself, with qualitative research concerned with concepts that yield meaningful portraits and not statistically precise formulations derived from artificial fixed conditions. Sensitized concepts refer to an orientation short of formal definition, yet apropos enough to help us cultivate facts vigorously.

By sensitized concepts we mean taxonomical systems that discover an integrating scheme within the data themselves. Whether by minting special metaphors or creating analogies or using direct expressions, the qualitative researcher maps out territories by finding seminal ideas that become permanent intellectual contributions while unveiling the inner character of events or situations. A portrait, illustrative story, or description of ritual behavior that crystallizes sentiment and life-style—all such rhetorical devices are necessary for elaborating sensitized concepts.[51] Thus Jerzy Kosinski, wishing to express the nature of living in an electronic age, uses the short story with the central character appropriately named "Chance." Jack Richardson illuminates television news by calling it a form of "community worship," where "network shamans" and "holy men" lead us in a "communal liturgy."[52]

By stressing sensitized concepts as the building blocks of qualitative research, we do not mean something intellectually immature. We are simply taking seriously our repeated contention that all human activity is interpretive. Sensitized concepts capture meaning at different levels and label them accordingly.[53] We can peel the onion of reality down to different layers, depending on our purpose and expertise. By apprehending events at various stages of an ongoing centrifugal process, these cognitive frames suggest directions along which our inquiry should advance. From this perspective, research does not progress in a linear fashion. We speak here of phaselike, sequential theorizing,

[50]For elaboration, see Alfred Schutz, "Concepts and Theory Formation in the Social Sciences," *Journal of Philosophy*, 51: 257–73 (1954), and Stephen E. Toulmin, "Concepts and the Explanation of Human Behavior," in *Understanding Other Persons*, Theodore Mischel, ed. (Totowa, N.J.: Rowman and Littlefield, 1974), pp. 94–99.

[51]Jacques Barzun and Henry Graff devote a major section of their *The Modern Researcher* to suggestions for writing up humanistically oriented materials (New York: Harcourt Brace Jovanovich, Inc., 1970, rev. ed., pp. 255–379).

[52]"Six O'Clock Prayers: TV News as Pop Religion," *Harper's*, Dec. 1975, pp. 34–38.

[53]Howard L. Gossage, for example, suggests a sensitized concept when developing a perspective on advertising as "the gilded bough." Obviously, practical magic is only an elementary device for orienting our study of advertising, but this rubric does conceptualize a host of issues and as such it suggests an interesting pivot of reference; in "The Gilded Bough: Magic and Advertising," Floyd Matson and Ashley Montagu, eds., *The Human Dialogue: Perspectives on Communication* (New York: Free Press, 1967), pp. 363–70. Even conclusions of modest proportions can have an enduring quality.

where repeated observation is necessary to clarify an emerging concept, which in turn improves the quality of further observation. Sensitive concepts must be continually tested, improved, illustrated differently, and refined by further encounter with the situations they presume to cover. As impressions take conceptual form, the naturalistic investigator checks them out by triangulation, that is, by testing one source against another until confident that the conclusion is valid.[54] This style of research builds toward saturation, always replacing an accepted theory with more illuminating and parsimonious ones. Thus sensitized concepts reflect the perpetual dialectic that is the life of the cultivated mind.

We have stressed participation throughout our description of the research process so far. Sensitized concepts arising from careful observation warrant attention, too. Researchers identify with social meanings in their role as participants and formulate theory about them as observers. The best scholarship results from those who act as members of the culture being studied and simultaneously as trained anthropologists from another culture. Since the days of Plato, and certainly Kant, we have recognized that experience alone is not the same as understanding it. Quality interpretive research arises not simply from personal involvements, but from a fully developed introspective capacity that produces formulations which accurately and substantively make compelling generalizations.[55] Interpretive research, in Denzin's terms, means

the studied commitment to actively enter the worlds of native people and to render those worlds understandable from the standpoint of a theory that is grounded in the behaviors, languages, definitions, attitudes, and feelings of those studied. . . . It aims for viable social theory; it takes rich ethnographic description only as a point of departure.[56]

True to the humanities from which this chapter receives much of its bearing, the scholar's role is to make intelligible by providing prophetic density. Thus David Riesman's work in *The Lonely Crowd* (New Haven: Yale University Press, 1961)—his sensitized concepts of tradition-, inner-, and other-directedness—tilt naturally into a perspective on history. Oscar Lewis' *Children of Sanchez* (New York: Random House, 1961) is not simply the account of a particular family but a commentary on oral culture generally. Alvin Gouldner's study of one factory provides insight into corporate bureaucracy as a whole.[57] Though we

---

[54]Norman K. Denzin, *The Research Act* (Chicago: Aldine Publishing Co., 1970), chs. 11, 12.

[55]Elliot W. Eisner uses the term "connoisseurship" for the research ability to evaluate in a penetrating way; in *Designing and Evaluating Educational Programs* (New York: Macmillan, Inc., 1979).

[56]Norman K. Denzin, "The Logic of Naturalistic Inquiry," *Social Forces*, 50: 166–82 (December 1971).

[57]*Patterns of Industrial Bureaucracy* (New York: Free Press, 1954).

resist making every natural laboratory "the world in a teacup," in a profound sense major theoretical contributions arise from concrete studies that use "complex specifics" to support broad cultural assertions.[58] In this manner, qualitative inquiry brings the prophetic element into communication research, prophecy, that is, of a genuine sort (not prediction but forthtelling—speaking truth with insight and conviction). Sensitized concepts with a prophetic touch, chosen almost at random, are Cooley's "primary group," Ellul's "efficiency," Tocqueville's "equalitarianism," Rousseau's "noble savage," Kuhn's "paradigm," Veblen's "conspicuous consumption," Innis' "monopoly of knowledge," Maslow's "self-actualizing," and Janis's "group think."

Interpretive studies allow themselves a freedom here that is denied by the typical hard-line fact and theory dichotomy. The received view in social science places a fundamental cleavage between the two, insisting that the scientist gathers neutral fact without injecting bias, that is, interpretation. Conclusions are valid only as the reverse side of data, only if compelled inexorably by the data or if drawn in meticulous logicodeductive fashion. In other cases, theories are put up front as hypotheses to be validated. But by breaking the theory-data contradiction, the interpretive approach does not wish to be called nonscientific. On the contrary, it is committed to sophisticated explanatory schemes, to demanding comprehensive designs. It has simply replaced prediction with empathic understanding as its research aim. Maintaining scientific integrity while effectively involved in research is a difficult problem, but at stake here is a different world view yielding a different definition of science. From this viewpoint, science is broadly conceived as that powerful enterprise of interpreting large numbers of phenomena in terms of a relatively small number of propositions. The naturalistic inquiry advocated here is built on the assumption that the knower is inextricably part of what is known rather than being independent of the social action.

Certainly, the general and specific still live in tension. Getting our sensitized concepts appropriately focused is an enormously difficult matter.[59] Robert Redfield, for example, felt a continuous ambiguity about his work, trying always to strengthen the "shaky bridges between general propositions and . . . such special knowledge as we have of particular societies."[60] Above all, conclusions must be returned to the concrete level for substantiation. A down-to-earth layman's configuration must be our point of departure and constant touchstone as we pursue

[58]Geertz, "Thick Description," p. 28.

[59]Howard Becker, in fact, speaks of an irreducible conflict between an academically sound sociological perspective and that of everyday life, "Problems in the Publication of Field Studies," in Maurice Stein et al., eds., *Reflections on Community Studies* (New York: John Wiley & Sons, Inc., 1964), p. 273.

[60]*The Folk Culture of Yucatan* (Chicago: University of Chicago Press, 1941). As he writes about his book, "This is both a report about Yucatan communities and a book about some general notions about the nature of society and culture" (p. ix).

judicious systematic elaboration of enduring problems. We always stand in danger of our concepts becoming desensitized. They can be pushed beyond their range of application until they become commonplace or vacant.[61] In the process of weaving a tapestry, the researcher attempts to reduce as much as possible the distance between imposed concepts and those employed by the people being studied. Constantly moving between social theory and the immediate arena of social experience ensures that the conceptual indicators we formulate will ring true on both levels; that is, they will be theoretically sound and realistic to the natives.[62]

The essential vocation of qualitative studies is, in Geertz's words, "to enlarge the universe of human discourse" and expand the horizons of human existence by making publicly available the manner in which others "have guarded their sheep," thus "enriching the consultable record" of what people have said and done.[63] Prophetic sensitized concepts are the most lasting contribution qualitative research can make.

We have staked out a scholarly domain in this chapter that takes seriously the creative and interpretive processes as central to the human species. We have entertained the hope throughout that social science can be freed from exploitative uses and enlisted instead in the cause of freedom and justice.

We recognize that research built from these assumptions, noble as they may be, can be as sloppy and irresponsible as the worst of academic endeavors. Therefore, to ensure intellectual toughness and prophetic clarity, we have described four standards by which this type of investigation proceeds. Only to the degree that we take naturalistic observation seriously, locate contexts validly, make fruitful comparisons, and formulate imaginative sensitized concepts can qualitative research be considered respectable.

At some point, certainly, the research compiled in this manner must be folded into the wider context of academic life. We accept the maxim that any approach imprisoned within itself—outside all canons of appraisal and therefore self-validating—simply cannot claim to be scien-

---

[61]We take seriously Max Weber's warning that if we include "the common elements of the largest possible number of phenomena," we lose the "richness of reality" and our conclusions are "devoid of content" (*Methodology of the Social Sciences*, p. 80). Barzun insists also that the researcher do his grouping and tidying carefully: "The moment the picture begins to look like a checkerboard, he has overshot the mark; he is no longer on earth but on Mars, where everything is canals" ("Cultural History," p. 398).

[62]This is similar to Robert Stake's responsive model in which research converges (develops a category) and diverges (fleshes out the details) in response to the questions and informal logic of actual life, in "The Case Study Method in Social Inquiry," unpublished paper, February 1976, Centre for Applied Research in Education, University of East Anglia. Compare Pitirim Sorokin for an argument that our intellectual connections must be readily comprehensible, *Social and Cultural Dynamics* (New York: American Book Co., 1937), pp. 26 ff.

[63]"Thick Description," pp. 14, 30.

tific. Though interpretive research does not arrange its scholarship in a manner that is easily repeatable, it does agree with the public nature of our scholarship and does consent that we must make our methods as clear as we can so additional work can be done.[64] It realizes, as with all scientific endeavors, that we must enter the larger world of communication theory and social studies generally in order to contribute to those broad concerns that the larger public expects academia to illuminate.

[64]For a very useful account of procedures in researching a medical hospital, see Howard S. Becker and Blanche Geer, "Participant Observation: The Analysis of Qualitative Field Data," in Richard Adams and Jack Preiss, eds., *Human Organization Research* (Homewood, Ill.: Richard D. Irwin, Inc., 1960). Thus Jerome Mintz explains carefully how he collected and scrutinized Hasidic tales (*Legends of the Hasidim,* pp. 14 ff.), William F. Whyte does a poststudy reflection on his research orientation, "On the Evolution of Street Corner Society," in Maurice Stein et al., eds., *Reflections on Community Studies* (New York: John Wiley & Sons, Inc., 1964). T. Shibutani and K. M. Kwan self-consciously document all the material they use, including the *New York Times* files. *Ethnic Stratification: A Comparative Approach* (New York: Macmillan, Inc., 1965).

19

Separating Wheat from Chaff in Qualitative Studies

Robert S. Fortner and
Clifford G. Christians

Assessing the merit of our research and scholarship is a perennial dilemma. We insist on footnotes in essays so our arguments can be reviewed and our sources checked. We replicate experiments to verify their findings. Though the problem of proper assessment is inherent in all academic life, separating the wheat from chaff is particularly difficult in the humanities. And communication research that takes its inspiration from the humanities shares in this larger uneasiness. However, the vitality and continued development of "humanistic models"[1] depend greatly, it seems to us, on the manner in which qualitative communication research engages the ongoing problem of verifying results.

Our concern in this chapter is to suggest means for producing com-

[1]The qualitative orientation is clouded at present by ambiguous nomenclature. Paul Lazarsfeld, for instance, called it "critical research" back in 1941 ("Remarks on Administrative and Critical Communications Research," *Studies in Philosophy and Social Science* 9: 1, 2–16, 1941). A Qualitative Studies Division with some of these concerns emerged in AEJ in 1975. Perhaps the two most developed streams in communications research with a humanistic flavor are symbolic interactionism and cultural studies. See James W. Carey, "A Cultural Approach to Communication," *Communication* 2 (1975). Paul M. Hirsch in introducing "humanistic models of communication research" properly suggested that such studies "constitute a neglected resource in which theories and insights for systematic testing are easily located." See Hirsch and James W. Carey, "Communication and Culture: Humanistic Models in Research," *Communication Research:* Special Issue, July 1978, p. 236.

petent humanistic research, with particular reference to the cultural approach, or what is sometimes called qualitative studies. We want to become more precise about valid investigation in this area. Statistically verifiable results are not appropriate in qualitative studies, since they operate with a mentality rooted in the humanities. However, while this fact may mean that qualitative research will lack the elegance of statistical tests, it should not imply a lack of rigor.

Precision and verification are particularly elusive for culturalists because their concern is meaning that has been generated and used by persons who would influence others, by those who have created cultural materials as interpretations of existence (such as music, film, and newspapers), meaning that has been generated and used as explanation by human beings coping with daily existence (and its intrinsic components, such as work, play, family, and peers), meaning that has been produced and used by critics, historians, sociologists, and other scholars in their attempts to understand and explain events. Each meaning that can be identified helps form a matrix, a web, of meanings, which eventually allows the culturalist to explain the ways human beings have organized community and family life. Although meaning has increasingly become the lightning rod in several areas of scholarship, we mention it here because it is central to the culturalist's understanding of communication theory. Communication could be defined, from this perspective, as the process by which meanings are created and exchanged.

INTERNAL AND EXTERNAL VALIDITY

How can research make meaning such an all-encompassing notion and yet accept some recognizable boundaries within which to pursue this elusive term? Here we confront that question directly, suggesting that cultural studies need their own version of internal and external validity and must meet acceptable standards of logic.

It should be apparent that the cultural approach to communication research remains interested throughout in empirical data. It does not accumulate such data with a highly refined methodology, and it avoids what C. Wright Mills called abstracted empiricism,[2] yet the pursuit of evidentiary detail is as fundamental to the humanistic endeavor as it is to all academic life. Reliable data are crucial to responsible conclusions in this mode of scholarship, even though it does not aim to test hypotheses statistically but to gain sensitive understanding.

Instead of laboratory experiments and field surveys as traditionally understood, cultural analysis tends to favor natural, noncontrived settings. The Chicago School of Sociology in the early twentieth century, for example, treated the hobo, the street gang, an ethnic minority,

---

[2]C. Wright Mills, *The Sociological Imagination* (New York: Oxford University Press, Inc., 1967).

slum dwellers, the professional thief all in their natural habitats. Data were collected in the form of people's own words, gestures, and behavior. Personal documents are the mainstays in discovering how people experience life in concrete situations, as Florian Znaniecki illustrated so dramatically in his afterword to *The Polish Peasant*.[3] We mean, obviously, not just the self-revelations of geniuses or members of an elite class, but the folk wisdom of ordinary people. Thus archival searches for letters, diaries, autobiographical notes, memorabilia, memoirs, verbatim reports, artistic reports, and all manner of private records have special significance as inside revelations. They permit us to study intimate facets of human drama that are not directly observable.

In addition to first-person accounts, open-ended, unstructured interviewing plays a prominent role in discovering how people define their realities. The voluntary character of the interview process is considered paramount, so that the interaction occurs as freely and in as nonstandardized a fashion as interviewing can permit, given the inevitable awkwardness in the relationship of strangers. Moreover, participant observation is recommended for plumbing the depths of a group's experience. The ideal experimenter, in this view, is not an "immaculate perceiver of an objective reality,"[4] but a person so unobtrusively steeped in people or documents that the investigator becomes an intimate, even thinking in the language of those being studied.

Ideally, the data must always be collected unobtrusively; yet the culturalist still seeks to do so systematically. Even though it does not rise from randomized samples or within tightly controlled variables, the aim is solid data nonetheless. In fact, the overriding importance of concreteness and the goal of illuminating real-life situations place unusual demands on the researcher. The student of culture selects his material not by fixed rule, but by Pascal's *esprit de finesse*, not reducing it to isolated variables but consistently viewing it as a whole. The often unstructured nature of the qualitative approach demands that users be very self-conscious, even critically so, of their procedures. Along these lines we offer several suggestions for effective data gathering.

It is widely understood and accepted that field surveys and laboratory experiments must be externally and internally valid; cultural studies need to meet these criteria as well (albeit in a manner peculiar to their own assumptions). External validity forces naturalistic observers to be circumspect in generalizing to other situations; have they, this guideline asks, selected cases and illustrations that are representative of the class, social unit, tribe, or organization to which they properly belong? Cultural studies arise in natural settings and not contrived ones, yet overgeneralizing remains a danger. The more densely textured our specifics, the more we can maintain external validity. Our

---

[3]Robert Bierstedt, ed., *On Humanistic Sociology: Selected Papers* (of Florian Znaniecki) (Chicago: University of Chicago Press, 1969).

[4]Neil Friedman, *The Social Nature of Psychological Research* (New York: Basic Books, Inc., 1967), p. 179.

concern here is particularly apropos in preparing case studies, a favorite qualitative tool since it allows in-depth and holistic probing.[5] In Norman Denzin's felicitous phrasing, the objective is representative rather than anecdotal (i.e., spectacular but idiosyncratic) cases.[6]

Regarding internal validity, our research mode must satisfy the requirement that the observations reflect genuine features of the situation under study and not aberrations or hurried conclusions that merely represent observer opinion. We are not interested in gathering only measurable details such as mortality rates; the culturalist, instead, disentangles the several layers of meaning inherent in any human activity. As Clifford Geertz puts it, "What the ethnographer is in fact faced with is a multiplicity of complex conceptual structures, many of them superimposed upon or knotted into one another, which are at once strange, irregular, and inexplicit, and which he must contrive somehow first to grasp and then to render."[7] We ask, "Is there sympathetic immersion in the material until one establishes, in Blumer's phrase, 'poetic resonance' with it?" Do we know enough to establish the principal aspects of the event being studied and to distinguish these main features from digressions and parentheses? Using the body as an analogue, do we separate the blood and brain from fingernails and skin, all of which are parts of the whole organism but of differing significance? It is usually assumed that such participatory observation can only serve an exploratory function, but we consider this a false assumption. If true interiority has occurred, that is, if data accurately reflect the natural circumstances, those data are valid and reliable even though not based upon randomization, repeated and controlled observation, measurement, and statistical inference. Our concern is for a research style that reduces situations and simultaneously maintains a broad understanding.

Another guideline for unearthing evidence involves the practice of exegetics, our effort at reading situations or documents with grammatical precision. Cultural studies consider failure on this expository level to be especially debilitating since their objective is rich detail. Ability to do accurate exegetical work requires cultivation so that a twitching eyelid is correctly interpreted as either a mischievous wink or incipient conspiracy (or simply a twitch). Simile is distinguished from allegory. Erving Goffman's work excels primarily because it diligently attends to every behavioral nuance. Admittedly, this norm, a developed grammatical sense, can only be placed on a sliding scale from meager to rich, yet culturalists insist on its being an important axis separating competent from incompetent study. Too much cultural work appears

[5]Robert Stake, "The Case Study Method in Social Inquiry," unpublished paper, Center for Instructional Research and Curriculum Evaluation, University of Illinois at Urbana-Champaign, 1976.

[6]Norman K. Denzin, *The Research Act* (New York: McGraw-Hill, 1978), chaps. 4, 6.

[7]Clifford Geertz, *The Interpretation of Cultures* (New York: Basic Books, Inc., 1973), p. 10.

with blurred grammatical categories and without the laborious attention to lexical details which demonstrates that the analyst has distinguished literal and figurative, has established historical antecedents and origins, has discovered words and their social patterns, knows exact meanings of synonyms and parallels, and the like. Often qualitative research just proceeds arbitrarily and does haphazard exegesis of either documents or events (or both).

This attention to the character of expressions is not a scholastic exercise. In fact, we agree with the newer exegesis that goes beyond letters to capture the textual spirit. All the while, however, definitions or explanations that authors themselves give is the starting point of adequate investigation. No one knows better than the author what particular sense he or she attaches to a word; this is initially assumed to be authentic; judging the inauthentic comes later. The culturalist considers it the highest priority to see the world as the actors themselves imagine it to be. Intellectual movement is therefore centripetal; understanding subjectively through our own involvement with the culture must occur before these interpretations can be understood from any other viewpoint. Theorizing on all levels must always be grounded in actual human transactions in particular contexts.[8]

Cultural studies deliberately center on real-life settings and written personalia, but not to the total exclusion of secondary sources (those not directly expressing a meaning structure) and information abstracted from everyday events. In fact, the culturalist's historical penchant often allows no other choice but to pursue public archives in addition to private ones and encourages submersion in every kind of human record, no matter how far removed from real life.[9] Normally, the public archives yield only secondary material—court testimony, newspaper accounts, business documents, actuarial statements, budget records—and thus are incomplete by themselves. Because these items usually represent a peculiar motivation and posture toward the issues, the selective bias must be ferreted out by careful attention to contexts.

The researcher does not merely cite these secondary documents, but rather weighs, evaluates, and then reconstructs them fairly. That principle obviously holds for all secondary materials; researching them is worthwhile only to the extent that they are painstakingly contextualized. Therefore, in dealing with such secondary material, we must ask several pertinent questions in order to measure this material appropriately: Is the evidence verifiable from other sources or corroborated by similar material in other locations? Can the testimony of the evidence be explained by its own bias? Is the evidence internally consistent or do contradictions occur that cannot be logically resolved? As a detective follows clues and then evaluates the evidence according to established

---

[8]Barney G. Glaser and Anselm L. Strauss, *The Discovery of Grounded Theory: Strategies for Qualitative Research* (Chicago: Aldine Publishing Co., 1967).

[9]Jacques Barzun and Henry F. Graff, *The Modern Researcher*, 3rd ed. (New York: Harcourt Brace Jovanovich, Inc., 1977).

rules, so we insist on our secondary sources meeting certain basic requirements. Was the author an insider with credentials?[10] To whom were the materials addressed—to a confidant, the public, an official? Was the statement made only out of self-interest? Taking evidence away from its context is a cardinal sin. We must never lose the flavor of the original, even though our task is reconstructing the material into a usable approximation to the truth. Deliberate care in dealing with imperfectly constructed records will help achieve a more complete and accurate rendering of events. Secondary sources can be helpful in the triangulation process described next and in expanding the scope of the inquiry.

Effective use of triangulation is another mark of competent humanistic research. Norman Denzin elaborates the concept in detail.[11] The goal is to build up a fully rounded analysis of some phenomenon by combining all lines of attack, each probe only revealing certain dimensions of the symbolic reality. The point is not to advocate eclecticism as such, but to avoid the personal bias and superficiality that stem from one narrow probe. Triangulation takes seriously the way we attach meanings to social reality and the fundamental elements of symbolic interaction embedded in the research process. The assumption is that different lines of action each reveal different aspects of reality, "much as a kaleidoscope, depending on the angle at which it is held, will reveal different colors and configurations of objects to the viewer."[12]

Triangulation occurs in several forms. It may refer, for example, to method, that is, combining document analysis with unstructured interviewing with unobtrusive observation, and combining this mixture in order to improve perspective. One can also take a social problem, pornography in the media, for instance, and triangulate it by viewing it historically (how does our modern view differ from previous eras and cultures), synchronically (what are the relevant facts on the problem today), and theoretically (what ethical or anthropological system does one use in gaining perspective on it). Theoretical triangulation is an obvious possibility, too, focusing several theoretical outlooks on a single object to see which one explains more.

Beyond these approaches is a kind of multiple triangulation in which all the various facets and insights generated are placed in interaction and cross-fertilization until the structural features of a setting or event are illuminated. Comprehension of actual context only accumulates gradually, so the search is always an ongoing one until we finally reveal the exact contours of the facts unearthed. "The facts never 'speak for themselves.' They must be selected, marshalled, linked together, and given a voice."[13]

---

[10] As Barzun and Graff suggest, "The value of a piece of testimony usually increases in proportion to the nearness in time and space between the witness and the event about which he testifies," ibid., p. 135.

[11] Denzin, *Research Act,* pp. 291–307.

[12] Ibid., p. 298.

[13] Barzun and Graff, *Modern Researcher,* p. xii.

Total description is only possible to the anthropologist working on a limited tribal culture; yet depth and complete intelligibility remain the ideals in humanistic research. The process of disentangling from within is complicated by the fact that we are interpreting a world that has been interpreted already. Our aim, then, can only be increasing insight. Thus the emphasis in cultural studies is on discovery rather than applying routinized procedures. We concur with a key notion of John Dewey that research methods are really "intelligence in operation," with intelligence being Dewey's term for directed operations "which eventually transform unsettled doubtful situations into situations that are determinate."[14]

In gathering data from natural field settings, then, cultural studies must pass the tests outlined previously—external and internal validity, exegetical awareness, accurate assessment of secondary sources, and imaginative triangulation. By these indexes one cannot always separate the wheat from the chaff, nor always guarantee valid data, but conscientious attention to them will serve the more modest goal of improved authenticity and meaningfulness in our analysis, interpretations, and explanations. At a minimum our guidelines indicate that research should be cautious, deliberate, reasoned, and accurate. We oppose sloppiness as much as anyone. We raise these standards as a minimum basis for improving this type of research while keeping imagination and meaning genuinely central. Rather than presenting them as restraints, we view these standards instead as aids for maximizing the adventuresome scholar's productivity.

PRESENTATION OF RESULTS

We come now to the problem of presenting our research. At one level this activity is simply an extension of the search for verification that has been the nemesis of research activity all along. During the data-gathering phase the problems have been, as mentioned, separating the idiosyncratic from the representative, as well as recognizing the biases of the sources and of the researcher. When we reach the reporting stage, also, we must take care to identify our position in reference to the material. How have our predilections affected the conduct of the research? What a priori assumptions were confirmed or denied as the research progressed? What nagging doubts do we still have about our findings?[15]

On another level our presentation must be in a form that allows the scholarly community to make independent evaluations of the validity of our arguments. We should note, too, that even in the case of the

[14]John Dewey, *The Quest for Certainty* (New York: Minton Balch, 1929), especially Chapters 8 and 9.
[15]See the last chapter of Alvin W. Gouldner's *The Coming Crisis in Western Sociology* (New York: Equinox Books, 1970) for his attempt to state the prejudices with which he wrote the book.

presentation with a purely descriptive intent, we are making an argument for the validity of the description. At the other end of the presentation spectrum is the polemic, which is obviously argumentative in character. In other words, any claim we make, if challenged, must be of such a nature that it can be made good or justified.[16] Our task in this regard is well stated by Stephen Toulmin:

> A man who puts forward some proposition, with a claim to know that it is true, implies that the grounds which he could produce in support of the proposition are of the highest relevance and cogency; without the assurance of such grounds, he has no right to make any claim to knowledge. The question, when if ever the grounds on which we base our claims to knowledge are really adequate, may therefore be read as meaning, "Can the arguments by which we would back up our assertions ever reach the highest relevant standards?": and the general problem for comparative applied logic will be to decide what, if any particular field of argument, the highest relevant standards will be.
>
> Now there are two questions here. There is the question, what standards are the most rigorous, stringent or exacting; and there is the question, what standards we can take as relevant when judging arguments in any particular field.[17]

Toulmin also proposes a system of argumentation that we believe to be well suited for presenting the findings of cultural or qualitative studies. Our goal, obviously, is to move forward from the data we have collected to a claim, or a series of claims, about those data and our interpretations of their meanings. Toulmin's model for such an argument appears as follows:

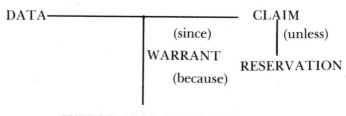

SUPPORT FOR WARRANT

The question, "Is that claim warranted?" captures nicely the notion of "warrant" in Toulmin's model. It is another way of asking, "Why do you think so?" We respond, "*Since* I know this to be the case, *because* this is true," or the like. We can stay on a correct path if we think in terms of justifying our claims by stating and demonstrating our assumptions to be true, or mapping out the cognitive process we use in

[16]Stephen E. Toulmin, *The Uses of Argument* (Cambridge, England: Cambridge University Press, 1958), p. 97.
[17]Ibid., p. 218.

verifying our intuition or revelation about the material we have studied. We can avoid making fundamental logical errors (*post hoc ergo propter hoc, argumentum ad hominem*, etc.) by continually questioning our own move from data to claim in the process of straining the move through the screens of "since" and "because."

The reservation to our claims is in the form of a qualifier or a condition or exception of rebuttal. It is such screens that prevent globalization of findings and that force us to recognize the existence of contrary facts, countercurrents, or explanations that offer alternatives to our own conclusions.

To give an example of this process at work, in the case of Canadian response to technological innovations in communications prior to World War I, the factual data seemed to indicate, *prima facie*, that Canadians had enthusiastically embraced the telegraph.

DATA ————————————————➤CLAIM

miles of telegraph line erected; growth in number of "telegraph towns"	Canadians enthusiastically embraced the telegraph

But why should such quantitative data necessarily lead to that conclusion? *Since* there would have been little continuing incentive for telegraph expansion into new areas if it were not being accepted and used, *because* the telegraph in Canada operated as part of the private economic sector and was dependent on revenues generated by its operation, any rapid expansion must indicate (*claim*) enthusiastic reception. But there are extenuating circumstances. Therefore, we admit that the claim is true *unless* the extension was due, for instance, to the growth in the west where towns were located at great distances from one another and where the government was involved in telegraph expansion for security purposes, and/or *unless* the usage was principally by government or business interests, which would have had little impact on public enthusiasm. What was, *prima facie*, a simple conclusion is made ever more complex by the use of such a system of argument. (The actual results are even more complex than this simple example indicates.)[18]

Of course, such a system makes the presentation of our findings much more complicated. But it also provides us with the means to validate our conclusions before we publish them and to defend them if they are challenged. The system also allows the community of scholars within which we work to confirm or deny our conclusions independently and to do so within a context that we understand and share. And finally this form facilitates the use of data, interpretations, and conclusions by other scholars who readily understand our work.[19]

That community may be thought of as an aspect of what Dewey

[18]Robert S. Fortner, "Messiahs and Monopolists: A Cultural History of Canadian Communications Systems 1846–1914" (Urbana, Ill.: Unpublished Ph.D. Thesis, 1978).
[19]See Chapter 3 of Toulmin's *Uses of Argument* for a more complete explanation of the system.

called "communal life," which he said was "moral," or "emotionally, intellectually, consciously sustained."[20] The implications of being part of such a communal enterprise in which one's work is subjected to community interpretation and judgment are profound. In the first place, it reminds us that we do not conduct our research in a vacuum: we are subject to communal "laws" of inquiry, which serve to validate or invalidate our work by adding or refusing imprimature to our personal revelations and conclusions. Our relevant community acts, in other words, as a mutual authority that judges the fruits of our endeavors.[21] Also, to be a part of such an enterprise implies that we have accepted both the historical and mythological constructs of the community to which we belong.

In the realm of historical constructs, Hirsch has noted that, "On the simplest level, the members of the community [of inquirers engaged in a communal enterprise] cannot even maintain an increasing body of evidence unless past evidence is stored and is brought to bear, when relevant, on hypotheses presently entertained."[22] Bloomfield has also addressed this aspect of the scholar's work, writing that, "Although nothing is enough, informed enjoyment and a historical dimension to one's experience, a conviction of accuracy, have the power to answer nagging questions and demands and can civilize a man more than destroy him."[23] We might call this phenomenon a historical imperative, for it compels all honest scholars to acknowledge history as it has been explained and interpreted for us by other members of the community of scholars. Because culturalism is necessarily a historical method, in the sense that any concern with meaning created as interpretive tool by people to deal with life is, ipso facto, historical, the scholar using the cultural method *must* address history that circumscribes, and which may impinge on, his or her interpretation and explanation of meaning. This is not to say that history is a dictator, for interpretations abound in this field, particularly over events or personalities that have been seen as axial by members of the history community; history is rather an arbiter that applies appropriate limits to imaginative scholarship, counseling caution to those heady from the brew of their own imaginings.

Because the conduct of cultural studies is one that borrows so heavily from historical methods, we need to be especially aware of the pitfalls that haunt historical research. Fischer has isolated a series of fallacies that infect historical study, dividing them into fallacies of inquiry,

[20]John Dewey, *The Public and Its Problems* (New York: Henry Holt and Co., 1927), p. 151.

[21]Michael Polanyi and Harry Prosch, *Meaning* (Chicago: University of Chicago Press, 1975), p. 194.

[22]E. D. Hirsch, Jr., "Value and Knowledge in the Humanities," Morton W. Bloomfield, ed., in *In Search of Literary Theory* (Ithaca, N.Y.: Cornell University Press, 1972), p. 65.

[23]Morton W. Bloomfield, "The Two Cognitive Dimensions of the Humanities," in Bloomfield, ibid., p. 79.

of explanation, and of argument.[24] Although all are of interest, we shall confine ourselves at this point to the fallacies of argument. Limitations of space prevent us, too, from reproducing Fischer's explanations, and his book is recommended as a necessary complement to this brief summary. Fischer acknowledges the need to "conform to a logic of argumentation" if the historian's arguments "are to cohere as truth."[25] But Fischer does not deal with formal fallacies of argument (a wise decision that we have decided to emulate), discussing, rather, informal fallacies of a semantic or substantive nature. The semantic fallacies include those of ambiguity, amphiboly (meaning muddled by slovenly syntax), figures (abuse of figurative language), accent (distortion by emphasis), equivocation, quibbling, and black-or-white (misconstruction of vague terms).[26] The remedy, Fischer says, for all semantic fallacies is "formal definition faithfully applied" (of which he provides multiple examples).[27] The second set of informal fallacies is substantive. "They all operate by shifting attention from a reasoned argument to other things which are irrelevant and often irrational."[28] He includes sixteen of the more common ones.[29] We have not been able to discuss in detail here all the problems with argument that we inevitably face in making interpretations. Nevertheless this all too brief discussion is intended to demonstrate the need for humanists to present research in a mode that responds to the standards of logic in both inquiry and argument. The positive results of such presentation will be a substantial difference in the acceptance of humanistic findings by the community of scholars, the tribunal of last resort. Acceptance of a more formal system for arguing positions will also lead to greater understanding of qualitative work as well as to the framework for more meaningful discussion of one another's work.

SUMMARY

We have reviewed in broad strokes some of the dynamics that characterize a qualitative, humanistic approach to communication research. In our summary we have emphasized the central role of imagination and meaning, and have suggested several minimum standards by which evidence is pursued and the results presented. We are concerned that many future academicians gather under the humanistic umbrella for practical reasons, rather than out of a philosophical sensitivity to humanistic aims. Thus we begin staking out in this essay a framework whereby cheap forms of culturalism can be exorcized.

[24]David Hackett Fischer, *Historians' Fallacies: Toward a Logic of Historical Thought* (New York: Harper & Row, Inc., 1970).
[25]Ibid., p. 263.
[26]Ibid., pp. 265–77.
[27]Ibid., pp. 277–80.
[28]Ibid., p. 282.
[29]Ibid., pp. 283–306.

Outside our arena, many who have questioned the use of cultural methods have done so not from malicious designs, but owing to a genuine desire to understand what we who practice it are doing and what our contributions to communication research are likely to be. Many of our colleagues, unfortunately, have misinterpreted the intent of these queries. As a final statement, therefore, on a philosophical plane, let us caution both our questioners and our defenders. We believe, with Hirsch, that total freedom of inquiry is necessary, particularly in communication research, owing to our very inability to predict the future value of any particular form of inquiry.[30] That being so, let us acknowledge that the choice of method is not the result of a conscious selection of an inherently superior tool, but of the selection of a tool most appropriate to our purposes. "Method is primordial judgment become cohesive, deliberate, and qualified within a specific perspective."[31]

Each of us, whatever our perspective, has something to offer the others, for, in the words of I. A. Richards, "the Total Meaning we are engaged with is, almost always, a blend, a combination of several contributory meanings or different types."[32] Qualitatively oriented offerings may not all be immediately important to everyone else, but they do deserve our attention and constructive criticism. Therefore, we should be able to resolve our differences through the application of that which we study, communication. Finally, we should each take to heart an explanation and admonition of Michael Polanyi:

> Man lives in the meanings he is able to discern. He extends himself into that which he finds coherent and is at home there. These meanings can be of many kinds and sorts. Men believe in the reality of these meanings whenever they perceive them—unless some intellectual myth in which they also come to believe denies reality to some of them.[33]

---

[30]*op. cit.*, p. 68.

[31]Justus Buchler, *The Concept of Method* (New York: Columbia University Press, 1961), p. 67.

[32]I. A. Richards, *Practical Criticism: A Study of Literary Judgment* (New York: Harcourt Brace Jovanovich, Inc., 1929), p. 174.

[33]In Polanyi and Prosch, *Meaning*, p. 66.

Presentation of Research Results

Guido H. Stempel III and
Bruce H. Westley

We began this book by talking about the rapid expansion of mass communication research and knowledge. The mass communication researcher is at the frontier of knowledge, and on this frontier, the pen truly is mightier than the sword.

Whatever techniques we develop and however many researchers are at work, knowledge in our field can progress only as rapidly and as effectively as we can communicate our findings. It is the journal article or the convention paper or the book that brings knowledge into our field. Without publication, any piece of knowledge is restricted to a few, and the growth of knowledge is impaired. To fail to publish is to fail to do one's elementary duty. (Whether the work is published, of course, depends on the judgment of colleagues as to its merit, or, in other words, their answer to the question of whether the scholar's product is indeed a contribution to knowledge.)

The mass communication researcher probably brings more training and experience to this task than researchers in most other fields. That edge, however, is at least partially offset by the diversity of audiences she or he must attempt to reach. That diversity is reflected in the wide range of publications that report research findings in mass communication. You may find yourself writing for the research-oriented audience of a publication like *Journalism Quarterly*. Such an audience can be expected to be at least as interested in the method as the findings. You may find yourself writing for a trade publication like *Editor & Publisher*. The reader of that publication probably hopes to find a practical application in your research that will make his or her paper better. Or you may find yourself writing for a daily newspaper. That audience will be interested in the results and little else about the study.

You will not be writing for all these publications or all these audiences at once, but at one time or another you may find that you want to reach each of them. That is not an easy assignment, but it is one that has been carried out well by a number of communication researchers.

FORMAT FOR THE RESEARCH ARTICLE

While format will necessarily vary as the research method varies, the standard format for empirical studies is a useful one that can be adapted to most other types of studies. It consists basically of four parts: statement of the problem, method, results, and conclusion. It may also include a summary at the end or an abstract at the beginning, but seldom both.

The statement of the problem consists largely of a sharply focused review of literature. As our field has grown, we have come to the point at which the literature review must be highly selective. A person doing a readership study of advertising 25 years ago might have included even studies of news-editorial readership in the review of literature. Today, the researcher should be prepared to limit it to something as narrow as the readership for four-color cigaret advertising in newspapers in the top 100 markets. Anything less narrow is likely to introduce studies that offer relatively little to the definition of the current research problem.

The literature review should provide a justification for the study's hypotheses. The author should put the existing studies together in logical sequence that leads to those hypotheses and in doing so make it clear what he or she proposes to accomplish with this study and in what way this study will add to the knowledge of the field. You may also want to draw on statements indicating the importance of the problem.

A major challenge in the statement of the problem is condensing the material so that only the essentials of each study mentioned are included. For most studies you will cite, that can be done in a single sentence.

Method

The method section has two purposes. The first is to give the readers an indication of what was done so that they can better understand the results. The second is to provide enough detail about what was done so that a researcher who wants to replicate the study will be able to do so. Many method sections achieve the former purpose, but not the latter one. Many writers do not take the matter of replication seriously and really do not attempt to provide such detail.

An important part of the method section is a clear explanation of the differences between various stimuli or experimental conditions. It is not enough to say that one group of respondents saw black-and-white ads while the other saw color ads. The reader is entitled to know whether color means four-color or one-color plus black-and-white. The reader also is entitled to know just how color was used. Are we talking about only the illustration, or were there tint blocks, colored body type, or some other nonpictoral use of color?

Likewise, we cannot simply tell the reader that we had a matched control group and experimental group. How were they selected? How were they matched? What measures are there of the similarity of the two groups?

In short, what we are looking for in a method section is analagous to what we find in a cookbook. Nothing should be left to the imagination. The reader should not have to guess what was done at a particular point in the experiment.

Results

In writing the results section, the author must be guided by his or her statement of hypotheses at the end of the statement-of-problem section. The hypotheses should be dealt with in sequential order, with a clear statement for each hypothesis as to whether it was accepted or rejected. Appropriate figures should be cited in the text, and reference should be made to the appropriate tables.

While there should be an interweaving of table and text, the author should avoid repeating large portions of the contents of the tables in the text. Only a few figures from each table should be included in the text.

When footnotes are called for in tables and figures, they should be given small letter designations (a, b) and be notated at the foot of the table or figure, not mixed with footnotes to the text.

The opening noun in the heading of a table or figure should refer directly to the data shown in the table. If percents, it should begin "Percents of . . . ," if frequencies, "Frequencies of. . . ."

When percents are given in tables, the table should make clear which way they add to 100, by rows or columns.

Put the legend for figures below the figure; put headings for tables above the table.

As a rule, when tables show the relationships between an independent variable and a dependent variable, the data should be tabled to show the dependent variables in columns and the independent variables in rows. E.g.:

| | Readership | |
	High	*Low*
Sex of respondent		
M		
F		
Social class		
Upper		
Middle		
Lower		

[handwritten annotation: "independent" pointing to left column; "dependent" pointing to Readership header]

In tabling correlations and proportions, you may omit decimal points.

As Danielson emphasized in Chapter 6, tables must "stand alone." That is, they should be meaningful to anyone who has not read the text. Many who "consult" articles turn to the tables first. They should not have to read columns of theory and method in order to understand exactly what the tables show.

In reporting differences in the hypothesized direction, the author should be careful to focus on those differences that are statistically significant. There are instances in which nonsignificant differences are of interest, but they are the exception. It is unfortunately not uncommon to find results sections that contain more references to differences that were not statistically significant than to those that were.

The author also should avoid introducing material that is unrelated to the hypotheses. Again, there may be a figure or two of interest even though they are unrelated to the hypotheses, but when such figures begin to dominate the results section, it disrupts the entire section.

In handling figures, the author also should keep in mind that the standard significance level in mass communication research is the 0.05 level. Anything with a higher chance probability than that should be considered potentially a chance difference. However tempting it may be with a given set of data, there can be no compromise on this standard. Reporting probabilities such as 0.10 will not be seen as innovative or insightful, but rather as an attempt to inflate the results.

Conclusions

Just as the results should be tied to the hypotheses, so should the conclusions. When the hypotheses are confirmed, that is a rather easy and obvious thing to do. Likewise, when none of the hypotheses is confirmed, it is relatively easy to deal with the conclusions in those terms.

What is more difficult and yet more urgent is to stick to that rule when some of the hypotheses are confirmed and some are not. The search for alternate conclusions has a built-in tendency to stray rather far afield. The danger is that a conclusion will be offered on the basis of limited support from the results and none at all from the literature cited at the outset.

Where the results are not clear-cut, some speculation and some opinion may be in order, but they should be limited. It is easy to find alternate explanations, given a set of data that turned out somewhat differently than predicted. The trouble is that the number of possible alternate explanations approaches infinity, and what may have great appeal to you as an explanation may strike the reader as grasping at straws.

The conclusions section can include a statement about future research. Such statements should be focused on what would seem to be the next logical thing to do in the particular area being studied. At the same time, the proposals should be plausible. In many cases, the next step is obvious, and suggestions for future research are superfluous.

If an abstract is to be included, it should be a miniature of the article not only in content but in form. It should follow the same pattern, starting with a summary statement of the problem, moving on to the method, the results, and the conclusions.

If a summary is included, it should be somewhat different from an abstract. It should focus more heavily on the results and the conclusions and give only passing notice, if any, to the statement of the problem and the method. Those matters should have been addressed adequately at their respective places, and we assume the summary's main function is to serve as a wrapup for someone who has read the article. It is true, of course, that some people scan summaries and do not read entire articles, but the writer's first responsibility is to those readers who arrive at the summary having read what has come before.

All this fits well the empirical study such as the experiment designed to determine whether the use of color in cigaret ads produces higher brand recognition. But what of the survey merely designed to find out what the readership of cigaret ads in color is or how the readership of color and black-and-white ads compares? These are merely descriptive studies, aren't they? There really isn't a hypothesis, is there?

We think there should be a hypothesis. If there is not, the absence of one most likely reflects the failure of the researcher to do his homework, to delve into the pertinent background. Few surveys in this day and age break completely new ground. Part of the meaning of most surveys comes from how the results compare with the results of similar surveys. That is just another way of saying that there is, or should be, a hypothesis provided by previous studies being tested by this study.

Take, for example, the frequent surveys of the popularity of the president of the United States. Are those merely descriptive studies of attitudes at a particular moment? Hardly. By now, those studies have been done long enough that the researcher knows what to expect. George Gallup does not tell you in his newspaper article that the hypothesis being tested was. He does, however, talk about how the current results compare with the pattern we have come to expect. A president's popularity is high when he takes office. It drops. It will rise again in a moment of genuine national crisis or national triumph. An assessment of current events tells us where we might expect to be in that model, and Gallup will tell us whether we are or not.

For most surveys, then, the empirical model will in fact fit pretty well. There may be some unexpected results. In particular, the inter-relationships may be hard to predict, but the more you know, the easier it is to predict. It may be argued that in any survey there are questions that are not directly related to the hypotheses. We would suggest that this is neither a necessary condition of a survey nor a sign of strength.

As we turn to studies without numerical data, it may be more difficult to see the connection with the empirical model. Yet, as Nelson and Nord and Yodelis and Gillmor and Dennis indicate in their discussions of historical and legal research, the movement in those fields is in the direction of the empirical model. Mountain climbers may still climb mountains because they are there, but historians no longer study newspapers or their editors just because they are there. The historical study is undertaken for a reason. Just as with the empirical study, the purpose of the study follows from the pertinent literature. The person writing the historical research article therefore should begin with a statement of purpose similar to that in the empirical study.

What comes next may be somewhat different. The need to elaborate on method is at least somewhat less. To the extent that the historical researcher quantifies, he or she will have the same need to explain sampling and measurement procedures as the experimental researcher. For many historical studies, however, the method may be self-evident and require little if any explanation.

The historical researcher should then move to an explication of what has been found. This may be organized in accord with the logic of the statement of the problem or it simply may be organized chronologically. In either case, the total evidence the researcher has on the problem should be presented, and the section should be restricted to that evidence. Subjective judgment and speculation do not belong here.

The conclusions section will more nearly resemble the conclusions section of the empirical article. Again the conclusions must be tied closely to the statement of the problem and to the evidence. Subjective statements that range far beyond the evidence should be avoided. Logical inference relating the various pieces of evidence is, however, highly appropriate.

The outline presented here for the historical research article also applies to legal studies and descriptive research. There always should be a clear statement of the problem. It must be based on an accurate and precise analysis of the literature on the topic. Evidence bearing on the problem should be presented, and it should be kept apart from the author's opinions about the evidence or the problem. The conclusions section should be tightly linked to the statement of the problem and to the evidence, but should go beyond the evidence to interpret meaning.

THESIS AND DISSERTATION WRITING

For many readers of this book, the research-writing task that lies immediately ahead is the master's thesis or doctoral dissertation. Much of what we have said about the research article holds for the thesis or dissertation as well, but there are differences. The basic scheme of organization remains the same. The usual chapter headings are Statement of Problem, Review of the Literature, Methodology, Results, and Conclusions.

One major difference is in the Review of the Literature, which becomes much more extensive than it can be in an article. The review reaches out farther away from the central topic of the study, and it discusses each piece of literature in more detail. It is not unusual for thirty or forty studies to be included and for this chapter to be twenty or twenty-five pages long.

Another major difference has to do with the details about methodology. We suggested earlier that it ought to be possible for someone to replicate your study on the basis of your description of the method. In a thesis or dissertation, this is normally carried to the point that the actual questionnaire, stimulus material, and the like are included. Most such material is put in appendixes, but it is available. Likewise, more statistical results are included, again in many cases in the appendixes.

While all this makes the thesis or dissertation longer, it probably does not make it any more difficult to write, because the writer does not have to make a lot of decisions about what to include and what to leave out. The rule on a thesis or dissertation is: If in doubt, include it.

WRITING STYLE

Good writing is clear thinking made visible. The format discussed in the preceding section will certainly promote clear thinking.[1] It is up to the researcher to carry it forward into the writing of the manuscript. He or she must begin where any writer begins—with a clear image of the audience.

Clarity of expression is especially important in scholarly publication because of its special character. Scholarly reporting is aimed at an audience of scholars and neophyte scholars. It is submitted in a form to answer the standard questions raised by all scholarship. Is the evidence to be believed? If one entertains doubts, how can it be checked? What assurance do we have that all precautions were taken to obtain the best

---

[1]We recommend three books that we believe will help authors increase clarity and improve writing style: John R. Trimble, *Writing with Style: Conversations on the Art of Writing* (Englewood Cliffs, N.J.: Prentice-Hall, Inc., 1975); William Strunk, Jr., and E. B. White, *The Elements of Style*, 2nd ed. (New York: Macmillan, Inc., 1972); and Rudolf Flesch, *The Art of Readable Writing* (New York: Harper & Row, Inc., 1949).

possible evidence? Do the author's conclusions flow logically from the evidence? Given the evidence, could other, even contradictory, conclusions be drawn? If the evidence is sound and the inferences reasonable, what does this study tell about how our present knowledge must be revised? Almost every feature of scholarly reporting may be traced to the researcher's attempts to answer these questions.

Clarity and precision as criteria arise from the need to impart to other scholars exactly what was done. For the historian this refers to what sources were consulted, for the legal scholar what cases and briefs were consulted. For the behavioral scientist it means telling exactly how many subjects were included in the control group, exactly how each concept was measured, how a sample was drawn, how a sample compared with parameters in the population from which it was drawn, and what rules governed the assignment of content to categories. The reader has a right to expect exact answers to such questions. In other words, the precision demanded by those who might want to repeat an experiment or to search a new source for further evidence is the kind of precision required of scholars in reporting their research. The clarity required is of the sort that answers these questions unambiguously.

Organization is critical because much scholarly writing is meant to be consulted by many and read by few and examined closely only by the very few who intend to abstract the essence of the study for their own purposes or to verify it by replication. Consultation is aided by several features of the organization of a research report, monograph, or journal article. First, there is the highly condensed account of the study provided by either an abstract at the top of the report or by a summary and conclusions section at the end. Both should give all essentials so that the reader may decide whether or not to look more closely. The next step may be to examine the tables. That is why the point is made elsewhere in this chapter that tables must be meaningful by themselves—must "stand alone." The reader may next be interested in how the hypotheses were derived. That points toward the formal statement of hypotheses, which should be found at the end of the problem statement section and just before the methodology section. Another reader might turn from the tables to the "operations" segment of the methodology or procedures section. The best service the writer can provide for the most important reader of the research is to specify exactly where everything can be found.

Most of the readers of this book will at this point in their lives have had too much experience writing for an audience of one—the instructor who assigned the paper. We have all lived through the frustration of discovering that this instructor evaluates our writing in a different way than the last instructor. That is frequently compounded by the failure of the instructor to articulate very clearly just what it is that is wanted. Frustrating as this is, it is instructional, if we care to let it be.

It tells us first of all that communicating is not a sure thing. What we feel we have made extremely clear may be totally misunderstood by our audience. We find that we must concentrate not merely on writing what sounds good to us, but on writing for others. We must think about how to communicate an idea. We must recognize that nobody else in the world has had exactly the experience that we have had. Nobody else perceives things in exactly the same context that we do.

Scholarly writing need not be dull. This particularly applies to the statement of the problem. The writer has considerable latitude here and should use it. It is not against the rules of scholarship to say something interesting. The writer who fails to do that is likely to leave the reader with the impression that the problem being studied is both uninteresting and unimportant.

We might profit by the example of Archimedes. He did not run through the streets of Athens shouting, "An interesting problem which has perplexed alchemists for generations is the measurement of the relative density of metallic substances." He yelled simply "Eureka." It is worth noting the the principle of Archimedes remains one of the most widely known scientific facts and the name of Archimedes one of the best-known names in the history of science.

The story of Archimedes also reminds us that the most powerful tool the researcher has at his or her disposal is the simple declarative sentence. Compound and complex sentences are used more often than they should be. Sometimes they are necessary, but the greatest need in scholarly writing is for greater use of the simple sentence.

Likewise, the use of common words is important. A reader who cannot understand the words you use cannot understand the idea you are trying to express. The scholarly writer cannot stay within the limits of commonly known words, but excursions outside that realm should be limited.

There is, of course, a language unique to the field of mass communication research. As is the case with most fields, that language is by now a mixture of sheer jargon and terms with a precise special meaning. It is important that you distinguish between the two and choose words accordingly. Rarely is it necessary to call it "media consumption" rather than "reading" or "listening." On the other hand "cognitive dissonance" may sound like jargon, but it is the most precise and concise way of expressing a concept that is important in our field.

Another matter worth some discussion is redundancy. The format we have described has redundancy built into it. The writer must be careful not to overdo it. If you find that you have written the same sentence for the third time in the same manuscript, you have a redundancy problem. To guard against this, you must constantly refer back and forth between sections. You may think you will remember everything you have written, but you may not.

SLANTING THE MANUSCRIPT

Every magazine writer knows that no two publications have the same editorial requirements or style or expectations. The writer's ability to succeed will depend a great deal on how well she or he understands the particular publication and can adjust and write accordingly. If it has not occurred to you that you cannot send the same manuscript to *National Geographic* and *Field and Stream,* you perhaps should pause to reflect on that.

Scholarly writing is no different. Different publications have different editorial requirements and different styles. They define different topics as being within their scope.

For the scholarly writer, this problem begins with the thesis. There are style requirements. There are specifications as to the size of margins and the weight of paper. In addition, there are the expectations of the members of the thesis committee as to what a thesis should be and how it should be presented. The problem, however, becomes more complex when we consider publications.

The most frequent problem of the writer who is submitting something to a particular journal for the first time is his or her unfamiliarity with that journal. As a journal editor, one of the authors has seen this unfamiliarity in a variety of ways, some amusing and some critical, but all detrimental to the prospects of the manuscript.

There are manuscripts addressed to the previous editor, who resigned eight years ago. There are those addressed to the business office. There are those addressed to a similar-named university and those to the right university, but the wrong city. All obviously were sent by people who did not look up the address that appears on the first editorial page of the journal. These errors are harmless except that they usually are harbingers of more serious ignorance of the publication.

On the more serious side, there are manuscripts sent with abstracts, which our publication has never used, and with references rather than footnotes, which our publication has not used for many years. There are manuscripts with footnotes not only in a style that is not our style, but which also do not contain the same information, so that it would be impossible for us to convert them. There are manuscripts with tables in formats that are so different from our normal formats that we could not possibly use them. All these things indicate that the author is not very familiar with the publication. All these matters could be ascertained rather readily by the author. The failure to do so makes his or her efforts look amateurish. While these are matters that concern us a good deal as editors, we have found that members of our editorial boards become almost as concerned as we do. Many are reluctant to even give serious consideration to a manuscript with such flaws.

The matter of topic is more subtle. There are certain topics that might logically appear in a number of journals, but there may be a tendency for a given topic to appear almost to be the exclusive property of one publication. Somehow articles on that topic naturally gravitate toward that journal. If you are writing on such a topic, you might as well take advantage of the natural tendency. A good rule of thumb on this matter is that you ought to consider what journals are cited in your footnotes. If you have not found references in *Journalism Quar-*

terly, but you have found a handful in *Public Opinion Quarterly,* chances are you should send your manuscript to *Public Opinion Quarterly* and not to *Journalism Quarterly.* Of course, this problem intensifies if both journals cover the topic equally, but you somehow found only the references in the one.

All this adds up to the simple fact that a little time spent learning something about the journal to which you plan to submit your manuscript is indispensable. The investment of an hour can protect or enhance the research investment that has already run into hundreds of hours. On that basis, it seems foolish not to take the time.

WHAT EDITORS LOOK FOR

In the previous section we have already indicated some of the things editors look for. They can be summed up under the heading of an indication that the manuscript was written specifically for their journal. There are, however, a number of other considerations.

Some of them, of course, have to do with the quality of the research itself. Each journal has certain standards with regard to methodology and scope of study. Again, the researcher certainly can sense some of this and would be well advised not to send a manuscript that clearly does not meet the journal's requirements. For one thing, it very well could hurt his or her chances with better manuscripts in the future.

At the same time, we should recognize that the topic may have a bearing in ways that the author really cannot predict. This can be either a plus or a minus. An editor may decide that she or he has had enough articles on a given topic, or feel that the real substance of the topic has been exhausted. Or the editor may be looking for a manuscript on a particular topic because it is timely in some sense and thus be highly receptive. (None of this is true of the "open channels" type of journal, which reviews all relevant manuscripts received and publishes them in order of acceptance, leaving little room for an editor's preferences.)

Beyond this, the quality of writing becomes a vital factor. This starts with such simple matters as correct spelling and grammatically correct sentences. This may seem almost trivial to some of you, but the unbelievable fact is that we have on occasion received manuscripts with between a dozen and two dozen errors in grammar and spelling. Those are fortunately rare and not really what we have in mind when we talk about quality of writing. Rather we are thinking of such things as clarity, conciseness, and aptness of phrasing. The clearer the manuscript, the better its chances of acceptance. We have suggested earlier that clarity is something you achieve by working at it.

Conciseness tends to reflect two things, the care the writer takes with each sentence and the degree to which the entire article has been organized. Some manuscripts turn out to be twice as long as they need to be because the writer does not have goals clearly in mind. If the writer is fortunate, the editor will give him or her the chance to cut it in half. The writer may, however, pay the price of rejection for failure to keep the manuscript within reasonable length limits. The writer should approach this question from a standpoint of maximum length, not minimum length. We see clear evidence in some instances that the author was striving to achieve a minimum length. That approach is likely to cause problems.

How well the writer turns a phrase is a matter of deeply rooted characteristics. The writer may not be able to do much to affect this, but it is a factor that will have something to do with the chance of acceptance of the manuscript. Attention to this may produce some small improvement, however.

The next thing the editor will look for is the reaction of the author to suggestions for revision and improvement of the manuscript. Relatively few manuscripts will be accepted without comment. It is up to the author to respond intelligently to the suggestions and thereby produce a better manuscript. If instead effort is spent in resisting the suggestions, the editor will not be favorably impressed. The author should remember that the suggestions come from established experts in the field. Some suggestions may be wrong and some may be based on misunderstanding, but most are not. The author should approach the suggestions with a positive frame of mind. The goal should be to gain as much as possible from the suggestions, not to debate them.

Editors want to be certain that what is offered them is original work and that it belongs exclusively to them. As to original work, we are not really talking about plagiarism, which is all but nonexistent, and we are not talking about originality in style or presentation. What we are talking about is that the work is that of the author and not a rewrite of someone else's work or closely similar to work already published or in press. *Journalism Quarterly*'s "Instructions to Contributors" emphasizes "original contributions" and "original investigations" and says, "A manuscript is accepted with the understanding that *Journalism Quarterly* has exclusive publication rights, which means that the manuscript has not been submitted, accepted for publication or published elsewhere."

The exclusivity issue is more complicated. Part of it is addressed in a note to contributors to *Journalism Monographs:*

> Authors are expected to be completely candid with the editor in matters pertaining to the origins and previous appearances of manuscripts, including their relationship to any thesis or dissertation, or any other use of the material, whether in the past or contemplated. It is our policy not to publish a long version of a study already published in a shorter version elsewhere, and the same applies to book chapters. These problems can be worked out, but the editor expects to be fully informed, including any use or contemplated use of the same material in trade or general publications.

Monographs, of course, present special problems. But the general problem applies to all scholarly publishing.

Thesis or dissertation completion does not constitute publication, but editors want writers to acknowledge the relationship between an article and its origins. Presentations to scholarly gatherings do not constitute publication either, but, again, such a history should be reported. (Published abstracts, as in *Dissertation Abstracts* and the proceedings of scholarly meetings, do not constitute publication, either, and need not be acknowedged.)

It is perfectly proper to spin off more than one article from a dissertation. What is not proper is to publish the same data in more than one periodical or serial. Where a methodological innovation is itself worthy of publication, there is nothing wrong with publishing it separately. The substantive article may then be reported elsewhere with a citation to the methodological piece.

ACKNOWLEDGING THE WORK OF OTHERS

Scholars are expected to pay their intellectual and pedagogical debts. The former involves giving credit for ideas, theoretical postures, even methodological innovations where they or some part of them originated with another scholar or in another laboratory. It is more a matter of reporting than an ethical obligation, but can be seen as both. Again, owing to the cumulative nature of a reasonably mature science, one traces connections between what is being reported now and what has been posited in the past. Paying pedagogical debts applies particularly to reporting work done under the supervision of others, as in work done for theses and dissertations. It is the student's own work, to be sure—or it had better be—but surely the student owes something to his or her mentor.

Sometimes work done under close supervision of a faculty member points to joint authorship, especially when the student work is part of a larger program of research directed by a faculty member. This brings us to the etiquette of joint authorship and sponsorship. To take the latter point first: The author should include in any submission to editors information about any assistance received that directly financed all or any part of the investigation being reported. Such assistance may have been provided by an outside funding source, such as a foundation, or by an agency of the university, college, school, or department where funds are granted to assist in the research. Normally this includes funding for specified costs, such as computer time, research assistants, even funds to hire interviewers and coders and to provide for publication costs, such as "page charges" required by some journals or "prior publication" offered by others.

The etiquette of collaboration is more complex. In some parts of the academic world it is traditional that, for all work carried out under the auspices of a research center or institute, the name of the head of the research team automatically goes on every article published. This is not usually the case in the behavioral sciences, where the issue usually turns on the question whether a major professor or the head of a research team does in fact deserve to be listed as an author. There are no hard and fast rules, but editors would like to believe that joint authorship signifies genuine collaboration, that both authors contributed significantly to the work. Supervision does not constitute participation. Some faculty members feel that they should not be listed as a co-author on any work based on a dissertation. The reasoning is quite compelling: a dissertation is a demonstration of ability to carry out independent scholarship. To share authorship of any article or monograph spun from a dissertation contradicts that principle. The same may be said of a master's thesis, except that often students carve out parts of a larger investigation and willingly share authorship with the senior person who heads the team, especially when the latter is actively involved with and responsible for the entire project.

Many of these problems do not arise in the pursuit of scholarship in history, law, and qualitative studies. Collaborations are rare in these fields because of the close intermingling of evidence and inference. In history, for example, the traditional scholar adduces evidence before subjecting it to interpretation, of course, but rarely farms out the gathering of evidence and separates it from the process of drawing conclusions, and the same may be said for original scholarship in law and qualitative studies. The latter, in fact, as Chapter 18 points out, are a highly individualized process.

Team research, on the other hand, and this could apply to the social science history described in Chapter 15, is the norm in behavioral science, and hence issues of collaboration and co-authorship are not hard to find. Even the order of names has potential significance. Here, especially, the rules are poorly drawn and exceptions abound. There is a tradition of "senior authorship," which assigns "first" authorship to the most senior and responsible member of the team. But there is also a contrary principle based on the magnitude of the contribution. One principle suggests that the head of the team should be listed first. The other principle suggests that the person who "did the work" should be listed first. The results are diametrically opposed. When co-equal colleagues collaborate, they may arrive at first authorship on the basis of who did the most work or whose idea the whole thing was. Or they may actually draw straws! One such team arrived at the solution of avoiding first authorship by arranging their names on the cover and title page in a circle, leaving it to librarians and others citing the work to decide what name to put first. (Librarians took the top name and went clockwise.) The sensible solution may be to list alphabetically. Where more than one publication results from a single collaboration, the authors' equality is signaled by alternating first authorship among them.

We may seem to be splitting hairs, but conscientious scholars nevertheless follow the etiquette of co-authorship as they know it.

A CONCLUDING COMMENT

We have stressed in this chapter that good writing does not just happen. Scholarly writing is demanding. It is also rewarding. There is to begin with the satisfaction the writer gets from putting thoughts down on paper and from finding that he or she can tie together the various aspects of the research. There is in addition the satisfaction obtained from seeing one's work in print. We might call this pride, in the most positive sense of that word. When you have achieved publication of a piece of research, you are entitled to feel some pride and personal satisfaction. Given the effort required, this seems only appropriate.

We recognize that writing research articles will be more rewarding for some people than others. We think, however, that how rewarding it turns out to be for you may depend a good deal on the extent to which you go in the directions suggested in this chapter. Our intent is to save the writer a good deal of wasted motion. Scholarly writing is, in the long run, one of those things that frequently takes less time and effort to do the right way.

Name Index

Subject Index